Personality Across Cultures

Personality Across Cultures
recent developments and debates

edited by

Jitendra Mohan

YMCA Library Building, Jai Singh Road, New Delhi 110001

Oxford University Press is a department of the University of Oxford. It furthers the University's objective of excellence in research, scholarship, and education by publishing worldwide in

Oxford New York
Athens Auckland Bangkok Bogota Buenos Aires Calcutta
Cape Town Chennai Dar es Salaam Delhi Florence Hong Kong Istanbul
Karachi Kuala Lumpur Madrid Melbourne Mexico City Mumbai
Nairobi Paris Sao Paolo Shanghai Singapore Taipei Tokyo Toronto Warsaw

with associated companies in

Berlin Ibadan

Published in India
By Oxford University Press, New Delhi

ISBN 0 19 565061 1

Typeset by InoSoft Systems, I. P. Extension, New Delhi 110092
Printed in India at Roopak Printers, Delhi 110032
and published by Manzar Khan, Oxford University Press
YMCA Library Building, Jai Singh Road, New Delhi 110 001

In Honour of

Professor H. J. Eysenck

Preface

Personality has retained its fascination for the thinkers all over the world. From the real self to the ideal role reported or projected self, the writings have created theories, models and methods. This book includes chapters written by some of the dominant signatures in psychology, some of whom are in the process of consolidating their work. I value their contributions.

My own serious concern in this field has also found its expression here. In the ongoing evolution of concepts, theories and instruments of personality research, I feel this work is a serious effort.

Ms Jayashree Mukhopadhyay, Oxford University Press and Mr Rakesh Sharma deserve a special mention for what they did for this volume. My special thanks are due to several people who have helped me in completing the book. But the most important was a little promise made to some Indian psychologists and Professor H.J. Eysenck, which sustained me all through in completing the book. This book ushers me to a new millennium of deeper, greater and stronger commitment to personality research!

Jitendra Mohan

Chandigarh
July, 2000

Contents

Contributors

Professor Alan Baddeley
Former Director,
M.R.C., Applied Psychology Unit, Chamcer Road,
Cambridge, UK

Dr Anuradha Bhandari
Reader, Department of Psychology, Panjab University
Chandigarh, INDIA

Professor B.C. Muthayya
Former Professor & Dean,
National Institute of Rural Development,
Hyderabad, INDIA

Professor B.S. Gupta
Department of Psychology, Banaras Hindu University,
Varanasi, INDIA

Professor Charles D. Spielberger
President: IAAP
Research Professor, University of South Florida,
Tampa, USA

Dr Chris Brand
Fellow, Galton Institute,
Edinburgh, Scotland, UK

Dr Devendra Agochia
Former Deputy Director,
Dn. Of Youth & Women Commonwealth Secretariat,
London, UK

Dr Glen Wilson
Institute of Psychiatry, Maudsley Hospital,
De Crespigny Park, Denmark Hill,
London, UK

Professor H.J. Eysenck (Late)
Professor Emiritus, Institute of Psychiatry,
Maudsley Hospital, De Crespigny Park, Denmark Hill,
London. UK

Professor Jeffrey A. Gray
Professor Emiritus, Institute of Psychiatry,
Maudsley Hospital, De Crespigny Park, Denmark Hill,
London, UK

Professor Jitendra Mohan
Department of Psychology, Panjab University
Chandigarh, INDIA

Dr Meena Sehgal
Department of Psychology, Panjab University,
Chandigarh, INDIA

Professor M.W. Eysenck
Head, Department of Psychology,
Royal Holloway College, Egham,
Surrey, UK

Professor Nathan Brody
Department of Psychology, Wesbyan University,
Mittle Town CT, USA

Professor Paul Kline (Late)
Professor of Psychology,
University of Exeter,
Exeter, UK

Dr Pittu Laungani
Reader, Department of Social Sciences, Southbank University,
London, UK

Professor V.V. Upmanyu
Department of Psychology, Panjab University,
Chandigarh, INDIA

1 The New Look in Personality and Intelligence Research: The Advent of the Paradigm

H. J. Eysenck

It is widely accepted that science proper begins with the appearance of a *paradigm,* that is, theories widely accepted and taught, and embodied in experiments and replications. Kuhn (1974) uses the terms 'exemplars' and 'disciplinary matrices' to denote these properties of a paradigm, and psychologists usually talk about *construct validity* when referring to attempts to demonstrate the truth value of a nomological network in terms of testable and verified deductions from a central theory (Garber and Strassberg, 1981). Unfortunately, much of psychology is in a pre-paradigmatic phase (Barnes, 1982), in particular, large areas of personality and intelligence, that is, important fields of individual differences. The reasons for this sad state of affairs was pointed out by Cronbach (1957) in his APA presidential address. As he said, there are two disciplines of scientific psychology—the experimental and the correlational—and it is only by bringing the two together will we be able to create a unified psychology with appropriate paradigms (Eysenck, 1984).

There clearly are weaknesses on all sides. Taxonomic studies of a correlational, factor analysis kind, clearly involve considerable subjective elements, and this subjectivity has prevented us from achieving agreement even at the most fundamental level. I have discussed this point in my paper 'Dimensions of Personality: 16, 5 or 3?' (Eysenck, 1991), and the choice available is obviously not limited to the three models discussed there. Without some resolution to this problem, personality study will remain pre-paradigmatic. Much of the same is true in the field of intelligence; although the Spearman–Thurstone hierarchic model of a number of correlated primaries leading up to a single g factor of general intelligence is widely accepted (Carroll, 1991), this acceptance is not universal, and many other models are still found in the market (Sternberg and Detterman, 1986).

To improve this situation, I have suggested that we should leave the purely phenotypic, descriptive taxonomy approach, and adopt a *causal* model, which incorporates explicit theories of causal significance, and testable deductions to access the truth value of the theories in question. This, after all, is the rationale of the hard sciences—a rationale, the outstanding success of which has given the term 'science' its well-deserved cachet. If this formula were followed, we would find the notion of *individual differences* firmly embedded in the set of laws and theories elaborated by psychologists relying on the *experimental method,* and usually devising their theories without regard to individual differences. The great advances in the determination of genetic contributions to both personality (Eaves, Eysenck and Martin, 1989) and intelligence differences (Plomin and McClearn, 1993) require us to construct a causal chain such as that shown in Figure 1, leading from DNA (distal antecedents) through biological intermediaries (proximal antecedents) to psychometric trait constellations, which constitute the central concepts of the model.

These constructs enable us to make testable predictions concerning proximal consequences, as in experimental studies, and distal consequences, that is, items of social behaviour.

A similar model can be constructed with regard to intelligence, and is shown in Figure 2 (Eysenck, 1983). Here the proximal antecedents are, of course, quite different from those theoretically linked with the major dimensions of personality, and the proximal and distal consequences too are very different. As regards the former, recent work has revitalized Galton's suggestion of using reaction-time and other elementary cognitive tasks (ECTs) (Eysenck, 1986, 1987), and there is now a large list of experiments linking this set of predictions experimentally with the biological theories. Distal consequences are, of course, the many social events linked with the very notion of 'intelligence'. Central to this is the Spearmanian notion of g, more particularly, the Cattellian construct of fluid intelligence (g^f). Here again, concepts arrived at theoretically—like Galton's notion of speed of information processing, which is fundamental to differences in intelligence—have been tested both correlationally *and* experimentally, to give the concept in question a much firmer

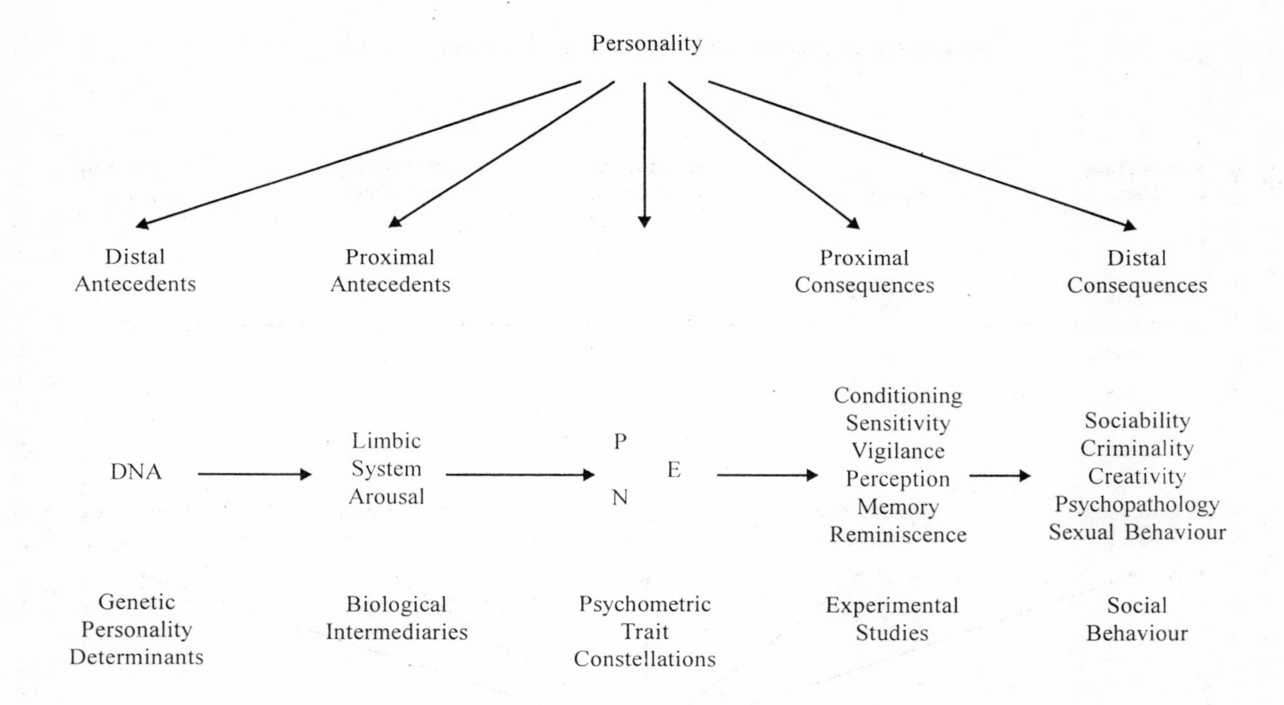

Figure 1. *Causal sequence defining personality constructs.*

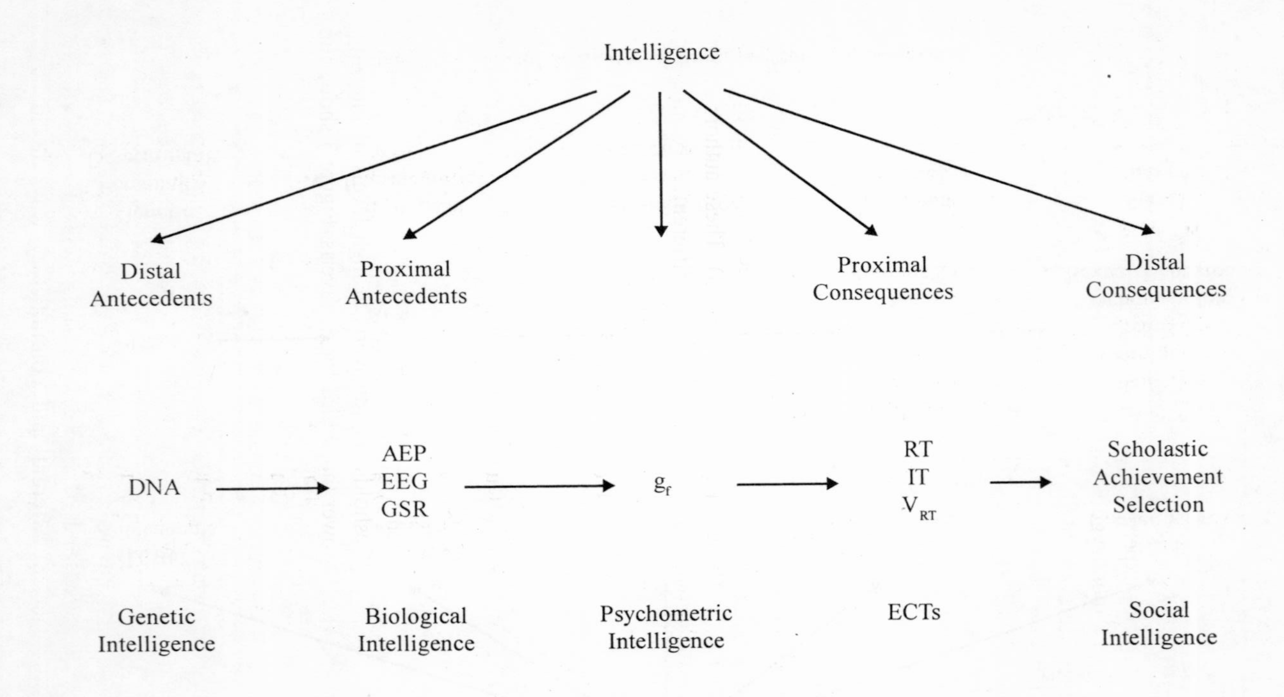

Figure 2. *Causal sequence defining the construct of intelligence.*

underpinning than would be possible by using only the methods of factor analysis.

From what I have said so far it might appear that from the proposed marriage of the correlational and experimental disciplines, only the former would have to gain. It is not so. In testing predictions from general theories experimentally, psychologists tend to treat subjects as if they were monozygotic twins, disregarding completely individual differences relevant to the theories tested. Usually, variance due to such individual differences is consigned to the error term, disregarding the major contribution it can often make, and the faulty conclusions it could often prevent. A few examples will illustrate this point; in each of these cases, a general theory has failed to predict the consequences correctly, and in each case, the addition of variables of individual differences implied in the concept under investigation has led to a solution of the problem. The first example is a prediction made by Urbantschitsch (1883) to the effect that thresholds for the perception of stimuli in one modality should be lowered by heteromodal stimulation. Divergent and contradictory results have been obtained by many experimentalists (Shigehisa and Symons, 1973). These authors argued that the discrepancy might be due to the differential response of extraverts and introverts to the stimuli in question, together with the intervention of Pavlov's law of transmarginal inhibition (law of inversion), according to which strong stimulation leads to defensive inhibition, that is, an inversion of the effects of weaker stimulation. The arousal theory of introversion (Eysenck and Eysenck, 1985) predicts that the point of inversion would be reached at a lower level of intensity of stimulation for introverts. Based on this theoretical argument, they predicted that visual stimulation would *lower* auditory thresholds at low intensities for extraverts and introverts, but would *increase* auditory thresholds for introverts at high levels of intensity, while continuing to lower thresholds for extraverts. Figure 3 shows the nature of the prediction.

The results supported the prediction in every detail. Shigehisa, Shigehisa and Symonds (1973) then repeated the experiment in reverse, measuring visual thresholds while varying auditory stimulation. Again, predictions from the personality theory were supported. Thus, this experiment not only supports the personality theory in question, but also explains why previous experimental studies have given varied and contradictory results. Where extraverts and introverts react in different and contradictory ways to identical stimuli, no simple linear experimental predictions are likely to be successful. Urbantschitsch's theory is correct when tested in the context of individual differences.

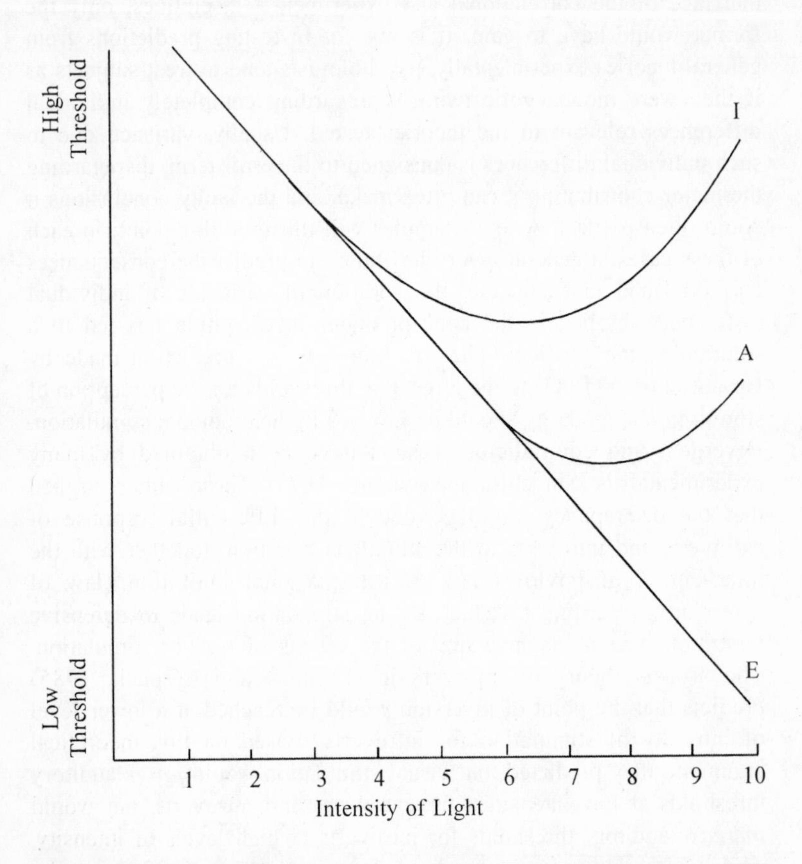

Figure 3. *Differential responding of introverts (I), ambiverts (A), and extraverts to heteromodal stimulation in terminal threshold response. The effects of heteromodal stimulation on auditory threshold.*

Another example relates to Kleinsmith and Kaplan's (1963, 1964) action decrement theory, according to which high arousal produces an active memory trace of longer duration; this, in turn, leads to enhanced consolidation. But during the consolidation phase there is a transient inhibition of retrieval, referred to as 'action decrement', which protects the actual memory trace from disruption. In consequence, while high arousal is beneficial for long-term retention, it impairs short-term retention for periods of time up to several minutes after learning. Given this general law, which has proved difficult to support experimentally, we would predict that introverts would show short-term memory impairment compared with extraverts, but long-term memory improvement. Howarth and Eysenck (1968) tested this prediction with positive results, as shown in Figure 4. Note again, that extraverts and introverts differ so profoundly in their reactions that mean effects would seem to disprove the general law by consigning individual differences to the error term. No wonder the law itself has been difficult to prove.

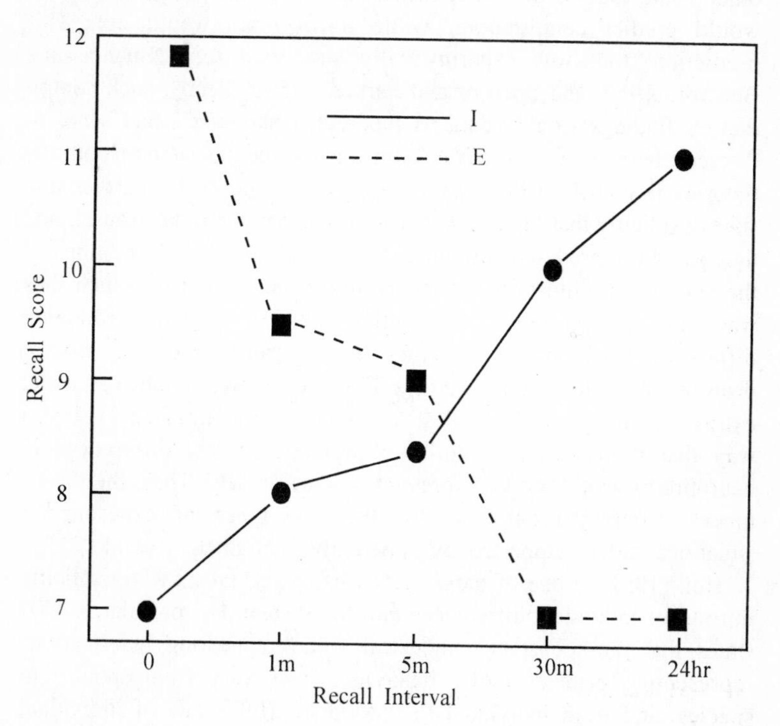

Figure 4. *'Action decrement' effects on recall in extraverts (E), and introverts (I). (Howarth and Eysenck, 1961).*

Many other examples could be given to show how often a proper understanding and testing of a general theory requires the addition of individual differences to make testable predictions that actually work

(Eysenck and Eysenck, 1985). Such a combination of the correlational and the experimental approaches can also often help to explain, in conformity with theory, apparently decisive disproofs of a given theory. This may happen when the theory predicts the *situation* in which certain predicted phenomena will occur, while predicting that in a different situation these phenomena would not occur.

Thus, Eysenck predicted that eyeblink conditioning should be correlated with introversion, but not with neuroticism; several studies gave support to this deduction (Eysenck and Levey, 1972; Jones *et al.*, 1981; Martin and Levey, 1969). Spence and Spence (1966), on the other hand, argued that high anxiety/neuroticism, acting as a drive, would predict conditioning, while introversion would not. This prediction, too, was experimentally supported (e.g., Spence and Beecroft, 1959; and Spencer and Parker, 1959). Clearly, such contradictory findings would count as theoretical anomalies, and serve to discredit both the theories. Yet, both sets of findings support both the theories (Eysenck, 1981). Eysenck's (1967) theory of introversion states explicitly that high limbic arousal increases cortical arousal, and thus should improve conditioning. In Spence's work the conditions of the experiment (situation factors) produced much anxiety, which thus was able to determine differential subject reactions producing differential rates of conditioning; these strong levels of arousal drowned out the much weaker differences between introverts and extraverts. In Eysenck's studies, the situation was arranged in such a way that there was no arousal of anxiety, so that differences in neuroticism would not be expressed in state anxiety. Thus, the theory makes different predictions for the two types of experimental situations and is supported by apparently contradictory results.

Hull (1951) is one of the very few experimentalists who explicitly introduces individual differences into his system. His postulate XVIII states that the 'constant' numerical values appearing in equations representing primary molar behaviour laws vary from species to species, and from individual to individual. Hull's law of individual differences expresses perfectly what I am trying to say; the science of individual differences must be integrated with the more general laws of the experimentalist, so that the 'constants' in the laws appear as the major concepts of the personality psychologist. For, 'drive' in Hull's system reads 'arousal' in mine, and many experimental consequences follow (Eysenck, 1973).

What would seem to follow from this argument would be certain criteria for any paradigm suggested in the fields of personality and intelligence. Consider one example from each of these fields. Eysenck and Barrett (1985) discuss the evidence for a certain theory of intelligence (g), involving evoked potential measures on the EEG. The resulting measure has been found to correlate quite highly (0.83) with total score on the WAIS. Regarding the latter as a reasonable approximation to g, we may regard the factor loadings of each of its eleven subtests as an index of the adequacy of that subtest as a measure of g. Similarly, we may regard the correlation of each subtest with our EEG measure as an index of the adequacy of that subtest as a measure of g, provided that our theory is correct, and the EEG measure is indeed a good measure of intelligence. The theory can be tested by correlating, over the eleven subtests, the factor loadings of the subtests with the correlations with the EEG test. This turned out to be 0.95, that is, as high as the unreliabilities of the measure used would permit (Eysenck, 1993). If the theory underlying the EEG measures were wrong, and if the notion of general intelligence were wrong, such a high concordance would be most unlikely. Thus, the experimental approach to the testing of theories of individual differences can give decisive support to such theories, and raise them above the purely descriptive, correlational level.

Consider, next, a problem raised by adherents of the Big Five system of personality description (Goldberg, 1993). In this system we have two factors, agreeableness (A) and conscientiousness (C), which, taken together, correlate 0.85 (disattenuated) with psychoticism (P) in the Eysenck system (Eysenck and Eysenck, 1985). Adherents of the Big Five suggest that P is formed by a shot-gun wedding of A and C, an arbitrarily statistical manipulation. I have suggested that A and C are, in fact, primary (low level) factors that form part of the various primary factors defining P, a higher-order factor. Goldberg (1993) declared the problem of deciding between these two formulations essentially insoluble, and in purely taxonomic, correlational terms, it undoubtedly is. Going beyond the purely correlational methodology, however, we may succeed in finding an answer by appealing to the nomological network surrounding the concept of P and making testable deductions which could not have been made by reference to A and C. I have tried to do this with reference to the notions of *creativity* and *genius* (Eysenck, 1995).

Very briefly, the arguments will run as follows: (1) Creativity consists essentially of bringing together (associating) two or more ideas that are usually kept apart, and whose association solves some scientific or artistic problem. (2) Creative people have consistently shallow associative gradients; that is, they form remote associations more readily than non-creative people with a steep associative gradient. (3) Schizophrenics have abnormally shallow associative gradients, leading to excessively 'original' productions (word salad) without social value. (4) High P scorers are similar to schizophrenics in having shallow associative gradients, but less extreme than schizophrenics, and, hence, are possibly creative. (5) High P scorers score highly on tests of creativity. There is evidence on all these points, with P showing quite high correlations with tests of creativity, as well as with the creation of high-value paintings and sculptures. There is nothing in the notion of A or C to predict these findings, and the fact that P is capable of mediating these predictions would seem sufficient support for its pre-eminence (Eysenck and Eysenck, 1976). But, so far, we have been only dealing with correlations, although the predictions are experimentally tested. But we can go further along strictly *causal* lines.

There is ample evidence that (6) overinclusion is causally related (negatively) to latent inhibition; that is, a tendency to inhibit remote associations through conditioning negative valences to previously non-reinforced stimuli (Lubow, 1989). Schizophrenics lack this inhibitory facility, and so do high P scorers. Further, it has been shown (7) that dopamine is involved in this process, and that this involvement is equally apparent in schizophrenics and in high P scorers (Gray, Pickering and Gray 1994). We thus have a proper causal chain from DNA through personality (P) to creativity and genius (Eysenck, 1995).

Can it be seriously maintained that A and C, each separately or in combination, could furnish us with a similar nomological network, or produce an equivalent testable (and tested!) causal chain? The answer is clearly negative, and I would suggest that it is possible along these lines to come to a decision concerning taxonomic claims based on correlational data. It seems to me that when two sets of taxonomic solutions are equally acceptable on correlational grounds, as the Big Five and the PEN system appear to be (Zuckerman, Kuhlman, and Camac, 1988), then the decision has to depend on the degree to which the respective solutions embody a proper nomological network, the degree to which they give rise to testable deductions, the degree to which the nomological network includes accepted theoretical concepts from within experimental psychology, and the degree to which deductions from the theory have been experimentally verified. Only in this way we can hope to achieve the status of a paradigmatic science.

The degree of unification offered by this procedure goes well beyond Cronbach's appeal to join together correlational and experimental psychology. We have other disciplines, notably physiological psychology, clinical psychology, and behaviour genetic psychology which deserve to be considered, but which are often treated as separate entities. The example of creativity has shown how these separate disciplines can be drawn into the construction of a nomological network, and how beneficial such a unification can be (Eysenck, 1995). In the days of Cronbach's (1957) presidential address, the supremacy of a fundamentalist type of behaviourism of the Watson–Skinner type excluded biological-psychophysiological notions and considerations of genetic factors from serious attention, and clinical psychology was still pre-empted by the vague, non-scientific subjectivity of Freud and the 'dynamic' schools (Eysenck, 1985). It is only in the past twelve years or so that these arbitrary and counterproductive limitations have been lifted, and that psychology has gained freedom from the shackels of behaviouristic orthodoxy. Such unification is essential if we are to have truly causal theories embracing the whole network of psychosomatic interactions that defines our behaviour.

References

Barnes, B. (1982). *T.S. Kuhn and Social Science,* London: Macmillan.

Carroll, J. (1993). *Human Cognitive Abilities,* Cambridge: Cambridge University Press.

Eaves, L.J., H.J. Eysenck, and N.G. Martin (1989). *Genes, Culture and Personality: An Empirical Approach,* New York: Academic Press.

Eysenck, H.J. (1973). 'Personality, Learning, and "Anxiety"', in H.J. Eysenck (ed.), *Handbook of Abnormal Psychology,* pp. 390–419.

Eysenck, H.J. (1981a). *A Model for Personality,* New York: Springer Verlag.

Eysenck, H.J. (1981b). 'General Features of the Model', in H.J. Eysenck (ed.), *A Model for Personality,* pp. 1–37, New York: Springer Verlag.

Eysenck, H.J. (1983). 'Revolution dans la theories et la mesure de l' intelligence', *La Revue Canadienne de Psycho-Education,* 12: 3–17.

Eysenck, H.J. (1983a). 'Psychopharmacology and Personality', in W. Janke (ed.), *Response Variability to Psychotropic Drugs,* pp. 127–54.

Eysenck, H.J. (1983b). 'Drugs as Research Tools in Psychology: Experiments with Drugs in Personality Research',. *Neuropsychology,* 10: 29–43.

Eysenck, H.J. (1984). 'The Place of Individual Differences in a Scientific Psychology', in J. Royce and L. Moos (eds.), *Annals of Theoretical Psychology,* pp. 233–314.

Eysenck, H.J. (1985). 'The Place of Theory in a World of Facts', in K.B. Madren and L. Moos (eds.), *Annals of Theoretical Psychology,* pp. 17–114.

Eysenck, H.J. (1985). *Decline and Fall of the Freudian Empire,* London and New York: Viking Press.

Eysenck, H.J. (1986). 'The Theory of Intelligence and the Psychophysiology of Cognition', in R. Sternberg (ed.), *Advances in the Psychology of Human Intelligence,* pp. 1–34. Hillsdale, NJ: Erlbaum.

Eysenck, H.J. (1987). 'Speed of Information Processing, Reaction Time, and the Theory of Intelligence', in P.A. Vernon (ed.), *Speed of Automation-Processing and Intelligence,* pp. 21–68. Hillsdale, NJ: Erlbaum.

Eysenck, H.J. (1991). 'Dimensions of Personality: 16, 5 or 3?– Criteria for a Taxonomic Paradigm', *Personality and Individual Differences,* 8: 773–90.

Eysenck, H.J. (1993). 'The Biological Basis of Intelligence', in P.A. Vernon (ed.), *Biological Approaches to the Study of Human Intelligence,* pp. 1–32, Norwood, NJ: Ablex.

Eysenck, H.J. (1985). *Genius: The Natural History of Creativity,* Cambridge: Cambridge University Press.

Eysenck, H.J. and P. Barrett (1985). 'Psychophysiology and the Measurement of Intelligence', in C.R. Reynolds and V. Willson (eds.), *Methodological and Statistical Advances in the Study of Individual Differences,* New York: Plenum Press.

Eysenck, H.J. and M.W. Eysenck (1985). *Personality and Individual Differences: A Natural Science Approach,* New York: Plenum Press.

Eysenck, H.J. and S.B.G. Eysenck (1976). *Psychoticism as a Dimension of Personality,* London: Hodder and Stoughton.

Eysenck, H.J. and A. Levey (1965). 'Alternation in choice behaviour and extraversion', *Life Sciences,* 4: 115–19.

Gray, N. A. Pickering and J. Gray (1994). 'Psychoticism and Dopamine D2 Binding in the Basal Ganglia using Single Photon Emission Tomography', *Personality and Individual Differences,* 17: 431–34.

Goldberg, L.R. (1993). 'The Structure of Phenotypic Personality in Traits', *American Psychologists,* 48: 26–34.

Howarth, E. and H.J. Eysenck (1968). 'Extraversion, Arousal, and Paired-Associate Recall', *Journal of Experimental Research in Personality,* 3: 114–16.

Hull, C. (1951). *Essentials of Behavior,* New Haven: Yale University Press.

Jones, J., H.J. Eysenck, I. Martin, and A. Levey (1981). 'Personality and the Topography of the Conditioned Eyelid Response', *Personality and Individual Differences,* 2: 61–83.

Kleinsmith and Kaplan (1963). 'Paired Associate Learning as a Function of Arousal and Interpolated Interval', *Journal of Experimental Psychology,* 65: 190–93.

Kleinsmith and Kaplan (1964). 'Interaction of Arousal and Recall Interval in Nonsense Syllable and Paired-Associate Learning', *Journal of Experimental Psychology,* 67: 124–6.

Lubow, R. (1989). *Latent Inhibition and Conditional Attention Theory,* New York: Cambridge University Press.

Martin, I. and A. Levey (1968). *The Genesis of the Classical Conditioned Response,* Oxford: Pergamon.

Plomin, R. and G. McClearn (1993). *Nature, Nurture and Psychology,* Washington DC: American Psychological Association.

Shigehisa, T. and J. Symons (1973). 'Effects of Intensity of Visual Stimulation on Auditory Sensitivity in Relation to Personality', *British Journal of Psychology,* 64: 205–13.

Shigehisa, P., T. Shigehisa and J. Symons (1973). 'Effects of Intensity of Auditory Stimulation on Photopic Visual Sensitivity in Relation to Personality', *Japanese Psychological Research,* 15: 164–72.

Spence, K. and R. Beecroft (1954). 'Differential Conditioning and Level of Anxiety', *Journal of Experimental Psychology,* 48: 399–403.

Spence, K. and I. Parker (1954). 'The Relation of Anxiety to Differential Eyelid Conditioning', *Journal of Experimental Psychology,* 47: 127–34.

Spence, J.T. and K. Spence (1966). 'The Motivational Components of Manifest Anxiety: Drive and Drive Stimuli', in C. Spielberger (ed.), *Anxiety and Behaviour,* 119–34, London: Academic Press.

Sternberg, R. and D. Detterman (1986). *What is Intelligence?* Norwood, NJ: Ablex.

Urbantschitsch, V. (1883). 'Uber den Einfluss von Trigeminus–Reizen auf die Sinnempfindungen insbesondere auf dem Gesichtsinn', *Archiv fur die Gesamte Physiologie,* 30: 129–75.

Zuckerman, M., D. Kuhlman and C. Camac (1988). 'What lies beyond E and N? Factor Analysis of Scales Believed to Measure Basic Dimensions of Personality', *Journal of Personality and Social Pathology,* 54: 96–107.

2 The Neuropsychology of Temperament

Jaffrey A. Gray

General Background

The term 'neuropsychology' is used to mean the study, quite generally, of the role played by the brain in behavioural and psychological functions, whether in human or animal subjects, and whether there is structural damage to the brain or not (as in Gray, 1982a). Since it is taken as axiomatic that all behavioural and psychological functions depend upon the activities of the brain, it follows that neuropsychology has a breadth which shadows that of psychology itself; if there is a psychology of hunger, intelligence, love, or learning French, then there is *ipso facto* a neuropsychology of the same.

Neuropsychology is a term of the same kind as physical chemistry or molecular genetics. It refers to a subject which arises at the frontier between two historically classical scientific disciplines as the barriers which (arbitrarily) divide their break down. In our case, the classical disciplines are psychology and neuroscience (the latter being itself a newly coined term, but covering the classical disciplines of neuroanatomy, neurophysiology, neurochemistry, etc.).

A major feature of the research strategies adopted in neuropsychology is that much reliance is necessarily placed upon experiments with animals. One advantage which flows from the use of such strategies is the need for simple operational and/or behavioural definitions of theoretical concepts, allowing them to be applied in the animal laboratory. Though, to be sure, this advantage is, to some extent, reduced by the subsequent need to demonstrate that there is sufficient continuity between animal and human neuropsychology, for the same concepts also to apply at the human level. The two assumptions that have guided my own thinking (and that of many others, e.g., Millenson, 1967; Mowrer, 1960; Newman, 1987; Shapiro *et al.,* 1988; and a number of authors in this volume) in thus rendering the term 'temperament' amenable to such simple definitions are: (1) that temperament reflects individual differences in predispositions towards particular kinds of emotion; and (2) that emotions are states of the Central (Conceptual) Nervous System (CNS), elicited by reinforcing events. It correctly captures the symbiosis between the study of the brain and behaviour that constitutes neuropsychology.

The Analysis of Emotion

Only in the animal learning theory, has there been a long reasonably clear consensus that emotions consist of states elicited by stimuli or events which have the capacity to serve as reinforcers for instrumental behaviour. This, for example, is the framework within which Miller (1951) and Mowrer (1947) analysed the concept of fear and its role in avoidance learning; Mowrer (1960) analysed the concept of relief, again in relation to avoidance learning; Amsel (1962) analysed the concept of frustration and its role in the extinction of rewarded behaviour; and Gray (1967, 1982a) analysed the concept of anxiety as an amalgam of fear and frustration.

The starting point for this analysis is the notion of an instrumental reinforcer. This has its standard Skinnerian definition: a reinforcer is any stimulus (or more complex event), which, if made contingent upon a response, alters the future probability of possible variants upon this definition, created by the intersection of (1) whether the putative reinforcer is presented, terminated, or omitted (when otherwise it would have occurred) contingent upon a response (the rows in Figure 1), and (2) whether the observed change is an increase or a decrease in the probability of emission of the response (the columns in Figure 1); if no change is observed, the stimulus is not a reinforcer at all. As a matter of empirical fact, it turns out that stimuli (if they are reinforcers at all) come in two kinds: those, which when presented contingent upon a response (top row), increase response probability and also, when terminated or omitted (bottom rows), decrease response probability; and those, which when presented, decrease response probability and also, when terminated or omitted, increase response probability. This gives rise to the distinction between (in various terminologies) positive (the former class of stimuli) and negative reinforcers (the latter), rewards and punishments, or appetitive and aversive stimuli. Since the termination and omission procedures usually give the same results, the figure may be collapsed into a 2×2 table: rewards, when presented, increase response probability and, when terminated/omitted, decrease it; punishments, when presented, decrease response probability and when terminated/omitted, increase it.

Procedure	Outcome $P^{(R)}\uparrow$	 $P^{(R)}\downarrow$
Presentation	Rew (Approach)	Pun! (Passive Avoidence)
Termination	Pun! (Escape)	Rew (Time-out)
Omission	Pun! (Active Avoidence)	Rew (Extinction)

S^{R+} S^{R-}

Figure 1. *The possible reinforcing events as defined operationally. Events may be presented, terminated, or omitted (rows) contingent upon a response, and response probablity (P^R) may, in consequence, increase or decrease (columns) S^{R+}, S^{R-}: positive and negative reinforcers, shown by cross-hatching.*

To this 2×2 table, one further complication has to be added: reinforcers may be primary (unconditioned) or secondary (conditioned). The former are stimuli or events which, without special learning, have innately reinforcing properties for the species concerned, for example, food, water, a sex partner, pain, etc. The latter are stimuli which are initially neutral (do not alter response probability), for example, a tone or light of moderate intensity, but take on reinforcing properties as a consequence of entering into an association (most probably by Pavlovian conditioning: Gray, 1975) with an unconditioned reinforcer.

We are now armed with most of the tools of conceptual analysis that we need. They are to be used to address the following questions: how many separate emotions are there, and how is each to be defined? Or, in terms of the argument being developed here, if, in general, emotions consist of states of the CNS elicited by reinforcing events, can we parcel out the total set of reinforcing events (as defined by Figure 1, together with the unconditioned/conditioned distinction) into subjects, each corresponding to a different emotion which members of only that subsect elicit?

At first, to someone steeped in human psychology, this question may seem too simplistic to the point of absurdity. After all, if one looks into any good dictionary, one will find hundreds of words describing (apparently) different emotions. Consider: regret, nostalgia, indignation, schadenfreude, etc. Yet, by the analysis developed here, there is only a maximum of eight (the multiple of 2×2×2 orthogonal distinctions) separate emotions possible. This problem, however, is more apparent than real. The analysis developed here is not aimed at human linguistic behavior. How we name emotions is as different from the way the CNS produces emotions, as is how we name colours from the mechanisms that underlie color vision; and, in both cases, the words we use reflect as much the particular circumstances which give rise to the experience (e.g., "nostalgia", "shocking pink") as the experience itself. Just as, in the case of color vision, a mechanism based initially on just three colour pigments is able to give rise to the great variety of experienced colours and thus to provide the basis for the larger variety of colour words, so (it is contended here) just a few emotion systems in the CNS are able to give rise to a variety of experienced emotional states, and then to provide the basis for the vocabulary used to describe those states (Gray, 1985).

How, then, are we to arrive at subsets of reinforcing events, each corresponding to a separate emotion and, therefore, to a separate system in the brain responsible for that emotion? The distinctions we have made above are largely of a purely operational kind. It is a matter of experimental convenience that we decide, for example, to measure changes in response probability separately as increases and decreases (the columns of Figure 1), or to classify stimuli as positive or negative reinforcers (the cross-hatching as shown in Figure 1). But we do not know in advance whether or not the brain makes the same distinctions that we do; it may or may not use different mechanisms to acquire new behaviour and to suppress the old, or to respond to positive and negative reinforcers, or to do both these things. Moreover, very different theoretical positions have been taken on just this sort of issue. Thus, some theorists suppose that the brain has a 'reward system' for dealing with positive reinforcers, no matter how they affect behaviour, together with a 'punishment system' which deals similarly with negative reinforcers (e.g., Olds and Olds, 1965); while others suppose that there is one system for acquisition of new behaviour and another for behavioural inhibition (e.g., Gray, 1975). These theories are quite different; though, they have often been confused with one another.

To take a position on these complex issues in the short space of a chapter inevitably appears arbitrary. However, the specific model I shall now present is based on an extensive database, culled from a wide variety of experimental approaches in the study of animal learning and behaviour, psychopharmacology, neuropsychology, and neuroscience (e.g., Gray, 1982a, 1987). A number of alternative models can be ruled out on the basis of the data from one or other of these disciplines; the model that remains is, by contrast, at least consistent with (though far from proved by) the bulk of the data from all of them (this multiplicity of sources of critical data is, indeed, one of the great advantages of the whole neuropsychological enterprise).

The model posits in the mammalian CNS three fundamental emotion systems, each of which (1) responds to a separate subset of reinforcing events with specific types of behaviour; and (2) is mediated by a separate set of interacting brain structures that processes specific types of information. The three systems are termed the behavioural inhibition system, the fight/flight system, and the behavioural approach system, respectively. The first of these has been extensively described before (see especially Gray, 1982a); the second has so far received little theoretical attention, especially at the cognitive level while the third has recently become the object of such attention (Gray *et al.,* 1991; Swerdlow and Koob, 1987). I shall therefore consider the fight/flight system only briefly, but the behavioural approach system in a little more detail than the other two systems. A further postulate, addressed at the end of the chapter, is that it is individual differences in the functioning of these three emotion systems, and their interaction, which underlie human temperament as measured by such dimensional analyses of personality as those of Eysenck (e.g., 1981) or Zuckerman, Kuhlman, and Camac (1988). There will be no attempt to present the data on which the model rests; portions of these data have been reviewed by Gray (1975, 1977, 1982a, 1987–1994), Gray and McNaughton (1983), and Gray *et al.* (1991).

The Model: I. The Behavioural Inhibition System

This is the best worked out part of the model, and the only one for which a corresponding human emotion (anxiety) can plausibly be identified. The behavioural inhibition is defined by the input-output relations. The critical eliciting stimuli are conditioned stimuli associated with punishment, conditioned stimuli associated with the omission or termination or reward ('frustrative nonreward'; Amsel, 1962), or novel stimuli. The appearance of novelty on this list may cause some surprise, since it is not at all at first obvious that this counts as a reinforcer.

In fact, however, novel stimuli possess rather complex reinforcing properties, which change as a function of the degree of novelty, and also interact with stimulus intensity as well as a number of other factors (Berlyne, 1960). At high values of novelty and intensity, the stimulus principally elicits the type of behaviour as (with stimulus prolongation or repetition) these values diminish, the elicited behaviour shifts to approach (see the section on the Behavioural Approach System, below); with still further stimulus prolongation or repetition, complete habituation sets in, and the stimulus ceases to elicit any response. The transition from behavioural inhibition to approach is not sudden; thus, over much of the range of values, novel stimuli elicit an approach-avoidance conflict (Gray, 1982a, 1987, Zuckerman, 1982).

The behaviour elicited by these stimuli consists in behavioural inhibition (interruption of any ongoing behaviour); an increment in the level of arousal, such that the next behaviour to occur (which may consist in a continuation of the action that was interrupted) is carried out with extra vigour and/or speed; and an increment in attention, such that more information is taken in, especially concerning novel features of the environment. Any one of the inputs to the BIS elicits all the outputs; furthermore, a range of interventions is capable of blocking all the outputs to any of the inputs, while leaving intact other input-output relationships (including some that involve inputs to or outputs from the BIS, but not both).

These are among the reasons for regarding the BIS as indeed a unified system, rather than a set of separate input-output relationships. Among the interventions which specifically abolish the input-output relationships that define the BIS is the administration of drugs, such as benzodiazepines, barbiturates, and alcohol, which reduce anxiety in human beings; indeed, the study of such drugs was a major impetus to the formation of the concept of the BIS (Gray, 1982a, b). On this basis, one may tentatively identify the subjective state that accompanies activity in the BIS, such as anxiety. This identification gains plausibility from the fact that it leads to a face-valid description of human anxiety; that is, a state in which one responds to threat (stimuli associated with punishment or nonreward) or uncertainty (novelty) with the reaction, 'stop, look and listen, and get ready for action' (Gray, 1982a, b, c).

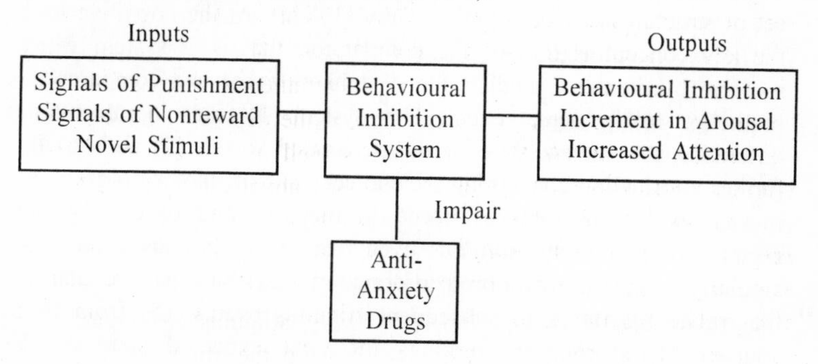

Figure 2. *The Behavioural Inhibition System (BIS) as defined by its inputs and outputs.*

The (tentative) identification of the BIS with activity in this set of structures depends upon a variety of sources of information (Gray, 1982a). Now, from the point of view of a psychologist attempting to understand temperament, it is, on its own, of no great importance to be told that one set of brain structures rather than another mediates the functions of the BIS. Indeed, there have been a number of valuable attempts to test, at the human level, predictions derived from the general concept of the BIS, together with related ideas, without reference to its supposed neurological under-pinning (e.g., Boddy *et al.,* 1986). There is, however, a value to the psychologist in such 'neurologizing'. First, in the actual construction of a concept such as that of the BIS, the utilization of data from the neurosciences as well as from psychology is likely to lead to a more robust basis for further, purely psychological theorizing. Second, understanding of the neural basis of a system such as the BIS can lead to specific psychological questions or hypotheses that would otherwise be unlikely to arise; we shall see some examples of this later in the chapter. Third, the neurological level leads inevitably back to mainstream issues in psychology. For, the main function of the brain is to process information; and the task of describing how that information is processed, in other than neurological terms, belongs to cognitive psychology. Thus, faced with the kind of neurological flow diagram shown in Figure 3, one should ask not only how the structures illustrated therein produce the behavioural outputs of the BIS (Figure 2), but also what cognitive (i.e., information-processing) operations they perform in order to do so.

The information-processing functions attributed to the interlinked set of structures can be found in Gray (1982a). At the cognitive level, the key concept is that of the comparator, that is, a system which, moment by moment, predicts the next likely event and compares this prediction to the actual event. This system (1) takes in information describing the current state of the perceptual world; (2) adds to this further information concerning the subject's current motor program; (3) makes use of information stored in memory and describing past regularities that relate stimulus events to other stimulus events; (4) similarly, makes use of stored information describing past regularities that relate responses to subsequent stimulus events; (5) from these sources of information, predicts the next expected state of the perceptual world; (6) compares the predicted to the actual next state of the perceptual world; (7) decides either that there is a match or that there is a mismatch between the predicted and the actual states of the world; (8) if there is a match, proceeds to run through steps (1) to (7) again; but (9) if there is a mismatch, brings the current motor program to a halt, that is, operates the outputs of the BIS so as to take in further information and resolve the difficulty that has interrupted this program.

In the application of this model to anxiety, the focus of the analysis was on step (9) and the further consequences of this step (Gray, 1982a). More recently, Gray *et al.* (1991) have been concerned with the details of the monitoring process itself, and the way in which this interacts with the running of motor programs; we turn to this aspect of the problem later, in the section on the Behavioural Approach System.

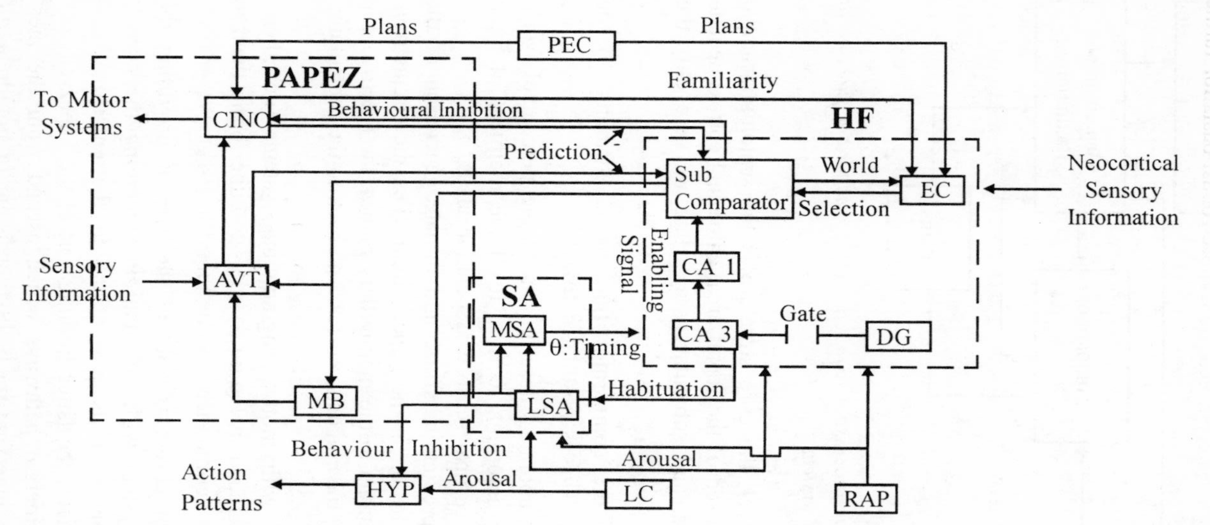

Figure 3. *The Septohippocampal System: Major structures composing the neural basis of the Behavioural Inhibition Stystem. The three major buildings are shown in heavy print: HF, the hippocampal formation, made up of the entorhinal cortex, EC, the denate gyrus, DG, CA 3, CA 1, and the subicular area, SUB. SA; the septal area, containing the medial and latera septal areas, MSA and LSA: and the Papez circuit, which receives projections from and returns them to the subicular area via the mammillary bodies. MB. Anteroventral thalamus, AVT, and cingulate cortex, CING. Other structures shown are the hypothalames, HYP, the locus coeruleus, LC, the raphe nuclei, RAP, and the prefrontal cortex, PFC. Arrows show direction of projection; the projection from SUB to MSA lacks anatomical confirmation. Words in lower case show postulated functions; behavioural inhibition.*

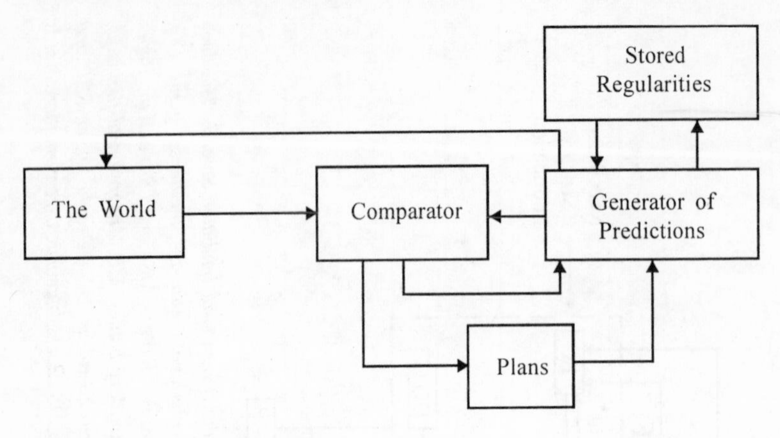

Figure 4. *Information processing required for the comparator function of the septohippocampal system.*

At the neural level, the core structure is the septohippocampal system (SHS, composed of the septal area, entorhinal cortex, dentate gyrus, hippocampus, and subicular area). Here we note only the following points:

1. The heart of the comparator function is attributed to the subicular area. This is postulated to:
   (a) receive elaborated descriptions of the perceptual world from the entorhinal cortex, itself the recipient of input from all cortical sensory association areas.
   (b) receive predictions from, and initiate generation of the next prediction in the Papez circuit (i.e., the circuit from the subiculum to the mammillary bodies, the anteroventral thalamus, the cingulate cortex, and back to the subiculum); and
   (c) interface with motor programming systems (not themselves included in Figure 3) so as to either bring them to a halt or permit them to continue.
2. The prefrontal cortex is allotted the role of providing the comparator system with information concerning the current motor program (via its projections to the entorhinal and cingulate cortices, the latter forming part of the Papez circuit).
3. The monoaminergic pathways which ascend from the mesencephalon to innervate the SHS (consisting of noradrenergic

fibres originating in the median raphe), are charged with alerting the whole system under conditions of threat and diverting its activities to deal with the threat; in the absence of threat, the information-processing activities of the system can be put to other, non-emotional purposes (Gray, 1984).

4. The system needs to be quantized in time, to allow appropriate comparison between specific states of the world and the corresponding predictions, followed by initiation of the next prediction and next intake of information describing the world. This function is attributed to the hippocampal theta rhythm in this model, giving rise to an 'instant' of about one-tenth of a second.

Much of the above analysis is inevitably speculative. Even so, the existence of a reasonably detailed sketch map of an emotion system covering several levels of analysis—behavioural, neural, and cognitive—together with a plausible identification of a subjective state associated with the activity of this system (i.e., anxiety), has, I believe, heuristic value in indicating what a developed theory of a particular emotion might look like. In particular, we can now flesh out a little the notion of an 'emotion system'. Behaviourally, this consists, as we have seen, of a set of outputs jointly elicited by any one of the several types of inputs. The plausibility of attributing such input-output relationships to an underlying system is increased by evidence that, say, certain drugs (e.g., Gray, 1977) or lesions to the brain (e.g., Gray and McNaughton, 1983) selectively alter these but not other input-output relationships; especially, if one can show by independent arguments from neuroscientific data that the drugs and lesions concerned affect function in only a particular subset of neural structures (e.g., Gray, 1982a). The concept of a system gathers further strength from a consideration of the particular cognitive (information-processing) functions that it is likely to discharge; especially, if such ideas can then be tested at the human level, as has recently been done for anxiety and the BIS (Mathews, 1988). Further important evidence at the human level comes from the recent application of imaging techniques to the living brain: using positron emission tomography, Reiman *et al.* (1984) have showed that patients diagnosed as having panic disorder differed from normal controls in only one brain region containing the entorhinal cortex (the major input to the SHS) and the subicular area (the major output station from the SHS). Thus, the program of research that commenced with the study, in animals, of drugs that reduce anxiety in human patients has come almost full circle back to the clinic.

The Model: II. The Fight/Flight System

The input-output relationships which define the fight/flight system (F/FLS) are a tentative and highly schematic neurology (Adams, 1979; Graeff, 1987). Whereas the BIS responds to conditioned aversive stimuli, the F/FLS responds to unconditioned aversive stimuli; and, whereas the BIS responds with the reaction 'Stop, look, and listen, and get ready for action', the F/FLS responds with unconditioned defensive aggression or escape behaviour (Adams, 1979). Moreover, to these different patterns of behaviour there correspond different pharmacologies. Thus, as noted above, the anti-anxiety drugs reduce the responses of the BIS to its adequate inputs, but these drugs do not reduce responses to unconditioned aversive (painful) stimuli, analgesics such as morphine reduce responses to painful stimuli, conversely, but do not affect reactions to conditioned aversive stimuli (for review, see Gray, 1982a). Similarly, as will be evident from a comparison of the two systems, the BIS and F/FLS have different neurologies, with very little overlap (which is not to say with little interaction; see below). There are three important levels in the neuraxis at which stimulation and lesion experiments have pinpointed structures which appear to have the functions of the F/FLS: the amygdala, which inhibits the medial hypothalamus, which, in turn, inhibits the final output pathway in the central gray. As yet, there has been little if any work on the information-processing activities of the F/FLS, nor any direct link with a corresponding human emotion (though anger and/or terror are obvious possibilities).

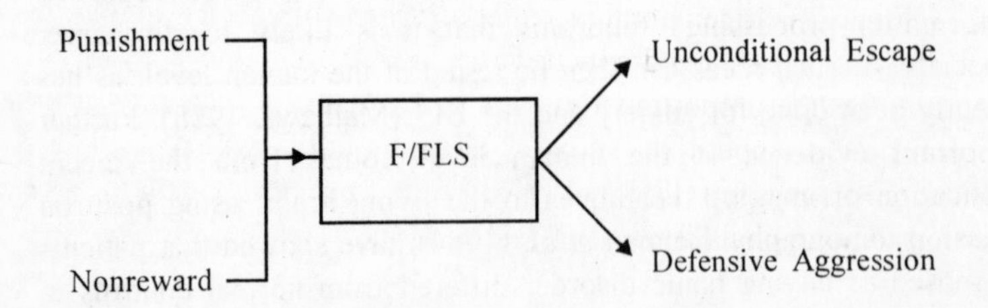

Figure 5. *The Fight/Flight System (F/FLS) as defined by its inputs and outputs.*

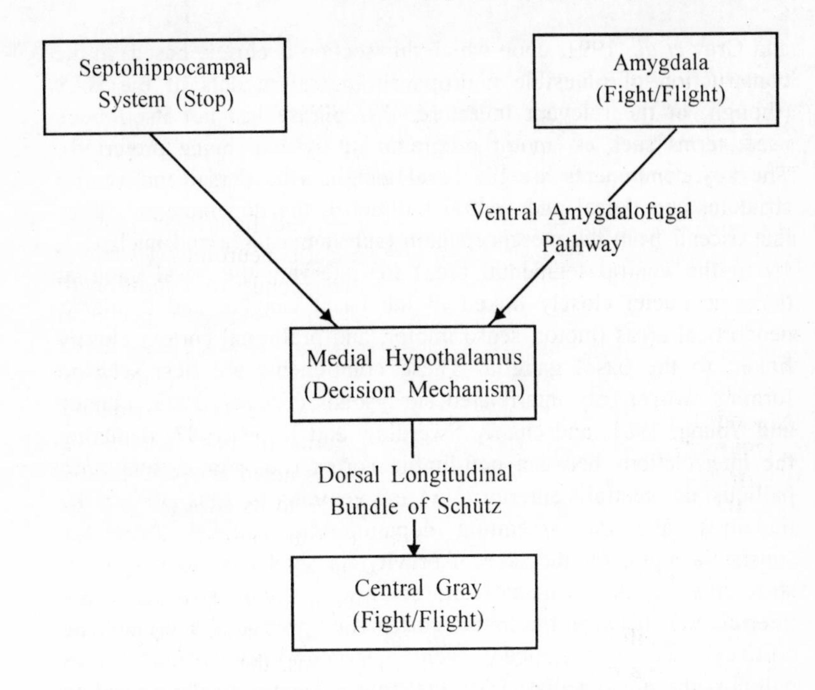

Figure 6. *Major structures composing the neural basis of the Fight/Flight System.*

The Model: III. The Behavioural Approach System

The input-output relations that define the behavioural approach system (BAS) or behavioural activation (Fowles, 1980). In essence, this depicts a simple positive feedback system, activated by stimuli associated with reward or with the termination/omission of punishment ('relieving non-punishment'; Mowrer, 1960), and operating so as to increase spatiotemporal proximity to such stimuli. By adding the postulate that conditioned appetitive stimuli of this kind activate the BAS to a degree proportional to their spatiotemporal proximity to the unconditioned appetitive stimulus ('goal') with which they are associated, a system that is, in general, capable of guiding the organism to the goals it needs to attain (food, water, etc.) for survival (Deutsch, 1964; Gray, 1975)

At the neurological level, the last decade has seen rapid progress (Groves, 1983; Penney and Young, 1981; Swerdlow and Koob, 1987;

and Gray *et al.*, 1991, upon which this section is closely based) in the construction of plausible neuropsychological models of the BAS (though, in the relevant literature, this phrase has not itself been used, terms such as 'motor programming system' being preferred). The key components are the basal ganglia (the dorsal and ventral striatum, and dorsal and ventral pallidum); the dopaminergic fibres that ascend from the mesencephalon (substantia nigra and nucleus A 10 in the ventral tegmental area) to innervate the basal ganglia; thalamic nuclei closely linked to the basal ganglia; and similarly, neocortical areas (motor, sensorimotor, and prefrontal cortex) closely linked to the basal ganglia. These components are best seen as forming two closely interrelated subsystems (Groves, 1983; Penney and Young, 1981; and chiefly Swerdlow and Koob, 1987) depicting the interrelations between non-limbic cortex (i.e., motor, senglobus pallidus, nn. ventralis anterior (VA) and ventralis lateralis (VL) of the thalamus, and the ascending dopaminergic pathway from the substantia nigra; for the sake of brevity we shall refer to this set of structures as the 'caudate' motor system. Similarly, there are interrelations between the limbic cortex (i.e., prefrontal and cingulate cortices), nucleus accumbens (ventral striatum), the ventral globus pallidus, the dorsomedial (DM) thalamic nucleus, and the ascending dopaminergic projection from A 10; for brevity we shall call this set of structures the 'accumbens' motor system. Importantly, nucleus accumbens also receives projections from two major limbic structures; the subiculum (output station for the SHS) and the amygdala.

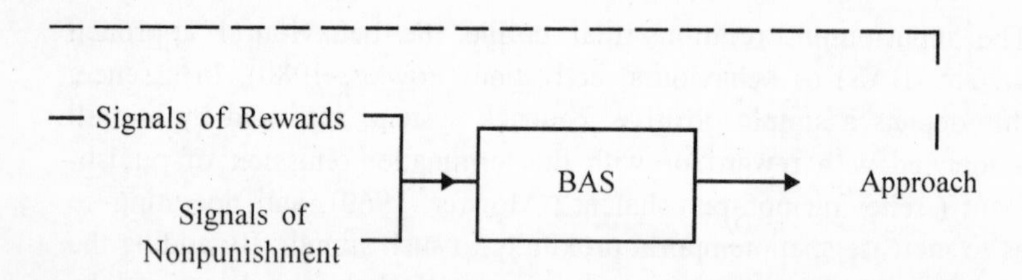

Figure 7. *The Behavioural Approach System (BAS) as defined by its inputs and outputs.*

As proposed by Swerdlow and Koob (1987), one can regard both the caudate and accumbens systems as being composed of three interacting feedback loops: a cortico-thalamo-cortical positive feedback loop (I); a cortico-striato-pallido-thalamo-cortical positive

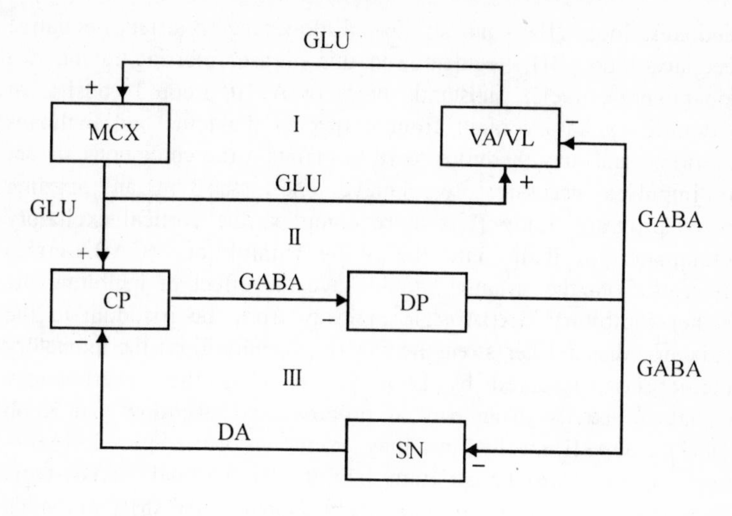

Figure 8. *The Caudate Motor System.*

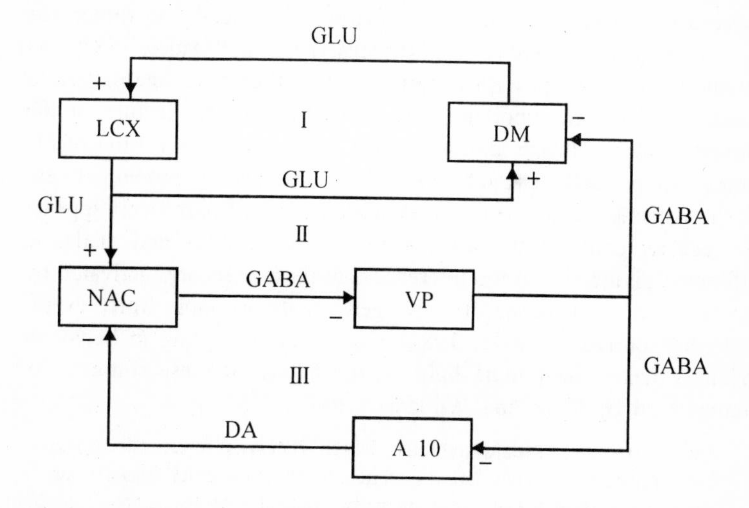

Figure 9. *The Accumbens Motor System. Limbic cortico-striato-pallido-thalamic-midbrain circuitry making up the 5 accumbens component of the Behavioural Approach System. LCX: limbic cortex, including prefrontal and cingulate areas. DM: dorsomedial thalamic nucleus. NAC: nucleus accumbens (ventral striatum). VP: ventral pallidum. A 10: dopaminergic nucleus A 10 in the ventral tegmental area. Neurotransmitters and feedback loops, as in Figure 8. Based on Swerdlow and Koob (1987).*

feedback loop (II); and striato-pallido-tegmento-striatal negative feedback loop (III), 'tegmento' in this phrase referring to the two dopaminergic nuclei, substantia nigra or A 10. Loop I consists of a double excitatory input from cortex to thalamus and thalamus to cortex, and may therefore serve to maintain the continuous stream of impulses necessary to achieve one 'step' in an ongoing motor program. Loop II is more complex: the cortical excitatory (glutamatergic) input onto the Spiny I inhibitory (GABA-ergic) efferents from the striatum should have the effect of inhibiting the further inhibitory GABA-ergic pathway from the pallidum to the thalamus, thus further strengthening (by disinhibition) the excitatory interactions subserved by Loop I. To bring this reverberatory excitatory activity to an end, as proposed by Swerdlow and Koob (1987), Loop III is called into play: excitation of the Spiny I GABA-ergic output from the striatum inhibits the pallidal GABA-ergic inhibition of the ascending dopaminergic input to the striatum, which is therefore increased. Since this dopaminergic input is itself also inhibitory, striatal activity is accordingly reduced; or rather (as proposed by, e.g. Evenden and Robbins, 1983 and Oades, 1985, and developed further below) it is permitted to switch from one pattern to another. A further important anatomico-physiological feature of the caudate and accumbens motor systems lies in the organization of the Spiny I output cells (Groves, 1983). These comprise about 96 per cent of the entire population of striatal neurons. Each Spiny I cell appears to receive convergent inputs from many cortical and thalamic afferents, giving rise to the inference that these cells are 'activated by the temporal coincidence of convergent excitatory input from several different sources' (Groves, 1982) Single unit recording in behaving primates has thrown some light on the nature of these sources. As summarized by Rolls and Williams (1987):

> Neurons in the caudate nucleus, which receives inputs from the association cortex, have activity related to environmental stimuli that signal preparation for or initiation of behavioral responses... Neurons in the putamen, which receive inputs from the sensorimotor cortex, have activity related to movements. Neurons in the ventral striatum (including the nucleus accumbens), which receive inputs from limbic structures such as the amygdala and hippocampus, respond to emotion-provoking or novel stimuli.

The firing of some particular subset of Spiny I striatal neurons, then, will be triggered by a particular combination of environmental stimulation and patterns of movement. The excitatory loops (I and II) described above will ensure that this same subset will continue to fire for a period of time. Continuity of this pattern of activity is further assured by the interrelations between the Spiny I cells themselves. These are organized in the form of a lateral inhibitory network; thus, whichever subset of Spiny I cells is active at any one time, it will tend to inhibit firing in other such cells outside the set.

It remains to be considered as to what might be represented by the particular set of cells that are active at a given moment. Basing their arguments both on the anatomical organization of the basal ganglia as described above, and on the general theory of random associative networks (Rolls, 1986a), Rolls and Williams (1987) have proposed an interesting answer to this question. Their proposal relates to the selection of an active subset of cells, not only in the striatum itself, but at all levels of the cortico-thalamo-pallidal midbrain circuitry. I shall not here go into the details of this proposal. In brief, however, Rolls and Williams (1987) consider cells, which, because of the particular chance patterns of connections they possess, receive inputs from both: (1) neurons that respond to environmental cues associated with reinforcement (i.e., reward or the avoidance of punishment); and (2) other neurons that fire when the animal makes a movement that affects the occurrence of this reinforcement; and they show how such cells might initially respond only to the conjunction of cue plus movement, but could come eventually to be activated by the clue alone, and so to participate in the production of the appropriate movement, given the cue. Thus, the particular set of neurons firing at a particular time in the basal ganglia can be seen (1) as representing a step in a goal-directed motor program; and (2) as having been selected for this function by instrumental reinforcement mediated by the connectivity of the neurons that make up the set.

The discussion so far has distinguished anatomically between the caudate and accumbens motor systems, but not yet functionally. In now making this distinction, I shall concentrate on the functions of the accumbens system; the function of the caudate system has already been given an adequate description, that is, that of encoding the specific content (in terms of relationships between stimuli, responses, and reinforcement) of successive steps in a goal-directed motor program. What, then, are the additional functions discharged by the accumbens system? A possible answer to this question (Gray *et al.*,

1991) is two-fold: (1) switching between steps in the motor program; and (2) in interaction with the SHS, monitoring the smooth running of the motor program in terms of progress towards the intended goal.

We have supposed above that the firing of a particular subset of output neurons in the dorsal striatum and its associated neurons in other related structures (pallidal, thalamic, etc.) represents a particular step in a motor program; and that the firing of the set is maintained for a period of time by the positive feedback loops designated I and II. For a motor program conceived in this way, to proceed as an integrated whole, there has to be an orderly transition from one step in the program to the next. The 'orderliness' of such a transition can best be defined in terms of spatiotemporal progression towards the reinforcer, or 'goal', to which the program is directed and by mediation of which it was originally established, that is to say, the 'next' step must be the one which will most effectively bring the subject into greater spatiotemporal proximity to the relevant goal. How is this next step to be determined?

Within the context of animal learning theory, the most common answers that have been given to this question depend upon the concepts of the goal gradient and incentive motivation. In essence, the theories that employ these concepts make the following assumptions:

1. Stimuli which do not initially possess positively reinforcing properties come to acquire them as the result of Pavlovian conditioning, in which they serve as conditioned stimuli (CS) for an unconditioned positive reinforcer; the latter may be either a definite reward such as food or water (providing the basis for approach behaviour), or the omission of an expected punishment (providing the basis for active avoidance).
2. The degree to which such CS possess positively reinforcing properties is a direct function of their proximity (in terms of time, space, or position in a series of chained stimulus-response links) to the initial unconditioned stimulus (UCS).
3. If the subject is simultaneously in the presence of more than one such CS, he/she directs his/her behaviour towards the one with the highest reinforcing power.

These assumptions can, in principle, generate behaviour that maximizes positive reinforcement (by approach to reward) and minimizes negative reinforcement (by active avoidance of punishment) (Gray, 1975).

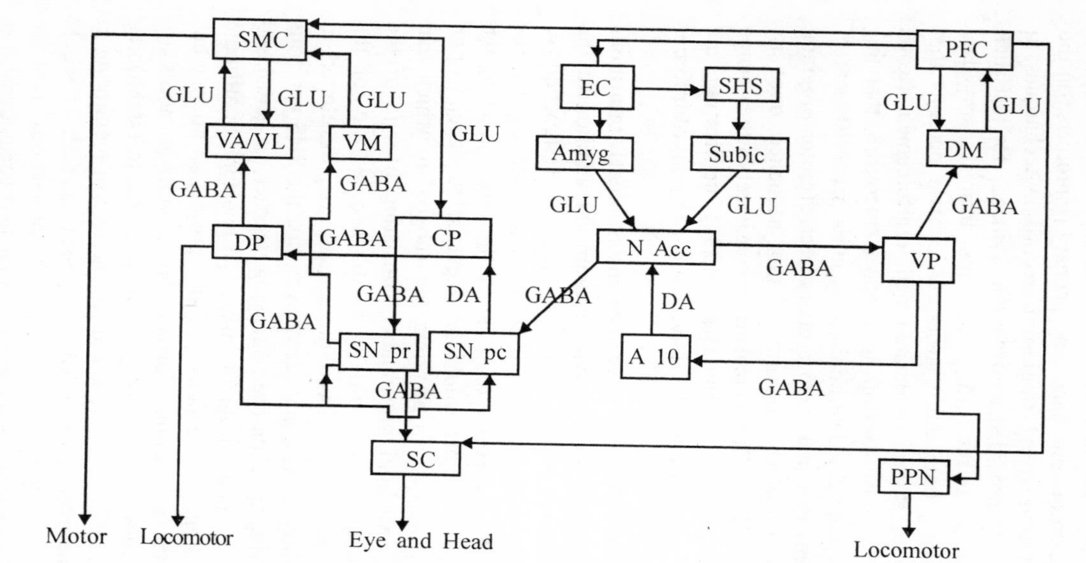

Figure 10. *Major structures composing the neural basis of the Behavioural Approach System and its interrelations with the Behavioural Inhibition System. Structures: SMC = sensorimotor cortex; PFC = prefrontal Cortex; EC = entorhinal cortex; SHS = septohippocampal system; Subic= subicular area; Amyg = amygdala; VA/VL = N. ventrails anterror and ventrals lateralis thalami; VM = N ventralis medialis thalami; DM = N, dorsalis medialis thalami; DP = dorsal palladium; VP = ventral paladium; CP = caudate-patamen; N. Acc = N. accumbens; SNpr = substantia nigra, pars reticulata; SNpc = substantia nigra, pars compacta; A 10 = N. A 10 in ventral tegmental area; SC = superior colliculus, PPN = penduculopontine nucleus. Transmitters: GLU = glutamate; DA = dopamine; GABA = gamma–aminobutyric acid.*

If we use these notions to guide us to a means by which the basal ganglia can assure orderly transitions from one step to the next in their motor programs, we should seek, then, a source of information concerning relationships between environmental stimuli that are not innately reinforcing, on the one hand, and primary reinforcers, on the other. The Rolls' group, using single-unit recording techniques in behaving monkeys, has provided considerable evidence for just such a source of information, in the form of the input from the amygdala to nucleus accumbens; both these structures contain neurons that respond selectively to stimuli associated with reinforcement (Rolls and Williams, 1987). It is plausible to suppose, therefore, that this input is responsible both for determining the initial establishment of the sequence of steps that makes up a goal-directed motor program, and for guiding the orderly running of this sequence once its establishment is complete. This postulate is consistent with a range of other evidence (Rolls, 1986b; Gray, 1987) implicating the amygdala in the formation of Pavlovian stimulus–reinforcer association.

However, this is not all that is needed to ensure orderly transitions from one step to another in a motor program. In addition to the selection and initiation of the next step in the program (a function we have just attributed to the input from the amygdala to nucleus accumbens), it is also necessary to consider the termination of the step that is in progress. This would be expected to depend upon feedback indicating success in attaining the subgoal to which that step is directed (a subgoal presumably consisting of one of the secondary reinforcing stimuli initially established by way of the amygdala–accumbens input). Given the assumption, developed in detail elsewhere (Gray, 1982a; and see above), that the SHS performs just such a monitoring function (i.e., checking whether the actual and expected outcomes of motor programs match), it is natural to attribute the role of providing this feedback to the projection to nucleus accumbens from the subiculum. Furthermore, given the necessary correspondence between (1) the role of reinforcement in establishing an orderly sequence of motor steps; and (2) the role of monitoring in determining that the expected subgoals have been attained, we would expect a considerable degree of overlap in the projections from the subiculum and the amygdala, respectively, to nucleus accumbens. It is indeed known that both these projections are densest in the same, caudomedial, region of the nucleus accumbens (Phillipson and

Griffiths, 1985), but information is as yet unavailable concerning the interrelations between them at the ultrastructural level.

These, then, are the major building blocks, both conceptual and anatomical, which make up the BAS. The chief assumptions they embody may be summarized as follows:

1. The caudate system, by way of its connections with sensory and motor cortices, encodes the specific content of each step in a motor program (e.g., for a rat, turn left at a junction in a maze; or, for a human being, the next word to be spoken in a sentence).
2. The accumbens system operates in tandem with the caudate system so as to permit switching from one step to the next in a motor program.
3. Both, the establishment of the sequence of steps that makes up a given motor program, and the subsequent orderly running of the program, are guided by the projection to nucleus accumbens from the amygdala; this projection conveys information concerning cue-reinforcement associations.
4. The SHS is responsible for checking whether the actual outcome of a particular motor step matches the expected outcome; this information is transmitted to nucleus accumbens by the projection from the subiculum.
5. Activities of the caudate, accumbens and SHS are co-ordinated and kept in step with one another by the prefrontal cortex, acting by way of its interconnections, respectively, with (a) the cortical components of the caudate system, (b) nucleus accumbens, dorsomedial thalamus and amygdala; and (c) the entorhinal and cingulate cortices.
6. The maintenance of the patterns of activity in a subset of striatal, thalamic, and cortical neurons that makes up a motor step is due to the reverberatory excitatory activity in Loops I and II, together with lateral inhibition in the striatum. These patterns of activity are periodically interrupted by the firing of the dopaminergic inputs to the striatum at the termination of Loop III.
7. The duration of a step in a motor program corresponds to the joint operation, in both the caudate and accumbens systems, of Loops I–III.
8. The timing is co-ordinated between the septohippocampal motor programming system and the basal ganglia motor programming

system. Given assumptions 6 and 7 above, and given the assumption that time is quantized in the SHS by the theta rhythm (Gray, 1982a), corresponding to an 'instant' of about a tenth of a second, this must also be the duration of a motor step.

Further details of this model of the BAS are available in Gray *et al.,* (1991). There has been little work relating the BAS to human emotion; given the functions attributed to this system, we might expect it to underlie such states as pleasurable anticipation ('hope'; Mowrer, 1960), elation, or happiness. More dangerously, it is likely that the activity in the BAS underlies the 'high' experienced by users of a variety of recreational drugs. There is good evidence that conventional positive reinforcers such as food or a sexually receptive member of the opposite sex elicit the release of dopamine from the terminals of A 10 neurons in nucleus accumbens, and that this neurochemical effect is closely related to the approach behaviour that such stimuli also elicit (and which, indeed, defines them as being positive reinforcers). It is significant, therefore, that compounds as chemically diverse as heroin, amphetamines, and cocaine (Stewart, de Wit, and Eikelboom, 1984), alcohol (Di Chiara and Imperato, 1985), and nicotine (Imperato, Mulas and Di Chiara, 1986; Mitchell *et al.,* 1989) have in common, the capacity to cause the release of dopamine in nucleus accumbens, and sometimes very selectively, in this region (e.g., Mitchell *et al.,* 1989). It has also been reported that animals will work to self-administer the dopamine-releasing drug, amphetamine, into nucleus accumbens (Hoebel *et al.,* 1981). It seems probable, therefore, that the powerful reinforcing effects of the common drugs of abuse stem, at least in part, from their capacity to release dopamine in nucleus accumbens and so to activate (in manner whose details, are as yet obscure) the BAS.

Personality

These, then, are the three postulated fundamental emotion systems, each: (1) defined in terms of a set of behavioural input–output relationships, in which the inputs consist of specific subsets of reinforcing events; and (2) attributed to the functioning of a particular subsystem in the brain. In the case of two of these systems (the BIS and BAS), the analysis (speculative as it is) has been extended also to the third, cognitive level, at which specific information-processing functions are attributed to the neural system concerned. Next we turn to the relation between these three systems and temperament (it should be noted that, in what follows, I use the terms 'temperament' and 'personality' interchangeably; I take them both to mean what remains of individual differences, once general intelligence and such special cognitive characteristics as visuo-spatial or verbal ability have been removed.

As noted, at the outset of the chapter, it is assumed that temperament reflects individual differences in predispositions towards particular kinds of emotion. We may now rephrase that assumption thus: temperament reflects parameter values (Gray, 1967) that determine, for a particular individual, the operating characteristics of our three emotion systems, alone and in interaction with one another. A further basic assumption is that the major dimensions of personality, as measured by such multivariate statistical techniques as factor analysis (e.g., Eysenck and Eysenck, 1985; Zuckerman *et al.*, 1988), are created by individual differences in such parameter values. However, while these techniques are able to determine the number of independent sources of variation in a given matrix of correlations (obtained, for example, from a battery of questionnaires or other instruments for the measurement of personality), they cannot by themselves establish a nonarbitrary location of the factors used to describe these sources of variation. Thus, it cannot be assumed that a particular dimensional description of personality, for example, introversion-extraversion (E), neuroticism (N) and psychoticism (P) in the Eysenckian system, embodies a one-to-one correspondence between the dimensions employed and the fundamental emotion systems, whose variation between individuals gives rise, *ex hypothesi,* to personality.

Analyses of personality such as those offered by Eysenck and Eysenck (1985) or Zuckerman *et al.* (1988) start from human individual differences measured directly, but in tests whose relation to the postulated underlying emotion systems is unknown. Suppose, instead, that we start the other way round and use our current understanding of these systems to predict the likely structure of human personality. We would then expect to observe dimensions of personality that correspond to individual differences in the functioning of each of our three emotion systems. In other words, we would expect to see: (1) a dimension of personality corresponding to individual differences in the intensity of functioning of the BIS, of which the high pole would presumably correspond to high-trait anxiety (Gray, 1982a); (2) a dimension corresponding to individual differences in the functioning of the F/FLS, of which the high pole might correspond to a high propensity to aggressive-defensive behaviour; and (3) a dimension corresponding to individual differences in the functioning of the BAS, of which the high pole might correspond to a high propensity to behaviour motivated by positive reinforcement and to the accompanying pleasurable emotions (hope, happiness, elation).

It is in connection with the first of these postulated dimensions (trait anxiety) that most progress has been made in bringing these general notions into the laboratory. This process has been aided by the existence of good instruments for measuring trait anxiety at the human level (e.g., Spence and Spence, 1966; Spielberger, 1976); and also by the fact that the location of this trait within an overall three-dimensional personality space is well established. Thus, in terms of the Eysenckian axes, high trait anxiety corresponds to high N, low E and low P, the alignment with N being the closest. These known correspondences have permitted a series of laboratory tests designed to pit predictions from Eysenck's (e.g., 1981) theory against those derived from the BIS model. The key predictions concern learning and performance in tasks which use either positive or negative reinforcers (Gray, 1970).

Trait anxiety is depicted in Figure 11 as a diagonal (from high N, low E, to low N, high E) running across the Eysenckian two-dimensional space defined by N and E. In addition, a second theoretical personality dimension derived from the emotion-system approach, impulsivity, orthogonal to trait anxiety, is postulated as reflecting individual differences in the functioning of the BAS. When this proposal was first made (Gray, 1970), it took no account of third Eysenckian dimension, nor of individual differences in the F/FLS. Since there is still no clear indication as to how best to extend the model into this necessary third dimension (though, see Gray, 1983, for one suggestion), I shall continue here to leave it out of account. The simplified two-dimensional model has the advantage that, predictions from Eysenck's (1981) theory (far and away the best validated of those that have emerged from the direct study of human individual differences) are clearly different from those derived from the emotion-system approach.

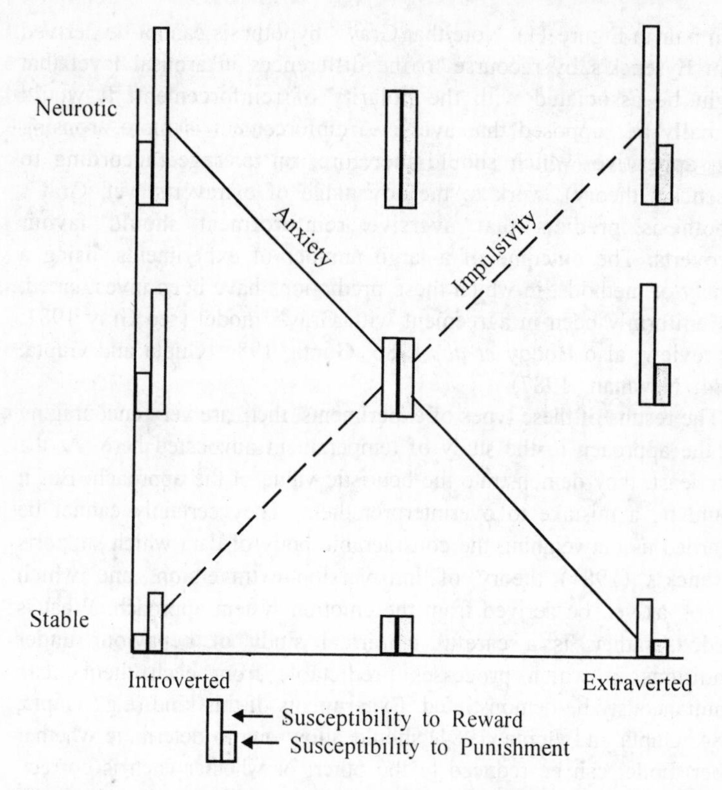

Figure 11. *Relations between sensitivity to stimuli associated with reward (impulsivity) and with punishment (anxiety), neuroticism and introversion–extraversion.*

According to Eysenck (1981) and Eysenck and Eysenck (1985), introverts should show superior conditioning and learning, relative to extraverts, unless level of arousal is high, in which case the relationship between E and conditioning is reversed. This hypothesis takes no account of the difference between conditioning and learning based on appetitive or aversive reinforcers, respectively. Gray's (1970) hypothesis, in contrast, critically depends on the latter distinction: it predicts that, other things being equal, performance and learning will be facilitated for introverts if aversive rather than appetitive reinforcers are used; while for extraverts performance and learning will be facilitated if appetitive rather than aversive reinforcers are used (compare the heights of adjacent bars making up each pair in Figure 11). Note that Gray's hypothesis cannot be derived from Eysenck's by recourse to the differences in arousal level that might be associated with the polarity of reinforcement. It would normally be supposed that aversive reinforcement is more arousing than appetitive, which should therefore, on average (according to Eysenck's theory), work to the advantage of extraverts; yet, Gray's hypothesis predicts that aversive reinforcement should favour introverts. The outcome of a large number of experiments, using a variety of methods, in which these predictions have been investigated, has uniformly been in agreement with Gray's model (see Gray 1981, for review; also Boddy *et al.,* 1986; Gupta, 1984; Gupta and Gupta, 1984; Newman, 1987).

The results of these types of experiments, then, are very encouraging for the approach to the study of temperament advocated here. At the very least, they demonstrate the heuristic value of the approach. But it would be a mistake to overinterpret them. They certainly cannot be regarded as outweighing the considerable body of data which supports Eysenck's (1981) theory of introversion–extraversion, and which cannot, as yet, be derived from the emotion-system approach. What is needed, rather, is a careful empirical study of behaviour under conditions in which processes predictable from each theory can simultaneously be demonstrated. Experiments of this kind (e.g., Gupta, 1984; Gupta and Gupta, 1984) should allow one to determine whether either model can be reduced to the other; or whether each is correct, but with a different domain of applicability, perhaps because each reflects the operation of different brain mechanisms.

One possibility of the former kind is that the level of arousal (the key concept in Eysenck's 1981 theory) is determined by the relative balance between the BIS and BAS. The possibility follows naturally, in fact, from the assumption (see above) that, other things being equal, aversive reinforcers are more arousing than those of the appetitive variety. Suppose that for any given situation there exists a range of actual and potential reinforcing events; and that, on average, across all situations, positive and negative reinforcers are roughly equal in frequency and potency. Then, on an average, an individual who is relatively more sensitive to aversive reinforcers (i.e., an introvert) will be at a higher level of arousal than the one who is relatively more sensitive to appetitive reinforcers (i.e., an extravert). In this way, it might be possible to deduce the fundamental Eysenckian postulate (that introverts are normally at a higher level of arousal than extraverts) from the relationships between, on the one hand, E, and, on the other, the reactivities of the BIS and BAS, as depicted in Figure 11.

While perhaps plausible, this proposal is at present quite speculative; it lacks detailed theoretical analysis, let alone empirical support. But is in this direction, I believe, that the most promising lines of investigation are to be found. The analysis of temperament would take a great stride forward if one could properly relate fundamental biological data, of the kind with which this chapter has mostly been concerned, to the great storehouse of information about human individual differences, which, while described by the current dimensional models, are still difficult to link to the workings of the brain.

References

Adams, D.B. (1979). 'Brain Mechanisms for Offence, Defense, and Submission', *Behavioral and Brain Sciences,* 2: 201–41.

Amsel, A. (1962). 'Frustrative Nonreward in Partial Reinforcement and Discrimination Learning: Some Recent History and a Theoretical Extension', *Psychological Review,* 69: 306–20.

Berlyne, D.E. (1960). *Conflict, Arousal and Curiosity,* New York: McGraw-Hill.

Boddy, J., A. Carver and K. Rowley (1986). 'Effect of Positive and Negative Verbal Reinforcement on Performance as a Function of Extraversion-Introversion: Some Tests of Gray's Theory', *Personality and Individual Differences,* 7: 81–8.

Deutch, J.A. (1964). *The Structural Basis of Behaviour,* Cambridge: Cambridge University Press.

Di Chiara, G. and A. Imperatc (1985). 'Ethanol Preferentially Stimulates Dopamine Release in the Nucleus Accumbens of Freely Moving Rats', *European Journal of Pharmacology,* 115: 131–2.

Evenden, J.L. and T.N. Robbins (1983). 'Increased Response Switching, Perseveration and Perseverative Switching Following d-Amphetamine in the Rat', *Psychopharmacology,* 80: 67–73.

Eysenck, H.J. (ed.). (1981). *A Model for Personality,* New York: Springer.

Eysenck, H.J. and M.W. Eysenck (1985). *Personality and Individual Differences: A Natural Science Approach,* New York: Plenum.

Fowles, D. (1980) 'The Three Arousal Model: Implications of Gray's Two-Factor Learning Theory for Heart Rate, Electrodermal Activity and Psychopathy', *Psychophysiology,* 17: 87–104.

Graeff, F.G. (1987). 'The Anti-Aversive Action of Drugs', in T. Thompson, P.B. Dews and J. Barrnett (eds), *Advances in Behavioural Pharmacoogy,* Vol. 6, Hillsadale, NJ: Erlbaum.

Gray, J.A. (1967). 'Disappointment and Drugs in the Rat', *Advancement of Science,* 23: 595–605.

Gray J.A. (1970). 'The Psychophysiological Basis of Introversion-Extraversion', *Behaviour Research and Therapy,* 8: 249–66.

Gray, J.A. (1972). 'Learning Theory, the Conceptual Nervous System and Personality', in V.D. Nebylitsyn and J.A. Gray (eds), *The Biological Bases of Individual Behaviour,* New York: Academic Press.

Gray, J.A. (1975). *Elements of a Two-Process Theory of Learning,* London: Academic Press.

Gray, J.A. (1977). 'Drugs Effects on Fear and Frustration: Possible Limbic Site of Action of Minor Tranquillizers', in L.L. Iversen and S.D. Snyder (eds), *Handbook of Psychopharmacology,* Vol. 8, New York: Plenum.

Gray, J.A. (1981). 'A Critique of Eysenck's Theory of Personality', in H.J. Eysenck (ed.), *A Model for Personality,* New York: Springer.

Gray, J.A. (1982a). *The Neuropsychology of Anxiety: An Enquiry into the Functions of the Septo-Hippocampal System,* Oxford: Oxford University Press.

Gray, J.A. (1982b). 'Precis of 'The Neuropsychology of Anxiety: An Enquiry into the Functions of the Septo-Hippocamal System', *Behavioral and Brain Sciences,* 5: 469–84.

Gray, J.A. (1982c). 'On Mapping Anxiety', *Behavioral and Brain Sciences,* 5: 506–25.

Gray, J.A. (1983). 'Where Should we Search for Biologically Based Dimensions of Personality?', *Zeitschrift fur Differentielle and Diagnostische Psychologie,* 4: 165–76.

Gray, J.A. (1984). 'The Hippocampus as an Interface Between Cognition and Emotion', in H.L. Roitblat, T.G. Bever and H.S. Terrace (eds), *Animal Cognition,* Hillsdale, NJ: Erlbaum.

Gray, J.A. (1985). 'Anxiety and the Brain: Pigments Aren't Colour Names', *Bulletin of the British Psychological Society,* 38: 299–300.

Gray, J.A. (1987). *The Psychology of Fear and Stress,* 2nd ed., Cambridge: Cambridge University Press.

Gray, J.A. (1994). 'Three Fundamental Emotion System', in P. Ekman and R.J. Davidson (eds), *The Nature of Emotion: Fundamental Questions,* Series in Affective Science, New York: Oxford University Press.

Gray, J.A., J. Feldon, J.N.P. Rawlins, D.R. Hemsley and A.D. Smith (1991). 'The Neuropsychology of Schizophrenia', *Behavioral and Brain Sciences,* Monograph 14.

Gray, J.A. and N. McNaughton (1983). 'Comparison Between the Behavioral Effects of Septal and Hippocampal Lesions: A review', *Neuroscience and Biobehavioral Reviews,* 7: 119–88.

Groves, P.M. (1983). 'A Theory of the Functional Organization of the Neostriatum and the Neostriatal Control of Voluntary Movement', *Brain Research Reviews,* 5: 109–32.

Gupta, U. (1984). 'Phenobarbitone and the Relationship Between Extraversion and Reinforcement in Verbal Operant Conditioning', *British Journal of Psychology,* 75: 499–506.

Gupta, B.S. and U. Gupta (1984). 'Dextroamphetamine and Individual Susceptibility to Reinforcement in Verbal Operant Conditioning', *British Journal of Psychology,* 75: 201–6.

Hebb, D.O. (1955). 'Drives and the C.N.S. (Conceptual Nervous System)', *Psychological Review,* 62: 243–59.

Hoebel, B.G., L. Hernandez, S. McLean, B.G. Stanley, E.F. Aulissi, P. Glimcher and D. Margolin (1981). 'Catecholamines, Enkephatin, and Neurotensin in Feeding and Reward', in B.G. Hoebel and D. Novin (eds), *The Neural Basis of Feeding and Reward,* Brunswick, GE: Haer Institute.

Imperato, A., A. Mulas and G. Di Chiara (1986). 'Nicotine Preferentially Stimulates Dopamine Release in the Limbic System of Freely Moving Rats', *European Journal of Pharmacology,* 132: 337–38.

Mathews, A. (1988). 'Anxiety and the Processing of Threatening Information', in V. Hamilton, G.H. Bower and N. Frijda (eds), *Cognitive Perspectives on Emotion and Motivation,* Dordrecht: Kluwer Academic Publishers.

Millenson, J.R. (1967). *Principles of Behavioral Analysis,* New York: Macmillan.

Miller, N.E. (1951). 'Learnable Drives and Rewards', in S.S. Stevens (ed), *Handbook of Experimental Psychology,* New York: Wiley.

Mitchell, S.N., M.P. Brazell, M.H. Joseph, M.S. Alavijeh and J.A. Gray (1989). 'Regionally Specific Effects of Acute and Chronic Nicotine on Rates of Catecholamine and Indoleamine Synthesis in Rat Brain', *European Journal of Pharmacology,* 167: 311–22.

Mowrer, O.H. (1947). 'On the Dual Nature of Learning: A Re-interpretation of "Conditioning" and "Problem-Solving"', *Harvard Education Review,* 17: 102–48.

Mowrer, O.H. (1960). *Learning Theory and Behavior,* New York: Wiley.

Newman, J.P. (1987). 'Reaction to Punishment in Extraverts and Psychopaths: Implications for the Impulsive Behavior of Disinhibited Individuals', *Journal of Research in Personality,* 21: 464–80.

Oades, R.D. (1985). 'The Role of NA in Tuning and DA in Switching Between Signals in the CNS', *Neuroscience and Biobehavioral Reviews,* 9: 261–82.

Olds, J. and M. Olds (1965). 'Drives, Rewards, and the Brain', in F. Barron, W.C. Dement, W. Edwards, H. Lindmann, L.D. Phillips J. Olds and M. Olds (eds), *New Directions in Psychology,* Vol. 2, New York: Holt, Rinehart and Winston.

Penney, J.B. and A.B. Young (1981). 'GABA as the Pallidothalmic Neurotransmitter: Implications for Basal Ganglia Function', *Brain Research,* 207: 195–99.

Phillipson, O.T. and A.C. Griffiths (1985). 'The Topographical Order of Inputs to Nucleus Accumbens in the Rat', *Neuroscience,* 16: 275–96.

Reiman, E.M., M.E. Raichle, F.K. Butler, P. Hersovitch and E. Robins, (1984). 'A Focal Brain Abnormality in Panic Disorder, a Severe Form of Anxiety', *Nature,* 310: 683–85.

Rolls, E.T. (1986a). 'Information Representation, Processing and Storage in the Brain: Analysis at the Single Neuro-Level', in R. Ritter and S. Ritter (eds), *Neural and Molecular Mechanisms of Learning,* New York: Springer.

Rolls, E.T. (1986b). 'A Theory of Emotion, and its Application to Understanding the Neural Basis of Emotion', in Y. Oomura (ed.), *Emotions: Neural and Chemical Control,* Tokyo: Japan Scientific Societies Press, and Basel: Karger.

Rolls, E.T. and G.V. Williams (1987). 'Sensory and Movement-Related Neuronal Activity in Different Regions of the Primatestriatum', in J.S. Schneider and T.I. Kidsky (eds), *Basal Ganglia and Behaviour: Sensory Aspects and Motor Functioning,* Bern: Hans Huber.

Shapiro, S.K., H. Quay, A. Hogan and K. Schwartz (1988). 'Response Perseveration and Delayed Responding in Undersocialized Aggressive Conduct Disorder', *Journal of Abnormal Psychology,* 97: 251–64.

Spence, J.T. and Spence K.W. (1966). 'The Motivational Components of Manifest Anxiety: Drive and Drive Stimuli', in C.D. Spielberger (ed.), *Anxiety and Behavior,* New York: Academic Press.

Spielberger, C.D. (1976). 'The Nature and Measurement of Anxiety', in C.D. Speilberger and R. Diaz-Guerrero (eds), *Cross-Cultural Anxiety,* Washington: Hemisphere.

Stewart, J., H. de Wit and R. Eikelboom (1984). 'Role of Unconditioned and Conditioned Drug Effects in the Self-Administration of Opiates and Stimulants', *Psychological Review,* 91: 251–68.

Swerdflow, N.R. and G.F. Koob (1987). 'Dopamine, Schizophrenia, Mania and Depression: Toward a Unified Hypothesis of Cortico-Striato-Pallido-Thalamic Function', *Behavioral and Brain Sciences,* 10: 215–17.

Zuckerman, M. (1982). 'Leaping up the Phylogenetic Scale in Explaining Anxiety: Perils and Possibilities', *Behavioral and Brain Sciences,* 5: 505–6.

Zuckerman, M., D.M. Kuhlman and C. Camac (1988). 'What Lies Beyond E and N? Factor Analyses of Scales Believed to Measure Basic Dimensions of Personality', *Journal of Personality and Social Psychology,* 54: 96–107.

3 Gender Differences in Occupational Stress

Charles D. Spielberger and Eric C. Reheiser

It is well-known that stress in the workplace adversely affects productivity, absenteeism, worker turnover, and employee health and well-being (e.g., Copper and Payne, 1988; Kahn *et al.*, 1964; Karasek and Theorell, 1990; Keita and Sauter, 1992; Levi, 1981; Matteson and Ivancevich, 1982; Perrewe, 1991; Quick, Murphy and Hurrell, 1992). For example, in a recent nation-wide study of occupational stress, the proportion of workers who reported 'feeling highly stressed' had more than doubled from 1985 to 1990; those reporting 'having multiple stress-related illnesses' increased from 13 per cent to 25 per cent (Northwestern National Life, 1991). Moreover, 69 per cent of the 600 workers surveyed in the Northwestern National Life study reported that their productivity was reduced because of high stress levels, and 'one in three say job stress is the single greatest stress in their lives' (1991).

The affects of occupational stress on absenteeism and worker turnover were also clearly reflected in the same study (Northwestern National Life, 1991). Of the participants, 17 per cent reported missing one or more days of work each year due to high stress levels, and 14 per cent indicated that stress had caused them to quit or change jobs in the preceding two years. In a similar study of more than 1200 full-time, private-sector employees, 40 per cent reported that their jobs were 'very' or 'extremely' stressful (Northwestern National Life, 1992). Compared with workers reporting lower levels of job stress, the employees who perceived their jobs as highly stressful were twice as likely to: work overtime frequently (62 per cent vs. 34 per cent); think about quitting their job (59 per cent vs. 26 per cent); suffer stress-related medical problems (55 per cent vs. 21 per cent); and experience burnout on the job (50 per cent vs. 19 per cent).

Absenteeism, employee turnover and stress-related medical problems are clear-cut direct costs to employers. In addition, reduced productivity and diminished customer services are hidden costs that often result from 'exhausted or depressed employees (who) are not energetic, accurate, or innovative at work' (Karasek and Theorell, 1990: 167). According to Matteson and Ivancevich (1987), preventable cost in the 1987 US economy, relating to reduced productivity, absenteeism, and worker turnover, is estimated to be approximately $2800 per year per employee. Many employees with stress-related workplace problems also expect compensation, and seek disability payments and early retirement benefits. Sauter (1992: 14) has observed that, each year in the US, 'nearly 600,000 workers are disabled for reasons of psychological disorders', costing $5.5 billion in annual payments to individuals and their families.

Growing concern over the consequences of job stress for both employees and organizations has stimulated efforts to understand the sources and consequences of stressors in the workplace. These concerns are dramatically reflected in the increasing number of studies of occupational stress that have appeared in the psychological, organizational, and medical literature over the past 20 years. Publications listed in Psychlit' with titles that specifically included 'job stress', 'work stress', 'occupational stress', or 'family stress' are presented in Figure 1 for each three-year period from 1971 to 1992, the latter being the last full year for which relatively complete data was available. Investigations in all three workplace-related stress categories have increased more than fifty-fold over the past two decades. The total number of studies in 1990–92 (N=169) was more than eight times greater than during the entire decade of the seventies (N=19). In contrast, research relating to family stress has increased to a much lesser degree.

Unfortunately, the explosive increase in research on stress in the workplace has not clarified the interpretations of the findings in these studies because of ambiguity in the conceptual definition of occupational stress, which often differs from study to study (Kasl, 1978; Schuler, 1980). As Schuler (1991) recently noted, a major source of confusion in occupational stress research stems from the fact that some investigators have focused mainly on the antecedent conditions and pressures associated with the characteristics of a particular job;

others have been primarily concerned with the consequences of work-related stress. Such differences in approaches to stress in the workplace have greatly influenced the procedures used to measure occupational stress.

In this chapter, influential conceptions of occupational stress are briefly reviewed, and stress measures emanating from these conceptions are evaluated. Gender differences in occupational stress are also examined. Finally, a new psychometric measure for assessing job stress, the Job Stress Survey (Spielberger, 1994), is described in some detail. Research findings with this instrument, that demonstrate substantial gender differences in occupational stress, are then reported.

Person–Environment Fit Theory

Person-Environment Fit Theory (French and Caplan, 1972; French, Caplan and Harrison, 1982) is among the most utilized and widely accepted approaches to conceptualizing the nature of occupational stress (Chemers *et al.,* 1985). In the context of this theoretical orientation, occupational stress is defined in terms of job characteristics that pose a threat to the individual because of a poor match between the abilities of the employee and the demands of the job (French and Caplan, 1972). The workplace stress that results from an incompatible person–environment fit produces psychological strain and stress-related physical disorders (French, Caplan and Harrison, 1982).

In early studies guided by the Person–Environment Fit Theory, differences in sources of job stress, and in stressful work-related events were investigated for a variety of occupations (e.g., Caplan *et al.,* 1975). The concepts of role ambiguity and role conflict, and how they differed for various organizational settings and occupational groups were prominent in this research (Fisher and Gitelson, 1983; Jackson and Schuler, 1985). For example, in studies of sources of stress for different occupational levels, executives and managers tended to perceive more role ambiguity. Employees in less responsible positions experienced more role conflict (Hamner and Tosi, 1974; Kahn *et al.,* 1964). It should be noted, however, that Jackson and Schuler (1985) found no relationship between occupational level and either role conflict or ambiguity, and little evidence that these variables influenced job performances or worker satisfaction.

Karasek (1979) proposed a variant of the Person–Environment Fit theory, in which interactions between level of control and job demands are emphasized as determinants of work-related psychological strain. For example, low control and high demand appear to contribute to lowered productivity and a greater risk of health problems. Sauter and Hurrel (1989) also recognized the importance of worker autonomy and control, noting that lack of control inhibits learning and undermines the motivation that is generally needed to overcome the stress associated with demanding work. However, they also pointed out that 'fundamental questions remain concerning the conceptualization and operationalization of the construct (of job control)' (1989: XVI).

Other job conditions such as workload and interpersonal conflict also contribute to person–environment fit problems, which often have adverse effects on job satisfaction and employee well-being. Spector (1987) reported significant positive correlations of excessive work-load and work-related interpersonal conflicts with anxiety, frustration, job dissatisfaction, health symptoms, and depression (Ganster, Fusilier and Mayes, 1986). The concepts of work overload and underload are similar to work demands, as this concept is related to job control.

Findings that support a person–environment fit model of occupational stress have been reported by Chemers *et al.* (1985). They also observed that interactions between person and environment variables predict job strain better than either person or environment variables separately (Caplan *et al.*, 1975; Harrison, 1978; Locke, 1969; Porter, 1961). Chemers *et al.* (1985: 628) conclude that although the Person-Environment Fit theory provides a useful approach to conceptualizing and measuring occupational stress, '... (the) theory has not yielded a highly focused approach'.

Measurement Issues

In researches guided by the Person-Environment Fit theory, measures of occupational stress have encompassed a wide range of contents. These have included the assessment of: job and organizational characteristics; employee skills; job satisfaction; individual differences in attitudes and personality traits; and health status (Beehr and Newman, 1978; Sharit and Salvendy, 1982). Control over how job demands are met (autonomy) is also emphasised in the assessment of occupational stress (Karasek and Theorell, 1990). Unfortunately, such diverse aspects of stress in the workplace are often confounded in the operational measures that are used to assess job stress, which makes it difficult to know what is being measured.

Environmental antecedents of stress in the workplace have been measured primarily in terms of general role demands or expectations. Specific job pressures and task characteristics tend to be neglected. Within the context of his general theory of stress, Lazarus (1994) has recently explained his approach to conceptualizing occupational stress as a process involving a transaction between an individual and his/her work environment.

Lazarus' Transactional Process Theory

Lazarus' theory distinguishes between stressful antecedent conditions ('stressors'), how these are perceived and cognitively appraised by a particular person, and the consequent emotional reactions when a stressor is perceived as threatening and the individual is not able to cope effectively with it. His theoretical approach requires a detailed analysis of the specific stressors that are associated with a particular job, and how different workers react to these stressors, taking into account the individual's coping skills and past experiences. Thus, Lazarus conceptualizes stress in the work-related stressor events on emotions and behaviour are mediated by an employee's perceptions and appraisals of particular stressors and her/his coping skills for dealing with them.

Brief and George (1994) criticize Lazarus' emphasis on the idiographic nature of occupational stress. They argue that it is especially important to discover those working conditions that are likely to adversely affect groups of employees who are exposed to them. In a similar critique of Lazarus' model, Harris (1994) has noted that occupational stressors associated with the climate and culture of an organization can have profound effects on employees, and that these may differ as a function of gender and individual differences in personality and coping skills.

In summary, Lazarus' conception of occupational stress and the Person–Environment Fit theory, both have merits and limitations, and they can be construed as complimentary rather than contradictory in providing a meaningful conceptual framework for understanding stress in the workplace. A major difference between these perspectives is in the specificity and size of the unit of measurement for assessing the components of job stress. Whereas the Person–Environment Fit theory identifies the general conditions that produce job strain (work demands), Lazarus' transactional process model focuses on how a particular stressor event is perceived and appraised, noting that these mediating processes are strongly influenced by the worker's coping skills and previous experiences. A comprehensive assessment of occupational stress as a transactional process requires taking into account the nature of the stressor event, how it is perceived and appraised, and the consequent emotional reactions of the worker.

Gender Differences in Occupational Stress

On the basis of a comprehensive review of stress in organizations, Beehr and Schuler (1980) concluded that there was little evidence that gender influences stress-related symptoms in the workplace. Similarly, Di Salvo *et al.* (1994), in a study of gender and work-related stress, observed that 'from a broad perspective, men and women perceive stressors quite similarly. No gender differences were found in the overall clusters (of stressors)' (p. 48). Martocchio and O'Leary (1989) came to a similar conclusion based on the results of a meta-analytic evaluation of 15 studies which examined gender differences in occupational stress. In their words: 'There are no sex differences in experienced and perceived work stress' (p. 495).

Jick and Mitz (1985) suggest that the difficulty in identifying gender-related differences in workplace stress may be due to sampling problems, noting that men are over-represented in managerial positions, while more women hold clerical and service jobs. In their review of empirical evidence of sex differences in workplace stress, they identified numerous 'gaps, ambiguity, and inconsistencies in the existing research' (1985: 408). Nevertheless, despite the oft-quoted findings of no gender-related differences in occupational stress, but also as a moderator affecting how stress is perceived, what coping skills are called upon, and how stress is manifest' (p. 409). In supporting this conclusion, they call attention to evidence that women report more symptoms of psychological distress (e.g., emotional discomfort and depression), whereas men are more prone to develop severe stress-related physical illnesses, as reflected by a higher incidence of heart disease and cirrhosis of the liver due to alcohol abuse.

Nelson and Quick (1985) also reviewed research on gender differences in workplace stress, and concluded that women experience greater occupational stress than men because of the unique sources of job stress typically faced by women—for example, lower salaries, career blocks, discrimination and sterotyping, and the interface of marriage and work (cf. Goldsmith, 1988). Although no inherent gender differences have been found in research on job-related burnout, there may be differences in the causes of burnout for men and women and in their coping strategies for handling burnout symptoms, with men choosing more active and direct coping strategies (Lowman, 1993).

Although Di Salvo *et al.* (1994) found no overall gender differences in broad clusters of workplace stressors, they noted that the 'frequency of specific causes of stress for men and women did differ in four out of the 14 cases' (p. 48). Workload factors such as too much or too little work were twice as likely to be reported by women than men. Stresses relating to power, such as lacking or expressing power, were mentioned more than twice as often by men.

Measuring Occupational Stress

In addition to differences in gender representation at higher and lower occupational levels, and in broader versus narrower definitions of stressor events, job stress measures tend to confound the perceived severity of a stressful event with the frequency of its occurrence. The perceived severity of a stressor will greatly influence the intensity of an emotional reaction when that stressor occurs. However, even though a specific stressor even may be perceived as highly stressful, if it occurs infrequently, it will have limited impact as a source of stress. Consequently, it is important to assess not only the perceived severity of a stressor, but also how often it occurs.

Jackson and Schuler (1985: 47) contended that research on occupational stress should focus on '*...the development of good diagnostic tools for pinpointing specific aspects about one's job that are ambiguous or conflicting*'. In a similar vein, Beehr and Newman (1978) argued that work environment variables should be measured both objectively and subjectively in stress research; and Murphy and Hurrell (1987) called for the construction of a generic questionnaire or core set of questions to facilitate comparing stress levels in specific occupational groups. Barone *et al.* (1988) also affirmed the need to develop valid psychometric questionnaires for assessing occupational stress. In their words, 'One would expect this burgeoning literature to be grounded in a sophisticated assessment of work stress; however, most of the literature has relied on answers to only one or a few questions about experienced stress' (pp. 141–42).

Noting such criticisms of existing job stress measures, Osipow and Spokane (1981) developed a promising generic measure to assess person–environment fit variables, such as role overload, role ambiguity, and psychological strain across different occupational levels and work environments. Consistent with Lazarus' transactional process theory, Spielberger and his colleagues (Spielberger *et al.,* 1981) developed the Police Stress Survey (PSS) to evaluate the perceived severity and frequency of occurrence of 60 specific stressors encountered by law enforcement officers. Most of these specific sources of stress in police work had been previously identified by Kroes (1976) and his colleagues (Kroes and Gould, 1979; Kroes, Margolis and Hurrell, 1974).

The PSS was field-tested with 50 Florida law enforcement officers from seven geographically diverse locations. Data were subsequently collected for a representative sample of 233 officers. Findings with the PSS are reported in a monograph by Spielberger *et al.* (1981), and in several brief reports (Spielberger, Grier and Pate, 1980). Since the representative sample of law enforcement officers included only 15 females, no gender differences were reported.

Teacher Stress Survey (TSS) was designed to evaluate sources of stress relevant to secondary school teachers, and to compare teacher stress with police stress (Grier, 1982). Of the 60 TSS items, 39 were selected from the PSS on the basis of their applicability to both teaching and police work. These TSS items were identical to the corresponding PSS items, except that 'teacher' and 'school' were routinely substituted for 'police' and 'department'. Twenty-one additional items were generated from the teacher stress literature in consultation with experienced high school teachers. Research findings with the TSS have been reported by Grier (1982), who found only one main effect of gender, but a number of sex-by-age and sex-by-experience interactions.

Brantly and Jones (1989) constructed a psychometric instrument designed to monitor and evaluate the frequency and impact of daily stressors. Commenting in general on the potential utility of self-report measures of occupational stress, Spector, Dwyer, and Jex (1988) noted that the validity of such instruments is supported by studies reporting findings of significant correlations between them and objective measures of stressful job conditions (Algera, 1983; Gerhart, 1986).

Barone (1994) and his colleagues (Barone *et al.*, 1988) developed the Work Stress Inventory (WSI), a psychometric instrument similar to the PSS and TSS, to assess the frequency and intensity of stressors in the workplace. Designed with the intent of assessing stress associated with a wide range of circumstances for various occupations (Barone *et al.*, 1988), the WSI consists of 40 items, each rated for both intensity and frequency. Components of occupational stress are assessed with two WSI 20-item subscales: Organizational Stress (OS) and Job Risk (JR). Females scored higher than males on the WSI Intensity indices, and lower on Frequency of Job Risk, which Barone *et al.* (1988) attributed to the over-representation of women in lower-risk jobs. No differences were found between men and women on the WSI frequency subscales.

Job Stress Survey (JSS)

The Job Stress Survey (JSS) was designed to address the shortcomings that have been noted in the existing measure of occupational stress (Spielberger, 1994; Spielberger and Reheiser, 1994; Turnage and Spielberger, 1991). The JSS was adapted from the earlier surveys that evaluated sources of stress specific to law enforcement officers (Spielberger *et al.*, 1981) and high school teachers (Grier, 1982). This 30-item psychometric instrument was designed to assess the perceived intensity (severity) and frequency of occurrence of working conditions that are likely to adversely affect the psychological well-being of employees who are exposed to them (Spielberger, 1994). Items describing general sources of stress commonly experienced by mana-gerial, professional and clerical employees in a variety of occupational settings were selected to form a generic job stress measure.

The format for responding to the JSS Severity Scale is similar to the procedure employed by Holmes and Rahe (1967) in the Social Readjustment Rating Scale for rating stressful life events. Subjects first rate, on a 9-point scale, the relative amount (severity) of stress that they perceive to be associated with each of the 30 JSS job stressors (e.g., 'Excessive paperwork', 'Working overtime'), as compared to a standard stressor event, 'Assignment of disagreeable duties' which was assigned a value of '5'. In research with the PSS and the TSS, this item was rated near the middle of the range in stress severity by both police officers and teachers.

In addition to rating the perceived severity of each stressor as compared to the standard stressor event, the JSS takes into account the state-trait distinction, that has proved important in the assessment of anxiety (Spielberger, 1972, 1983), by requiring the respondents to indicate how frequently each stressor event was encountered. Respondents are asked to report, on a scale from 0 to 9+ days, the number of days on which each workplace stressor was experienced during the preceding six months. Thus, ratings of the individual JSS items provide useful information regarding the perceived severity of each of the 30 stressor situations, and how often a particular person experiences each stressor event.

Summing the ratings for each individual JSS item yields overall Severity (JSS-S) and Frequency (JSS-F) scores based on all 30 items, and an overall Job Stress Index (JSS-X), which is based on the sum of the cross-products of the Severity and Frequency scores. Stress Severity and Frequency scores are also computed for the 10-item Job Pressure and Organizational Support subscales, which were derived in factor analyses of the 30 JSS items (Spielberger, 1994).

Turnage and Spielberger (1991) administered the JSS to white-collar employees of a large manufacturing firm to investigate differences in specific sources of job stress experienced by managerial, professional, and clerical personnel. They found that the professionals rated job pressures as more intense than the other groups, and had higher overall Job Stress Index scores than the clerical employees. Managers reported experiencing a greater number of job pressures more frequently than the professional personnel, who, in turn, reported more frequent job pressures than the clerical personnel. Specific sources of stress, such as meeting deadlines, periods of inactivity, and frequent changes from boring to demanding activities, were reported significantly more often by females than by males. Spielberger and Reheiser (1994) also identified a number of significant gender differences relating to the perceived severity and frequency of occurrence of specific stressors.

Gender Differences in JSS Severity, Frequency and Index Scores

Gender differences in scores on the JSS evaluated for a sample of 1,781 working adults (922 females, 859 males) employed in university and corporate work settings. These groups included 1,387 faculty and staff from a large state university (579 males, 808 females); and 450 managerial, professional, and clerical employees (280 males, 114 females) located at the corporate headquarters of two large industrial companies.

All participants responded anonymously to the JSS, and were informed that their responses would be confidential, and would contribute to the development of university's or company's stress management program. In addition to responding to the JSS, they were asked to report their age, gender, professional classification, and the number of years they had been employed in their present work settings. The rate of return was approximately 60 per cent for the corporate employees, and 70 per cent for the university personnel.

The means and standard deviations for the perceived Severity and Frequency scores of females and males are reported in Table 1 for each of the 30 JSS items, except for item 1, for which only the assigned score of 5 is reported. The items are listed in descending order of the mean Severity scores for the females. It is interesting to note that item 1, 'Assignment of disagreeable duties', the standard on the basis of which the perceived severity of the other 29 items was rated, ranked 13th in severity for females and 16th for males. This finding provides additional evidence that the standard is about 'average' in perceived severity as compared to the other JSS items.

The most striking finding in the results of the ANOVAs for the item data is the number of items for which significant gender differences were found. Differences were found for almost half of the JSS Severity items (14 of 29), and for 60 per cent of the Frequency items (18 of 30). Moreover, the probability level for 19 of the 32 items for which significant gender differences were found was less than 0.001. It is interesting to note that both men and women rated the same 6 items as highest in perceived severity, and that both sexes rated the same 5 items as lowest in severity.

For both men and women, 'Inadequate salary' and 'Lack of opportunity for advancement' ranked highest in severity. The former also ranked relatively high in frequency of occurrence. These findings probably reflect the fact that more than three-fourths of the subjects were employed in a state university, where salaries for both faculty and staff are relatively low, with minimum raises during the several years before this study was conducted.

'Working overtime' was ranked very low in perceived severity by both men and women, whose mean scores for this item were essentially the same. The relative rank given to this stressor event in terms of its frequency of occurrence was much higher, especially for the males. Gender differences in Frequency scores for 'Working overtime' appeared to be greater than for any other stressor event ($F=70.28$, $p<0.001$), with males ranking this item 3rd in frequency of occurrence and females ranking it 15th.

Gender Differences in Job Pressures and Organizational Support

On the basis of the information provided by each respondent, employees were classified as either managerial, professional, clerical or maintenance personnel. University administrators, deans, and department chairs were classified as managers; and, professors and mid-level administrators were assigned to the professional group. However, in order to have a sufficient number of subjects for more stable analyses of the data in terms of gender and occupational levels, the participants assigned to the two higher levels (managers and professionals) and the two lower levels (clerical and maintenance) were combined to form two occupational levels.

For the total sample, the number of men and women was relatively equal, but there were nearly twice as many men in the higher occupational level group, and more than twice as many women in the lower group. As was previously noted, such differences in the proportion of females to males in the managerial/professional and clerical groups are generally consistent with the prevailing gender representation in different occupational levels.

Means, standard deviations, and alpha coefficients for the JSS Severity, Frequency, and Index scales are reported in Table 2 for the total sample. The alpha coefficients for all three JSS scales were remarkably high, especially for the relatively brief 10-item JSS Severity and Frequency scales. The mean JSS Severity and Index scores for men and women were quite similar for the total sample, and for the subsamples of managerial/professional and clerical/maintenance personnel, as can be noted in Table 2. Differences in these means were evaluated in 2×2 ANOVAs, for which the results are also reported in Table 2.

The results of the ANOVAs indicated no main effects for gender, nor any gender-by-occupational level interactions for the total sample. Moreover, no significant main effects or interactions were found for the JSS Severity and Index scores for the two occupational groups.

However, the main effect for occupational level was highly significant ($p<0.001$), indicating that both female and male managerial/professional employees reported experiencing the occurrence of the 30 JSS stressor events much more frequently than clerical/maintenance workers. Thus, in marked contrast to the numerous differences that were found in both the perceived severity and the frequency of occurrence of specific JSS stressor events, no differences were found in the JSS scale scores as a function of gender, nor any interactions of gender with occupational level.

The findings of numerous differences in the perceived severity and frequency of occurrence of specific JSS stressors, and the failure to find any gender-related differences in JSS Severity, Frequency and Stress Index scores, at first seems paradoxical. However, these results are actually quite consistent with, and help to clarify, the results reported by other investigators. Gender-related differences in occupational stress appear to be determined by differences in the perceived severity of specific stressors, and in the frequency that these stressors are experienced by men and women.

Of the 14 JSS stressor events reported in Table 1 for which significant differences in perceived severity were found, women rated 9 of these stressors as significantly more severe than men, whereas men perceived 5 of them as more severe. Of the 18 JSS stressor events for which significant differences in frequency of occurrence were found, men reported experiencing 10 of these stressors more frequently than women, and women had higher Frequency scores for 8 of the JSS stressors. When scores on the specific JSS stressor events for which significant differences were found were summed up to form Severity or Frequency scales, these differences tended to cancel out.

Summary and Conclusions

Evidence of adverse effects of stress in the workplace on employee productivity, absenteeism, worker turnover, and stress-related medical problems was examined. Direct and indirect costs to both workers and employers were noted. Person–Environment Fit theory and other current conceptions of occupational stress were briefly reviewed, and a number of measures that have been used to assess stress in the workplace were critically evaluated.

It was noted that ambiguity and inconsistencies in the prevailing theories of stress in the workplace are reflected in the wide range of heterogeneous contents that are assessed by measures of occupational stress. Confusion in occupational stress research has also resulted from the fact that some investigators have focused on job pressures, whereas others have been concerned primarily with the consequences of work-related stress. The importance of developing good diagnostic tools for assessing specific job pressures and organizational factors that contribute to stress in the workplace is now recognized as a major priority by occupational stress researchers.

Inconsistencies in research on gender differences in occupational stress were attributed to sampling problems and limitations in the instruments that have been used to measure stress in the workplace. The Job Stress Survey assesses the perceived severity of specific stressor events and how frequently they occur. Numerous gender differences in the severity and frequency of occurrence of specific JSS stressors were found, along with consistencies in perceived severity and frequency of specific stressors. It can be concluded that gender is extremely important in determining how different workplace stressors are perceived, and that men and women experience different stressors more or less often, depending to some extent on their occupational level.

References

Algera, J.A. (1983). '"Objective" and Perceived Task Characteristics as a Determinant of Reactions by Task Performers', *Journal of Occupational Psychology,* 56: 95–107.

Barone, D.F. (1994). 'Developing a Transactional Psychology of Work Stress', in P.L. Perrewe and R. Crandall (eds), *Occupational Stress: A Handbook,* pp. 29–37, New York: Taylor and Francis.

Barone, D.F., G.R. Caddy and A.D. Kathell, F.B. Roselione and R.A. Hamilton (1988). 'The Work Stress Inventory: Organizational Stress and Job Risk', *Educational and Psychological Measurement,* 48: 141–54.

Beehr, T.A. and J.E. Newman (1978). 'Job Stress, Employee Health, and Organizational Effectiveness: A Facet Analysis, Model, and Literature Review', *Personnel Psychology,* 31: 665–99.

Beehr, T.A. and R. Schuler (1980). 'Stress in Organizations', K. Rowland and G. Ferris (eds), *Personnel Management,* pp. 390–419, Boston: Allyn and Bacon.

Brantly, F.J. and G.N. Jones (1989). *Daily Stress Inventory Professional Manual,* Odessa, FL: Psychological Assessment Resources.

Brief, A.P. and J.M. George (1994). 'Psychological Stress in the Workplace: A Brief Comment on Lazarus' Outlook', in P.L. Perrewe and R. Crandall (eds), *Occupational Stress: A Handbook,* pp. 15–19, New York: Taylor and Francis.

Caplan, R.D., S. Cobb, J.R.P. French, Jr. R.V. Harrison and S.R. Pinneau (1975). *Job Demands and Worker Health: Main Effects and Occupational Differences,* Washington, DC: National Institute of Occupational Safety and Health (NIOSH).

Chemers, M.M., R.B. Hayes, F. Rhodewalt and J. Wysocki (1985). 'A Person–Environment Analysis of Job Stress: A Contingency Model Explanation', *Journal of Personality and Social Psychology,* 49: 628–35.

Cooper, C.L. and R. Payne (eds) (1988). *Causes, Coping and Consequences of Stress at Work,* Chichester, England: Willey.

Di Salvo, V., C. Lubbers, A.M. Rossi and J. Lewis (1994). 'The Impact of Gender on Work-Related Stress', in P.L. Perrewe and R. Crandall (eds), *Occupational Stress: A Handbook,* pp. 39–50, New York: Taylor and Francis.

Fisher, C.D. and R. Gitelson (1983). 'A Meta-Analysis of the Correlates of Role Conflict and Ambiguity', *Journal of Applied Psychology,* 68: 320–33.

French, J.R.P., Jr. and R.D. Caplan (1972). 'Occupational Stress and Individual Strain', in A.J. Marrow (ed.), *The Failure of Success,* pp. 30–66, New York: Amacom.

French, J.R.P., Jr., R.D. Caplan and R.V. Harrison (1982). *The Mechanisms of Job Stress and Strain,* Chichester, England: Willey.

Gangster, D.C., M.R. Fusilier and B.T. Mayes (1986). 'Role of Social Support in the Experience of Stress at Work', *Journal of Applied Psychology,* 71: 102–10.

Gerhart, B. (1986). 'Sources of Variance in Incumbent Perceptions of Job Complexity', Paper presented at the annual meeting of the Academy of Management, August, Chicago.

Goldsmith, E.B. (ed.) (1988). 'Work and Family: Theory, Research and Applications' (Special issue), *Journal of Social Behavior and Personality,* 3(4).

Grier, K.S. (1982). 'A Comparison of Job Stress in Law Enforcement and Teaching' (Doctoral dissertation, University of South Florida, 1981), *Dissertation Abstracts International,* 43: 870B.

Hamner, W.C. and H.L. Tosi (1974). 'Relationship of Role Conflict and Role Ambiguity to Job Involvèment Measures', *Journal of Applied Psychology,* 59: 497–99.

Harris, J.R. (1994). 'The utility of the Transaction Approach for Occupational Stress Research', in P.L. Perrewe and R. Crandall (eds), *Occupational Stress: A Handbook,* pp. 21–8, New York: Taylor and Francis.

Harrison, R.V. (1978). 'Person–Environment Fit and Job Stress', in C.L. Cooper and R. Payne (eds), *Stress at Work,* pp. 175–205, New York: Wiley.

Holmes, T.H. and R.H. Rahe (1967). 'The Social Readjustment Rating Scale: A Cross-Cultural Study of Western Europeans and Americans', *Journal of Applied Psychology,* 59: 497–99.

Harris, J.R. (1994). 'The Utility of the Transaction Approach for Occupational Stress Research', in P.L. Perrewe and R. Crandall (eds), *Occupational Stress: A Handbook,* pp. 21–8, New York: Taylor and Francis.

Harrison, R.V. (1978). 'Person–Environment Fit and Job Stress', in C.L. Cooper and R. Payne (eds), *Stress at Work,* pp. 175–205, New York: Wiley.

Holmes, T.H. and R.H. Rahe (1967). 'The Social Readjustment Rating Scale: A Cross-Cultural Study of Western Europeans and Americans', *Journal of Psychosomatic Research,* 14: 391–400.

Jackson, S.E. and R.S. Schuler (1985). 'A Meta-Analysis and Conceptual Critique of Research on Role Ambiguity and Role Conflict in Work Settings', *Organizational Behavior and Human Decision Process,* 36: 16–78.

Jick, T.D. and L.E. Mitz (1985). 'Sex Differences in Work Stress', *Academy of Management Review,* 10: 408–20.

Kahn, R.L., D.M. Wolfe, R.P. Quinn, J.D. Snoek and R.A. Rosenthal (1964). *Organizational Stress: Studies in Role Conflict and Ambiguity,* New York: Wiley.

Karasek, R.A., Jr. (1979). 'Job Demands, Job Decision Latitude and Mental Strain: Implications for Job Redesign', *Administrative Science Quarterly,* 24: 285–308.

Karasek, R.A., Jr. and T. Theorell (1990). *Healthy Work: Stress, Productivity, and the Reconstruction of Working Life,* New York: Basic Books.

Kasal, S.V. (1978). 'Epidemiological Contributions to the Study of Work Stress', in C.L. Cooper and R.L. Payne (eds), *Stress at Work,* pp. 3–38, New York: Wiley.

Keita, G.P. and S.L. Sauter (eds) (1992). *Work and Well-Being: An Agenda for the 1990s,* Washington, DC: American Psychological Association.

Kroes, W.H. (1976). *Society's Victim—the Policeman: An Analysis of Job Stress in Policing,* Springfield: Charles C. Thomas.

Kroes, W.H. and S. Gould (1979). 'Job Stress in Policemen: An Empirical Study', *Police Stress,* 1: 9–10, 44.

Kroes, W.H., B. Margolis and J.J. Hurrell, Jr. (1974). 'Job Stress in Policemen', *Journal of Police Science and Administration,* 2: 145–55.

Lazarus, R.S. (1994). 'Psychological Stress in the Workplace', in P.L. Perrewe and R. Crandall (eds), *Occupational Stress: A Handbook,* pp. 3–14, New York: Taylor and Francis.

Levi, L. (1981). *Preventing Work Stress,* Reading, MA: Addison-Wesley.

Locke, E.A. (1969). 'What is Job Satisfaction?', *Organizational Behavior and Human Performance,* 4: 309–36.

Lowman, R.L. (1993). *Counseling and Psychotherapy of Work Dysfunction,* Washington, DC: American Psychological Association.

Martocchio, J.J. and A.M. O'Leary (1989). 'Sex Differences in Occupational Stress: A Meta-Analytic Review', *Journal of Applied Psychology,* 74: 495–501.

Matteson, M.T. and J.M. Ivancevich (1982). *Managing Job Stress and Health: The Intelligent Person's guide,* New York: Free Press.

Matteson, M.T. and J.M. Ivancevich (eds) (1987). *Controlling Work Stress: Effective Human Resource and Management Strategies,* San Francisco: Jossey-Bass.

Murphy, J.R. and J.J. Hurrell (1987). 'Stress Measurement and Management in Organizations: Development and Current Status', in A.W. Riley and S.J. Zaccharo (eds), *Occupational Stress and Organizational Effectiveness,* pp. 29–51, New York: Praegar.

Nelson, D.L. and J.C. Quick (1985). 'Professional women: Are Distress and Disease Inevitable?', *Academy of Management Review,* 10: 206–13.

Northwestern National Life (1991). *Employee Burnout: America's Newest Epidemic,* Minneapolis, MN: Northwestern National Life Insurance Company.

Northwestern National Life (1992). *Employee Burnout: Causes and Cures,* Minneapolis, MN: Northwestern National Life Insurance Company.

Osipow, S.J. and A.R. Spokane (1981). *Occupational Stress Inventory Manual Research Version,* Odessa, FL: Psychological Assessment Resources.

Perrewe, P.L. (ed) 1991. 'Handbook on Job Stress' (Special issue), *Journal of Social Behavior and Personality,* 6(7).

Porter, L.W. (1961). 'A Study of Perceived Need Satisfactions in Bottom and Middle Management Jobs', *Journal of Applied Psychology,* 45: 1–10.

Quick, J.C., L.R. Murphy and J.J. Hurrell, Jr. (eds) (1992). *Stress and Well-Being of Work: Assessments and Interventions for Occupational Mental Health,* Washington, DC: American Psychological Association.

Sauter, S.L. (1992). 'Introduction to the NIOSH Proposed National Strategy', in G.P. Keita and S.L. Sauter (eds), *Work and Well-Being: An Agenda for the 1990s,* pp. 11–16, Washington, DC: American Psychological Association.

Sauter, S.L. and J.J. Hurrell, Jr. (1989). 'Introduction', in S.L. Sauter, J.J. Hurrell, Jr. and C.L. Cooper (eds), *Job Control and Worker Health,* pp. XIII–XX, Chichester, England, Wiley.

Schuler, R.S. (1980). 'Definition and Conceptualization of Stress in Organizations', *Organizational Behavior and Human Performance,* 25: 184–215.

Schuler, R.S. (1991). 'Foreword', in P.L. Parrewe (ed), Handbook on Job Stress (Special issue), *Journal of Social Behavior and Personality,* 6(7): v–vi.

Sharit, J. and G. Salvendy (1982). 'Occupational Stress: Review and Reappraisal', *Human Factors,* 24: 129–62.

Spector, P.E. (1987). 'Interactive Effects of Perceived Control and Job Stressors on Affective Reactions and Health Outcomes for Clerical Workers', *Work and Stress,* 1: 155–62.

Spector, P.E., D.J. Dwyer and S.M. Jex (1988). 'Relation of Job Stressors to Affective, Health, and Performance Outcomes: A Comparison of Multiple Data Sources', *Journal of Applied Psychology,* 73: 11–19.

Spielberger, C.D. (1972). 'Anxiety as an Emotional State', in C.D. Spielberger (ed), *Anxiety: Current Trends in Theory and research,* Vol. 1, pp. 23–49, New York: Academic Press.

Spielberger, C.D. (1983). *Manual for the State-Trait Anxiety Inventory (Form Y),* Palo Alto, CA: Consulting Psychologists Press.

Spielberger, C.D. (1994). *Professional Manual for the Job Stress Survey (JSS),* Odessa, FL: Psychological Assessment Resources.

Spielberger, C.D., K.S. Grier and G. Greenfield (1982). 'Major Dimensions of Stress in Law Enforcement', *Florida Fraternal Order of Police Journal,* Spring, pp. 10–12.

Spielberger, C.D., K.S. Grier and J.M. Pate (1980). 'The Police Stress Survey', *Florida Fraternal Order of Police Journal,* Winter, pp. 66–7.

Spielberger, C.D. and E.C. Reheiser (1994). 'Job Stress in University, Corporate and Military Personnel', *International Journal of Stress Management,* 1: 19–31.

Spielberger, C.D., L.G. Westberry, K.S. Grier and G. Greenfield (1981). 'The Police Stress Survey: Sources of Stress in Law Enforcement', Human Resources Institute Monograph Series Three, No. 6, Tampa, FL: University of South Florida, College of Social and Behavioral Sciences.

Turnage, J.J. and C.D. Spielberger (1991). 'Job Stress in Managers, Professionals, and Clerical Workers', *Work and Stress,* 5: 165–76.

4 Short-Term Phonological Memory for Language Development

Alan Baddeley, Susan Gathercole and Costanza Papagno

Overview

It is suggested that short-term phonological memory, as represented by the phonological loop component of working memory, plays a crucial role in the long-term acquisition and development of language. It is demonstrated, first, that a neuropsychological patient with a very pure and specific deficit in phonological short-term memory was dramatically impaired at new phonological learning, while showing a normal capacity for learning pairs of already familiar, meaningful words, secondly, it is presented that children who were identified as having a specific disorder in language development prove to have a particularly marked deficit in short-term phonological memory, performing at a substantially poorer level than younger children who were matched with them for degree of language development.

In case of normal children, a close association in shown between a short-term phonological task—the capacity to echo back an unfamiliar non-word, and level of vocabulary development, together with cross-legged correlational evidence, suggesting that non-word repetition is the driving force behind vocabulary acquisition, rather than the reverse. It is presented that children selected as having poor non-word repetition demonstrate impaired new learning of unfamiliar names when compared to children of equal intelligence but with higher non-word repetition capacity. Finally, a parallel study on learning of a second language is outlined. It is concluded that the short-term phonological loop component of working memory plays a crucial role in the acquisition of language.

Short-Term Phonological Memory and Language Development

During the 1960s, there was considerable controversy as to whether human memory should be regarded as a unitary system, or dichotomized into separated long-term and short-term memory systems. By the late 1960s, the evidence seemed to be pointing strongly in the direction of a dichotomy. Most notably, evidence from neuropsychological patients pointed to two contrasting subgroups, those suffering from the classic amnesic syndrome, in which long-term learning is grossly impaired, but short-term memory preserved (Baddeley and Warrington, 1970), and patients who showed the opposite pattern, with apparently normal long-term learning coupled with a grossly defective capacity for short-term storage (Shallice and Warrington, 1970). For example, in the digit-span task, in which the subject hears a sequence of numbers and attempts to repeat them back, such patients typically fail to repeat sequences of more than one or possibly two digits. In due course, however, the idea that the short-term memory system itself was unitary encountered difficulties, and Baddeley and Hitch (1974) proposed that the earlier concept of a unitary short-term memory be replaced by a multi-component system they termed 'working memory'. This was assumed to involve three major components—an executive attentional controlling system, aided by two slave systems. One of these, the visuo-spatial sketchpad was assumed to be capable of storing and manipulating visuo-spatial information, while the other, the articulatory or phonological loop was assumed to store speech-based information.

The phonological loop is assumed to comprise two components: a phonological store that is capable of holding information, via a trace that fades over a time-course of about two seconds, coupled with a subvocal articulatory control process. This represents a form of 'inner speech' that is capable both of maintaining information in the store through rehearsal, and also of talking visually presented a very recent accomplishment, and it seems implausible to assume that it could have had any substantial influence on the evolution of cognitive structures. An alternative possibility, however, is that the phonological loop could possibly play a part in long-term phonological learning, as part of the system whereby a child acquire as language, and that this system, in turn, plays a role in the development of reading.

This simple model is able to handle a rich array of well-established short-term memory phenomena (Badeley, 1986), and, in addition, provides a good account of the deficits shown by short-term memory patients, who are assumed to have a defective phonological store (Vallar and Baddeley, 1984). Such patients do, however, raise an intriguing question about the function of this store, since, apart from their difficulty in performing laboratory memory tasks dependent on short-term memory, they appear to have remarkably few problems in coping with everyday life. This raises the question of the functional significance of the phonological loop system.

One possibility is that it plays an important role in language comprehension. Some early theories would certainly predict this, since they assumed the need to hold whole sentences in order to parse them adequately. Such a view is clearly over-simplified, since patients with a short-term memory deficit can understand sentences that are considerably longer than they are able to repeat. There is evidence to suggest a more subtle impairment, but the extent of the role of short-term phonological memory in normal comprehension remains controversial (Howard and Butterworth, 1989; Vallar and Baddeley, 1989).

A second possible line of investigation was suggested by the widespread association between developmental dyslexia and reduced digit span, suggesting the involvement of the phonological loop system in the process of learning to read. Such an association has been noted by many investigators, although the exact process whereby phonological memory is necessary for reading is rarely well specified (Jorm, 1983). It is, however, not legitimate to draw the conclusion from a simple correlation such as this, that good non-word repetition reflects a system that is causally necessary for vocabulary development. One might equally plausibly argue that the causal link operates in the reverse direction, with a good vocabulary allowing more efficient performance of the non-word repetition test.

One problem with this view is that patients with short-term memory deficits have shown apparently normal long-term learning (Shallice and Warrrington, 1970; Vallar and Baddeley, 1984). However, the learning tasks used have tended to require the subject to learn meaningful material, or visual material such as faces or patterns, with no studies of phonological learning such as faces or patterns, with no studies of phonological learning. We, therefore, decided to carry out such a study.

Short-Term Phonological Memory and Long-Term Learning

A single case, P.V., who had been extensively investigated, and found to have a very pure deficit of short-term phonological memory following a vascular incident was tested. She was intellectually unimpaired, and had been shown to have normal language and normal general long-term learning abilities, but to have a memory span of only two digits in contrast to the normal span of six or seven digits. We tested her phonological memory by attempting to teach her Russian vocabulary, associating each of eight words of her native Italian with a Russian word selected as being dissimilar to Italian with a Russian word selected as being dissimilar to Italian, but nonetheless easily pronounced. It was contrasted with her capacity to learn to associate pairs of Italian word, and her performance was compared with that of subjects matched for age and education. The results of the study are shown in Figure 1, from which it is clear that she was quite normal in her capacity to learn pairs of material such as a printed word, and registering it in the store by means of subvocalization.

This result, therefore, is entirely consistent with the hypothesis that P.V. would have a specific problem in new phonological learning; she had no difficulty in perceiving and discriminating speech sounds, and showed no problem in retrieving already learned material from long-term memory, as evidenced by her normal vocabulary and speech rate. However, P.V. was only a single case, leaving open the possibility that she might have just happened to have two separated deficits, one in short-term phonological memory, and the other in long-term phonological learning.

It was attempted to simulate the deficit shown by P.V. using normal subjects in whom phonological coding is disrupted by the process known as articulatory suppression. This involves requiring the subjects to utter repeatedly some redundant speech sounds such as the word 'the' while attempting to remember or learn new material. There is abundant evidence to suggest that this effectively blocks the articulatory rehearsal process, and furthermore, prevents visually-presented items being registered in the phonological store (Baddeley,

1990). Typically, its effects are considerably less drastic than one would expect from the neurological destruction of the store, since the visual presentation means that items are encoded visually. Nevertheless, one might reasonably expect articulatory suppression to differentially impair the occurrence of new phonological learning, given visual presentation.

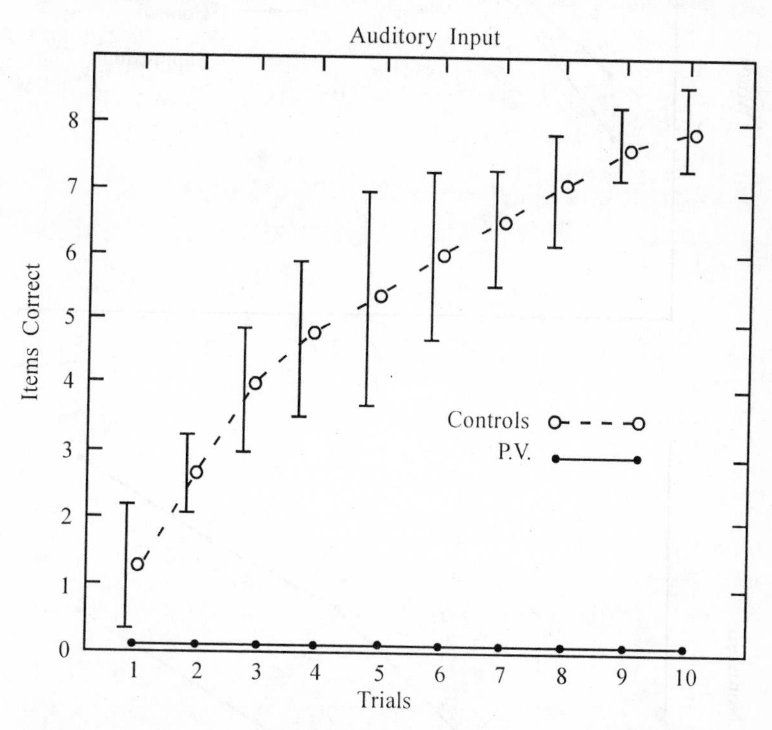

Figure 1. *Acquisition of foreign-language vocabulary by control subjects and by P.V., a patient with a specific deficit in short-term phonological memory.*

A total of 24 Italian subjects were presented with the pairs of words and Russian vocabulary pairs used in the previous study. Under one condition, they were required to continually repeat the sound 'bla', while in the other they were free to subvocalize if they so wished (Papagno, Baddeley, and Valentine, 1989). The results of this study are shown in Figure 2, from which it is clear that the effects obtained were analogous to the deficit shown by P.V., with articulatory suppression differentially impairing the learning of the unfamiliar Russian vocabulary.

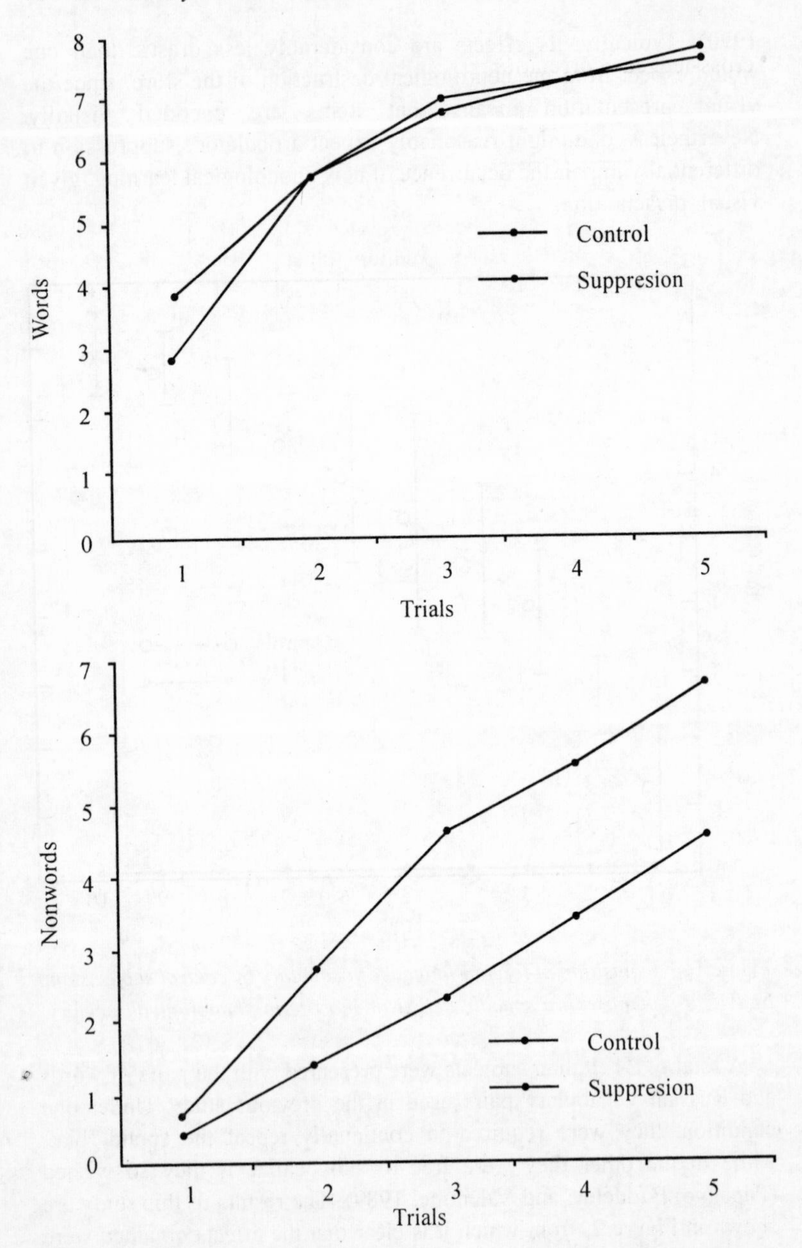

Figure 2. *Effect of suppression of subvocal rehearsal on learning pairs of familiar words and foreign vocabulary.*

One way of attempting to resolve this dilemma is via the process of cross-legged correlation. This involves studying the correlation between the two capacities, that is, non-word repetition and vocabulary development, two successive points in development. If the capacity for non-word repetition indicates a system that is necessary for vocabulary learning, then one might expect the subject's repetition performance to predict subsequent vocabulary one year later significantly more highly than the reverse pattern of correlation between initial vocabulary score and subsequent non-word repetition. On the other hand, if vocabulary is the crucial driving factor, then one would expect the reverse pattern of correlation magnitudes. We therefore conducted cross-lagged correlations between non-word repetition and vocabulary at ages 4 and 5. The results indicated a higher correlation between non-word repetition and subsequent vocabulary than was found for the reverse pattern, supporting the view that phonological short-term memory capacity is necessary for vocabulary development, rather than the reverse.

Phonological Memory and Normal Language Development

The presence of a short-term phonological processing deficit in our language-disordered children, that is substantially more severe than their general language deficit, strongly suggests that it may have a causative role. Such a conclusion, however, would not necessarily imply that the capacity of phonological memory places a major constraint upon the language development of normal children. We decide to explore this in a sample of 4-year-olds who were tested on starting school, and re-tested one and two years later (Gathercole and Baddeley, 1989).

We chose children who showed no evidence of any capacity to read at this stage, measuring their non-verbal intelligence by means of Raven's Progressive Matrices, their phonological memory by means of a non-word repetition task in which they repeat back non-words increasing in length and complexity, and their vocabulary in terms of the British Picture Vocabulary Scale. This involves presenting the child with a set of four pictures, naming one of them and asking the child to point to that item. Table 1 shows the correlation between vocabulary and performance on various other tasks. It is clear that at all three stages, non-word repetition is the best predictor of vocabulary. When step-wise regression was performed, taking out differences in vocabulary performance attributable to non-verbal intelligence, there still remained a very substantial contribution from non-word repetition to vocabulary score.

Table 1

Correlation between vocabulary scores at ages 4 and 5 and other variables together with percentage variance accounted for by each based on simple and fixed-order stepwise regression.

Measure	Correlation Coffiecient	Simple Regression (% Variance)	Stepwise Regression (% Variance)
AGE 4			
Chronological	0.218	5*	5*
Nonverbal intelligence	0.388	15**	13**
Nonword repetition	0.525	27**	15**
Sound mimicry	0.295	9**	0
Total	0.578	33**	–
AGE 5			
Chronological age	0.007	0	0
Nonverbal intelligence	0.164	3	3
Nonword repetition	0.492	24**	21**
Sound mimicry	0.366	13**	1
Reading	0.277	5**	0
Total	0.503	25**	–

* $p < 0.05$
** $p < 0.01$

A consistent and high correlation between vocabulary and non-word repetition is clearly consistent with the expectation.

Phonological Storage and Language Development

While conducting these experiments, the memory capacities of children who had been categorized as 'language-disordered' were also studied. Vocabulary and reading ages of these children were at least two years behind their age expectations, despite their having normal or above normal non-verbal intelligence. We found that the single most striking deficit that these children showed was in their capacity to echo back unfamiliar pseudo-words. These 8-year-old children performed this task at the level of 4-year-old, indicating an impairment that was substantially greater than the reading and vocabulary deficit for which they had been referred for special schooling. Further investigation indicated that their impaired performance was unlikely to be attributable to problems in auditory perception or in speed or fluency of articulation, and suggested that the root problem was probably one of short-term phonological memory (Gathercole and Baddeley, 1989). This is consistent with he hypothesis that the phonological loop component of working memory plays an important role in children's language acquisition.

Non-Word Repetition and Second Language Learning

While we were conducting our study of vocabulary development in English children, a parallel independent study of second language learning was carried out by Service (1989) in Helsinki. This formed a part of a study investigating the desirability of beginning the teaching of English as a second language to children several years younger than is currently the case. As one component of her study, Service measured the capacity of her children to repeat back immediately unfamiliar English words, a task that was equivalent to our own non-word repetition test. She correlated performance on this task in 7-year-old children with their performance on a range of English language tests two years later. Her results showed non-word repetition to be an excellent predictor of subsequent language performance.

Conclusions

The hypothesized link between short-term phonological memory and language acquisition is supported by evidence from both normal and neurologically-impaired adults and children. Given the proposed link between long and short-term memory systems, do we need to continue to assume a distinction? There is nothing from our evidence that suggests that this distinction should be abandoned. Impaired short-term storage appears to result in an impairment in new leaning but has no consistent effect on the speed or accuracy of retrieving old memories. Conversely, amnesic patients with clear deficits in long-term learning and retrieval typically show no impairment in the performance of short-term tasks such as those involved in auditory or visuo-spatial memory span. Clearly, however, as our data indicate, the two systems operate highly interactively. More specifically, they are consistent with the hypothesis that adequate short-term phonological storage is necessary for normal acquisition of language.

REFERENCES

Baddeley, A.D. (1990). *Human Memory: Theory and Practice,* London: Lawrence Erbaum Associates.

Baddeley A.D. and G. Hitch (1974). 'Working memory', in G.A. Bower (ed.), *Recent Advances in Learning and Motivation,* Vol. 8, New York; Academic Press.

Baddeley A.D., G. Papagno and G. Vallar (1988). 'When Long Term Learning Depends on Short-Term Storage', *Journal of Memory and Language,* 27: 586–95.

Baddeley A.D. and E.D. Warrington (1970). 'Amnesia and the Distinction Between Long and Short-Term Memory', *Journal of Verbal Learning and Verbal Behaviour,* 9: 176–89.

Gathercole, S.E. and A.D. Baddeley (1980). 'The Role of Phonological Memory in Normal and Disordered Language Development' in C. von Bulr, I. Lundberg, and G. Lennerstrand (eds), *Brain and Reading,* London; Macmillan Press, pp. 245–55.

Gathercole, S. and A.D. Baddeley (1989). 'Evaluation of the Role of Phonological STM in the Development of Vocabulary in Children: A Longitudinal Study', *Journal of Memory and Language,* 28: 200–13.

Howard, D. and B. Butterworth (1989). 'Short-Term Memory and Sentence Comprehension: A Reply to Vallar and Baddeley, 1987', *Cognitive Neuropsychology,* 6: 455–63.

Jorm, A.F. (1983). 'Specific Reading Retardation and Working Memory: A Review', *British Journal of Psychology,* 74: 311–42.

Papagno. C., A.D. Baddeley and T. Valentie (1989). 'Memoria Fonological a Breave Termine e Apendimento Verbale', *Achivio di Psicologia Neurologia e Psichiatria,* 3: 542–57.

Service, E. (1989). 'Phonological Coding in Working Memory and Foreign Language Learning', Helsinki, University of Helsinki General Psychology Monographs, No. B9.

Shallice, T. and E.K. Warrington (1970). 'Independent Functioning of Verbal Memory Stories: A Neuropsychological Study', *Quarterly Journal of Experimental Psychology,* 22: 262–73.

Vallar, G. and A.D. Baddeley (1984) 'Fractionation of Working Memory: Neuropsychological Evidence for a Phonological Short-Term Store', *Journal of Verbal Learning and Verbal Behavior,* 23: 151–61.

Vallar, G. and A.D. Baddeley (1989). 'Development Disorders of Verbal Short-Term Memory and their Relation to Sentence Comprehension: A Reply to Howard and Butterworth', *Cognitive Neuropsychology,* 6: 465–73.

5 The Processing Efficiency Theory of Anxiety

Michael W. Eysenck and Manuel G. Calvo

Anxiety and performance research focuses on two major issues: (1) complexity and apparent inconsistency of the findings; and (2) conceptual definition of task difficulty. Some theorists (e.g., Humphreys and Revelle, 1984; Sarason, 1988) argue that anxiety causes worry, and worry always impairs performance on tasks with high attentional or short-term memory demands. According to the processing efficiency theory, worry has two main effects: (1) a reduction in the storage and processing capacity of the working memory system available for a concurrent task; and (2) an increment in on-task effort and activities designed to improve performance. The theory distinguishes between performance effectiveness (quality of performance) and processing efficiency (performance effectiveness divided by effort). It is believed that anxiety characteristically impairs efficiency more than effectiveness.

INTRODUCTION

There is profound evidence showing that performance on many tasks varies as a function of individual differences in trait and test anxiety (Eysenck, 1982). It is typically found that high-trait and/or text-anxious individuals have a lower level of performance than low-trait and/or test-anxious individuals, especially under stressful conditions. However, this impaired performance is found more consistently when the task is difficult than when it is easy. Eysenck (1982) discussed a total of 24 experiments in which there was a significant interaction between trait or test anxiety and task difficulty; in 22 of those experiments, the pattern of interaction was as anticipated.

Of course, there are numerous exceptions to this anticipated interaction pattern between anxiety and performance in a variety of tasks. Eysenck (1985) reported that anxiety impaired performance in only 3 of the 12 component processes involved in a difficult version of a letter-transformation task under stress conditions. In a study by Calvo (1985), high- and low-anxiety subjects performed similarly in the difficult part of a non-verbal inductive reasoning task under test conditions without any reward, although with reward the performance of high-anxiety subjects was worse than that of low-anxiety subjects. As far as motor tasks are concerned, a number of studies indicate not only that anxiety sometimes has no effect on performance, but also that the effect is positive in some cases (Calvo and Alamo, 1987; see Weinberg, 1990).

These empirical complexities raise two problems, that is, to explain the relationship between anxiety and performance, and the notion of task difficulty, which is the main factor that interacts with anxiety to determine individual differences in performance.

Many theories have been proposed to account for the effects of anxiety on performance. Two of the most influential theoretical approaches deserve special mention.

Worry and Attentional Interference

Liebert and Morris (1967) argued that test anxiety can be divided into the two components of worry and emotionality. Most of the research indicated that the negative effects of anxiety on performance were attributable to worry rather than to emotionality (Deffenbacher, 1980; Morris, Davis and Hutchings, 1981). This finding led some theorists to define test anxiety mainly as proneness to self-preoccupation and, more specifically, as worry over evaluation (Sarason, 1988). In this approach (e.g., Sarason, 1984, 1986; Wine, 1971, 1982), the effects of worry on performance have been explained in terms of an interference effect of worry on attention. Worrisome thoughts interfere with attention to task-relevant information, thus reducing the cognitive resources available for task-processing activities. As a consequence, performance is impaired.

This approach led to two predictions. First, as worry is the critical factor responsible for performance decrements, it follows that individuals high in test anxiety will generally perform at an inferior level to those low in test anxiety, provided that the former subjects have a higher level of worry than the latter. Second, the more difficult the task is, the greater will be the detrimental effect of worry on performance, assuming that difficulty is related to the amount of attentional resources demanded by the task.

The first prediction was found consistent with a number of findings (Deffenbacher, 1978; Sarason and Stoops, 1978; Morris, Kellaway, and Smith, 1978). However, there is evidence that test anxiety is not always related to performance, even when there is a positive relationship between test anxiety and worry. Calvo and Ramos (1989) and Calvo, Alamo and Ramos (1990) reported that significantly higher worry scores by high-anxious than by low-anxious subjects were obtained on difficult tasks on which the performance of the two groups was equivalent. In similar fashion, Blankstein, Toner and Flett (1989) discovered that high-test-anxious subjects have a higher ratio of negative thoughts about themselves and a lower ratio of positive thoughts about an anagram task performance than did low-test-anxious subjects, but the two groups did not actually differ in performance. Blankstein *et al.* (1990) found in a difficult analogies task performed under evaluative stress that high-test-anxious subjects made more unfavourable and fewer favourable statements about themselves than did low-test-anxious subjects, but again there was no difference in performance. The problem with the first prediction lies in the conceptualization of worry as a factor with only one method of influence, namely, attentional interference.

The second prediction is confirmed by the data based on interaction between task difficulty and anxiety (Eysenck, 1982). Defining task difficulty is a problem by itself as it is equated with the amount of attentional resources demanded by a task. In fact, tasks can be difficult because of their demands on either processing resources or on transient storage capacity, and this distinction between processing and storage is important within the processing efficiency theory of anxiety.

Anxiety, Avoidance Motivation and Arousal

Humphreys and Revelle (1984), and Revelle and Loftus (1990) developed a comprehensive theory of the relationship among individual differences in personality, motivation and cognitive performance, including the role of anxiety. According to these authors, state anxiety has a cognitive component, worry which can be 'equated with avoidance motivation, which produces a subsequent decrease in resources allocated to the task (on-task effort)' (Humphreys and Revelle, 1984: 176). In addition, state anxiety has an arousal component, defined as a state of 'alertness, vigor, peppiness and activation' (p. 176). Secondly, they made a distinction between sustained information transfer (SIT) tasks and short-term memory (STM) tasks. In SIT tasks, 'the subject is required to process a stimulus, associate an arbitrary response to the stimulus, and execute the response. Furthermore, there is no appreciable retention required...' (p. 161). Simple reaction time is an example of SIT tasks. STM tasks 'require subjects to either maintain information in an available state through rehearsal or other processes or retrieve information that has not been attended for a short time' (p. 164). Revelle (1987) made a further distinction based on long-term memory tasks.

In general, those tasks with a substantial short-term memory component are relatively much more adversely affected than those with a minimal involvement of short-term memory. The worry component, as well as interfering with attention, reduces on-task effort, and so produces performance decrements in STM and SIT tasks. The arousal component impairs STM performance, but it can facilitate SIT performance. Therefore, STM performance will always be impaired, but performance decrements in SIT tasks induced by worry can be counteracted by high arousal.

The theory proposed by Humphreys and Revelle (1984) has two main advantages over the attentional interference theory: (1) the activational influence of anxiety is considered as well as the cognitive influence; and (2) tasks are distinguished in more specific ways than simply in terms of their dependence on attentional resources; this permits a more precise account of task difficulty, and facilitates accounting for interactions between anxiety and task difficulty.

In the light of the efficiency theory, Eysenck (1992) criticizes the approach of Humphreys and Revelle. Firstly, the hypothesis that anxiety promotes task-avoidance motivation and reduces on-task effort overestimates the negative motivational influence of anxiety. If anxiety typically reduces on-task effort, then performance should generally be impaired, at least in tasks with substantial short-term memory demands. However, there is evidence contrary to this prediction (Calvo, 1985; Eysenck, 1985). The crucial weakness may be the conceptualization of avoidance motivation as characterizing high-anxious individuals. If high-anxious subjects are allowed to avoid or escape from a threatening or stressful situation, and this behaviour has no aversive consequences, they will probably do it (Geen, 1987). However, most stressful situations in daily life and experimental settings (e.g., examinations, participations in experiments, speaking in public) represent not only a threat, but a challenge (Jerusalem, 1990). If high-anxious individuals avoid or escape from the situation, there may be aversive consequences (e.g., negative evaluation by others, self-esteem decrements, material losses, failure to obtain a grade). In those situations, when anxious individuals perceive the threat, they are motivated to avoid the aversive consequences of poor task performance. Therefore, anxiety does not so much produce task-avoidance activation, as Humphreys and Revelle (1984) claim, but motivation to avoid aversive consequences. Furthermore, this form of motivation typically increases effort on the task instead of decreasing it. This compensatory effort can prevent the performance of anxious subjects from deteriorating.

Secondly, the role of arousal may not be as important as Humphreys and Revelle (1984) assumed. It has proved extremely difficult to find any consistent psychophysiological differences between groups high and low in trait anxiety, or in the closely related personality dimension of neuroticism. Holroyd *et al.* (1978) and Holroyd and Appel (1980) found that high- and low-anxiety subjects showed comparable changes in objective electrodermal activity and heart rate response to the stress of a testing situation, but high-anxiety subjects reported higher levels of self-perceived arousal than low-anxiety subjects. Further evidence indicates that, although high-anxiety subjects report higher levels of subjective arousal, it is not associated with impaired performance in either cognitive or fine motor tasks (Calvo and Ramos, 1989; Calvo *et al.*, 1990). Fahrenberg (1987) reviewed the relevant literature, and came to the following conclusion: 'Psychophysiological research on physiological correlates of the established emotionality (neuroticism) trait dimension has come to a standstill. Findings of questionnaire studies generally support the postulated psychophysiological relationship, but research that employs objectively measured physiological parameters in large scale, methodologically well-controlled and replicated investigations has not substantiated these hypotheses.' Therefore, arousal, as it is assessed by physiological measures of activation, seems to make no more than a minor contribution to the anxiety–performance relationship.

Thirdly, the theoretical approach of Humphreys and Revelle (1984) appears to assume that individuals behave in a passive and mechanistic fashion, in which they simply respond to situations. Within this approach, active compensatory operations and resources are not considered. The processing efficiency theory, proposes a contrasting position.

THE PROCESSING EFFICIENCY THEORY

The processing efficiency theory (which represents an extension of earlier theoretical statements by Eysenck, 1979, 1982) is basically designed to provide an explanation of the effects of state anxiety on performance. It is intended to have general applicability, but may in practice have most relevance to cognitive-task performance, to high anxiety in normal populations rather than clinical populations, and to test or evaluative stress conditions.

It is assumed within processing efficiency theory that state anxiety is determined interactively by trait anxiety and by situational threat or stress. It is also assumed that it is the level of state anxiety which is generally crucial in determining individual differences in internal processing and performance. However, it should be noted that it is often difficult to distinguish between trait and state anxiety at an empirical level. The reason for this is because they correlate as highly as 0.70 or more with each other.

Worry (e.g. self-preoccupation, concern over evaluation, concern over level of performance) is an important construct within the theory; it is regarded as forming the conginitive component of state anxiety (cf. Morris *et al.*, 1981). The essential features of a working memory-system is that it is concerned with both active processing and the transient storage of information. The specific version of a working memory system put forward by Baddeley (1986) consists of three components, all of which have limited capacity: a modality-free central executive resembling attention, which is involved in active processing; an articulatory loop specializing in rote verbal rehearsal, which is used for transient storage of verbal material, and a visuo-spatial sketch pad specializing in visual and/or spatial information. The central executive is the most important part of the working memory system.

According to Baddeley (1986), it is used on tasks requiring planning or decision-making, in situations where poorly-mastered response sequences are involved, and acts as a trouble-shooter when lower processing systems seem inadequate.

According to the processing efficiency theory, one of the major effects of worry about task performance is to pre-empt some of the processing and storage resources of the working memory system. It is assumed that the main effects of worry are on the central executive, although the articulatory loop is also probably implicated. As a consequence, any adverse effects of state anxiety on performance tend to be greater on tasks which impose substantial demands on the capacity of the working memory system, especially if those demands are primarily on the central executive and the articulatory loop.

Worry about task performance has a second effect within the theory. It serves a motivational function via a control system probably located within the working memory system (see below). The functioning of this system leads to the allocation of additional processing resources (i.e., effort) and to the initiation of processing activities (e.g., strategies) designed to improve performance (see later). In order to escape from the state of apprehension associated with worrisome thoughts, and to avoid the likely aversive consequences of poor performance, anxious subjects try to cope with threat and worry by allocating additional resources (i.e., effort) and/or initiating processing activities (i.e., strategies). Such attempts, if successful, increase available working memory capacity. As a consequence, potential performance impairments caused by the utilization of working memory resources can be compensated for by the allocation of additional resources or activities.

A central contention of the processing efficiency theory is that there is a control or self-regulatory system which is involved in mediating the effects of anxiety on processing and on performance. Hockey (1986) has speculated on the details of how such a system might operate. There is evidence that such a system is responsive to indications (e.g., failure feedback) that the current level of task performance is falling below that required by the subject. There are two major types of reactions to poor performance which are initiated by the control system. First, it is sometimes possible to cope directly with the current level of threat and/or worry. There is a consequent reduction in worry and an increase in the available capacity of the working memory. Second, it is often possible to reduce or eliminate the negative effects of worry on task performance by applying additional effort (extra processing resources) to the task. The complex nature of the various functions of the control system indicate that it is located within the working memory system.

There is evidence that such a control system is implicated in metacognitive activities during learning and performance, for example, during reading (Baker and Brown, 1984; see Britton and Glynn, 1987). Presumably, this system has two major functions: awareness and regulation of the ongoing cognitive processes. More specifically, learners have some awareness of their own cognitive processes and efficiency, and monitor their progress sufficiently to detect a problem in processing or performance. They can also introduce remedial or corrective strategies and deploy compensatory resources to overcome the problem that has been detected. Thus, the cognitive system is flexibly directed by self-regulatory mechanisms which monitor and evaluate current or previous outcomes, and which actively deploy resources or strategies to improve performance.

As far as anxiety is concerned, the control system is sensitive to failure feedback, indicating that the current level of task performance is falling below the required level, and to estimates of the likelihood and intensity of aversive consequences if the task is avoided and if the task is approached. Subsequently, there are two major types of reaction to poor performance and threat of aversive consequences: (1) coping directly with the current level of threat and worry (e.g., repression or denial, calming down, and self-revalorization) (Rost and Schermer, 1989b); (2) reduction or elimination of the negative effects of worry on performance by applying additional resources (e.g., effort or time) or activities (e.g., rote learning, articulatory rehearsal, seeking external assistance) to the task.

In general terms, additional processing resources or activities initiated by the control system to the current task will be found more frequently in high-anxious individuals than in low-anxious individuals. There are various reasons for this. First, the presence of worry about the current level of performance has direct motivational consequences. It leads to active and effortful responses designed to improve performance, and to reduce threat and worry. Second, the fact that high-anxious individuals tend to devote more of their processing resources than low-anxious individuals to worry and to other task-irrelevant processing can lead to impaired performance. This increases the probability of detecting a mismatch between the expected and actual performance. Third, high-trait-anxious individuals are faster than low-trait-anxious ones at detecting threat-related stimuli of various kinds, and the former subjects selectively allocate more attention to those stimuli (Eysenck, MacLeod and Mathews, 1987). They are also more likely to interpret ambiguous sentences in a threatening fashion than the latter (Eysenck *et al.,* 1987). In test situations specifically, high-anxious subjects are much more sensitive than low-anxious subjects to failure feedback (Jerusalem, 1990). This means that they are more likely to detect a mismatch between performance and expectation, and to process threat-related information, and that they are much more motivated than low-anxious subjects to allocate additional effort to task performance. Fourth, anxious individuals may set themselves unrealistically high standards of performance, thus increasing the probability of a performance-expectation mismatch.

The above theoretical analysis leads to a fundamental theoretical distinction between performance effectiveness and processing efficiency. Performance effectiveness simply refers to the quality of task performance, whereas processing efficiency refers to the relationship between the effectiveness of performance and the effort or amount of processing resources invested. In other words, processing efficiency is defined by performance effectiveness divided by effort. It seems to be implicit in most theories (e.g., that of Sarason, 1984, 1988; Humphreys and Revelle, 1984; Revelle, 1987) that anxiety has comparable adverse effects on both processing efficiency and performance effectiveness. As a result, processing efficiency can readily be inferred from performance effectiveness. In contrast, it is argued within the processing efficiency theory that, the effects of anxiety on processing efficiency and on performance effectiveness are frequently rather different. More specifically, the greater use of the control system by anxious individuals means that the adverse effects of anxiety on performance effectiveness are often less than those on processing efficiency. As a consequence, it is necessary to obtain separate measures of processing efficiency and performance effectiveness in order to understand the full range of effects of anxiety.

This can be difficult to achieve in practice. Performance effectiveness can generally be measured fairly precisely, but effort (which is relevant to processing efficiency) can be assessed only in approximate terms, and efficiency even more approximately. The main reason why efficiency is so difficult to assess accurately is because the notion that efficiency is effectiveness divided by effort cannot be taken in any strict mathematical sense. For example, if high-anxious subjects have higher performance effectiveness and exert greater effort on a task than low-anxious subjects, it is extremely difficult to decide which group has shown superior processing efficiency.

Contrasts Among Theories

The processing efficiency theory differs from other theories of anxiety and performance in a number of different ways. First, worry has motivational as well as attentional interference effects in contrast to Sarason's (1984, 1988) theory. Second, the motivational effect is generally positive in that it leads to increased effort or compensatory strategies, which contrasts with the theory of Humphreys and Revelle (1984). Third, the notion that the effects of anxiety on performance differ from those on efficiency is not considered within the other theories. Fourth, anxiety affects both the storage and the processing capacity of the working memory system which are available for task performance rather than simply the storage capacity of short-term memory (Humphreys and Revelle, 1984) or attentional resources (e.g., Sarason, 1988).

At a more general conceptual level, it is assumed within other theories (e.g., Sarason, 1988) that stressful situations or threats cause anxious individuals to respond relatively passively with self-preoccupation.

Processing Efficiency Theory

Prediction 1: *Anxiety typically impairs processing efficiency more than performance effectiveness.*

In order to facilitate the testing of this prediction, it makes sense to focus on those situations in which high- and low-anxious subjects have comparable performance effectiveness. The prediction then becomes straightforward. The high-anxious subjects will generally exert more effort, and thus show lower processing efficiency. As processing efficiency depends on performance effectiveness as well as effort, it is only when the two groups of subjects have equivalent levels of performance effectiveness that there is a simple and direct relationship between effort and efficiency.

The methods to test the above prediction include: assessment of subjective effort; use of a secondary task; probe-latency assessment of spare processing capacity; motivational manipulations; the loading paradigm; assessment of processing time; and psychophysiological measures. Each of these methods is discussed below.

Prediction 1.1: *High-anxious subjects should report higher levels of subjective effort than low-anxious subjects on tasks on which their performance is comparable.*

Research of relevance to Prediction 1.1 was reported by Dornic (1977, 1980). Dornic (1977) compared stable extraverts (i.e., those low in trait anxiety) with neurotic introverts (i.e., those high in trait anxiety) on the performance of four versions of a closed-system thinking task varying in terms of task load and extra-task load. The two personality groups did not differ significantly in their performance on any of the four versions of the task. In terms of subjective efforts, however, the high-anxious subjects (i.e., the neurotic introverts) expended significantly more effort than the low-anxious subjects (i.e., the stable extroverts) when there was high task load and high extra-task load.

Dornic (1980) assessed levels of subjective effort in neurotic introverts and stable extraverts performing a visual search task and a task which involved counting backwards. With both tasks, the high-anxious subjects reported higher levels of effort expenditure, especially in the case of more demanding task conditions.

It is possible that high-trait-anxious subjects are inclined to exaggerate their reported level of effort, so that any given effort rating has different significance for individuals high and low in trait anxiety. However, the data cannot be accounted for purely in these terms. High- and low-trait-anxious subjects differed in their ratings of subjective effort only on certain tasks, and this pattern of findings is more consistent with the view that the ratings are valid than with the notion that they reflect individual differences in the tendency to exaggerate.

Prediction 1.2: *Anxiety will typically have an adverse effect on a secondary task performed currently with a primary task.*

According to Kahneman (1973), the amount of spare processing capacity available during the performance of a task is inversely related to the effort or resources applied to that task. One way of assessing this processing capacity is by means of a concurrent secondary or subsidiary task. Consider the case in which the performance of high-

and low-anxious groups is comparable on the primary task. According to the processing efficiency hypothesis, the high-anxious group probably applies greater effort to that task than the low-anxious group. This leaves less spare processing capacity for the subsidiary task, whose performance should thus suffer, if the assumption is made that the initial amount of allocatable resources is comparable in high- and low-anxious groups.

Erysenck (1982) identified 16 experiments involving concurrent primary and secondary tasks administered to high- and low-anxious or stress groups. The most commonly used secondary task was incidental learning of apparently irrelevant peripheral stimuli. In 11 of the 16 experiments, anxiety or stress had a significantly detrimental effect on the performance of the secondary task. In the remaining five experiments, anxiety or stress had no effect on the secondary task performance.

As a consequence of definite methodological limitations in these studies, it is not clear whether the poor performance of anxious or stressed subjects on the secondary tasks occurred because they could not process the secondary task stimuli thoroughly or because they chose not to.

> Prediction 1.3: *Anxiety will reduce spare processing capacity (assessed by responding to probes) during the performance of a central task.*

A modified version of the secondary task method, known as the probe technique, provides a superior way of assessing spare processing capacity. In essence, subjects are instructed to perform the central task as well as possible, diverting only spare processing capacity to the secondary task. The secondary task consists of responding to an occasional probe stimulus as rapidly as possible in the circumstances. The probe technique has the advantages of providing strong constraints on the subject's allocation of processing resources, and of providing a direct, on-line assessment of spare processing capacity.

Hamilton (1978) made use of the probe technique on a digit-span task, with the probe being interpolated between presentation of the digit string and its subsequent recall. Probe response latencies were considered only from those trials on which the digits were recalled correctly, so that performance on the central task was equated for high- and low-anxious subjects. High-anxious subjects as compared with low-anxious subjects had significantly slower response latencies to the probe when the digit-span task consisted of seven digits (the most difficult condition), which implies that the high-anxious subjects had less spare processing capacity than the low-anxious subjects.

Eysenck (1989) used the probe technique on simple versions of the letter-transformation task. High- and low-trait-anxious subjects did not differ in their performance on one- and two-letter problems. However, the high-anxious subjects had significantly longer probe reaction time than the low-anxious subjects during the performance of two-letter problems. As Eysenck (1989) concluded, 'While the high- and low-anxious groups exhibited equal performance effectiveness on two-letter problems, the high-anxious group was actually performing with lower processing efficiency.'

Prediction 1.4: *Motivational factors enhancing effort typically benefit the performance of low-anxious individuals more than high-anxious individuals.*

According to the processing efficiency theory, high-anxious individuals under low-motivational conditions, perform poorly than the low anxious individuals. This is because the worry experienced by the high-anxious individuals reduces their available working memory capacity and leads them to utilize compensatory processing resources (e.g., effort). As a consequence of their elevated effort expenditure under low-motivational conditions, the high-anxious individuals are less able than the low-anxious ones to respond to motivational conditions by increased effort, and so their performance should benefit less than that of low-anxious individuals from conditions designed to increase motivation.

There are various ways in which motivational levels can be manipulated. One method is to compare performance following ego-involving or challenging instructions (e.g., 'This is an intelligence test') with those following task-involving instructions. The typical finding in studies of this type is an anxiety by instructions interaction: the performance of low-anxious subjects is either unaffected by the instructions, or they perform better after ego-involving instructions, whereas high-anxious subjects tend to perform worse under ego-involving instructions (e.g., Calvo and Alamo, 1987; Deffenbacher, 1978; Nicholson, 1958; Sarason, 1956, 1957, 1972). Although these findings are consistent with the above prediction, there are difficulties of interpretation. The effects of ego-involving instructions are not limited to motivation, but may also include increased worry (e.g., concern over evaluation). Accordingly, it is not easy to provide an unequivocal interpretation of the data.

Monetary or other incentives provide a way of enhancing motivation without increasing worry. Calvo (1985) provided monetary incentive for good performance on a non-verbal inductive reasoning test. Trait anxiety interacted significantly with incentive under test or ego-involving conditions. Low-trait-anxious subjects had better performance with incentives, whereas incentives tended to impair performance of high-trait-anxious subjects.

Eysenck (1985) compared the performance of high- and low-trait-anxious subjects on a letter-transformation task under conditions of high and low monetary incentive. Because the presence of monetary incentive had no effect on state anxiety, it is reasonable to assume that it did not increase worry. However, there was a significantly interaction between trait anxiety and incentive: low-trait-anxious subjects performed much better under incentive conditions, whereas the performance of high-trait-anxious subjects was unaffected by incentive.

Prediction 1.5: *The performance of a central task will be adversely affected by an additional load to a greater extent in anxious rather than in non-anxious groups.*

The essence of the loading paradigm is that a central task is performed either on its own or concurrently with a second task or load must be performed to some criterion. According to the processing efficiency theory, if high- and low-anxious groups perform the central task at an equivalent level when it is performed on its own, it is assumed that the high-anxious group has achieved this by investing more processing resources than the low-anxious group. If the presence of a load task prevents extra resources from being allocated to the central task, then the performance of high-anxious individuals should be impaired.

Eliatamby (1984) used the loading paradigm to examine the effects of an additional load on the performance of an anagram task. Anagrams were solved on their own, concurrently with articulatory suppression, or concurrently with counting backwards by threes. High- and low-trait-anxious groups did not differ in their median solution times on five-letter anagrams when the anagram task was performed on its own. However, the high-trait-anxious subjects performed the same anagram task considerably more slowly than the low-trait-anxious subjects when it was combined with the load of counting backwards by threes.

Calvo and Ramos (1989) used the loading paradigm to investigate the effects of anxiety on motor learning. In their first experiment, high- and low-test-anxious subjects performed four motor tasks which varied in their attentional demands and in their muscular requirements. There was a practice trial, followed by a transfer trail on these tasks, with performance being assessed only on the transfer trail. Trait anxiety had no effect on performance. In their second experiment, the same motor tasks were performed.

However, there was also a task or load during the practice trial, consisting of repeating sentences. As a consequence of this load, the transfer-trial performance of the high-trait-anxious subjects on the attentionally demanding motor tasks was significantly inferior to that of the low-trait-anxious subjects.

Prediction 1.6: *Impaired processing efficiency produced by anxiety can be detected by lengthened processing time.*

The time taken to process information can be regarded as a measure of processing efficiency. Given that there are no effects on accuracy, then greater processing time is associated with lower efficiency. Culler and Hollahan (1980) and Benjamin *et al.* (1981) provided indirect support for Prediction 1.6. They discovered that high-test-anxious students reported spending more time studying during several phases of a course than did their low-test-anxious counterparts.

Calvo, Ramos, and Estevez (1999) made use of a reading task on which processing time could be measured very precisely, and on which the comprehension performance of high- and low-anxious subjects had previously been found to be comparable. Several expository and narrative texts with or without summaries were presented to subjects, under instructions to obtain as high a level of comprehension as possible in the least possible time. The reading of the texts was self-paced, word-by-word, using the moving-window technique (e.g., Haberlandt and Graesser, 1985). Performance-effectiveness was measured by means of comprehension tests, and processing-efficiency was assessed by relating comprehension performance to reading times (dividing performance scores by word reading times).

There were no significant effects of anxiety on comprehension performance. However, there was a significant interaction among anxiety, narrativity, and summary for processing efficiency. In this interaction, the high-test-anxious subjects had inferior efficiency as compared to the low-test-anxious subjects, especially with expository texts without a summary. These findings indicate that high-anxious readers require additional processing time to acquire an amount of information equivalent to that acquired by low-anxious readers. Thus, anxiety reduces comprehension efficiency, but not effectiveness. It is presumably the case that efficiency is impaired by anxiety when reading expository rather than narrative texts and texts without rather than with a summary, because many cognitive resources are required to handle expository texts without a summary. It has been found that reading texts without a summary and reading expository texts is more demanding than reading texts with a summary (de Vega *et al.*, 1990) or than reading narrative texts (Haberlandt and Graesser, 1985; de Vega *et al.*, 1990)

Prediction 1.7: *The greater impairment effect of anxiety on efficiency than on effectiveness can be detected by psycho-physiological measures.*

Weinberg and Hunt (1976) used electromyography (EMG) to provide several measures of muscle activity during a throwing task. Trait anxiety had no effect on throwing performance prior to the introduction of feedback, but there were several effects on the EMG. According to Weinberg and Hunt (1976: 223), 'High-anxious subjects anticipated significantly longer with the agonists and shorter with the antagonists than did the low-anxious group. Therefore, they were preparing for the throw in all of the muscles while low-anxious subjects were preparing mostly with the antagonist muscles. This implies that high-anxious subjects were using more energy than necessary, and expending it over a greater period of time, than were low-anxious subjects.'

Rather similar findings were reported by Weinberg (1978), using the same task. Again, there were no effects of trait anxiety on performance prior to feedback. However, there were significant effects on various EMG measures. These included co-contraction (simultaneous contraction of the antagonists and agonists), duration (time of major muscle contraction), and perseveration (continued contraction of decreasing amplitude following the major muscle contraction). The EMG of high-anxious subjects indicated less efficiency than that of low-anxious subjects with respect to each of these measures.

Prediction 2: *Adverse effects of anxiety on task performance generally become stronger as task demands on working memory capacity increase.*

According to the processing efficiency theory, anxious individuals engage in more worry (i.e., self-preoccupation, concern over evaluation, concern over performance) than non-anxious individuals, and worry pre-empts some of the resources of the central executive and of the articulatory loop. As a consequence, tasks requiring the resources of either the central executive or of the articulatory loop should be more vulnerable to anxiety than tasks which do not require the resources of these two components of the working memory. However, it should be noted that attempts to predict the effects of anxiety on performance are rendered more difficult because of the complex effects of increased effort and compensatory activities.

In view of these complexities, it is desirable to consider primarily those tasks which make considerable demands on either the processing resources of the central executive or the storage capacity of the articulatory loop. Of course, the adverse effects of anxiety on performance should be greatest on the tasks placing substantial demands on both storage and processing.

It should be noted that this part of the processing efficiency theory may facilitate understanding of the common finding that anxiety interacts with task difficulty. The notion of 'task difficulty' leaves it unclear as to which cognitive processes or mechanisms are particularly affected by anxiety. According to the processing efficiency theory, task difficulty is important only to the extent that demands on the central executive and/or articulatory loop are affected.

Prediction 2.1: *The effects of anxiety on task performance depend on the amount of resources required by the task (measurable by the susceptibility of that task to interference by a concurrent load).*

Calvo *et al.* (1999) adopted an empirically and conceptually convergent approach to the issue of making sense of anxiety-by-task difficulty interactions in terms of task-processing demands. In one study (Calvo and Alamo, 1987), the processing demands of two tasks (i.e., building a small toy with screws and nuts, which involved finger movements, and typewriting with only one finger, which involved arm movements) were established. Subjects performed each task either on its own or concurrently with an interference task (verbally repeating series of numbers immediately after their presentation). Conceptually, the high-demanding version of each task required more extensive response selection for each stimulus than the low-demanding version. Empirically, the high-demanding version of each task was the one which was more impaired by the concurrent task than the low-demanding one. In a subsequent experiment, these tasks were presented alone under evaluative conditions. High-anxious subjects had a lower level of performance than low-anxious subjects on the high-demanding tasks, but the two groups were comparable in their performance on the low-demanding tasks.

In a different series of experiments, Calvo *et al.* (1990) used four versions of a task which involved manipulating small or large geometrical pieces with two fingers or with two hands. In the low-demanding versions, each piece had to be placed in a separate position, whereas in the high-demanding versions all of the pieces had to be assembled. Conceptually, the response movement for each stimulus was perceptually discriminable in the former versions, but had to be inferred in the latter. Empirically, the high-demanding versions were impaired by a concurrent loading task (verbal shadowing of sentences), but the low-demanding versions were not impaired. In a subsequent experiment with evaluative instructions and no concurrent load, high-anxious subjects had a significant performance impairment only on the high-demanding tasks on the practice trial, but not on a transfer trial. According to the logic of the transfer paradigm (Schmidt, 1988: 358–63), the effects of anxiety were on performances rather on learning *per se.*

Prediction 2.2: *Anxiety reduces transient storage capacity.*

The digit-span task requires maximal utilization of transient storage capacity, and imposes great demands on the capacity of the articulatory loop (Baddeley, 1986). It therefore follows from the processing efficiency theory that high levels of state anxiety should be associated with impaired digit span. There are several studies in which this finding was obtained (see Eysenck, 1979). There are also a number of studies in which digit span was impaired by stress (see Eysenck, 1979).

According to the processing efficiency theory, internal processing and performance are determined by state anxiety rather than by trait anxiety *per se.* As a consequence, any effects of trait anxiety on digit-span performance should be relatively weak and inconsistent.

Eysenck (1979) reviewed the experimental evidence from a total of 16 studies. There were non-significant effects of trait anxiety on digit-span in nine studies, a significant relationship between trait anxiety and digit span in two studies, a significant negative relationship in three studies, and complex relationships between trait-anxiety and digit-span in the remaining two studies. Recent research has produced inconsistent findings. Darke (1988a) reported that test anxiety was associated with a moderate negative effect on the performance of a digit-span task under ego-threat conditions. However, in a study by Calvo *et al.* (1990) there was no difference between high- and low-test-anxious students in letter-span under either evaluative conditions.

Prediction 2.3: *Anxiety has powerful adverse effects on tasks with storage and processing demands.*

One of the main predictions from the processing efficiency theory is that adverse effects of anxiety on task performance should be greatest when the task makes considerable demands on both the central executive and the articulatory loop. It follows that adverse effects of anxiety on tasks primarily involving the articulatory loop should be less than on those tasks also having a substantial involvement of the central executive. The effects of anxiety on the storage and processing capacity of working memory have been compared in a number of studies.

The above predictions were investigated by Darke (1988a). He used ego-threatening conditions, and found that the digit-span performance of low-test-anxious subjects was approximately 20 per cent higher than that of high-test-anxious subjects. He also used a modified version of a reading-span task specifically designed to measure the capacity (processing plus storage) of working memory. Up to six consecutive sentences were presented for comprehension, followed by a recall test for the last word in each sentence. The number of trials on which all of the last words were recalled provided a measure of the working memory capacity. This task clearly places more demands on working memory than does digit-span, because a high storage load is combined with the high processing requirements of the comprehension task. Therefore, the adverse effects of test anxiety should be greater on this reading-span task than on digit-span. As predicted, superiority of the low-test-anxious subjects over the high-test-anxious subjects was much greater on this task (68 per cent correct trials) than on digit-span.

More evidence on the role of working memory in mediating the effects of anxiety on performance was obtained by Calvo *et al.* They assessed the letter span and reading span of high- and low-test-anxious subjects. Unlike Darke (1988a), they made use of both evaluative and non-evaluative testing conditions. There was no effect of test anxiety on letter span under either evaluative or non-evaluative testing conditions. However, there was a highly significant interaction between test anxiety and testing conditions on the reading-span task. The performance of low-test-anxious subjects was 64 per cent better than that of high-test-anxious subjects under evaluative testing conditions, but the performance of the two groups did not differ under non-evaluative conditions.

The findings of Calvo *et al.* (1990) replicated and extended those of Darke (1988a). It was not clear from the findings of Darke (1988a) whether the poor reading span of high-anxious subjects was due to a basic deficit in working memory, or whether it was due to a transitory working memory deficit stemming from the worry produced by being evaluated. Calvo *et al's* data clearly support the latter interpretation.

An alternative way of testing Prediction 2.3 is to make use of a series of related tasks differing in the demands they place on the central executive and the articulatory loop. The expectation is that the adverse effects of anxiety on performance will become more apparent as the demands on working memory (and especially the central executive component) increase. The letter-transformation paradigm (Hamilton, Hockey and Rejman, 1977) provides a suitable range of tasks to test this prediction. The basic version of the task involves transforming a single letter by moving a given distance through the alphabet, and then producing the result of the transformation as the answer (e.g., the answer to 'M+2' is 'O'). As the number of letters needing to be transformed increases, the task makes progressively greater demands on both the processing and storage capacities of working memory. There were between one and four letters per problem, and the time to produce the correct answer was the dependent variable.

There was a highly significant interaction between trait anxiety and the number of letters in the problem. High-trait-anxious subjects were markedly slower than low-trait-anxious subjects with three- and four-letter problems, but the two groups did not differ on one- and two-letter problems. These findings support the prediction that anxiety has a greater adverse effect on tasks making substantial demands on working memory capacity. However, the findings can readily be accounted for by other theories. For example, Humphreys and Revelle (1984) argued that anxiety reduces short-term memory capacity, and the demands on the short-term memory capacity are greater for three- and four-letter problems than for one- and two-letter problems. Accordingly, Eysenck (1985) carried out a second experiment to provide evidence to discriminate between alternative theories.

Only four-letter problems were used in this second experiment. The time taken to perform each of the following componential processes for each of the four letters was recorded: access to the long-term representation of the alphabet; performance of the transformation; and rehearsal and storage of the accumulating answer. Thus, 12 separate component times were recorded. According to the theory proposed by Humphreys and Revelle (1984), anxiety should affect all of the component times for the third and fourth letters because of the high demands on short-term memory. In contrast, it is emphasized within the processing efficiency theory that anxiety mainly affects complex processing involving the central executive. The organizational processes involved in rehearsal and storage of the accumulating answer, especially towards the end of each problem, place the greatest demands on the central executive. As predicted by this analysis, high-trait-anxious subjects were significantly slower than low-trait-anxious subjects in their rehearsal and storage times for the second, third, and fourth letters, but did not differ with respect to the other nine componential processing times.

Prediction 2.4: *Anxiety does not generally impair performance on tasks not involving the central executive and/or articulatory loop components of the working memory system.*

Because the main adverse effects of anxiety on performance occur because worry pre-empts some of the processing resources of working memory, it follows that tasks making either no or minimal demands on working memory should typically not be impaired by anxiety. In practice, it is rather difficult to test this prediction, because there are probably very few tasks which make no demands at all on the working memory system. Another reason why it is difficult to test the prediction is that non-significant effects of anxiety on task performance can either be due to the non-involvement of working memory in the task, or due to the compensatory activities initiated by the control system.

Darke (1988b) attempted to test Prediction 2.4. He argued that only automatic processes are involved when drawing necessary inferences, and he discovered that comprehension speed on a task requiring the drawing of necessary inferences was unaffected by test anxiety. In contrast, high-test-anxious subjects were much slower than low-test-anxious subjects on a task requiring the drawing of unnecessary inferences, presumably because this task involves working memory.

Darke (1988b: 504) drew the following conclusion from these findings: 'High anxiety subjects are disadvantaged vis-à-vis low anxiety subjects in their ability to infer implicit facts from explicit text only when the processing involved in such inferential reasoning relies on the working memory.' This conclusion appears to be somewhat over-stated. It is probable that drawing necessary inferences requires modest use of the resources of working memory rather than none at all.

There are several other studies in which anxiety has no effect on the performance of tasks apparently involving few of the resources of working memory. For example, Mayer (1977) found that groups high and low in trait anxiety did not differ in their performance of relatively undemanding tasks such as searching text for the letter 'a' or deciding whether pairs of numbers were identical. In contrast, the same high-trait-anxious subjects produced only half as many correct solutions as low-trait-anxious subjects on problems (e.g., anagram solving; water-jar problems) requiring extensive use of working memory.

Eysenck (1989) compared subjects high and low in trait anxiety on the one-letter version of the letter-transformation task. This version requires only the highly over-learned skill of working through the alphabet a short distance in the forward direction, and so places minimal demands on working memory. The two groups did not differ in their performance. In addition, there were no effects of anxiety on the performance of a concurrent probe task designed to assess spare processing capacity. This suggests that the two groups did not differ in the resources which they allocated to the letter-transformation task.

Conclusions and Future Developments

The empirical evidence relating to different aspects of the processing efficiency theory and the relationship between anxiety and task performance permits one to draw the following conclusions: (1) state anxiety is generally associated with poor processing efficiency under test conditions, as high-anxious individuals use more processing resources than low-anxious individuals; and (2) the effects of state anxiety on performance effectiveness depend on (a) the availability and utilization of additional resources; and (b) the demands of the task on working memory.

Several issues await clarification. First, the negative effects of anxiety on performance as a function of task demands on working memory need to be separated from those negative effects which are attributable to the unavailability (or non-utilization) of compensatory resources. A related issue here is that of identifying more precisely the mechanisms involved in interactions between anxiety and task difficulty. Second, performance decrements can be compensated for by specific cognitive processes (e.g., use of more optimal strategies) as well as by enhanced effort, and these specific processes need to be identified. Third, more research needs to address the factors which produce the processing inefficiency associated with high anxiety. Fourth, there are clear similarities between the account of the effects of anxiety on performance offered by the processing efficiency theory and the account of the effects of depressed mood on memory provided by Ellis and Ashbrook (1988) in their resource allocation model. It would be of considerable theoretical interest to compare the processes underlying anxiety- and depression-mediated effects on performance.

Recent research on anxiety and reading by Calvo and his colleagues is of relevance to the first two issues identified above. In a series of studies by Calvo and Ramos (in prep.), high- and low-test anxious students were asked to read and comprehend several texts under evaluative and non-evaluative conditions. The texts were presented by means of a computer under several different conditions: word-by-word, sentence-by-sentence, or the complete text; self-paced or experimenter-paced, with or without the possibility of reading regressions; and with articulatory suppression, verbal distraction, or no concurrent task. Spontaneous lip movements and utterances were recorded during reading, and the measure of reading times and comprehension performance were taken. It was thus possible to detect the use of several compensatory activities (regressions and the use of articulatory rehearsal). The conditions differed systematically in their demands on working memory, with the demands increasing from complete text presentation on a self-paced basis to word-by-word presentation on an experimenter-paced basis, and from no concurrent articulatory suppression task.

The above studies by Calvo and Ramos (1999) appear to indicate that high-anxious subjects used more additional reading time than low-anxious subjects as the demands on working memory increased. They also made more regressions and used more articulatory rehearsal when compensatory time or regressions were not possible. Comprehension performance was not affected by anxiety when time, regressions, or articulatory rehearsal were available.

With respect to the third issue, the immediate determinant of processing inefficiency in anxious individuals is sometimes a transitory state of cognitive interference caused by the appraisal of ego-threat and by worry, as is accepted by several theorists (e.g., Humphreys and Revelle, 1984; Sarason, 1986). In order to compensate for that interference, high-anxious subjects have to employ extra resources. According to this view, the reduction in processing efficiency should be restricted to situations inducing ego-threat and worry, that is, evaluative or test conditions. Another possibility, however, is that inefficiency has a more long-term basis. For example, high-anxious subjects could have a basic deficit in processing capacity within working memory, prior knowledge, or in the skills (e.g., study habits, problem-solving strategies) which they usually employ for task-performance. If this were the case, then the high-anxious individuals would have to spend extra processing resources to compensate for their basic processing deficit.

With respect to working memory capacity, Calvo *et al.* (1999) found that high- and low-anxious subjects had comparable reading spans under non-evaluative conditions, although anxiety impaired reading span under test conditions. These results are consistent with the transitory interference hypothesis. As far as prior knowledge is concerned, Covington and Omelich (1987) and Calvo *et al.* (1999) obtained significant negative correlations between several vocabulary measures and test anxiety under non-evaluative conditions, which is in accordance with the basic deficit hypothesis. Moreover, in the study by Calvo *et al.* (1999), this knowledge deficit accounted for the increasing reading time shown by the high-anxious subjects reading texts relevant to the vocabulary measures. As far as the skills deficit is concerned, there is evidence indicating that high-anxious students have poorer study habits than low-anxious students (Culler and Holahan, 1980, see Tobias, 1986), a finding which is consistent with the basic deficit hypothesis. These different sources of inefficiency associated with anxiety probably have reciprocal effects on each other. For example, the awareness of basic deficits may make the high- anxious subjects worry about likely failures on task performance. As a consequence, they would need to utilize additional resources to compensate for both the transitory interference caused by worry and for the basic deficits.

So far as the fourth issue (i.e., the relationship between anxiety and depression) is concerned, Ellis and Asbrook (1988) proposed that depression can have adverse effects on performance, because depressed individuals allocate some processing capacity to their own concerns and because they put less cognitive effort into task performance. The notion that depressed individuals exert less effort than non-depressed individuals, whereas anxious individuals frequently exert more effort than non-anxious ones makes theoretical sense, and deserves detailed investigation.

In sum, the processing efficiency theory can be integrated into a general conceptualization of the anxiety-performance relationship as a dynamic process, in which there are interactions between cognitions and motives over time during task performance (e.g., Covington and Omelich, 1988; Schwarzer, 1986), with an appraisal function to monitor and evaluate current threat and task performance (Jerusalem, 1990), and a self-regulatory function aimed at coping with task demands and personal feelings of inefficiency (Rost and Schermer, 1989a). However, the processing efficiency theory goes further: (1) by positing specific predictions regarding the adaptive resources and actions initiated by anxiety to cope with the threat and overcome performance difficulties; and (2) by considering the cognitive mechanisms whose efficiency is affected by anxiety, and which thus cause performance decrements.

References

Baddeley, A.D. (1986). *Working Memory,* Oxford: Clarendon Press.

Baker, L. and A.L. Brown (1984). 'Metacognitive Skills and Reading', in P.D. Pearson (ed.), *The Handbook of Reading Research,* New York: Longman.

Benjamin, M., W.J. McKeachie, Y.G. Lin and D.P. Holinger (1981). 'Test Anxiety: Deficits in Information Processing', *Journal of Educational Psychology,* 73: 816–24.

Blankstein, K.R., B.B. Toner and G.L. Flett (1989). 'Test Anxiety and the Contents of Consciousness: Thought Listing and Endorsement Measures', *Journal of Research in Personality,* 23: 269–86.

Blankstein, K.R., G.L. Flett, P. Boase and B.B. Toner (1990). 'Thought Listing and Endorsement Measures of Self-Referential Thinking in Test Anxiety', *Anxiety Research,* 2: 103–11.

Britton, B.K. and S.M. Glynn (1987). *Executive Control Processes in Reading,* Hillsdale, NJ: Lawrence Erlbaum Associates Inc.

Calvo, M.G. (1985). 'Effort, Aversive Representations and Performance in Test Anxiety', *Personality and Individual Differences,* 6: 563–71.

Calvo, M.G. and L Alamo (1987). 'Test Anxiety and Motor Performance: The Role of Muscular and Attentional Demands', *International Journal of Psychology,* 22: 165–77.

Calvo, M.G. and P.M. Ramos (1989). 'Effects of Test Anxiety on Motor Learning: The Processing Efficiency Hypothesis', *Anxiety Research,* 2: 45–55.

Calvo, M.G. and P. Ramos (1999). 'Compensatory Cognitive Resources During Reading as a Function of Test Anxiety and Task Demands on Working Memory', *Private Communication.*

Calvo, M.G., L. Alamo and P.M. Ramos (1990). 'Test Anxiety, Motor Performance and Learning: Attentional and Somatic Interference', *Personality and Individual Differences,* 11: 29–38.

Calvo, M.G., P. Ramos and A. Estevez (1999). 'Test-Anxiety and Comprehension Efficiency: The Role of Prior Knowledge and Working Memory Deficits', *Private Communication.*

Covington, M.V. and C.L. Omelich (1987). '"I knew it could before the exam": A Test of the Anxiety-Blockage Hypothesis', *Journal of Educational Psychology,* 79: 393–400.

Covington, M.V. and C.L. Omelich (1988). 'Achievement Dynamics: The Interaction of Motives, Cognitions, and Emotions Over Time', *Anxiety Research,* 1: 165–83.

Culler, R.E. and C.J. Holahan (1980). 'Test Anxiety and Academic Performance: The Effects of Study Related Behaviors', *Journal of Educational Psychology,* 72: 16–20.

Darke, S. (1988a). 'Anxiety and Working Memory Capacity', *Cognition and Emotion,* 2: 145–54.

Darke, S. (1988b). 'Effects of Anxiety on Inferential Reasoning Task Performance', *Journal of Personality and Social Psychology,* 55: 499–505.

Deffenbacher, J.L. (1978). 'Worry, Emotionality and Task Generated Interference: An Empirical Test of Attentional Theory', *Journal of Educational Psychology,* 70: 248–54.

Deffenbacher, J.L. (1980). 'Worry and Emotionality in Test Anxiety', in I.G. Sarason (ed.), *Test Anxiety: Theory, Research and Applications,* Hillsdale, NJ: Lawrence Erlbaum Associates Inc.

De Vega, M., M. Carreiras, M. Calvo and M. Alonso (1990). *Lecture y comprehension: Una perspectiva cognitiva,* Madri: Alianza.

Dornic, S. (1977). 'Mental Load, Effort, and Individual Differences', Reports from the Department of Psychology, University of Stockholm, No. 509.

Dornic, S. (1980). 'Efficiency vs. Effectiveness in Mental Work: The Differential Effect of Stress', Reports from the Department of Psychology, University of Stockholm, No. 568.

Ellis, H.C. and P.W. Ashbrook (1988). 'Resource Allocation Model of the Effects of Depressed Mood States on Memory', in K. Fiedler and J. Forgas (eds), *Affect, Cognition and Social Behaviour,* Toronto: Hogrefe.

Eysenck, M.W. (1979). 'Anxiety, Learning and Memory: A Reconceptualization', *Journal of Research in Personality,* 13: 363–85.

Eysenck, M.W. (1982). *Attention and Arousal: Cognition and Performance,* Berlin: Springer.

Eysenck, M.W. (1985). 'Anxiety and Cognitive-Task Performance', *Personality and Individual Differences,* 6: 579–86.

Eysenck, M.W. (1992). 'The Nature of Anxiety' in A. Gale and M.W. Eysenck, *Handbook of Individual Differences: Biological Perspectives,* pp. 157–78, Chichester: Wiley.

Eysenck, M.W. (1989). 'Stress, Anxiety, and Intelligent Performance', in D. Vickers and P.L. Smith (eds), *Human Information Processing: Measures, Mechanisms and Models,* Amsterdam: North-Holland.

Eysenck, M.W. (1992). *Anxiety: The Cognitive Perspective,* Hove: Lawrence Erlbaum Associates Ltd.

Eysenck, M.W., C. MacLeod and A. Mathews (1987). 'Cognitive Functioning and Anxiety', *Psychological Research,* 49: 189–95.

Fahrenberg, (1987). The Psychophysiology of Neuroticism, in H.J. Eysenck and J. Strelau (eds), *Personality Dimensions and Arousal,* New York: Plenum.

Geen, R.G. (1987). 'Test Anxiety and Behavioral Avoidance', *Journal of Research in Personality,* 21: 481–88.

Haberlandt, K. and A.C. Graesser (1985). 'Component Processes in Text Comprehension and Some of Their Interactions', *Journal of Experimental Psychology: General,* 114: 357–74.

Hamilton, P., G.R.J. Hockey and M. Rajman (1977). 'The Place of the Concept of Activation in Human Information Processing Theory: An Integrative Approach', in S. Dornic (ed.), *Attention and Performance,* Vol. VI., Hillsdale, NJ: Lawrence Erlbaum Associates Inc.

Hamilton, V. (1978). 'The Cognitive Analysis of Personality Related to Information-Processing Deficits with Stress and Anxiety', Paper presented at the British Psychological Society meeting, London.

Hockey, G.R.J. (1986). 'A State Control Theory of Adaptation to Stress and Individual Differences in Stress Management', in G.R.J. Hockey, A.W.K. Gaillard and M.G.H. Coles (eds), *Energetics and Human Information Processing,* Dordrecht: Martinus Nijhoff.

Holroyd, K. and M. Appel (1980). 'Test Anxiety and Physiological Responding', in I.G. Sarason (ed.), *Test Anxiety: Theory, Research, and Applications,* Hillsdale, NJ: Lawrence Erlbaum Associates Inc.

Holroyd, K., T. Westbrook, M. Wolf and E. Badhorn (1978). 'Performance, Cognition, and Physiological Responding in Test Anxiety', *Journal of Abnormal Psychology,* 87: 442–51.

Humphreys, M.S. and W. Revelle (1984). 'Personality, Motivation, and Performance: A Theory of the Relationship Between Individual Differences and Information Processing', *Psychological Review,* 91: 153–84.

Jerusalem, M. (1990). 'Temporal Patterns of Stress Appraisals for High- and Low-Anxious Individuals', *Anxiety Research,* 3: 113–29.

Kahneman, D. (1973). *Attention and Effort,* Englewood Cliffs: Prentice Hall.

Liebert, R.M. and L.W. Morris (1967). 'Cognitive and Emotional Components of Test Anxiety: A Distinction and Some Data', *Psychological Reports,* 20: 975–78.

Mayer, R.E. (1977). 'Problem-Solving Performance with Task Overload: Effects of Self-Pacing and Trait Anxiety', *Bulletin of the Psychonomic Society,* 9: 282–86.

Morris, L.W., D.S. Kellaway, and D.H. Smith (1978). 'Mathematics Anxiety Rating Scale: Predicting Anxiety Experiences and Academic Performance in Two Groups of Students', *Journal of Educational Psychology,* 70: 589–94.

Morris, L.W., M.A. Davis, and C.H. Hutchings (1981). 'Cognitive and Emotional Components of Anxiety: Literature Review and a

Revised Worry-Emotionality Scale', *Journal of Educational Psychology,* 73: 541–55.

Nicholson, W.M. (1958). 'The Influence of Anxiety Upon Learning: Interference or Drive Increment?', *Journal of Personality,* 26: 303–19.

Revelle, W. (1987). 'Personality and Motivation: Sources of Inefficiency in Cognitive Performance', *Journal of Research in Personality,* 21: 436–52.

Revelle, W. and D.A. Loftus (1990). 'Individual Differences and Arousal: Implications for the Study of Mood and Memory', *Cognition and Emotion,* 4: 209–37.

Rost, D.H. and F.J. Schermer (1989a). 'The Various Facets of Test Anxiety: A Subcomponent Model of Test Anxiety Measurement', in R. Schwarzer, H.M. van der Ploeg, and C.D. Spielberger (eds), *Advances in Test Anxiety Research,* Vol. 6, Amsterdam: Swets and Zeitlinger.

Rost, D.H. and F.J. Schermer (1989b). 'The Assessment of Coping with Test Anxiety', in R. Schwarzer, H.M. van der Ploeg and C.D. Spielberger (eds), *Advances in Test Anxiety Research,* Vol. 6, Amsterdam: Swets and Zeitlinger.

Sarason, I.G. (1956). 'Effect of Anxiety, Motivational Instructions, and Failure on Serial Learning', *Journal of Experimental Psychology,* 51: 253–60.

Sarason, I.G. (1957). 'The Effect of Associative Value and Differential Motivating Instructions on Serial Learning', *American Journal of Psychology,* 70: 620–23.

Sarason, I.G. (1972). 'Experimental Approaches in Test Anxiety: Attention and the Uses of Information', in C.D. Spielberger (ed.), *Anxiety: Current Trends in Theory and Research,* New York: Academic Press.

Sarason, I.G. (1984). 'Stress, Anxiety, and Cognitive Interference: Reactions to Tests', *Journal of Personality and Social Psychology,* 46: 929–38.

Sarason, I.G. (1986). 'Test Anxiety, Worry, and Cognitive Interference', in R. Schwarzer (ed.), *Self-Related Cognitions in Anxiety and Motivation,* Hillsdale, NJ: Lawrence Erlbaum Associates Inc.

Sarason, I.G. (1988). 'Anxiety, Self-Preoccupation and Attention', *Anxiety Research,* 1: 3–7.

Sarason, I.G. and R. Stoops (1978). 'Test Anxiety and the Passage of Time', *Journal of Consulting and Clinical Psychology,* 46: 102–9.

Schmidt, R.A. (1988). *Motor Control and Learning: A Behavioral Emphasis,* Champaign, IL: Human Kinetics.

Schwarzer, R. (1986). 'Self-Related Cognitions in Anxiety and Motivation: An Introduction', in R. Schwarzer (ed.), *Self-Related Cognitions in Anxiety and Motivation,* Hillsdale, NJ: Lawrence Erlbaum Associates Inc.

Schwarzer, R., M. Jerusalem and H.A. Stiksrud (1984). 'The Developmental Relationship Between Test Anxiety and Helplessness', in H.M. van der Ploeg, R. Schwarzer, and C.D. Spielberger (eds), *Advances in Test Anxiety Research,* Vol. 3, Hillsdale, NJ: Lawrence Erlbaum Associates Inc.

Tobias, S. (1986). 'Anxiety and Cognitive Processing of Instruction', in R. Schwarzer (ed.), *Self-Related Cognitions in Anxiety and Motivation,* Hillsdale, NJ: Lawrence Erlbaum Associates Inc.

Weinberg, R.S. (1978). 'The Effects of Success and Failure on the Patterning of Neuro-Muscular Energy', *Journal of Motor Behavior,* 10: 53–61.

Weinberg, R.S. (1990). 'Anxiety and Motor Performance: Where to From Here?', *Anxiety Research,* 2: 227–42.

Weinberg, R.S. and V. Hunt (1976). 'The Interrelationships Between Anxiety, Motor Performance, and Electromyography', *Journal of Motor Behavior,* 8: 219–24.

Wine, J.D. (1971). 'Test Anxiety and Direction of Attention', *Psychological Bulletin,* 76: 92–104.

Wine, J.D. (1982). 'Evaluation Anxiety: A Cognitive-Attentional Construct', in W. Krohne and L. Laux (eds), *Achievement, Stress and Anxiety,* New York: Hemisphere.

6 Altruism Among Youth Workers: An Appraisal

Devendra Agochia, Jitendra Mohan and Neeraj Kakkar

INTRODUCTION

Recent advances in personality research have selected many unorthodox aspects for its focus. Altruism is one of those aspects of human behaviour which is equally significant as aggression or violence on which positive social order is developed. Helping others, especially those in distress, is not only considered a 'good turn' or moral act, but also a socially responsible behaviour. According to Berkowitz and Daniel (1963), the social responsibility norms prescribe that people should help those who are dependent upon them. In almost all the religions also there is special exhortation to the followers to help the poor and the needy, and a helping act is considered godly or religious; people who do not help others are called selfish.

Buck and Ginsburg (1991) opined that altruism is the tendency of one organism to act to increase the welfare of another organism, with no obvious benefit, and, often, at a cost to the helper. According to Grusec (1991), altruism refers to acts of concern for others—such as sharing, helping, showing concern and consideration, reassuring, and defending—that are performed independent of hope of reward or fear of punishment from external sources.

Many investigators use the term 'altruism' and 'prosocial behaviour' interchangeably. These terms are used to describe a wide spectrum of behaviours, ranging from helping an old person cross the street to saving the life of a drowning stranger. Therefore, these terms may denote a heroic deed or a seemingly mudane or casual act.

However, many researchers distinguish between prosocial and altruistic behaviour. Prosocial behaviour refers to acts that bring benefit to other people. Prosocial behaviour can involve actions that are planned and formal, or spontaneous and informal; and may require direct or indirect aid giving (Smithson, Amato, and Paerce, 1983). Prosocial behaviour could result in benefit to another person, without there being any real intent to help. Or, there could even be some material gain expected by the initiators of the behaviour. They may be motivated by a desire to get something in return, or by nothing more than the personal satisfaction of having helped. The only requirement for a behaviour to be labelled prosocial is that it be 'other directed in a positive sense' (Wispe, 1978).

Altruism, on the other hand, can be termed as a special kind of prosocial behaviour. Altruism is typically defined as an action carried out with the intent to benefit others without the desire to receive benefit from others in return (Staub, 1978; Rushton, 1980). Unlike instances of helping behaviour where a person may be tempted to help because the costs are low and the possibility for receiving material as social benefits are high, altruistic behaviour involves helping even by taking grave risks, even though the act is not likely to be rewarded, recognized, or even appreciated. While some forms of helping may involve selfish motives, the altruistic act is selfless (Saks and Krupt, 1988).

According to Freud, the superego develops as a child learns values from his/her parents and cultures. These values are internalized and become part of the individual, serving as ideals and internal sources of rewards and punishment. The necessary conditions for such strong internalization of values include exposure to a set of standards in the context of a close, loving parent–child relationship (Staub, 1975). Prosocial behaviour was thought to be determined by this process initiated by the development of the superego. Freud borrowed the commonly accepted idea of 'conscience'. An alternative way of conceptualizing the growth of a conscience and internal standards is through cognitive development. Both Piaget (1965) and Kohlberg (1969) have proposed that as children grow and interact with the environment, there is a natural progression from primitive notions of morality to highly sophisticated ones. As children grow older, they begin to grasp the fact that there are other perspectives beside their own. These stages of development are found to be influenced to some degree by culture (Salili, Maehr, and Gillmore, 1976). Research supports the notion that as children grow older, they progress to higher levels of cognitive development and different sorts of moral reasoning, but these cognitive differences do not seem to be particularly helpful in predicting actual altruistic behaviour (Emler and Rushton, 1974; Rushton and Weiner, 1975).

A theory of moral conduct developed by Hogan (1973) combines the idea of cognitive development and the kind of internalization process emphasized by Freud. He describes several dimensions of morality based on development and internalization; he points out the consequences of the various patterns that can emerge when some dimensions are stronger than others. Hogan, thus, describes prosocial behaviour as a somewhat complex combination of independent characteristics. From the point of view of learning theory, prosocial responses occur because they have been rewarded in the past. In addition to this direct influence, people are also guided by expectations about future rewards and punishment. As altruistic intentions can arouse unpleasant expectations, one's perceptions of this unpleasantness may interfere with prosocial actions (Pomazal and Jaccord, 1976). One prediction that stems from the reinforcement conceptualization is that prosocial behaviour can be increased or decreased by associating rewards or punishment with it. Helping can be made to vary as a function of reinforcement. Findings consistent with these were reported in a laboratory investigation by McGover, Ditzian and Taylor (1975). This does not, however, resolve the dilemma, because if an altruistic act is considered selfless, where is the question of rewards and punishments. The easy answer is that the person gains a feeling of well-being or is motivated by internal, intangible goals that cannot be defined in material terms.

Empathy has long been implicated as a factor in the expression of altruism. Several researchers (Batson and Coke, 1981; Batson, Dorley, and Coke, 1975) have suggested that empathetic emotion leads to motivation directed toward the altruistic goal of increasing others' welfare. This suggestion has been called the empathy–altruism hypothesis (Batson and Coke, 1981). Studies have reported that empathy evokes genuinely altruistic motivation to reduce others' distress (Fultz *et al.,* 1986). Working on the previous research, which focussed on the motivational role of empathy within the altruistic personality, Romer, Gruder, and Lizzadro (1986) found that the altruists and receptive givers (nurturant type) may be more empathetic than selfish and inner-sustaining people (succorant type), at least with regard to empathetic concern, fantasy and perspective-taking (Davis, 1983).

Batson and Olesan (1991) suggested that the human capacity for altruism is limited to those for whom we feel empathy. When empathy for the person in need is low, the pattern of helping suggest underlying egoistic motivation. According to them, it is not that we never help people for whom we feel little empathy—we often do, but only when it is in our best interest. Simon (1990) argued that 'docility'—the tendency to believe what one is expected to learn and believe—can account for persons behaving altruistically in the biological-genetic sense of risking their own reproductive fitness in order to benefit others.

Simon (1990) found that if altruism results from docility, then the fitness of altruists will actually exceed the fitness of selfish individuals, as long as the demands of altruism that the society imposes on docile individuals are not excessive compared with the advantageous knowledge and skills acquired through docility.

Johnson *et al.* (1992) commented that 'docility produces altruism' position is viable only when the one assumes that powerful sources of influence in a given society are more strongly supportive of altruism than of a lack of altruism, and that altruism towards other persons, even when these others are not friends or relatives of the altruist, results in an increased reproductive fitness. A review of studies of correlates of human altruism favour reciprocal altruism over docility as an explanation for individual differences in altruism toward non-kin.

According to Buck and Ginsburg (1991), altruism and other kinds of social behaviours involve species-specific behaviour systems that derive from and are based upon affective bonds or affinities, often hierarchically structured, that characterize the social system of the species. Such bonds are species-typical, and range from those involved in mating, parenting, and peer coalitions to the more complex social roles that are central to the formation and maintenance of socially-cohesive groups. These bonds, in turn, are based upon experiences with spontaneous affective communication over the course of development.

Buck and Ginsburg (1991) proposed the communicative gene hypothesis, which posits that there are communicative genetic systems at the root of spontaneous affective communication, which, in turn, form the basis of all social behaviours, including empathic emotions and altruism. This spontaneous communication normally is sufficient to produce social bonds such that individuals act in concert and individuate social roles that are beneficial to the group, but not necessarily to each individual within it. Rushton *et al.* (1989) studied the relationships among age and aggressive, assertive, and altruistic tendencies with the dimensions of Eysenck Personality Questionnaire for 573 pairs of adult twins. The results revealed that assertiveness and most measures of altruism were linked to extraversion, while empathy was linked to neuroticism. They also found that prosocial tendencies increased with age whereas antisocial and extraverted tendencies decreased with age.

Grusec (1991) mentions that the agents of socialization include parents, siblings, peers, teachers, school, organizers of extracurricular activities, and the media. In some cases, attempts to foster altruism are deliberate; in others, they are the result of experiences that may not be aimed directly at encouraging prosocial proclivities in the child, but that are, nevertheless, potent.

Fabes, Einsberg and Miller (1990) found significant relationship between boys, emotional responses and their helpfulness; boys who expressed more negative affect tended to be more helpful.

Cliver and Oliver (1988) studied people who rescued Jews from Nazi's during World War II. They interviewed and administered personality tests to both rescuers and non-rescuers (controls). Analysis showed that empathy or internalized altruistic values were related to rescuing behaviour for some people, whereas feelings of obligation to a valued social group (such as church or community group) and its explicit and implicit expectations seemed to play an important role for others.

Youth Work and Altruism

The youth have always been a valuable and vibrant segment of society. The concern for youth and youth work has been almost universal. However, in the last three decades, issues, problems, potential and roles of the youth have received unprecedented focus, resulting in major political, social, educational and cultural transformations. There are several factors responsible for bringing the focus on youth. This group is important not only from social and economic standpoints, but is also politically a very significant (and volatile) section of the population, especially in countries where the minimum age for voting is 18 years. As Mollar (1974) commented, a large youth population always carries the potential for cultural and social innovation, but it also may turn to acting out violence, bent on dismantling old institutions and putting a new elite into power. By the 1980s, a world system had developed that was becoming increasingly interconnected economically, culturally, socially and politically. Even the goals of nation-states through the world have now become rather uniform, all struggling for economic might and political power in an international stratification system (Boli-Bennett, 1980; Meyer and Hanhan, 1979). Young people cannot remain insulated from this situation.

The youth are deemed as a national resource, which needs to be not only preserved, but also enriched through appropriately identified and well-directed inputs. The development growth of young people is seen as arising out of the objectives of youth work lies in its attempt to integrate the youth into society. Every nation faces the problem of incorporating the young and the young adults into society. Indeed, the continuity and vitality of a nation depends upon how well young people are integrated into the primary, social, political and economic institutions (Coleman, 1974; National Commission on Youth, 1980; United Nations, 1985).

The selection of youth workers, their education and training have been closely linked to the functions which they are expected to perform, which, in turn, are dependent on the activities carried out within the overall framework of youth work in a particular country. In some countries where youth work included working with problem youth, the emphasis on possession of special skills was far more pronounced, and, in many cases, those with social work background or with counselling skills were preferred. In countries where the efforts to mobilize youth energies for constructive community activities were a part of youth work, organizing skills were considered important. Thus, it is abundantly clear that if youth workers are to become effective functionaries of the present day youth work, they should not only be in a position to organize activities for the youth, but also be endowed with the necessary skills to enable them to work with the beneficiary groups, to maintain close liaison with the youth, and to assist them in the resolution of their problems and realization of their aspirations. Thus, broadly speaking, youth workers facilitate the development of the youth, individually and in groups, and seek to harness their energies and resources for the good of the community in which they live. An important aspect of the conceptual base for youth workers is that they are committed to enabling young people to contribute to the resolution of problems and to the improvement of the society. They believe in an active participative society. This calls for an intimate knowledge of the special characteristics of the target group, its subculture, and of the skills which are required to deal with the youth.

An important aspect of the work of a youth worker is his motivation, a desire to work with the youth and be of help to them. He should be pro-youth, having a positive attitude towards them, and should be able to identify with their problems. He should have full faith in their potential, and confidence in his ability to work with them. There is no doubt that youth work thrives on the mutually reinforcing bonds between a youth worker and his client groups. He should be guided by firm belief that youth work can bring about qualitative change in the life of youth and help them become assets, not only to their families but to the society as a whole. Career aspirations of a youth worker cannot be delinked from the special demands which youth work makes on the associated functionaries. A harmonious blend of these two (aspirations and demands) will, to a substantial extent, ensure the effectiveness of the youth worker. Undoubtedly, his vision of his career will be greatly influenced by the values he has imbibed during the process of socialization and interaction with peers. Thus, unhesitatingly, one may premise that the dispositions of a youth worker (towards youth and youth work) will be influenced by the values, including prosocial, which are close to his heart. These values will guide his interactions with the youth; of course, these may either reinforce his values and strengthen his commitment to the job or bring in a certain degree of disillusionment.

The positive meaning of youth work can never be denied, because it attempts to solve major youth issues like unemployment, drug abuse, alienation, crime, health and education. Youth worker is the key per-son, totally involved in such an activity on a voluntary or non-voluntary basis. The youth worker, on voluntary or non-voluntary basis is totally involved in such an activity. Therefore, understanding the youth worker has been both academic as well as of applied value. This can work as a model or standard, having implications for selection, training, evaluation, and even revising a system if diagnosis indicates shortcomings. When youth work emphasizes all round development of the youth, it may be deemed as a helping process, in which the youth worker is the nurturer and benefactor. The helping process can thrive if the youth worker has an empathetic understanding of the needs and problems of the client group (the youth), and has a positive disposition towards the youth. Above all, the youth worker must have faith in this helping process and also in the potential of his/her beneficiaries.

Is there an 'altruistic personality'? Staub (1974) argues that personality characteristics also affect helping behaviour, and they may modify the influence of (situational) determinants. The 'prosocial orientation' that exerts its influence probably represents, primarily, a way of looking at and thinking about other people's welfare, and one's own responsibility towards other people. Rushton, Chrisjohn and Feeken (1981) have, like Staub, argued that there is a personality trait of altruism. They state that 'such people are consistently more generous, helping, and kind than others.' Basically, the question is whether or not certain traits or characteristics of individuals are related to altruistic behaviour consistently across situations. While the evidence is not firmly assertive and the question remains controversial, it does appear that there is some relationship between certain personality characteristics and the degree to which a person engages in helping behaviour.

Work on the 'altruistic personality' or on 'prosocial orientation' seems promising in demonstrating what so many sensed—that some people are, over a range of situations and time periods, more likely to offer help than are others.

In India, very recently, some work in the field of altruistic behaviour has been published, in which self report method has been used. Mohan and associates reported researches on different groups, that is, adolescents, doctors, engineers, lawyers and others, and suggested a positive relationship between altruistic behaviour and personality measures.

Study of Youth Workers

The present investigation was designed as a cross-cultural study of altruistic behaviour of youth workers in relation to Eysenckian dimensions of personality, viz., Psychoticism, Extraversion, Neuroticism and Lie (Social Desirability) scale, and values, viz., Theoretical, Economic, Aesthetic, Social, Political and Religious. The sample comprised of 140 youth workers from eight different countries of the

Asia-Pacific region, namely Bangladesh, Hong Kong, India, Malaysia, Singapore, Sri Lanka, and Australia–New Zealand.

The Eysenck Personality Questionnaire developed by Eysenck and Eysenck (1975) was used to measure the personality dimensions, and Allport *et al.* (1960) study of values was used to measure the six values. Altruism was measured by the Self Report Altruism Scale (Rushton *et al.,* 1981).

Results revealed that youth workers from Australia and New Zealand scored the highest on altruism, followed by those from Sri Lanka, Bangladesh, India, Singapore and Malaysia. Youth workers from Hong Kong scored the lowest on altruism.

The t-ratios were computed to see whether these differences were statistically significantly, and the results revealed that the youth workers from Bangladesh scored significantly higher than those from Hong Kong on altruism. However, youth workers of Australia–New Zealand were found to be significantly higher on altruism in comparison to the Bangladesh group. Furthermore, Hong Kong youth workers were significantly lower on altruism in comparison to Sri Lanka and Australia–New Zealand workers. Similarly, Malaysian youth workers as well as Singapore youth workers were significantly lower on altruism than the Sri Lankan and Australia–New Zealand youth workers.

Regarding the personality dimension of Psychoticism, comparison of means of youth workers of different countries revealed that the Australia–New Zealand youth workers scored the highest on Psychoticism, followed by those from Bangladesh, Sri Lanka, India, Malaysia and Singapore, while Hong Kong workers scored the least on Psychoticism. However, these differences were found to be statistically insignificant.

On the personality dimension of Extraversion, the means indicated that the Australia and New Zealand group obtained the highest score on Extraversion, followed by the groups from Malaysia, Singapore, Bangladesh and India, whereas the Hong Kong youth workers obtained the lowest scores on this personality dimension. The country-wise t-values showed significant differences between Bangladesh and Hong Kong, Bangladesh and Australia–New Zealand, Hong Kong and India, Hong Kong and Malaysia, Hong Kong and Singapore, Hong Kong and Sri Lanka, Hong Kong and Australia–New Zealand, India and Malaysia, India and Australia–New Zealand, and Sri Lanka and Australia–New Zealand.

A comparison of the means on the Neuroticism dimension of personality revealed that both the Malaysia as well as the Singapore group scored the highest on Neuroticism, followed by groups of youth workers from Bangladesh, Sri Lanka, India and Hong Kong. The Australia–New Zealand group scored the lowest on this personality dimension. The countrywise t-values revealed significant differences between Bangladesh and Hong Kong, Bangladesh and Australia–New Zealand, Hong Kong and Malaysia, Hong Kong and Singapore, India and Malaysia, India and Singapore, Malaysia and Australia–New Zealand, and Singapore and Australia–New Zealand.

On the Lie (Social Desirability) scale, means of the youth workers from different countries showed that Singapore workers obtained the highest score on this, followed by the youth workers from Bangladesh, Sri Lanka, Malaysia, India and Hong Kong. The Australia–New Zealand group obtained the lowest mean scores on the Lie (Social Desirability) scale in comparison to all the other countries, viz. Bangladesh, Hong Kong, India, Malaysia, Singapore and Sri Lanka.

Some of the differences in personality observed in different countries (particularly on the dimensions of Extraversion and Social Desirability) have been explained by Eysenck and Eysenck (1975) and Barret and Eysenck (1984) in terms of the inherent differences in social and cultural practices specific to these countries. The permissive versus highly-controlled cultures could influence the development of personality, resulting into pretentious self-report on social desirability.

The results also revealed that altruism was found to be significantly and positively correlated with Extraversion in the groups of youth workers from Hong Kong, India, Singapore and Australia–New Zealand. This is in accordance with the findings of several studies conducted by Mohan and Behl (1986), Mohan and Sheoran (1987), Mohan and Kapila (1987), and Rushton *et al.* (1989). According to Rushton *et al.* (1989), Extraversion predisposes an individual to good mood and happiness; and, mood and altruism are clearly related.

The only other positive correlation to emerge was between altruism and Psychoticism, and that too in the non-government officers only. This is contrary to the findings of earlier researches (Mohan and Kapila, 1987; Mohan and Sethi, 1988; Mohan and Bhatia, 1987). However, Mohan and Behl (1986) have also reported a positive correlation between Psychoticism and altruism.

Regarding values, comparison of means of youth workers on Theoretical values indicated that the Bangladesh group scored the highest, followed by groups from India, Sri Lanka, Singapore, Hong Kong and Malaysia, whereas the Australia–New Zealand group scored the lowest on Theoretical values. The countrywise t-ratios on Theoretical values showed significant differences between Bangladesh and Hong Kong, Bangladesh and Malaysia, Bangladesh and Australia–New Zealand, India and Malaysia, India and Australia–New Zealand, and Singapore and Australia–New Zealand.

On Economic values, Hong Kong subjects obtained the highest mean scores, followed by those from Bangladesh, Singapore, India, Malaysia and Sri Lanka. The Australia–New Zealand subjects obtained the lowest scores on Economic values. The countrywise t-ratios showed significant differences only between Australia–New Zealand and five other countries, viz. Bangladesh, Hong Kong, India, Malaysia, and Singapore.

Comparison of mean scores on Aesthetic values indicated that the Australia–New Zealand youth workers scored the highest, followed by the youth workers from Hong Kong, Singapore, Sri Lanka, Bangladesh, and Malaysia. The Indian youth workers scored the lowest. The countrywise t-ratios showed significant differences between Hong Kong and India, Hong Kong and Malaysia, India and Singapore, India and Australia–New Zealand, and Malaysia and Australia–New Zealand.

Mean scores of different countries on Social values revealed that the Australia–New Zealand group obtained the highest scores, followed by the groups of workers from India, Sri Lanka, Hong Kong, Singapore and Malaysia. The workers from Bangladesh obtained the lowest scores on Social values. Significant differences emerged between Bangladesh and India, Bangladesh and Sri Lanka, Bangladesh and Australia–New Zealand, and Singapore and Australia–New Zealand.

On Political values, the youth workers from Bangladesh were found to be scoring the highest, followed by those from Hong Kong, Sri Lanka, India, Singapore and Australia–New Zealand. The youth workers of Malaysia scored the lowest on Political values. Statistically significant differences emerged only between Bangladesh and five other countries, with the youth workers from Bangladesh scoring significantly higher in comparison to those from India, Malaysia, Singapore, Sri Lanka and Australia–New Zealand.

On Religious values, the youth workers from Malaysia scored the highest, followed by those from Australia–New Zealand, Singapore, Sri Lanka, Bangladesh and India, while the Hong Kong group scored the least. The countrywise t-ratios on Religious values showed that significant differences emerged between Bangladesh and Australia–

New Zealand, Hong Kong and Malaysia, Hong Kong and Singapore, Hong Kong and Australia–New Zealand, India and Malaysia, India and Australia–New Zealand, Malaysia and Singapore, and Malaysia and Sri Lanka.

Sex Differences

It was hypothesized that the results would show definite differences among male and female youth workers. Regarding altruism, males were found to score significantly higher in comparison to females. These results are contrary to the findings of Midlarsky and Bryan (1972) and Dlugokinski and Firestone (1973, 1974), who reported females to be more altruistic than males. Mohan and Behl (1986) and Mohan and Sheoran (1987) have, however, reported no sex differences on altruism in university students and adolescents, respectively. No significant differences between males and females were found on any of the Eysenckian dimension of personality, viz., Psychoticism, Extraversion, Neuroticism and Lie (Social Desirability) scale. On the test of values, males were found to be higher on Theoretical values and females to be higher on Aesthetic values. Egan (1977) and Greenfield (1977) have also reported males to be higher on Theoretical values and females to be higher on Aesthetic values. Mohan and Sheoran (1987) did not find any significant sex differences on all the six values for adolescents.

Government vs Non-Government Youth Workers

It was expected that the results would show definite differences between the government and non-government officers (GOs and NGOs). The results of the present investigation revealed that GOs and NGOs differed significantly only on the personality dimension of 'Social Desirability' with the GOs scoring significantly higher than the NGOs. Interestingly, no significant differences emerged in any of the other variables between the two groups.

In the light of the review of literature and the results of the present investigation, it can be concluded that altruistic behaviour is an important field of psychological concern and deserves to be studied in greater detail. It also warrants that if it is determined by some socio-economic-cultural correlates, those aspects should be taken into account while developing training programs for the professionals aiming to work in the areas of human concern, assistance, help and care.

References

Barret, P. and S.B.G. Eysenck (1984). 'The Assessment of Personality Factors—Across 25 Countries', *Personality and Individual Differences,* 5: 615–32.

Batson, C.D. and J.S. Coke (1981). 'Empathy: A Source of Altruistic Motivation for Helping', in J.P. Rushton and R.M. Sorrentino (eds), *Altruism and Helping Behaviour: Social Personality, and Development Perspective,* pp. 167–87, Hillsdale, NJ: Erlbaum.

Batson, C.D., J.M. Dorley and J.S. Coke (1975). 'Altruism and Human Kindness: Internal and External Determinants of Helping Behaviour', in L. Pervin and M. Lewis (eds), *Perspectives in Interactional Psychology,* 111–40, New York: Plenum Press.

Batson, C.D. and K.C. Olesan (1991). 'Current Status of Empathy Altruism, Hypothesis', in M.S. Clark (ed.), *Prosocial behaviour,* London: Sage Publications.

Berkowitz, L. and L.R. Daniel (1963). 'Responsibility and Dependency', *Journal of Abnormal and Social Psychology,* 66: 429–36.

Buck, R. and B. Ginsburg (1991). 'Spontaneous Communication and Altruism: The Communicative Gene Hypothesis', in M.S. Clark (ed.), *Prosocial Behaviour,* London: Sage Publications.

Boli-Bennett, J. (1980). 'Global Integration and the Universal Increase of State Dominance', in A. Bergesen (ed.), *Studies of the Modern World System,* New York: Academic Press.

Coleman, J.S. (ed.) (1974). *Transition to Adulthood,* Chicago: University of Chicago Press.

Davis, M.H. (1983). 'Empathic Concern and the Muscular Dystrophy Telethon: Empathy as a Multidimensional Construct', *Personality and Social Psychology Bulletin,* 9: 223–29.

Dlugokinski, E. and I.J. Firestone (1973). 'Congruence Among Four Methods of Measuring Other-Centredness', *Child Development,* 44: 304–8.

Dlugokinski, E. and I.J. Firestone (1974). 'Other Centredness and Susceptibility to Charitable Appeals Effects of Perceived Discipline', *Development Psychology,* 10: 21–28.

Egan, M.J. (1977). 'A Study of the Effect of Educational Level, Age and Sex on the Values and Self-Concepts of Adult Students and Alumni of an Adult', *Baccalaureate Degree Programme,* 1 May, 37 (11-A): 7034–35.

Emler, N.P. and J.P. Rushton (1974). 'Cognitive Development Factors in Children's Generosity', *British Journal of Social and Clinical Psychology,* 13: 277–81.

Eysenck, H.J. and S.B.G. Eysenck (1975). *Manual of the Eysenck Personality Questionnaire,* London: Hodder and Stronghton Educational.

Fabes, R.A., N. Eisenberg and P.A. Miller (1990). 'Maternal Correlates of Children's Vicacious Emotional Responsiveness', *Development Psychology,* 26(4): 639–48.

Fultz, J., C.D. Batson, V.A. Fortenback, P.M., McCathy and L.L. Varney (1986). 'Social Evaluation and the Empathy Altruism Hypothesis', *Journal of Personality and Social Psychology,* 50: 761–69.

Greenfield, N. (1977). 'A Study of Student Values', *Theo. Journal of Psychology, The general field of Psychology,* 79: 85–96.

Grusec, J.E. (1991). 'The Socialization of Altruism', in M.S. Clark (ed.), *Prosocial Behaviour,* London: Sage Publications.

Hogan, R. (1973). 'Moral Conduct and Moral Character: A Psychological Perspective', *Psychological Bulletin,* 79: 217–32.

Johnson, R.C., G.P. Danko, T.J. Darvill and C.T. Nagashi (1992). '"Docility" versus Reciprocity as an Explanation for Evolutionary Selection for Altruistic Behaviour', *Personality and Individual Differences,* 13 (3): 263–67.

Kohlberg, L. (1969). 'Stage and Sequence, the Cognitive Developmental Approach to Socialization', in D.A. Goslin (ed.), *Handbook of Socialization Theory and Research,* Chicago: Rand Mentally, 347–480.

McGovern, L.P., J.L. Ditizian and S.P. Taylor (1975). 'The Effect of one Positive Reinforcement on Helping with Const.', *Bulletin of the Psychonomic Society,* 5: 421–23.

Meyer, L.P. and M.T. Hanhan (eds) (1979). *National Development and the World System,* Chicago: University of Chicago Press.

Midlarsky, E. and J.H. Bryan (1972). 'Affect Expressions and Children's Initiative Altruism', *Journal of Experimental Research in Personality,* 61: 195–203.

Mohan, J. and A. Behl (1980). 'A Study of Altruism in Relation to Personality, Locus of Control, Alienation and Academic Achievement of the University Students', Unpublished M.Phil thesis, P.U.: Chandigarh.

Mohan, J. and S. Bhatia (1987). 'Altruistic Behaviour of Engineers and Teachers in Relation to their Personality', *Indian Journal of Applied Psychology,* 24(2): 87–90.

Mohan, J. and N. Kapila (1987). 'A Study of Altruism, Personality, Achievement Motivation and Adjustment of Doctors', Unpublished Ph.D. thesis, Punjab University: Chandigarh.

Mohan J. and S. Sethi (1988). 'Altruistic Behaviour of Males and Females in Relation to their Personality', *Indian Psychological Review,* 33 (10–12): 1–5.

Mohan, J. and R.S. Sheoran (1987). 'Altruism and Values of Adolescents', *Manodarpan,* 3 (1–2): 19–23.

Mollar, H. (1974). 'Rebellious Youth as a Force of Change', in A. Esler (ed.), *The Conflict of Generations in History,* Lexington, MA: D.C. Health.

National Commission on Youth (1980). *Transition of Youth to Adulthood: A Bridge too Long,* Boulder, Co: Westview Press.

Oliver, S.P. and P.M. Oliver (1988). *The Altruistic Personality: Rescuers of Jews in Nazi Europe,* New York: Free Press.

Piaget, J. (1965). *The Moral Judgement of the Child,* New York: Free Press (originally published, 1932).

Pomazal, R.J. and J.J. Jaccord (1976). 'An Informational Approach to Altruistic Behaviour', *Journal of Personality and Social Psychology,* 33: 317–26.

Romer, D., C.L. Gruder and T. Lizzadro (1986). 'A Person-Situation Approach to Altruistic Behaviour', *Journal of Personality and Social Psychology,* 51: 1001–12.

Rushton, J.P. (1980). *Altruism, Socialization, and Society,* Englewood Cliffs, NY: Prentice Hall.

Rushton, J.P., R.D. Chrisjohn and G.C. Feeken (1981). 'The Altruistic Personality and the Self-Report Altruism Scale', *Personality and Social Difference,* 2: 293–302.

Rushton, J.P., D.W., Fulker, M.C. Neale, D.K.B. Neas and H.J. Eysenck (1989). 'Ageing and the Relation of Aggression, Altruism and Assertiveness Scales to the Eysenck Personality Questionnaire', *Personality and Individual Differences,* 10 (2): 261–63.

Rushton, J.P. and J. Weiner (1975). 'Altruism and Cognitive Development in Children', *British Journal of Social and Clinical Psychology,* (141, 341–49).

Saks, M.J. and E. Krupt (1988). *Social Psychology and its Applications,* New York: Harper & Row.

Salili, F. M.L. Maehr and G. Gillmore (1976). 'Achievement and Morality: A Cross Cultural Analysis of Casual Attribution and Evaluation', *Journal of Personality and Social Psychology,* 331: 327–37.

Simon, H.A. (1990). 'A Mechanism for Social Selection and Successful Altruism', *Sciences,* 250: 1665–68.

Smithson, M., P. Amato and P. Pearce (1983). *Dimensions of Helping Behaviour,* Oxford: Pergannon Press.

Staub, E. (1974). 'Helping a Distressed Person: Social Personality and Stimulus Determinants', in L. Berkowitz (ed.), *Advances in Experimental Social Psychology,* Vol. 7, 293–341, New York: Academic Press.

Staub, E. (1975). *The Development of Prosocial Behaviour in Children,* Morriston, NJ: Lawrence Erlbaum.

Staub, E. (1978). *Positive Social Behaviour and Morality,* Vol. 1, Social & Personal influences, New York: Academic Press.

United Nations (1985). 'Youth in the 1980's: Social and Health Concerns', *Population Reports,* 13-IV: 350–79.

Wispe, L. (1978). *Altruism, Sympathy and Helping: Psychological and Sociological Principles,* New York: Academic Press.

7 Spearman Reconsidered

Nathan Brody

Abstract

Spearman's paper on General Intelligence, published in 1904, is described, and its metatheoretical and substantive contributions are evaluated. Spearman's theory is related to contemporary research. It is concluded that Spearman's theory is congruent with contemporary theoretical developments. Spearman's paper, "General Intelligence, Objectively Determined and Measured", published in 1904, has a unique position in psychological science. It is difficult, if not impossible, to think of a single paper as old as Spearman's that is as relevant to contemporary theory and research. In this chapter, I attempt to assess Spearman's contributions with the benefits of hindsight derived from contemporary research on intelligence.

Description of Spearman's Paper

Spearman's paper reported that results of an empirical investigation of a hypothesis developed by Galton (1883). Galton believed that individual differences in intelligence were related to individual differences in sensory acuity. In a note to a paper written by James McKeen Cattell (1890), Galton suggested that it would be useful to relate measures of sensory acuity to ratings of individual differences. Spearman's paper was similar to a paper published by Wissler (1901). Wissler found that there was little or no relationship between performance on experimental tasks and the academic achievement of

Columbia University students. Spearman was not aware of Wissler's results at the time he collected his data (Spearman, 1930). He wrote that he would not have conducted his research if he had been aware of Wissler's negative results (Spearman, 1930).

Spearman's paper contained a review of the previous literature on the subject, a description of a series of empirical studies, and an innovative method of analyzing his data leading to the development of his two-factor theory of intelligence. Spearman had four major criticisms of the research he reviewed. First, with the exception of Wissler, statistical analyses were not reported relating scores on measures of sensory functioning to various indices of intelligence. For the most part, researchers relied on impressions rather than systematic analyses of data. Second, there was no attempt to calculate probable errors to determine the statistical reliability of obtained results. Third, previous investigators relied on unsystematic samples. Fourth, there were few controls, and little concern with using the most reliable methods of observation.

Spearman attempted to remedy the defects of the previous studies he reviewed. He measured pitch discrimination using a monochord; visual discrimination thresholds were obtained using gray cards; and weight discrimination thresholds were obtained using identical appearing cartridges differing in weight. He obtained data from five samples of adults and children using individual- or group-administered sensory discrimination procedures. 'Intelligence' was assessed by peer ratings or by indices of scholastic performance.

It is clear that Spearman's research topic was not extraordinarily innovative. And, while his research may have been more adequate than that of his contemporaries, it was still far from adequate if judged by modern standards. Why then is this paper of enduring significance? The importance of Spearman's research rests on his innovative data analyses, and on his theoretical interpretations of the results he obtained.

Spearman noted that the correlations he obtained among measures of discrimination tended to be positive, and the correlations between these indices and various indices of intelligence and scholastic performance were also positive. Since the correlations were positive, he aggregated the results to obtain general indices of discrimination ability and intellectual ability. He obtained correlations between various aggregate indices. Spearman's paper on general intelligence was accompanied by a paper written by him in the same issue of the

American Journal of Psychology (Spearman, 1904b). In this paper, Spearman developed the correction for attenuation, which results in an estimate of a hypothetical correlation corrected for unreliability of measurement in each of the indices from which the obtained correlations were derived. When this correction was applied to the correlation for aggregate indices of intelligence and discrimination, the resulting hypothetical correlation was 1.00. Spearman concluded that general intelligence and general discrimination ability were different manifestations of the same theoretical entity. In his words, *'the common and essential element in the Intelligences wholly coincides with the common and essential element in the Sensory Functions.'* (Spearman, 1904a: 269).

Spearman extended his analysis of the unity between discrimination ability and intelligence to a consideration of unities among various manifestations of intelligence. He examined correlations among measures of different categories of intellectual functioning. He noted that correlations between aggregate indices of particular categories of intellectual functioning, when corrected for attenuation by a consideration of within category correlations, tended to be less than 1.00. He assumed that the commonalities between dissimilar disattenuated aggregates were all attributable to a common general intellectual capacity, and the difference between the disattenuated correlations and the value of 1.00 were attributable to the influence of specific non-general intellectual capacities attributable primarily to 'favoring circumstance' or environmental advantage (see Spearman, 1904a: 273, footnote 2). Spearman's analysis is contained in the following passage:

> Though the range of this central Function appears so universal, and that of the specific functions so vanishingly minute, the latter must not be supposed to be altogether non-existent. We can always come to them eventually, if we sufficiently narrow our field of view and consider branches of activity closely enough resembling one another. When, for instance in the same preparatory school we take on the one side Latin translation with Latin grammar and on the other side French prose with French diction, then our formula gives us a new result; for the two Latin studies correlate with the French ones by an average of 0.59, while the former correlate together by 0.66 and the latter by 0.71; so that the element common to the Latin correlates with the element common to the French by

$$\frac{0.59}{\sqrt{0.66 \times 0.71}} = 0.86 \text{ only}$$

> That is to say, the two common elements by no means coincide completely this time, but only to the extent of 0.86 or 74%; so that in the remaining 26%, each pair must possess a community purely specific and unshared by the other pair. (Spearman 1904a: 273)

This quotation from Spearman elucidates the foundation of the two-factor theory of intelligence. The variance of all measures of intelligence may be partitioned into two components—g, a component that is common to all measures of intelligence, and s, a specific component that influences narrowly similar measures. Correlations between dissimilar measures are attributable to the extent to which they share g variance. Measures of intelligence differ with respect to the proportion of common to specific variance they contain, that is, their g to s ratio. The g to s ratio of a measure may be estimated by examining the average correlation between the measure and all other measures of intellectual functioning. Measures of intellectual functioning may be rank-ordered with respect to their g to s ratio, and a correlation matrix may be obtained in which the rank-ordered measures are arrayed horizontally and vertically in a descending order. The correlations in this matrix should decline across rows or down columns, since correlations between measures with lower g to s ratios are assumed to be lower than correlations between measures with high g to s ratios. Spearman's calculations led him to assert that Classics had the highest g to s ratio (99 to 1) and weight discrimination had the lowest g to s ratio (19 to 81) in his set of measures. Spearman later proposed a more rigorous test of the values of correlations derived from the two-factor theory. The theory implied for correlations among all possible sets of four intellectual variables that $r_{12} \times r_{34} = r_{13} \times r_{24}$. This is called the law of tetrad differences (Spearman and Holzinger, 1924).

Spearman's Metatheoretical Contributions

Spearman's paper may be viewed as having five metatheoretical contributions. First, Spearman distinguished between a construct and a measure of the construct. General intelligence is the common element in any and all possible measures of intelligence, including measures of intelligence that have not been invented. It cannot be identified with any particular measure. A definition of intelligence as something that is identical to a particular test score would, from Spearman's perspective, be an intellectual absurdity. Spearman argued that there were errors of measurement, and it is only through a process of refinement that is possible to make statements about the theoretical construct whose values are inferred from imperfect indices (Spearman, 1904b). Spearman's paper assessed the construct validity of measures of intelligence.

Second, Spearman's paper reported the first analysis of a correlation matrix that resembles factor analysis. It should be noted that Spearman's analysis procedures were quite different from most of the analyses of the statistical structure of correlation matrices that followed his work. Spearman's analyses were only partially inductive. He examined the correlation matrix he obtained in order to test a theory. His theory specified expected quantitative relationships that obtain among the correlations in the matrix. In this respect, Spearman's analyses may be viewed as being analogous to the contemporary use of LISREL procedures to examine the relationship between obtained and expected correlation matrices.

Third, Spearman used aggregate procedures. More accurate measures of psychological functioning may be obtained by aggregating or compositing several measures. Spearman was later to make this notion explicit in the development of Spearman-Brown prophecy formula that specifies the relationship between the number of observations and the true score variance of the aggregate derived score for these observations. Spearman called the principle of aggregation the 'hotchpotch' principle. Spearman's theory provided a theoretical justification for the use of aggregate measures of intelligence, and also provided a rationale for the equivalence of different measures of intelligence. It was stated that aggregate indices of diverse measures of intelligence will be saturated with the common true score variance. Different measures of intelligence that contain a non-overlapping diverse set of particular indices of intelligence will have high true score variance, and therefore will exhibit high positive correlations. Spearman's theory supported the principle of the 'indifference of the indicator'. If Spearman's theory is correct, it does not matter which tests are included in a battery. As long as each battery of tests contains many subtests (or individual items) that each measure general intelligence, the aggregate index will be highly related to any other aggregate index derived from an independent subtest or items.

Fourth, Spearman's paper provided a rationale for the construction of measures of intelligence—use measures that have a high g to s ratio. The use of such measures will provide gains in efficiency since they will permit an accurate estimate of general intelligence using a limited number of measures. It is interesting to note that this principle is violated in the construction of widely used tests of intelligence such as the Wechsler tests.

Fifth, Spearman believed that individual difference, psychology should be allied with experimental psychology. He used the techniques of experimental psychology to measure intelligence in an objective manner. Spearman's research was published one year before the development of the first intelligence test. Following Binet's work, research on intelligence was dominated by Binet's approach to measurement. Binet's tests did not require the use of elaborate laboratory facilities, and were originally designed to be administered in school settings. The attempt to relate individual differences in intelligence to measures derived from performance on tasks used to assess psychological functioning in laboratory settings became less prominent after the development of tests of intelligence. And, it is only in the last 15 years that this approach to the study of intelligence has been pursued vigorously. In this respect, Spearman's approach to research in intelligence is in vogue.

Substantive Contribution

Spearman's paper contained two empirical claims: (1) sensory discrimination ability is related to general intelligence; and (2) all measures of intelligence measure a common intellectual function (or group of functions).

Structure of the Correlation Matrix

The resolution of the optimal structure of correlation matrices of scores on different measures of intellectual ability and the relative importance of general and specific abilities continues to be a topic of controversy. A review of this issue is beyond the scope of this paper (see Brody, 1992). Spearman knew that g does not account for all of the common variance in the matrix. An appropriate resolution of this issue that is partially congruent with contemporary research was proposed by

Eysenck in 1939. Eysenck reanalysed the data collected by Thurstone in support of the notion of separate primary abilities (Thurstone, 1938). Thurstone's data were obtained from college students, and were based on a sample that was restricted for a range of talent. This restriction would decrease the magnitude of correlations between tests and lead to a decrease in the presence of g in the matrix. Nevertheless, Eysenck's reanalysis of these data indicated that the g variance of the measures used by Thurstone varied from 0.237 to 0.868. Although Thurstone initially advocated an analysis that postulated the existence of several independent ability factors, his data matrix provided ample support for the presence of a general factor. Eysenck's analysis indicated that g accounted for 30.8 per cent of the common variance in the matrix. Eysenck also found evidence for the presence of Thurstone type ability factors in the residual variance in the matrix and defined eight such factors that accounted for 23.55 per cent of the variance. On his analysis, g accounted for more variance than all of the special factors combined. The variance of each of the special factors ranged from 6.61 to 0.97 per cent of the common variance in the matrix. The common variance among these measures are dramatically higher than the amount of variance attributable to any single residual factor. Carroll (1988) analysed this same matrix, and noted that Eysenck's analysis also provided considerable evidence in support of the importance of special factors. He noted that the proportion of common factor (g) variance in individual tests to specific factor variance ranged from 0.44 to 0.59. Thus, for the tests included in Thurstone's classic study, g and specific factors accounted for roughly equal proportions of the variance.

Among the most sophisticated contemporary analyses of ability matrices are a series of studies by Gustafsson (1988). He used confirmatory factor analyses to test different hierarchical models of the structure of intellect based on Cattell's attempts to distinguish between two g components—fluid intelligence and crystallized intelligence (Cattell, 1963, 1971; Horn, 1985). He found that the only model that would fit his matrices was one in which fluid intelligence was identical with the g factor, and crystallized ability had a different status in the hierarchical structure. The model that fits the data was one that was partially congruent with the hierarchical analysis proposed by Eysenck. That is, a model in which g is at the apex of a hierarchical structure that included several narrower factors at a lower level of the hierarchy. This solution is congruent with analyses based on multidimensional scaling. Marshalek, Lohman and Snow (1983) factor, analysed a battery of tests and derived g loadings for each of the tests in the matrix. They used a multidimensional scaling program to determine the distance between tests in the matrix. Their solution grouped tests with high g loading in the centre of a radex (Guttman, 1954, 1965, 1970). This implies that tests with high g loadings are, on average, closer to the location of other tests in the set. Tests with low g are found on the periphery of the conceptual map and are, on average, not close to all other tests in location. Various specialized factors form a circumplicial ordering in the radex. The radex representation of distances among tests derived from multidimensional scaling analyses is analogous to the hierarchical ordering derived from confirmatory factor analyses. Both analyses provide a prominent role for g, and allow for a number of more specialized narrow factors that occupy a different conceptual order in the analysis. The picture that has emerged from some contemporary statistical analyses, according to a more prominent role to narrow factors, agrees with that contained in the quotation taken from page 273 in Spearman's paper; in that g is assumed to account for a substantial portion of the common variance in correlation matrices of ability measures.

Discrimination and Intelligence

Spearman's empirical findings relating discrimination ability to general intelligence, in contradistinction to his theory of the statistical structure of correlation matrices of ability measures, had relatively little impact on subsequent research and theory. It is possible to speculate on the reasons for the neglect of this aspect of Spearman's paper. The development of the first test of intelligence by Binet and Simon in 1905 changed the direction of subsequent research on intelligence. Binet's research provided an impetus to study intelligence in non-laboratory contexts, and to use measures of complex as opposed to simple psychological processes. Binet (1905) believed that Spearman's attempt to relate intelligence to discrimination ability was mistaken. He characterized Spearman's research as defective, and asserted that he was *profoundly* astonished at the conclusion (Binet, 1905, see p. 624). In addition to Binet's skepticism, contemporary researchers placed great reliance on Wissler's study (Wissler, 1901). Wissler reported that the correlations between scholastic performance and a variety of simple laboratory measures were close to zero. His work was influential, and has been repeatedly cited by psychologists. His negative results, representing the culmination of James Mckeen Cattell's influential research program at Columbia, did much to turn American psychologists away from the study of the elementary information processing correlates of intelligence. Wissler's work continues to be cited in contemporary sources. I encountered a reference to his study in a recently published Introductory Psychology textbook (Darley, Glucksberg, and Kinchla, 1991). Although Wissler's research was probably more influential than Spearman's, it is possible to argue that Spearman's research was closer to being empirically correct. Spearman presented two criticisms of Wissler's research in his 1904 paper. First, Wissler used only Columbia University students, and the restriction in range of talent would reduce the magnitude of the obtained correlations. Second, the experimental procedures used by Wissler were far from ideal. Subjects, or reagents as Spearman called them, were tested in groups of three. They were presented with 22 tests in 45 minutes. In addition, the experimenter measured head circumference and head length, and noted other physical features of the subjects in the experiment. Deary (in press) and Jensen (1980: 687) reviewed Wissler's study. Wissler measured reaction time using 3 to 5 reactions. Jensen estimated that the test-retest reliability correlation for such measures would be approximately 0.35, thus attenuating any possible correlation with scholastic performance. Also, Wissler calculated only 42 of the correlations in the matrix—less than 7 per cent of the total set. There may have been statistical irregularities in the matrix that were overlooked in Wissler's analysis.

Deary (in press) reviewed the research of Spearman and his contemporaries on the relationship between discrimination ability and intelligence. Spearman had miscalculated the correlations (Fancher, 1985). Spearman actually obtained correlations ranging from 0.25 to 0.47 for his different measures of sensory discrimination and his ratings of intelligence. The best research of Spearman's contemporaries, although frequently interpreted in contradictory ways, actually obtained findings that were congruent with those reported by Spearman. For example, Burt (1909–10) found correlations of 0.40 and 0.37 in two groups between ratings of intelligence and measures of pitch discrimination. Weight discrimination correlated close to zero with intelligence. Thorndike, Lay and Dean (1909) reported a correlation of 0.23 between intelligence and ability to discriminate line length and weight. Deary concluded that Spearman's research was the first methodologically adequate study of the relation between sensory discrimination and ratings of intelligence. Spearman's findings of a moderate positive correlation between discrimination ability and intelligence were supported by the research of his contemporaries.

Of greater significance for contemporary analysis, is the research demonstrating relationships between measures of discrimination ability and general intelligence. Discrimination measures have been found to be related to general intelligence. Nettlebeck (1973) developed a measure of 'inspection time' that is typically defined as the duration threshold for ability to discriminate between two backwardly masked lines differing in lengths. Kranzler and Jensen (1989) reported a meta-analysis of studies relating some variant of the inspection time measure to performance on tests of intelligence. They reported that the average correlation was –0.29. The average correlation after correction of restrictions in a range of talent and attenuation was –0.49. These analyses suggest that as much as 25 per cent of the variance of scores on tests of intelligence may be predictable from performance on tests of rapid discrimination of such simple stimuli as line lengths. Raz and Willerman and their associates obtained correlations between a variety of auditory discrimination measures and intelligence that were somewhat higher than those found in most of the inspection time literature (Raz and Willerman, 1985; Raz *et al.*, 1983; Raz, Willerman and Yama, 1987). They derived thresholds for the duration of presentation required to discriminate between two backwardly masked tones that clearly differed in pitch, and they obtained pitch discrimination thresholds for tones presented for 10 or 20 milliseconds. Their various measures of duration thresholds or pitch discrimination thresholds correlated with measures of intelligence in college samples (some of whom were selected for extreme scores) between –0.33 and –0.73. Most of the uncorrected values were close to –0.5, suggesting that the ability to discriminate between briefly presented tones that differ in pitch predicts more than 25 per cent of the variance on tests of intelligence. These data indicate that the contemporary versions of discrimination tasks do predict performance on tests of intelligence. Spearman's empirical results are closer to contemporary findings than Wissler's results.

CONCLUSIONS

Spearman argued that discrimination ability, ability to reason, and scholastic achievement were reflections of a common underlying intellectual disposition. It is possible to relate Spearman's theory to contemporary behaviour genetic research. Behaviour genetic methods are typically used to partition the variance associated with a particular phenotype. It is also possible to use behaviour genetic analyses to partition the covariance between phenotypic measures. For example, if the correlation between two measures is higher among monozygotic twin pairs than dizygotic twin pairs, it is possible to infer that variance in genetic similarity are related to the covariance among measures. Such analyses may, in principle, result in a partitioning of the co-variance between measures, allocating their covariance to various genetic and environmental components of variance. Such analyses have been reported for the relationship between elementary information processing tasks and general intelligence, and for the relationships between intelligence and academic performance. For example, Ho, Baker and Decker (1988) presented monozygotic and dizygotic twin pairs with several elementary information processing tasks. Among the tasks they used were rapid naming tasks that required subjects to rapidly name familiar objects, colors, numbers and letters. They found that between 57 and 70 per cent of the covariance between performance on these tasks and general intelligence was attributable to genetic covariance, implying that the genetic characteristics that influence performance on the elementary information processing tasks over-lapped with the genetic characteristics that influenced performance on the tests of intelligence. The remaining covariance was attributable to non-shared environmental influences, that is, environmental influences that were not shared by siblings reared together. Such influences would act to make siblings reared in the same family different from each other. Although the elementary information processing tasks used in this study were not those that were similar to the discrimination tasks used by Spearman, the study does provide a tentative suggestion that the relationship between an elementary information processing task and intelligence may be partially mediated by genetic covariance.

Thompson, Detterman and Plomin (1991) reported a behaviour genetic covariance analysis for the relationship between intelligence and scholastic performance for a sample of 6–12-year-old twins. They found the correlations between measures of academic performance and various intellectual ability indices was higher for monozygotic twin pairs than for dizygotic twin pairs. Their analysis were compatible with a model that estimated a genetic correlation of 0.80 for the phenotypic correlation between intelligence and academic performance. Their model is also compatible with the assumption that shared environmental events that contribute to similarity between siblings reared in the same family have no influence on the relationship between intelligence and scholastic performance.

Pedersen *et al.* (1992) reported lower heritability of narrow factors than of g in a study of twins reared together and apart. In addition, they reported that the g loadings of intellectual tests correlated 0.77 with the estimated heritability of these narrow factors. This suggests that variations among tests as well as the relationships among diverse manifestations of g are influenced (N.B. I do not use the term determined in this connection) by a genotypic characteristic of a person.

The genetic covariance analyses are tentative; it would be premature to assume that covariances between elementary information processing tasks and intelligence, and between intelligence and scholastic performance were substantially attributable to genetic covariance among these measures. At the same time it should be realized that these data are compatible with such an assumption, indicating that there may be individual dispositions that are influenced by genotypes that influence performance on elementary information processing tasks, tests of intelligence, and scholastic performance—a position similar to that advocated by Spearman in 1904. Spearman even hinted at the relationship between genotypes and general intelligence in his 1904 paper. Spearman attributed correlations between similar intellectual tasks (the specific or s component) to environmental circumstances. He wrote, 'Of course this specific community is further resolvable into natural talent and favoring circumstances of which factors the latter may often be paramount.' (Spearman, 1904a: 273, footnote 2). Spearman does not indicate that g, which he assumes is responsible for relationships between dissimilar measures of intelligence, is determined principally by 'natural talent'. It is possible that he might have found this view congenial. Spearman assumed that relationships between similar measures of intelligence were attributable to s, and s was determined by 'favoring circumstance'. For reasons of symmetry, it would have been natural for him to have assumed that g was influenced by natural talent.

In summary, contemporary research on intelligence provides tentative support for each of the following generalizations:

1. The matrix of relationships among intellectual tasks is resolvable into a hierarchical structure that includes a g factor at its apex that accounts for a substantial portion of the common variance in the matrix and specific narrow factor.

2. The variance in the g loadings of tests in the matrix are positively correlated with the heritability of narrow factors.
3. Some measures of the ability to discriminate stimuli are related to general intelligence.
4. The covariance between some elementary information processing tasks and intelligence may be partially mediated by genetic covariance.
5. The covariance between general intelligence and scholastic aptitude is partially mediated by genetic covariance.
6. The personal disposition that influences performances on tests of intelligence extends from the ability to solve the intellectual problems posed in tests of intelligence to performance on a class of 'elementary information processing tasks' to academic achievement. Variations in the disposition and the covariances among the diverse manifestations of the disposition may be partially determined by genotypes.

It is possible to argue that each of these tentative generalizations derived from contemporary research on intelligence is compatible with the theory of intelligence advanced in 1904 by Spearman.

References

Binet, A. (1905). 'Analyse de C.E. Spearman, the Proof and Measurement of Association Between Two Things and General Intelligence Objectively Determine and Measured', *L'Anneé Psychologique,* 11: 623–24.

Brody, N. (1992). *Intelligence,* 2nd edition, San Diego: Academic Press.

Burt, L. (1909–10). 'Experimental Tests of General Intelligence', *British Journal of Psychology,* 3: 94–177.

Carroll, J.B. (1988). *Yes, There's g, and What Else,* Unpublished manuscript based on a colloquium presented at the University of Delaware, 17 November.

Cattell, J.McK. (1890). 'Mental Tests and Measurements', *Mind,* 15: 373–81.

Cattell, R.B. (1963). 'Theory of Fluid and Crystallized Intelligence: A Critical Experiment', *Journal of Educational Psychology,* 54: 1–22.

Cattell, R.B. (1971). *Abilities: Their Structure, Growth and Action,* Boston: Houghton-Miflin.

Darley, J.M., S. Glucksberg and R.A. Kinchla (1991). *Psychology,* Englewood Cliffs, NJ: Prentice Hall.

Deary, I.J. (in press). 'The Nature of Intelligence: Simplicity to Complexity and Back Again', in M. Shepherd and D. Forshaw (eds), *Maudsley Essay Series in the History of Psychology and Psychiatry.*

Eysenck, H.J. (1939). 'Primary Mental Abilities', *British Journal of Educational Psychology,* 9: 260–65.

Francher, R.E. (1985). 'Spearman's Original Computation of g: A Model for Burt?', *British Journal of Psychology,* 76: 341–52.

Galton, F. (1883). *Inquiries into Human Faculty,* London: Dent.

Gustafsson, J.E. (1988). 'Hierarchical Models of Individual Differences', in R.J. Sternberg (ed.), *Advances in the Psychology of Human Intelligence,* Vol. 4, Hillsdale, NJ: Erlbaum.

Guttman, L. (1954). 'A New Approach to Factor Analysis: The Radex', in P.F. Lazarsfeld (ed.), *Mathematical Thinking in the Social Sciences,* Glencove, IL: Free Press.

Guttman, L. (1965). 'The Structure of the Interrelations Among Intelligence Tests', *Proceedings of the 1964 Invitational Conference on Testing Problems,* Princeton, NJ: Educational Testing Service.

Guttman, L. (1970). 'Integration of Test Design and Analysis', *Proceedings of the 1969 Invitational Conference on Testing Problems,* Princeton, NJ: Educational Testing Service.

Ho, H.Z., L. Baker and S.N. Decker (1988). 'Covariation Between Intelligence and Speed of Cognitive Processing: Genetic and Environmental Influences', *Behaviour Genetics,* 18: 247–61.

Horn, J.L. (1985). 'Remodeling Old Models of Intelligence', in B.B. Wolman (ed.), *Handbook of Intelligence: Theories, Measurements and Applications,* New York: Wiley.

Jensen, A.R. (1980). *Bias in Mental Testing,* New York: The Free Press.

Jensen, A.R. (1985). 'The Nature of the Black-White Difference on Various Psychometric Tests: Spearman's Hypothesis', *Behavioral and Brain Sciences,* 8: 193–263.

Kranzler, J.H. and A.R. Jensen (1989). 'Inspection Time and Intelligence: A Meta-Analysis', *Intelligence,* 13: 329–47.

Marshalek, B., D.F. Lohman and R.E. Snow (1983). 'The Complexity Continuum in the Radex and Hierarchical Models of Intelligence', *Intelligence,* 7: 107–27.

Nettlebeck, T. (1973). 'Individual Differences in Noise and Associated Perceptual Indices of Performance', *Perception,* 2: 11–21.

Pedersen, N.L., R. Plomin, J.R. Nesselroade and G.E. McLearn (1992). 'A Quantitative Genetic Analysis of Cognitive Abilities During the Second Half of the Life Span', *Psychological Science,* 3: 346–53.

Raz, N., L. Willerman, P. Igmundson and M. Hanlon (1983). 'Aptitude-Related Differences in Auditory Recognition Masking', *Intelligence,* 7: 71–90.

Raz, N. and L. Willerman (1985). 'Aptitude-Related Differences in Auditory Information Processing: Effects of Selective Attention and Tone Duration', *Personality and Individual Differences,* 6: 299–304.

Raz, N., L. Willerman and M. Yama (1987). 'On Sense and Senses: Intelligence and Auditory Information Processing', *Personality and Individual Differences,* 8: 201–10.

Spearman, C. (1904a). '"General Intelligence" Objectively Determined and Measured', *American Journal of Psychology,* 15: 201–93.

Spearman, C. (1904b). 'The Proof and Measurement of Association Between Two Things', *American Journal of Psychology,* 15: 72–101.

Spearman, C. (1930). 'C. Spearman', in C. Murchison (ed.), *A History of Psychology in Autobiography,* Vol. 1, Worcester, MA: Clark University Press.

Spearman, C. and K.J. Holzinger (1924). 'The Sampling Error in the Theory of Two Factors', *British Journal of Psychology,* 15: 17–19.

Spearman, C. and F. Krueger (1906). 'Die Korrelation zwischen Verschiedenen geistigen Leistungsfahigkeiten', *Zeitschrift fur Psychologie und Physiologie der Sinesorgane,* 44: 50–114.

Thompson, L.A., D.K. Detterman and R. Plomin (1991). 'Associations Between Cognitive Abilities and Scholastic Achievement: Genetic Overlap but Environmental Differences', *Psychological Science,* 2: 158–65.

Thorndike, E.L., W. Lay and P.R. Dean (1909). 'The Relation of Accuracy in Sensory Discrimination to General Intelligence', *American Journal of Psychology,* 20: 364–69.

Thurstone, L.L. (1938). *Primary Mental Abilities,* Chicago: The University of Chicago Press.

Wissler, C. (1901). 'The Correlates of Mental and Physical Tests', *Psychological Review,* Monograph No. 3.

8 Teacher Effectiveness and Personality

Meena Sehgal and Rajinder Kaur

INTRODUCTION

Education is a universal phenomenon of strategic value for all of us. The advancements in science and technology in recent times have put greater emphasis on improvement of education for realizing the dream of a progressive society. The role of education in development was recognized even by ancient philosophers like Plato, who considered education as indispensable to economic health of a good society, as education makes citizens reasonable individuals. It is probably in continuation with the same kind of thinking, that most of the enlightened governments of today have made education, at least till primary level, free and compulsory. The Indian Government also spends about 3 per cent of its national budget on education, and has set up numerous administrative bodies, such as Education Commissions, National Council for Educational Research and Training (NCERT) and National Council for Teacher Education (NCTE), whose primary function is to assess the changing needs of the society, which is an ongoing process, and produce corresponding changes in the educational curricula simultaneously to make education relevant to the needs of the society.

No one can question the statement that the success of educational endeavours depends to a very great extent on the teachers who are responsible for implementing the educational programs. In the process, which involves curriculum and syllabi, textbooks and policies, evaluation and feedback, the teacher's role is supreme. The teacher occupies the key position in promoting pupil adjustment too. In a narrow sense, the primary function of a teacher is to teach curriculum only and transmit knowledge, but in a broad sense, he is instrumental in developing the entire personality of his pupils—physical, social, emotional, intellectual, and spiritual. In the words of educationists Remmers and Gage (1955), pupil learning is conditioned not only by how much the teacher knows (subject matter) but also, to a considerable extent, by the personality of the teacher and his relationship with the pupil. No wonder there has been a systematic effort to identify characteristics of an effective teacher.

In the olden days, education was a family affair, and was linked to the socio-economic status of people. Religious education was most widespread and limited to inculcation of religious beliefs. In the 19th century, education became a mass movement, and in the 20th century one witnessed the phenomenon of compulsory schooling. With this changed scenario, there emerged a need for introducing changes in teacher training courses too. Mass literacy goals and the emergence of technology transformed the character of teacher training and philosophy. Till 1800, education could be provided in elementary schools by anyone who had a command of reading, writing and arithmetic (the three R's). Soon after, specific teacher training procedures were designed, which emphasized to the teachers that besides imparting subject matter and knowledge, their main tasks included creating an affective climate in the classroom to provide security to children; creating favourable situations for affective, cognitive and psychomotor development of pupils; enriching the social experience of pupils; helping in fostering readiness for social interactions; and helping the family in achieving these educational goals. This implies training teachers to be empathetic (Delandsheere, 1991). So vital is the contribution of a teacher to the society, that now teacher education for making a teacher effective is not limited to primary or secondary school teachers; but teacher training has become an ongoing process. The Government of India has created scores of Academic Staff Colleges under the aegis of University Grants Commission to train even college and University teachers. The main job of these Academic Staff Colleges is to update teachers' knowledge in the subject matter, as well as to focus on personality development and interpersonal skills of teachers to enhance their effectiveness.

This chapter presents a study on personality as a predictor of teacher effectiveness in the light of the review of related literature. The criteria for evaluating teacher effectiveness are discussed, and personality characteristics of an effective teacher are highlighted. The main aim is made to present a multi-dimensional perspective of the concept of teacher effectiveness to gain a better insight into this much relevant and oft-studied concept.

CONCEPT OF TEACHER EFFECTIVENESS

The Chambers Twentieth Century Dictionary defines effectiveness to mean causing something, successful in producing a result or effect. The Oxford dictionary defines the term 'Effective' as able to bring about the intended results. The search for identifying criteria to define an effective teacher has been on since ancient times. In the ancient Indian treatise, the Vedas-teacher was called Guru—the reverred one. In the Vedas, 'Gur' means darkness and 'ru' means destroyer—Guru or teacher was the destroyer of darkness.

Radhakrishnan, the late President of India and an eminent educationist, stated that a good teacher must know how to arouse the interest of pupils in the field of study for which he/she is responsible; he/she must himself be a master in the field and be in touch with the latest developments in his subject, and he/she must him/herself be a fellow traveller in the existing pursuit of knowledge.

Definitions

There hardly seems to be a decisive concurrence as to the concept of an effective teacher because its conception varies from person to person, place to place, and from one area of culture to that of another. According to Moore and Cole (1957), 'the definition of successful teaching probably always depends upon the specifics of the situation in which a given definition is developed.' It is very likely that what is found applicable in one setting with one type of students, one set of criteria and expectancies, may or may not be applicable elsewhere.

Despite complexities in arriving at a universally accepted definition of teacher effectiveness, some researchers made attempts to define and measure it; their views are presented below:

Remmers (1952) defined effectiveness as follows: 'Effectiveness is the degree of which an agent produces effects.' Three categories of effect in terms of objects affected were identified for teachers: (a) the pupil; (b) school operations; and (c) the school community. Effects on pupils have long been accepted as relevant criterion dimensions of teacher effectiveness. Pupil growth, change, gain, development, learning and the like have often been considered as the ultimate criteria of teacher effectiveness.

According to Scriven (1987), 'teachers are meritorious to the extent that they exert the maximum possible influence towards beneficial learning on the part of their students, subject to three conditions: (i) the teaching process used is ethical (ii) the curriculum coverage and the teaching process are consistent with what has been promised, and (iii) the teaching process and its foreseable effects are consistent with the appropriate institutional and professional goals and obligations.' Dickson and Wiersma (1984) defined teacher effectiveness as the repertoire of competencies involved with teaching plan, teaching material, classroom procedures, interpersonal skills, teacher's reinforcement and involvement.

According to Veerraghvan and Bhattacharya (1987), an effective teacher is one who not only can impart the entire educational curricula allotted to him in the best and most efficient manner, but also can ensure the best academic performance and optimal all-round development of the students. Sometimes, the term 'teacher' is expanded as:

T—Truthfulness
E—Efficiency
A—Affiliation
C—Control and Command
H—Healthy
E—Effectiveness
R—Resourcefulness

The first recorded study of teacher effectiveness was the one conducted by Kratz (1896). A large group of elementary school pupils were asked to try to remember the best teacher each of them had ever encountered, and to write down what made that teacher different from others. These descriptions were then collected and compared, and from them was derived a list of characteristics that supposedly distinguished effective teachers from ineffective. For the next half a century or so, this kind of study was repeated again and again with groups of chosen pupils currently attending schools, sometimes by persons considered to be experts, educators or teacher educators. Perhaps the most extensive and sophisticated example of this genre was the monumental Commonwealth Teacher Training Study (Charters and Waples, 1929), which used exhaustive and meticulous procedures to derive a number of lists of varying lengths. Typical of the characteristics listed for effective teachers were the following, which were the top six on a list of twenty-five: (1) adaptability, (2) considerateness, (3) enthusiasm, (4) good judgement, (5) honesty, and (6) magnetism.

It is important to bear in mind that, at no point in this series of studies was any attempt made to validate any of the characteristics by checking whether the pupils taught by teachers perceived as possessing the characteristics did in fact learn more than pupils taught by teachers not perceived as possessing them.

Riley and Schaffer (1979) conducted a research on self-certification, that is, accounting to oneself, and gave the following qualities of an effective teacher: he/she is creative and varies instructional approaches; maintains a warm and open classroom atmosphere; strives to meet individual student's needs; is self-confident, well-organized, and flexible; has knowledge of the subject matter; involves students in planning; co-operates with parents, co-workers and administration; is aware of students' home environment; has multitudes of educational experiences; knows different philosophies; derives own philosophy; is able to put theory into practice; is emotionally stable; offers a variety of meaningful experiences; is a good person; is able to challenge all children; has had a variety of creative experiences; communicates with students and faculty; is young at heart; recognizes and understands personal and learning problems; is humanistic; encourages independence; has perceptive understanding; continually searches for new knowledge; is aware of various resources; understands and copes with emotional needs of individuals; has patience; establishes rapport with students, parents and staff; knows resources available; is an entertainer; is dedicated; is aware of various aspects of child development (cognitive, social, physical and emotional); has a sense of humour; is aware of modelling effects upon children, other teachers, and parents; has a sincere interest in children; accepts individual differences; offers varied concrete experiences; is a good listener; builds self-confidence; and works towards self-employment.

Ashton (1984) reported that effective teachers were the ones who had strategies for achieving objectives, shared common goals with students, and were democratic in decision-making.

Miron (1985) conducted a study on the 'good professor', as perceived by university instructors, and reported that instructors attached primary importance to the professor's ability to spark intellectual growth; the method of instruction used by the professor was considered to be of secondary importance. The professor's traits, connected to his academic status and his personality, were of relatively little concern. A disparity existed between the instructors' and students' conceptions of the 'good professor'.

Effective teachers help in the development of problem-solving skills in students; they understand the importance of problem-solving in modern life and emphasize it in many ways in their instruction (Lesgold, 1988). Effective teachers also foster creative thinking; they understand the conditions that lead to creative thought, and arrange learning activities to help develop creativity. Effective teachers are able to communicate to the students what they are expected to learn.

Criteria of Teacher Effectiveness

The term 'criterion' is commonly attached to any set of observations that may be used as a standard for evaluative purposes, or as a frame of reference for judging or testing something. It is a base, often of a rather arbitrary nature, and ultimately involving value judgements, against which comparisons may be made. Thus, teacher effectiveness as a concept has no significance apart from the criterion measures used. It would perhaps be necessary, before embarking upon the present investigation on teacher effectiveness, to look into the question of the criterion measures of teacher effectiveness.

Klausmeier and Ripple (1971) reported that teacher effectiveness can be assessed through three types of criteria: process, product and presage. Individuals who prefer the criterion of product, which relates to what is learned, think that the best test of teacher effectiveness is how well the students achieve. Achievement tests and other measures in the cognitive, psychomotor and affective domains are used to measure teacher effectiveness, according to this criterion. Individuals who prefer the criterion of process think that the best test of teacher effectiveness is what the teacher does, what the students do, the interactions that occur between the teacher and the students, or all three. Observation of both teacher behaviour and student behaviour is used to measure teacher effectiveness, according to this criterion. Here, behaviour does not include behaviour indicative of subject-matter achievement. Individuals who use the criterion of presage prefer not to, or are unable to, observe the teacher's behaviour in the classroom. According to this criterion, measures of teacher's personality, intellectual ability, grades made in college, personal appearance, test scores, and ratings usually made outside the classroom are used to measure teacher effectiveness.'

In another study, Jenkins and Bausell (1974) surveyed the opinions of 264 teachers and administrators, who were asked to rank sixteen criteria for judging teacher effectiveness in order of importance. Table 1 presents these sixteen criteria of teacher effectiveness in order of importance.

Table 1

Teachers' Perceptions of the Relative Importance of Sixteen Criteria of Teacher Effectiveness.

Criteria	Mean Rating*
1. Relationship with class (good rapport)	8.3
2. Willingness to be flexible, to be direct or indirect as situation demands	8.2
3. Effectiveness in controlling class	7.9
4. Capacity to perceive the world from student's point of view	7.8
5. Personal adjustment and character	7.7
6. Influence on student's behaviour	7.6
7. Knowledge of subject matter and related areas	7.6
8. Ability to personalize teaching	7.6
9. Extent to which verbal behaviour in classroom is student-centred	7.3
10. Extent to which inductive (discovery) methods are used	7.0
11. Amounts students learn	6.9
12. General knowledge and understanding of educational facts	6.4
13. Civil responsibility (patriotism)	6.2
14. Performance in student teaching	5.7
15. Participation in community and professional activities	4.9
16. Years of teaching experience	3.9

*Rating was done on a nine-point scale, ranging from 9: 'extremely important' to 1: 'completely unimportant'. Any rating over 5, therefore, would indicate that a criterion was perceived as more important than unimportant.

Kundu (1988) reported that among the various criteria of judging success in teaching, the more frequently used criteria are students' grades; ratings by principals, supervisors or co-operating teachers; pupil growth; self-evaluation; peer rating; and objective tests. However, measures of pupil gain as a means of evaluating teacher success did not correlate highly with other criteria of success. Some studies, however, showed significant correlation among the ratings of varying administrators, supervisors and authorities. It seemed that most of the criteria of successful teaching were based upon different conceptions of success. This approach, that is measurement of pupil gain as a criterion of teacher effectiveness, is beset with a lot of methodological problems.

Students have varying abilities and motivations. Since some children, often whole groups of children, may be unwilling to learn in the institutions used to educate them, and some children learn in those institutions regardless of what happens to them, how does one go about attributing student achievement to what teachers do? Pupil achievement does not seem to be an adequate criteria of teacher effectiveness.

Pupil achievement, therefore, has not been used a criteria of teacher effectiveness in the present study.

How to evaluate/assess teacher effectiveness? There are various approaches to teacher evaluation. The most frequent criteria of teacher effectiveness have been self-evaluation and ratings made by a variety of judges, viz., principals, schools administrators, colleagues, and students (Lomak, 1973).

Self as a source/Teacher self-evaluation: Self-evaluation ranges from informal self-reflection to formal written appraisals penned for others as well as teachers' rating themselves. This method becomes a democratic process and shows that teachers are keen for self-improvement. Since a major goal of any evaluation program is to encourage faculty to become monitors of their own profession, self-evaluation provides opportunities for teachers to reflect on their own teaching.

Administrators/Principals as sources: Another way to evaluate different aspects of teachers is presumably related to ratings by school administrators/principals, who have the necessary expertise in the discipline of the faculty members, and are in an excellent position to judge their effectiveness.

Students as sources: Pupils have the maximum opportunity to observe a teacher in action. Consequently, teachers can be evaluated on the basis of pupil ratings on various aspects teaching merit. The unique value of pupil ratings stems from the direction of their approach to important factors in learning situation—attitudes or emotionally-toned feelings. Children's attitudes are of primary importance in the effective acquisition of knowledge skills, interests, attitudes, ideals, etc., with which school learning is concerned. Students as sources provide an important and unique perspective since they are the primary recipients of instruction. Students may be asked to give ratings or written appraisals of teachers.

Cooper, Stewart and Gudykunst (1982) reported in a study that, students' assessment of their relationship with the teacher is one of the best predictors of students' evaluation of the teacher. So, instructor/teacher evaluation appears, in part, to be measuring how effective a teacher is in maintaining good interpersonal relations with his/her students and not the amount of learning (task). Therefore, some people do opine that pupil ratings are not valid, as pupils cannot distinguish between task and relational concerns. However, Shepherd and Trank (1989) found that students can distinguish in their evaluations between (1) task dimension, which is concerned primarily with assessing how much learning took place in the class, and (2) a relational dimension, which is concerned primarily with teacher/student relationship. One needs to be cautious, though, in interpreting and evaluating student ratings of teacher effectiveness (Kundu, 1988)

The present study used three different sources of teacher evaluation, viz., self, principal and pupils. All the three were asked to rate the teachers on various dimensions of teacher effectiveness. In addition, a global measure of teacher effectiveness (addition of all three sources of teacher evaluation) was also included in the present study.

PREDICTORS OF TEACHER EFFECTIVENESS

Many efforts have been made in the past to ascertain predictors of teacher effectiveness. A number of factors like age, seniority, communication style, intelligence, training, stress, teaching styles and personality (Grewal, 1975; Kundu, 1988; Glover and Bruning, 1990; Mohan, 1993, 1994a, b, 1995a, b; Sehgal and Kaur, 1995; Sehgal, 1992, 1993a, b, 1994, 1995; and Sehgal and Kaur 1995) have been linked with teacher effectiveness; yet, personality characteristics of teachers, as predictors of teacher effectiveness, have been the main focus of research since decades. According to Dickson and Wiersma (1984) and Gibney and Wiersma (1986), there is ample evidence supporting the view that personality of a teacher is a very important determiner of successful teaching, and that teacher effectiveness is perceived to exist as a consequence of the characteristics of a teacher as a person.

Tracing the history of search for good teacher as a model person reminds one of the myths of the early 20th century, hypothesising teachers to be ideals, manifesting all noble virtues, and having no human frailties (Norman, 1990). The ideal teacher was one who manifested self-denial, abstinence and deprivation. No one understood at that time that denial of the basic needs of teachers may lead to dissatisfaction among teachers, which would be reflected in teacher's behaviour in the classroom and, thus, alienate pupils.

The search went on and myths gave way to reality, and research was revitalized using standardized personality assessment instruments. As a result, in the 1950s and 1960s thousands of studies attempted to predict teacher effectiveness from personality measures (Getzels and Jackson, 1963; Levis, 1992).

There are several reasons for attributing such immense importance to the personality of a teacher. The first and foremost is that the personality of the teacher influences his/her relationship with pupils. One is aware that faulty/pathological interaction patterns stemming from the disturbed personality of the teacher can cause immense harm to the mental and physical health status of pupils. In fact, in a recent survey of 1,000 adolescent school children, Sehgal (1995) found children liking those teachers best who were calm and relaxed, gave them a feeling of security, and used no physical punishment. A well-balanced, non-anxious teacher can create a healthy emotional climate of learning and would be at ease with his/her pupils. Researches show that learning in the classroom is an emotional experience, and the younger the people, the more true is this statement (Sehgal, 1995). The process of learning in the classroom is accompanied and accelerated by positive affect and relaxed atmosphere. Fear of teachers can inhibit learning. In another study, Sehgal (1994, 1996) discovered that pupils rated those teachers as most effective who were mentally healthy, stable, warm, and nurturant; and pupils scored maximum marks in subjects taught by the teachers they liked the most. An over-anxious teacher with negative attitude towards pupils may unconsciously transfer his/her tensions and unresolved neurotic conflicts to pupils via his/her disturbed emotional interactions with pupils, for example, he/she may continuously denigrate good pupils, and be overcritical, nagging, cynical, over-restrictive, and oppressive in the class. Such a teacher is also aggressive and hostile. Unresolved neurotic conflicts may force the teacher to be sadistic, and suppress creativity and spontaneity of pupils. An egocentric and narcisstic teacher may undermine brilliant students. Pupils are at the receiving end of these unhealthy behaviour patterns of teachers; and pupils' achievement, mental health and liking for a subject are invariably linked with the teacher's personality (Sehgal and Kaur, 1995; Sehgal, 1996).

No wonder, then, that a majority of earlier studies in the area of teacher effectiveness have linked teacher effectiveness with outgoing, extraverted tendencies, confidence (Soloman, 1965; Srivastava and Bhargava, 1984); emotional stability, emotional maturity, calmness, low anxiety, warm and empathetic personality, sensitivity and warmth (Gage, 1965); problem-solving ability (Gage, 1965; Matteson, 1974); less inhibition, control, less impulsive personality, sense of humour and flexibility.

Further, those teachers have also been found to be effective who are not dominated by a narcisstic self and a neurotic need for power and authority (Bhatia, 1977; Hamachek, 1969; Mohan, 1995).

In spite of volumunious research in the area, there is no consistency and no equivocal recommendation regarding which of the traits are more important to be an effective teacher. This is true both in developed and developing countries (Avalos and Hedded, 1981; Buch, 1974, 1979; Raina, 1981).

There seems to be an implicit assumption that a good teacher is an omni-competent person, a person who can teach all things to all persons in all circumstances. Researchers have been trying in vain to discover the characteristics that make this mythical person, thus treating all teachers as absolute generalists (Raina, 1983; Schofield and Start, 1980; Levis, 1992).

However, researchers have shown that perception of who is an effective teacher varies across rural/urban habitat (Matteson, 1974); school, college and university levels (Sehgal, 19995); gender (Sehgal, 1995); type of subject taught, that is, arts vs. science (Murray *et al.*, 1990; Sehgal, 1995); and experience and seniority (Sehgal and Kaur, 1995); and no simple generalization can be drawn in the field of personality and teacher effectiveness.

Other reasons for getting conflicting evidence in the field of personality traits, as related with teacher effectiveness, are: (1) wide range of meanings assigned to the team personality; (2) difficulties associated with selection of appropriate measures of personality; and (3) difficulty in establishing criteria of teacher effectiveness.

Relevance of the Present Study

The present study reviewed the earlier work and tried to take a fresh perspective of personality as a predictor of teacher effectiveness. As type of habitat, courses taught, gender, and seniority/experience of teachers have been found to be pertinent in the study of personality and teacher effectiveness, care was taken to select a large sample of female teachers only from arts, humanities and sciences groups; from both urban and rural habitats; and with teaching experience ranging from 10 to 20 years. The study was confined to female sample only as female teachers outnumber males (ratio 5:1). Also, as researches have revealed that the younger the children, the more crucial is the impact of the teacher's personality on the pupils, the present study was restricted to school teachers. A sample of 240 female (age = 30–45 years) secondary school teachers was chosen finally. To overcome ambiguities in the definition of personality, and measuring tools, the study used Eysenck's model of personality and Eysenckian personality questionnaires.

The personality dimensions used for predicting teacher effectivess were: Psychoticism, Extraversion, Neuroticism and Lie (Social Desirability) Scale assessed by EPQ-R; and Empathy, Impulsiveness, and Venturesomeness assessed by IVE (Eysenck and Eysenck 1978). Academic achievement was also used as a predictor of teacher effectiveness. To assess teacher effectiveness, self rating, principal's rating, and students' rating of teacher effectiveness were taken. In addition, a global measure of teacher effectiveness, that is, addition of all three ratings of teacher effectiveness, was also taken.

Hence, the present study focussed on assessing all four measures of teacher effectiveness in relation with Eysenckian personality dimensions, viz., Extraversion, Psychoticism, Neuroticism, Lie (Social Desirability) Scale, Empathy, Impulsiveness, Venturesomeness and Academic Achievement.

Results and Discussion

The present study took a multidimensional perspective of teacher effectiveness. After reviewing the relevant literature, four criteria were taken as measures of teacher effectiveness:

1. Principal-rated teacher effectiveness.
2. Student-rated teacher effectiveness.
3. Self-rated teacher effectiveness.
4. Global measure of teacher effectiveness.

Teacher effectiveness was related with Eysenckian personality dimensions of Extraversion, Neuroticism and Psychoticism; Empathy, Impulsiveness and Venturesomeness; and academic achievement.

Descriptive Statistics

Means and SDs for the sample are presented in Table 2 for all the variables, viz., Eysenckian personality dimensions, Empathy, Impulsiveness, Venturesomeness, academic achievement and the four measures of teacher effectiveness.

Multivariate Analyses

Inter-correlations were run between all the twelve variables as shown in Table 2. As can be seen, principal-rated teacher effectiveness was significantly and positively related with Extraversion, Empathy and other measures of teacher effectiveness, viz., pupil-rated, self-rated and global teacher effectiveness. It was significantly and negatively related with Neuroticism and Psychoticism.

Self-rated teacher effectiveness was significantly and positively related with Extraversion, Lie (Social Desirability) Scale, Empathy, and other measures of teacher effectiveness, and negatively with Psychoticism and academic achievement. Pupil-rated teacher effectiveness was significantly and positively related with other measures of teacher effectiveness only and with none of the personality dimensions taken. Global teacher effectiveness was significantly and positively related with Extraversion, Lie (Social Desirability) Scale, Empathy and other measures of teacher effectiveness. It was significantly and negatively associated with Psychoticism. All the measures of teacher effectiveness were positively related with each other.

Table 2
Means, SDs and Inter-Correlations

Variables	P	E	N	L	Empathy	I	V	Academic Achievement	Principal-rated Teacher Effectiveness	Self-rated Teacher Effectiveness	Student-rated Teacher Effectiveness	Global-rating Teacher Effectiveness	M	SD
Psychoticism	–	–09	09	–42	–27	25	17	18	–13	–53	06	–37	8.08	4.32
Extraversion		–	–19	–02	08	10	28	–04	12	17	09	20	12.55	3.78
Neuroticism			–	–23	16	12	–11	–07	–16	14	–08	–02	11.06	4.74
Lie (Social desirability) scale				–	19	–11	–08	–10	01	28	–09	19	13.95	3.49
Empathy					–	05	09	–07	15	39	–03	34	12.53	2.52
Impulsiveness						–	29	10	09	–09	02	–04	7.71	3.09
Venturesomeness							–	07	09	–04	–04	03	7.21	2.63
Academic Achievement								–	09	–19	02	–04	59.72	6.78
Principal-rated Teacher Effectiveness								–	14	08	67	269.29	34.48	
Self-rated Teacher Effectiveness										–	00	72	315.48	37.15
Student-rated Teacher Effectiveness										–	17	116.82	108.74	
Global-rating of Teacher Effectiveness											–	233.42	20.01	

0.05 level – 0.12 0.01 level – 0.16

Table 3

Multiple Regression analysis: Predicting Various Dimensions of Teacher Effectiveness

Dependent Variables	Step	IV	Beta	T	P	R^2
Principal-rated Teacher Effectiveness	1	Neuroticism	–0.17	2.57	0.005	0.02
	2	Empathy	0.17	2.54	0.05	0.06
	3	Academic Achievement	0.098	1.54	0.010	0.07
	4	Psychoticism	–0.12	1.66	0.010	0.07
	5	Lie (Social Desirability) Scale	–0.096	1.34	0.025	0.08
	6	Extraversion	0.07	1.06	0.100	0.08
		$R^2 = 0.08$	F = 3.60	df = (6, 233)	p	0.01
Self-rated Teacher Effectiveness	1	Psychoticism	–0.43	7.32	0.005	0.28
	2	Empathy	0.18	3.30	0.005	0.34
	3	Neuroticism	0.20	3.48	0.005	0.38
	4	Extraversion	0.13	2.38	0.005	0.39
	5	Lie (Social Desirability) Scale	0.10	1.76	0.010	0.40
		$R^2 = 0.40$	F = 25.83	df = (6, 233)	p	0.001
Student-rated Teacher Effectiveness	1	Lie (Social Desirability) Scale	–0.09	1.27	0.025	0.008
	2	Neuroticism	–0.10	1.54	0.010	0.020
	3	Extraversion	0.096	1.40	0.025	0.02
	4	Venturesomeness	–0.096	1.40	0.025	0.03
	5	Psychoticism	0.06	.80	–	0.03
		$R^2 = 0.03$	F = 1.59	df = (5, 234)	p	n.a.
Global rating	1	Psychoticism	–0.29	4.83	0.005	0.16
	2	Empathy	0.25	4.16	0.005	0.20
	3	Extraversion	0.15	2.57	0.005	0.22
		$R^2 = 0.22$	F = 22.16	df = (3, 236)	p	0.001

Further, to identify predictors of different measures of teacher effectiveness, stepwise multiple regression analyses were carried out. Four criterion variables (dependent variables) were identified, viz., principal-rated teacher effectiveness, self-rated teacher effectiveness, student-rated teacher effectiveness, and global measure of teacher effectiveness. Eight variables, viz., Eysenckian personality dimensions of Extraversion, Psychoticism, Neuroticism and Lie (Social Desirability) Scale; Empathy, Impulsiveness, Venturesomeness, and academic achievement were used as independent variables. Table 3 summarizes the results of regression analyses.

Criterion: Principal-Rated Teacher Effectiveness

A summary of Table 3 reveals that independent variables, viz., Neuroticism, Empathy, Psychoticism, Lie (Social Desirability) Scale, Extraversion, and academic achievement, emerged as significant predictors of principal-rated teacher effectiveness, and explained 8 per cent of the total variance. Personality dimensions of Impulsiveness and Venturesomeness did not emerge as significant predictors of this measure of teacher effectiveness. Table 3 also reveals that Extraversion, Empathy and academic achievement emerged as positive predictors of teacher effectiveness and Psychoticism, Lie (Social Desirability) Scale and Neuroticism emerged as negative predictors of principal-rated teacher effectiveness.

Criterion: Student-Rated Teacher Effectiveness

A summary of Table 3 reveals that the independent variables of Lie (Social Desirability) Scale, Neuroticism, Extraversion, and Venturesomeness emerged as significant predictors of student-rated teacher effectiveness, explaining only 3 per cent of the total variance. Out of these, Extraversion was a positive predictor of student-rated teacher effectiveness, and Lie (Social Desirability) Scale, Neuroticism and Venturesomeness emerged as negative predictors of this criterion.

Criterion: Self-Rated Teacher Effectiveness

Table 3 summarizes the results for the criterion of self-rated teacher effectiveness. Stepwise regression analyses showed that Psychoticism, Empathy, Neuroticism, Extraversion and Lie (Social desirability) Scale emerged as significant predictors of teacher effectiveness, explaining 40 per cent of the total variance. The beta coefficients revealed that Psychoticism was related negatively with self-rated teacher effectiveness, and Empathy, Neuroticism, Extraversion and Lie (Social Desirability) Scale were related positively with self-rated teacher effectiveness.

Criterion: Global Measures of Teacher Effectiveness

Table 3 summarizes the results for global measure of teacher effectiveness. Stepwise regression analyses revealed that only Psychoticism, Extraversion and Empathy emerged as significant predictors of global teacher effectiveness, explaining 22 per cent of the total variance. Psychoticism emerged as a negative predictor of global teacher effectiveness, and Extraversion and Empathy emerged as positive predictors of this criterion measure.

Overall, the pattern of results (see Table 3) clearly reveals that for all the criteria of teacher effectiveness, the strongest positive predictors of different measures of teacher effectiveness were Extraversion and Empathy. Psychoticism was a negative predictor of different measures of teacher effectiveness throughout, except for student-rated teacher effectiveness. Neuroticism was negatively related with principal-rated teacher effectiveness and student-rated teacher effectiveness, but positively with self-rated teacher effectiveness.

Lie (Social Desirability) Scale emerged as a negative predictor for principal-rated and student-rated teacher effectiveness.

By and large, Impulsiveness and Venturesomeness did not contribute to most measures of teacher effectiveness. Venturesomeness emerged as a negative predictor of teacher effectiveness only in the case of student-rated teacher effectiveness. The results are in line with some of the earlier studies.

One finding worth mentioning is that academic achievement did not emerge as a significant predictor of teacher effectiveness, except in the case of principal-rated teacher effectiveness. Besides the little contribution of academic achievement as a predictor of teacher effectiveness, another finding worth mentioning is the absence of any personality correlates associated with student-rated teacher effectiveness, as revealed by bivariate correlations (Table 2) and even in multivariate analyses. Variance explained in pupil-rated teacher effectiveness by personality variables is almost negligible (R^2 = 3 per cent); and this needs further probing.

One cannot help questioning the validity of pupils' ratings of teacher effectiveness. There are two schools of thoughts regarding this. One stream of thought maintains that student ratings are as reliable and valid as those of adult judges (Doyle and Whiteley, 1974; Misra, 1980; UmmeKusum and Khajapeer, 1985). Some authors, however, support the other school of thought and report that student ratings suffer from Halo effects (Marsh, 1984; Widmeyer and Loy, 1988). Does it imply that students cannot distinguish between task and relational concerns in their evaluation of teachers and, as a result, even if teachers teach nothing, those who can make good relations can assure themselves of high ratings from students?

Brown (1976), Gaski (1987) and Powell (1977) also found evidence regarding validity of student evaluation equivocal. Therefore, one should use student ratings cautiously in reaching decisions about faculty improvement/promotion and training. Present findings also raise doubts about using student rating criterion as a sole measure of teacher effectiveness, and recommend the use of multiple measures of teacher effectiveness. This may be more true for school children's rating as they are not cognitively mature enough to evaluate teachers without biases/mental sets.

Personality Characteristics of Effective Teachers

Wangoo (1986) in a study of Indian teachers found that Psychoticism, adjustment, democratic leadership behaviour and emotional stability emerged as the most important personality characteristics related with teacher effectiveness. He concluded that teachers who had an outgoing attitude, and who were less aggressive, more trusting, open, forthright, relaxed and group-dependent were highly successful.

Murray *et al.* (1990) stated that though the personality profile of an effective teacher differs markedly across different type of courses, in smaller, intensive level discussion-oriented classes, effective teachers were friendly, gregarious, flexible, adaptable and open to change. High and Katterns (1984) also opined that effective teachers are able to flexibly control a repertoire of strategies and tactical skills and are sensitive and flexible.

In the early 1960s, a survey was carried out in USA, sponsored by American Council on Education. In this survey, more than 6,000 teachers were surveyed for establishing characteristics needed in an effective teacher. Results revealed that emotionally stable, friendly, restrained and tolerant teachers were rated as more effective. Pal and Bhagoliwal (1987) also found that more effective teachers were more expressive, socialized and expressed behaviour in a socially-approved way. Similar results, relating teacher effectiveness positively with Extraversion, were reported by Solomon (1965), Chhaya (1974), Gupta (1976) and Srivastava and Bhargava (1984).

Interestingly, results of a very recent survey carried out in India by Sehgal (1955), almost 35 years later than the American Survey, reveal the same conclusions. About 1,000 students from colleges and schools were asked to list the most important characteristics of teachers they perceived to be effective. Table 4 reveals several qualities of effective teachers as identified by college and school students, respectively.

Table 4

Characteristics listed by:

College Students	School Students
Encourages discussion and participation 70%	Knows the subject well 97%
Understands our problems 95%	Communication ability 95%
Knows subject well 85%	Understanding 85%
Friendly and treats us as equals 83%	Encourages discussion and participation 84%
Calm and relaxed 80%	Kind, loving and helpful 82%
Makes us relaxed in class 79%	Good support 80%
Punctual 78%	Links teaching to outside world 80%
Has excellent communication skills 73%	Calm, complex-free, self-accepting 80%
Impartial, objective 72%	Treats us with respect 75%
Has a sense of humour, helpful 65%	Patient 72%
	Impartial 70%
	Punctual 65%
	Others: Builds personality, loves his profession, makes us relaxed 50%
	Uses variety in instructional mode 50%

The present study also found similar results, translated into formal personality testing measures, as revealed by students in the above-quoted survey. In the present investigation, Extraversion and Empathy emerged as positive predictors of teacher effectiveness. Psychoticism and Neuroticism emerged as negative predictors of various measures of teacher effectiveness.

The results of the present study, showing Neuroticism to be a negative predictor of teacher effectiveness for principal-rated teacher effectiveness, is in consonance with early findings which reveal that highly anxious, neurotic teachers transfer their conflicts to pupils via disturbed interactions patterns and by being faulty models (Bhatia, 1977; Rushton *et al.*, 1987; Mohan, 1995; Sehgal and Kaur, 1995). Only in case of self-rated teacher effectiveness, Neuroticism emerged as a positive predictor of teacher effectiveness. Maybe in this case, neuroticism is acting as a motivator for putting in more effort to be better prepared for teaching. Neuroticism in moderation acts as a motivator (Eysenck & Eysenck, 1985).

In the end, one may reiterate that extraversion was chosen as a predictor as it constitutes one of the most widely researched traits in the field of personality and has been linked with individual differences in expressive behaviour similar to classroom teaching behaviour (Campbell & Rushton, 1978; Wilson, 1981; Eysenck & Eysenck, 1985; Rushton *et al.,* 1987; Mohan, 1995; Fritz *et al.,* 1995). Extraversion may be related positively with teacher effectiveness as extraverts have an advantage in being more effective communicators, outgoing, people-oriented and optimistic.

In fact, it is not surprising that extraverted and empathetic teachers emerge as more effective in the present study. More and more studies reveal that being sensitive to the needs of the students, being understanding in managing classrooms is in fact a sign of maturity (Bramald, *et al.,* 1995; Jones & Vesilind, 1995).

School situation is interactive and people oriented. As part of their daily routine, teachers are surrounded by students and may have to meet multitudes of people, for example, teacher aides, pupils, parents, principals, clerks, cleaners, colleagues, school staff, administrators, etc. Therefore, it is important for teachers to create a positive interpersonal environment. For a teacher, being emotionally stable, sensitive, empa-thetic, outgoing, less harsh, tenderminded, socialized, less impulsive and less hostile is necessary for being an effective teacher. Today, there is a lot of stress in society; families are breaking down, and single parent families and divorced families are on the increase. Hence, as pointed out by Kelly and Berthelsen (1995), a teacher has an additional role to perform; that is, extend his/her role from just being transmitter of knowledge to being caring, nurturing and understanding.

Three different models of teaching have been identified:

1. Teacher as a transmitter of knowledge. This model, in which the teacher gives pupils facts and information, has the longest tradition.
2. Teacher as a developer of students' inductive reasoning.
3. Model of interpersonal learning.

Each of these models has assets and drawbacks, and there is a need to blend all three. Yet, looking at wholistic results of recent surveys as well as the present results, the role of interpersonal learning model of teaching, which emphasizes the development of warm human relationships between the teacher and pupils, has been validated. According to this model, if a teacher can create warm empathetic classroom climate, pupil learning is faster.

Empathy and Teacher Effectiveness

A leading exponent of this model of teaching is Carl Rogers, who emphasized that a teacher should pay more attention to creating conditions for experiential learning, and emphasize experience and feeling more than just thinking or reading as pathways to acquiring knowledge. Traditional learning is impersonal, cold and aloof. In his classic work *Freedom to Learn*, Rogers presents three necessary and sufficient conditions for the promotion of learning: empathy, unconditional positive regard, and genuineness (Rogers, 1969). Empathy enables a teacher to convey to pupils: 'We understand.' According to Norman (1990), non-verbal communication is very important in classroom as 90 per cent of message's impact is trans-mitted non-verbally. Empathy reflects a positive attitude towards pupils. Unconditional positive regard permits teachers to accept pupils for what they are without passing judgement; acceptance of pupils is unconditional. Genuineness implies that one should be real and unpretending.

Ryans and Cooper (1979), Miron (1985), Pal and Bhogliwala (1987), O'Keefe and Johnston (1989) and Sethi (1996) also reported empathy to be positively related with teacher effectiveness.

Conclusions and Implications

The present study may be characterized as an exploratory effort, and the results are tentative, requiring further investigation and verification. Nevertheless, a limited number of implications can be drawn from analyses, and suggestions for future research may be given. The present findings have implications both for selection and training of teachers.

The present results reveal that the quality of positive human interaction is the key to pupil learning and the crux of teacher effectiveness. Although disseminating of appropriate information is important, classroom atmosphere, positive human interactions, and interpersonal skills are more important.

A teacher high on Neuroticism creates anxiety and a teacher high on Psychoticism may create fear and negative feelings among students, which may inhibit learning. Stress emanating from fear of teachers and negative effect in the classroom may create a host of psychosomatic complaints in adolescents (Mohan 1995) and inhibit pupil achievement.

Present results clearly reveal that teachers high on Extraversion and empathy, and low on Psychoticism and Neuroticism would be highly effective. Based on these results, one of the challenges of teacher training, then, is to develop/sensitize teachers' thinking about role of affect in learning and teaching, and the role of teachers' personality in pupil learning.

Carkhuff (1982) conducted a large survey relating teacher effectiveness with interpersonal skills. In a summary of 28 studies involving more than 1,000 teachers and 30,000 students, teachers with high levels of affective interpersonal skills were found to be more effective teachers. Similar results have been reported by Newberg and Loue (1982), Aspy and Roebuck (1982) and Sehgal and Kaur (1995).

Implications for Teacher Educator to Enhance Teacher Effectiveness

The study has many theoretical and practical implications. Anderson and Ching (1995) opined that three goals have to be achieved in planning teacher education, which relate to enhancing teachers' (1) knowledge; (2) feelings and self-awareness; and (3) interpersonal skills and human relations skills. The second and third goals are goals of affective teacher education. The next question is, can training be given for empathy?

Research shows that teachers can acquire appropriate feelings and interpersonal skills by participating in training programmes for at least 18 hours. (Brown, 1975; Aspy and Roebuck, 1982). They also found that student achievement improved significantly after working with affectively trained teachers. Students of such teachers were found to be less destructive in class. One-third of students' disruptive behaviour in the class can be accounted for by the variance in teachers' level of interpersonal skills.

Again, proof that empathy can be learnt is borne out by the fact that therapists/counsellors receive training to become effective communicators (Macfarland, 1985). A person high on empathy can identify with others' feelings; can accept what other persons say without making a judgement; likes a high degree of interpersonal interactions; does not act on impulse; is not rigid, cynical, doubting; does not scoff at someone's self-disclosure; and is sensitive and flexible. One can educate teachers for these dimensions of empathy (Tomic, 1991). As Rogers put it, empathy is more readily caught than taught. It can be caught through observation of those who have it and demonstrate it. Empathy is a human competence which is worth striving for.

In addition, teacher trainees can be given training for non-verbal communication also.

In summary, interpersonal skills can be transmitted to teachers economically and effectively. Also teachers who possess these skills are more effective. Empirical support is there for relationships between teacher behaviour, interpersonal skills' and student development. Hence, personality of a teacher is as important in selection as his/her cognitive ability. Training programmes can enhance teacher effectiveness by training them in empathy and interpersonal skills.

The review of related research and present results clearly highlight that personality is a more important predictor of teacher effectiveness than cognitive dimension; and this statement has cross-cultural validity. Also, as there are some differences in predictors of various measures of teacher effectiveness, one may take teacher effectiveness to be a multi-dimensional concept, where teacher effectiveness must be assessed from different sources rather than a single source to be more valid.

However, results also show that personality variables as predictors accounted for only 3–8 per cent variance in pupil-rated principal-rated teacher effectiveness. In the case of self-related teacher effectiveness, and global measure of teacher effectiveness, personality variables accounted for up to 40 per cent variance, implying more important role of personality in the latter category. It may not be out of place to suggest that additional variables such as attitude towards teaching and quality of working life may be included in future research endeavours, and, together, these variables may account for greater variance in teacher effectiveness.

The results of the present study also imply that there be a departure from the conventional criteria of teacher selection, that is, selecting teachers merely on the basis of grades/academic achievement. Contrary to expectations, academic achievement did not show a positive correlation with teacher effectiveness. It is suggested that assessment of teacher's personality and interpersonal skills be made an integral part of teachers' selection along with academic achievement. Training in interpersonal skills and empathy should be made a part of course content of teacher education programmes and in-service teacher training programmes. Similar studies of this nature need to be conducted in colleges and universities to develop a broad-based model of teacher effectiveness.

References

Anderson, L.W. and Ching M. (1995). 'Affective Teacher Education', *Encyclopaedia of Education,* K.U. N.Y.

Ashton, P.T. (1984). 'Teacher Efficacy: A Motivational Paradigm for Effective Teacher Education', *Journal of Teacher Education,* 35(5): 28–32.

Aspy, D.N. and F.N. Roebuck (1982). 'Affective Education: Sound Investment', *Educational leadership,* 39: 489–93.

Avalos, B. and W. Haddad (1981). *A Review of Teacher Effectiveness Research in Africa, India, Latin America, Middle East, Malaysia, Philippine, and Thailand: Synthesis of Results,* Ottawa: Ontario International Development Research Centre.

Bhatia, H.J. (1977). *A Textbook of Educational Psychology,* New Delhi: Macmillan Company of India.

Birkinshaw (1935). Quoted in G.N.P. Srivastava and A. Bhargava (1984), 'Personality Factors and Teaching Effectiveness of Science Pupil-Teachers', *Journal of Educational Research and Extension,* 21 (2): 103–11.

Bramald, R., F. Hardman, and D. Least (1995). 'Initial Teacher Trainees and Their Views of Teaching and Learning', *Teaching and Teacher Education,* 11(1): 23–31.

Brown, D.L. (1976). 'Faculty Ratings and Student Grades: A University-Wide Multiple Regression Analysis', *Journal of Educational Psychology,* 68: 573–78.

Brown, G.I. (1975). 'The Training of Teachers for Affective Roles', in K. Ryan (ed.), Fourth Yearbook of the National Society for the Study of Education, Part 2, Chicago, Illinois: University of Chicago Press.

Buch, M.B. (1974). *A Survey of Research in Education,* Baroda: M.S. University.

Buch, MB. (1979). *Second Survey of Research in Education (1972–78),* Baroda: Society for Educational Research and Development.

Campbell, A. and J.P. Rushton (1978). 'Bodily Communication and personality', *British Journal of Social and Clinical Psychology,* 17: 31–36.

Carkhuff, R.R. (1982). 'Affective Education in the Age of Productivity', *Educational Leadership,* 39: 484–87.

Charters, W.W. and D. Waples (1929). *The Commonwealth Teacher Training Study,* Chicago: University of Chicago Press.

Chhaya (1974). 'An Investigation Into Certain Psychological Characteristics of an Effective School Teacher', Doctoral Dissertation, Kanpur University.

Cooper, P.J., L.P. Stewart and W.B. Gudykunst (1982). 'Relationship with Instructor and Other Variables Influencing Student Evaluations of Instruction', *Communication Quarterly,* 30: 308–15.

DeLandsheere, G. (1991). 'Concepts of Teacher Education', *Encyclopaedia of Education,* K.U.

Dickson, G.E. and W. Wiersma (1984). *Empirical Measurement of Teacher Performance,* Toledo, OH: The University of Toledo, The Centre for Educational Research and Services College of Education and Allied Professions.

Doyle, K.L., Jr. and S.E. Whiteley (1974). 'Student Rating a Criterion for Effective Teaching', *American Research Journal,* 2: 259–74.

Education and National Development Report of the Education Commission, 1964–66, Delhi: NCERT.

Evertson, S. and V.B. Smylie (1987). Quoted in J.A. Glover and R.H. Bruning (1990), *Educational Psychology: Principles and Applications,* 3rd edn., London: Freeman and Company.

Eysenck, H.J. and M.W. Eysenck (1985). *Personality and Individual Differences,* New York: Plenum Press.

Eysenck, S.B.G. and H.J. Eysenck (1978). 'Impulsiveness and Venturesomeness: Their Position in Dimensional System of Personality Description', *Psychological Reports,* 43: 1247–55.

Eysenck, S.B.G. and H.J. Eysenck and R. Barrett (1985). 'A Revised Version of the Psychoticism Scale', *Personality and Individual Differences,* 6(1): 21–9.

Flanders, N.A. (1970). *Analyzing Teacher Behaviour,* Reading, Mass: Addison-Wesley.

Fritz, J.J., J. Miller-Heyl, J.C. Kreutzer and D. MacPhee (1995). 'Fostering Personal Teaching Efficacy Through Staff Development and Classroom Activities', *The Journal of Educational Research,* 88(4): 200–8.

Gage, M.L. (1965). 'Desirable Behaviour of Teacher', *Urban Education,* 1: 85–95.

Gagne, A. and P. Driscoll (1988). Quoted in J.A. Glover and R.H. Bruning (1990), *Educational Psychology: Principles and Applications,* London: Freeman and Company.

Government of India (1985). Challenge of Education—A Policy Perspective, Ministry of Education.

Grewal, S.S. (1975). 'Intellectual and Personality Correlates of Teacher Effectiveness at the Higher Secondary School Stage', Unpublished Ph.D. thesis, Punjab University, Chandigarh.

Glover, J.A. and R.H. Bruning (1990). *Educational Psychology: Principles and Applications,* London: Freeman and Company.

Gaski, J.F. (1987). 'Comments on Construct Validity of Measures of College Teaching Effectiveness', *Journal of Educational Psychology,* 79(3): 326–30.

Getzels, J.W. and P.W. Jackson (1963). 'The Teachers Personality Characteristic', in N.L. Gage (ed.), *Handbook of Research on Teaching,* Chicago: Rand McNally.

Gupta, R.C. (1976). 'Predicting of Teacher Effectiveness Through Personality Tests', Second Survey of Research in Education, Buch, M.B., Mumbai: Popular Prakashan.

Gibney, T. and W. Wiersma (1986). 'Using Profile Analysis for Student Teacher Evaluation', *Journal of Teacher Education,* May–June.

Hamacheck, D.E. (1969). 'Characteristics of Good Teachers and Implications for Teacher Education', *Phi Delta Kappa,* 50: 341–44.

Jena, B. (1993). 'The Effect of Organizational Climate, Stress, Coping Mechanisms on Teacher Effectiveness: A Study of Male and Female Teachers', Unpublished Ph.D. thesis, Delhi University.

Jenkins, J.R. and R.B. Bausell (1974). 'How Teachers View the Effective Teacher: Student Learning is not the Top Criterion', *Phi Delta Kappa,* 55: 572–73.

Jones, M.G. and E. Vesilind (1995). 'Preservice Teachers' Cognitive Frameworks for Class Management', *Teaching and Teacher Education,* 11(4): 313–30.

Kelly, A.L. and D.C. Berthelsen (1995). 'Preschool Teachers' Experiences of Stress', *Teaching and Teacher Education,* 11(4): 347–57.

Klausmeier, Herbert J. (1961). 'Learning and Human Abilities': Educational Psychology, New York: Harper & Row.

Kratz, H.E. (1896). 'Characteristics of the Best Teachers as Recognized by Children', *Pedagogical Summary,* 3: 413–18.

Kumar, P. and D.N. Mutha (1985). *Revised Manual for Teacher Effectiveness,* Vallabh, Vidya Nagar: Sardar Patel University.

Kundu, C.L. (1988). *Indian Year Book on Teacher Education,* New Delhi: Sterling Publishers Private Limited.

Lesgold J.P. (1988). Quoted in J.A. Glover and R.H. Bruning (1990). *Educational Psychology: Principles and Applications,* 3rd Edition, London: Freeman and Company.

Levis, D.S. (1992). 'Teacher's Personality', *Encyclopaedia of Education,* K.U.

Lomax, D. (1973). 'Teacher Education', in H.J. Butcher and H.B. Pont (eds), *Educational Research in Britain,* Vol. 3, London: University of London Press, pp. 301–27.

Macfarland, C. (1985). 'Education for Empathy', *New Frontiers in Education,* 15(1): 91–7.

Marsh, H.W. (1984). 'Students Evaluations of University Teaching: Dimensionality, Reliability, Validity, Potential Biases and Utility', *Journal of Educational Psychology,* 76(5): 707–54.

Matteson, D.K. (1974). 'Personality Traits Associated with Effective Teaching in Rural and Urban Secondary Schools', *Journal of Educational Psychology,* 66(1): 123–28.

Miron, M. (1985). 'The "Good Professor": As Perceived by University Instructors', *Higher Education,* 14: 211–15.

Misra, S.P. (1980). 'Correlates of Effective Teaching as Measured by Student Rating', *Journal of Experimental Education,* 49(1): 59–62.

Mitzel, H.E. (1960). 'Teacher Effectiveness', in C.W. Harris, *Encyclopedia of Educational Research,* New York: The MacMillan, 1486–91.

Mohan, J. (1992). 'Personality & Teacher Effectiveness', Special Lecture, Government College of Education, Jalandhar.

Mohan, J. (1993). Workshop on Management of Classroom Problem by Teachers', Academic Staff College, Punjab University, Chandigarh.

Mohan, J. (1994). 'Teacher Effectiveness & the Correlates', STAR Conference, Madrid.

Mohan, J. (1995a). Stress Among University Teachers, ASC Reference Course in Education, Punjab University, Chandigarh.

Mohan, J. (1995b). Teacher Effectiveness Workshop, Academic Staff College, Punjab University, Chandigarh.

Mohan, J. (1995c). 'Teacher Effectiveness and Curriculum', Government College of Education, Jalandhar.

Mohan, J. (1995d). 'STRESS: An Indian Perspective', STAR Conference, Prague, 1995.

Mohan, J. (1995e). 'Enchancing Effectiveness by Successful Stress Management', ASC Refersher Course in Management.

Moore, C.H. and D. Cole (1957). 'The relation of MMPI Scores to Practice Teacher Ratings', *Journal of Education and Research,* 50: 711–16.

Murray, H.G., J.P. Rushton and S.V. Paunonen (1990). 'Teacher Personality Traits and Student Instructional Ratings in Six Types of University Courses', *Journal of Educational Psychology,* 82(2): 250–61.

Newberg, N.A. and W.E. Loue (1982). 'Affective Education Addresses the Basics', *Educational Leadership,* 39: 498–500.

Norman, S., P. Sprinthall and R.C. Sprinthall (1990). *Educational Pychology: A Developmental Approach,* 5th ed., New York: Mcgraw Hill.

O'Keefe, P. and M. Johnston (1989). 'Perspective Taking and Teacher Effectiveness: A Connecting Thread Through Three Developmental Literatures', *Journal of Teacher Education,* 3: 20–25.

Pal, S.K. and S. Bhagoliwal (1987). 'Personality Characteristics Associated with Teacher Effectiveness as seen Through the Rorschach Technique', *Indian Educational Review,* 22(3): 17–29.

Panda, S.K. and R.K. Mishra (1983). 'Effect of Sex, Training and Experience on the Personality Development of Teachers', *Indian Educational Review,* 18(4): 111–15.

Powel, M.L. (1977). 'Perceptions of Organisational Climate as Mediators of Relationships Between Individual Need and Job-

Satisfaction of Counsellors in the North Carolina Community College System', *Dissertation Abstracts,* 138(2): 77, 638-A.

Raina, V.K. (1981). 'Relationship Between Personality Measures and Teaching Ability', *Journal of Psychological Researches,* 25: 18–22.

Raina, V.K. (1983). 'A Factorial Study of Personalities, Attitudes to Teaching and Creativity of Inservice and Student-Teachers Belonging to Three Subject Areas', *Indian Educational Review, July,* 76–84.

Remmers, H.H. (1952). 'Report of the Committee on the Criteria of Teacher Effectiveness', *Review of Educational Research,* 22: 238–368.

Remmers, H.H. and N.L. Gage (1955). *Educational Measurement and Evaluation,* New York: Harper and Brothers Publishers.

Riley, R.D. and E.C. Schaffer (1979). 'Self Certification: Accounting to Oneself', *Journal of Teacher Education,* 2: 23–26.

Rogers, C.R. (1969). *Freedom to Learn,* Columbus, Ohio: Merrill.

Rushton, J.P., H.G. Murray and S. Erdle (1987). 'Combining Trait Consistency and Learning Specificity Approaches to Personality with Illustrative Data on Faculty Teaching Performance', *Personality and Individual Differences,* 8(1): 59–66.

Ryans, K. and J.M. Cooper (1979). *Those Who can Teach,* Dallas: Houghton Mifflin.

Schofield, H.L. and K.B. Start (1980). 'Product Variable as Criteria of Teacher Effectiveness', *Journal of Experimental Education,* 48: 130–36.

Scriven, M. (1987). 'Summative Teacher Evaluation', in J. Millman (ed.), *Handbook of Teacher Evaluation,* Sage Publications.

Sehgal, M. (1982). 'Psychosocial Aspects of Occupational Stress in Teachers', Proceedings of Annual Conference of Behavioral Medicine, Society of India, Nimbans, June.

Sehgal, M. (1992). 'Psychosocial Aspects of Occupational Stress in Teachers', Proceedings of the Annual Conference on Behavioural Medicine Society of India, Nimbans, June.

Sehgal, M. (1993a). 'Teacher's Personality, Job-Satisfaction and Pupil-Achievement', Proceedings of the 30th Annual Conference of Indian Academy of Applied Psychology, November.

Sehgal, M. (1993b). 'Dynamics of Teacher Effectiveness: A Human Resource Developmental Model', Proceedings of Golden Jubilee Sourvenir of Clinical Psychology, Madras, December.

Sehgal, M. (1994). 'A Study of Effects of Yogic Relaxation on Anxiety and Occupational Stress among Working Women', Proceedings of the 15th International Conference on Stress and Anxiety Research, July.

Sehgal, M. (1995). 'Stress & Illness: A Mental Health Perspective in Working Women', Proceedings of 21st Annual National Conference of Clinical Psychology, February.

Sehgal, M. and Kaur (1995). 'Teacher as an Agent of Mental Health: A Cross Cultural Confirmation', Proceedings of World Congress of Cultural Psychiatry, March.

Sehgal, M. (1996). 'Adolescent Stress: A Review of its Determinants', Paper presented at India Science Congress, Patiala, 3–8 January.

Sethi, A. (1996). 'Creativity in Relation to Intelligence, Classroom & Home Environment During Plus 2 Stage', Paper presented at Indian Science Congress, Patiala, 3–8, January.

Shepherd, G.J. and D.M. Trank (1989). 'Individual Differences in Consistency of Evaluation: Student Perceptions of Teacher Effectiveness', *Journal of Research and Development in Education,* 22(3): 45–52.

Solomon, D. (1965). 'Teacher Behaviour and Student Training', *Journal of Education and Psychology,* 55: 23–30.

Srivastava, G.N.P. and A. Bhargava (1984). 'Personality Factors and Teaching Effectiveness of Science Pupil-Teachers', *Journal of Educational Research and Extension,* 21(2): 103–11.

Taylor, P.H. (1962). 'Children's Evaluations of the Characteristics of the Good Teacher', *British Journal of Educational Psychology,* 32: 58–66.

Tomic, W. (1991). 'Training Programmes in Research into the Effectiveness of Teacher Behaviour', *Journal of Education for Teaching,* 17(2).

UmmeKusum and M. Khajapeer (1985). 'Teacher-Educators' Effectiveness: A Research Study', *Indian Educational Review,* 20(2): 51–63.

Veerraghvan, V. and R. Bhattacharya (1987). 'Correlates of Teacher Effectiveness', *Perspectives in Education,* 3: 161–67.

Veldman *et al.* (1965). Quoted in G.N.P. Srivastava and A. Bharyava (1984), 'Personality Factors and Teaching Effectiveness of Science Pupil-Teachers', *Journal of Educational Research and Extension,* 21(2): 103–11.

Walberg, H. (1986). 'Synthesis of Research on Teaching', in M.C. Witrock (ed.), *Handbook of Research on Teaching,* New York: Macmillan, 214–29.

Wangoo, M.L. (1986). 'Teacher Personality Correlates and Scholastic Competence as Related to Teacher Effectiveness', *Indian Educational Review,* 2(3): 78–81.

Warburton, F.W., H.I. Buthher and G.M. Forret (1961). 'Predicting Student Performance in a University Department of Education', *British Journal of Educational Psychology,* 33: 68–79.

Widmeyer, W.N. and J.W. Loy (1988). 'When You're Hot, You're Hot: Warm-Cold Effects in First Impressions of the Persons and Teaching Effectiveness', *Journal of Educational Psychology,* 80(1): 118–21.

Wilson, G.D. (1981). 'Personality and Social Behaviour', in H.J. Eysenck (ed.), *A Model for Personality,* New York: Springer.

Witty, P.A. (1947). 'The Teacher Who has Helped Me Most', *Elementary English,* 24: 45–54.

9 Drugs in Personality Research: A Review of Indian Studies

B.S. Gupta and Uma Gupta

Abstract

The review of studies presented in this article, especially that of studies where multiple doses of a drug were used in experimentation, reveals the following main trends: (1) stimulant and depressant drugs produce differential effects in introverts and extraverts, introverts being affected more by depressant drugs and extraverts by stimulant drugs; (2) the effects of phenobarbital, a central depressant, are biphasic in extraverts; smaller doses have excitatory effects while larger doses produce depressing effects; (3) individual sensitivity to signals of reward and punishment, in terms of Gray's conceptualization of personality, undergoes a change under the influence of stimulant and depressant drugs; and (4) the effects of drugs are, in general, task-specific, that is, the effects are likely to be expressed into behaviour on certain tasks but not on others. The importance of conducting dose-response studies in subjects having different personality characteristics is emphasized with a view to gaining greater insight into the biological bases of personality.

Introduction

The three major Eysenckian dimensions of personality, namely, extraversion, neuroticism and psychoticism have been found to emerge in a large number of studies carried out in many countries. A vast body of literature demonstrates that these personality dimensions operate consistently over time and across situations. A variety of substances have been used by mankind since antiquity for producing subjective effects that are pleasurable and euphoric in nature. These substances alter behaviour, at least temporarily, in such a way that an individual's position within this three-dimensional framework appears to undergo a change. For instance, barbiturates and alcohol may shift behaviour in the direction of greater Extraversion, anxiolytic drugs in the direction of greater emotional stability, and LSD and other hallucinogenic drugs in the direction of greater psychoticism. Thus, drugs producing change, though over short periods of time, in personality characteristics assumed to be consistent over time (i.e., state variables affecting trait variables) appear to be of considerable interest to a person doing research in personality. And, the effect of drugs on behaviour can be influenced by the personality characteristics of the subject administered the drugs. Hence, the interaction between drugs and personality is of interest in two ways: (1) how drugs change behaviour along the axes defining personality; and (2) how personality determines the way drugs affect behaviour. The other confounding factors in drug research may be: habituation to drugs, initial response level, personal characteristics associated with drug metabolism, withdrawal symptoms, dosage, and diurnal arousal variations. Moreover, the drug-effects may be biphasic in certain situations.

In India, experimentation with drugs for testing various predictions from personality theory has been done mainly within the framework of Eysenckian personality dimensions of extraversion and neuroticism; work has mostly been done with the former. Two deductions emerge from Eysenck's (1957, 1963) drug postulates:

1. The depressant drugs increase cortical inhibition, decreases cortical excitation, and thereby produce extraverted behaviour patterns, while the stimulant drugs decrease cortical inhibition, increase cortical excitation, and thereby produce introverted behaviour patterns. It was probably McDougall (1929) who for the first time predicted such relationship: '....the markedly extraverted personality is very much susceptible to the influence of alcohol.... The introvert on the other hand is much more resistant to alcohol.' In the same context, McDougall further states '....extraverts need less alcohol to reach a point of intoxication than do introverts, who with the same amount of alcohol simply become more extraverted.' About the relationship between neuroticism and drug-effects,

Eysenck (1960) states that stimulant drugs increase and depressant drugs decrease neuroticism, and affect, in a predictable manner, all the objective tests known to measure this dimension. Similarly, Shagass (1960) also conceptualizes that there may be some general factor of cerebral resistance to drugs, which is related to personality.
2. The susceptibility to the action of drugs is determined by an individual's temperamental characteristics.

The central objective of most of the studies reviewed in the following sections has been to discover the occurrence of personality-by-drug interactional effects, if any, on the dependent variable. The direct or indirect focus has been to gain greater insight into the biological bases of at least one personality dimension, that is, extraversion. An attempt is also made to review important studies that aimed to test the deductions from Eysenck's theory.

Perceptual Judgement

In a recent study by Gupta, Dubey and Gupta (1994), the effects of caffeine on perceptual judgement were investigated employing a haptically presented task that successfully eliminates attentional biases associated with visual and auditory presentations. Four doses (1, 2, 3 and 4 mg/kg body weight) of caffeine and a placebo were administered. The subjects were high or low scorers on the scale of impulsivity. The study showed that caffeine, compared to the placebo, facilitated performance by reducing error in perceptual judgement in high impulsives but had no influence on the performance of low impulsives. The study also demonstrated that drug-effects accounted for 70.43 per cent of the variation in high impulsives; the corresponding figure for low impulsives was 29.57 per cent. The effects were dose-dependent for high impulsives but not for low impulsives. The authors propose this differential result to be a consequence of greater resistance to caffeine-provoked variations in the organismic state in highly aroused (lies impulsive) than in less aroused (high impulsive) subjects.

The effects of caffeine were also investigated by Gupta and Gupta (1994) in subjects classified into four groups on the basis of their scores on both neuroticism and extraversion dimensions of personality according to a procedure known as 'zone analysis' (Eysenck, 1967a). Subjects thus classified, presumably, have different positions on the scale of arousal (from low to high): stable extraverts (N–E+); stable introverts (N–E–) and neurotic extraverts (N+E+); and neurotic introverts (N+E–) (Eysenck, 1967b). Each of the two intermediate groups had larger scores on one personality dimension and smaller scores on the other. These two personality dimensions, however, do not refer to the same aspects of the concept of arousal, which, in fact, is multidimensional in nature (Thayer, 1978) and involves qualitatively distinct activation states (Hamilton, Hockey and Rejman, 1977). The results demonstrated that caffeine, as compared to placebo, reliably reduced judgement error in the felt width of haptically presented blocks, and thus facilitated performance of the subjects having relatively lower levels of basal arousal, that is, stables (N–), extraverts (E+) and stable extraverts (N–E+); the results were, however, more marked for the N–E+ group. The decrease in judgement, error of these groups was dose-dependent, followed a pattern of monotonic decrease, and showed a dominant linear trend. Caffeine did not produce any reliable effects in the intermediate and high arousal states. Trend components in caffeine effects also accounted for differential variation in the different personality groups.

Figural After-Effects

Gupta (1974) investigated the effects of 10 mg of dextroamphetamine and 100 mg of phenobarbital on kinesthetic figural after-effect (KFAE), a perceptual phenomenon related to distortion in the felt width of a standard block occurring as a consequence of induction experience with a block different in width from the standard block. The study was conducted on three groups of subjects having different positions on the scale of extraversion, namely introverted, ambiverted and extraverted. Compared with placebo, dextroamphetamine reduced and phenobarbital enhanced the magnitude of KFAE, with the main-effect of drug-treatments being statistically significant. No significant interaction between extraversion and drug-treatment was found, although in terms of Eysenckian theory the possibility of such an interaction showing differential drug-effects in the various extraversion groups could not be ruled out.

The failure to discover a significant interaction in the study by Gupta (1974) might have been due to the lack of optimum conditions for its occurrence, since only a single dose of each drug was used. In another experiment, Gupta and Kaur (1978) examined the effects of three doses (7.5 mg, 10.0 mg, and 12.5 mg) of dextroamphetamine on KFAE in three groups of subjects: low, intermediate and high scorers on the scale of extraversion. The study revealed the anticipated extraversion-by-dextroamphetamine interaction, specifying clearly that KFAE was reduced in the extraverted and enhanced in the introverted subjects under the influence of the drug. Moreover, the effects were dose-dependent in both the groups.

The dose-response relationship between phenobarbital, a central depressant, and KFAE was also examined in introverted and extraverted groups of subjects (Gupta, 1982). The drug was used in three doses: 30 mg, 60 mg and 100 mg. The study revealed a statistically significant interaction between extraversion and drug-treatments, showing that larger doses (60 mg and 100 mg), compared to placebo, significantly increased the extent of KFAE in the introverted group of subjects, whereas the smaller dose (30 mg) had no effect on the performance of this group. Contrarily, the smaller dose had no effect on the performance of this group. Contrarily, the smaller dose led to a significant reduction in KFAE in the extraverted group of subjects, whereas larger doses were ineffective. The KFAE was expected to increase under the influence of phenobarbital, but the drug-impact, especially with the smaller dose, observed in the form of reduction in KFAE, indicated that this dose acted like a stimulant in the extraverted group of subjects, and led to a decrement in KFAE. Citing Cohen (1975) and Franz (1975), who suggested that barbiturates at low concentrations generally produce an excitatory effect on some functions by depressing the ascending inhibitory system of the reticular formation, as well as Price (1975), who points out that at the highest levels there is a release from inhibition in the extra-limbical systems, the author suggests that these excitatory influences are likely to be expressed into behaviour only under suboptimal conditions as is the case with extraverts, who generally work suboptimally under normal conditions (Eysenck, 1967a, b).

In another study, the effects of caffeine, a potent stimulant of both CNS and ANS (Rall, 1980; Boulenger and Uhde, 1982; Dews, 1982), were investigated on the KFAE of subjects having extreme positions on the scale of impulsivity (Gupta and Gupta, 1990). Caffeine was administered in four doses (1, 2, 3 and 4 mg/kg body weight) along with a placebo. Caffeine in all doses, compared to the placebo, led to a decrease in the KFAE of subjects having high scores on the impulsivity scale. Conversely, the largest dose of caffeine (4 mg/kg body weight) enhanced KFAE in subjects having low scores on the impulsivity scale; the other caffeine doses did not produce any significant effect. The authors propose this differential result to be a consequence of greater resistance to caffeine-provoked variations in the organismic state in highly aroused (less impulsive) than in less aroused (high impulsive) subjects.

Singh and Gupta (1981) examined the effects of 10 mg of dextroamphetamine and 100 mg of phenobarbital on the visual figural after-effect (VFAE) of subjects having extreme scores on neuroticism and extraversion scales. A within-subject design was used. The study did not reveal any indication of an interaction existing between drug-treatments and personality characteristics; however, the main-effect of treatments was statistically significant. The study specifically demonstrated significant increase in VFAE under the influence of phenobarbital in the highly aroused (N+E– group) and less aroused (N–E+ group) subjects; the increase did not reach the accepted levels of significance in subjects having intermediate positions on the scale of arousal (N+E+ and N–E– groups) (Eysenck, 1967b). Dextro-amphetamine also tended to increase the VFAE scores of all groups, but the increases were statistically nonsignificant.

Short-Term Memory

In a recent dose-response study (Gupta, 1991), the effects of caffeine on free recall, immediately after acquisition of conceptual and acoustic tasks, were investigated in subjects having high or low scores on the scale of impulsivity. The study was carried out within the general framework of depth of processing, and explored the interactions, if any, occurring among caffeine effects, impulsivity, and tasks in their effects on free recall. Caffeine was used in four doses (1,2,3 and 4 mg/kg body weight) along with a placebo. The impulsivity-by-task, caffeine-by-task, and impulsivity-by-caffeine-by-task interactions were found to be statistically significant. Dose-response trend components for the two tasks accounted for differential variation in high and low impulsives. For high impulsives, the linear component accounted for most of the variation (77.05 per cent) in the conceptual task while the quadratic component was responsible for most of the variation (80.88 per cent) in the acoustic task; for low impulsives, the linear component accounted for almost all the variation (98.15 per cent) in the conceptual task while the linear (46.0 per cent) and quadratic (46.23 per cent) components accounted for most of the variation in the acoustic task. The study also demonstrated that: (1) caffeine, compared to the placebo, inhibited recall in high impulsives after conceptual acquisition, but facilitated it after acoustic acquisition; and (2) caffeine produced no effect on the recall of low impulsives, irrespective of whether the acquisition was done conceptually or acoustically. The author attributes these differential effects in high and low impulsives to greater resistance to organismic variations in high arousal states.

Gupta (1993) also examined the effects of caffeine on recognition performance of high and low impulsives on the conceptual and acoustic tasks. In this study also caffeine was used in four doses (1, 2, 3 and 4 mg/kg body weight) along with a placebo. The impulsivity-by-task, task-by-treatments, and impulsivity-by-task-by-treatments inter-actions were found to be statistically significant. The treatment-effect was, however, statistically significant for the high impulsives only; the drug, compared to the placebo, inhibited the recognition performance after conceptual acquisition, but facilitated it after acoustic acquisition. The author has attributed these findings to the inverted U-shaped relationship between arousal and performance, in which less impulsives (presumably highly aroused persons) have their position closer to the optimal level of performance, and a shift in either direction does not affect their performance.

Verbal Conditioning

Jawanda (1965) investigated the effects of single doses of dextroamphetamine, phenobarbital, ephedrine and chlorpromazine on verbal conditioning, employing Taffel's (1955) sentence-construction technique. The study was conducted on four groups of subjects: (1) neuroticism high, extraversion high (N+E+); (2) neuroticism low, extraversion high (N–E+); (3) neuroticism high, extraversion low (N+E–); and (4) neuroticism low, extraversion low (N–E–). The main-effect of treatment was statistically significant. As compared to the placebo, the stimulant drugs enhanced and the depressant drugs inhibited the amount of conditioning in all the personality groups. The personality-by-treatments interaction was statistically nonsignificant; the results were, however, indicative of such a possibility.

In a dose-response study, the effects of 50, 100, and 150 mg doses of phenobarbital were examined on verbal conditioning in subjects having high, moderate, or low scores on the extraversion dimension of personality (Gupta, 1968). The drug led to a significant decrease in verbal conditioning in all the extraversion groups, indicating no treatments-by-extraversion interaction.

In another dose-response study, the effects of three doses (60, 100, and 150 mg) of phenobarbital were tested on verbal conditioning in four groups of subjects: N+E+, N+E–, N–E+, and N–E– (Gupta and Singh, 1971). The personality-by-treatments interaction was statistically significant; the decrease in conditionability, produced by phenobarbital, was more pronounced in the introverted groups, than in the N+E– and N–E– groups.

Gupta (1970) investigated the effects of 10 mg of dextroamphetamine and 100 mg of phenobarbital on the verbal conditionability of subjects scoring high, moderate or low on the extraversion scale. The study showed the treatments-by-extraversion interaction to be statistically significant; dextroamphetamine led to an increase in the amount of verbal conditioning in the E+ and E (moderate scorers on extraversion) groups of subjects, and phenobarbitone decreased it in all the groups; but the decrease was more marked in the E+ and E– groups.

Gupta (1973) also examined the effects of 10 mg of dextroamphetamine, 100 mg of phenobarbital, 30 mg of ephedrine and 100 mg of chlorpromazine on verbal conditioning in subjects at three different levels (high, moderate, and low) on the extraversion dimension of personality. Dextroamphetamine facilitated conditioning in the E+ and E groups, but not in the E– group. Both phenobarbital and chlorpromazine led to a comparable decrease in the conditioning scores of all the groups; no interaction was, therefore, indicated between these two psycholeptic drugs and extraversion. Ephedrine did not produce significant effect in any of the extraversion groups.

Several experiments conducted by Gupta and colleagues (Gupta, 1976; Gupta and Nagpal, 1978; Nagpal and Gupta, 1979; Gupta and Shukla, 1989; Gupta, 1990) consistently indicated that rewarding cues (positive reinforcement) produced greater amount of verbal conditioning in extraverts while punishing cues (negative reinforcement) led to greater conditioning in introverts. Two more experiments were carried out by Gupta and colleagues (Gupta and Gupta, 1984; Gupta,

1984) to examine whether individual susceptibility to reinforcement, in terms of Gray's (1970, 1973) model of personality, undergoes a change under drug influence, and, as a consequence, whether the conditionability of extraverts and introverts with positive and negative reinforcers is affected. Gupta and Gupta (1984) investigated the effects of 7.5 mg and 12.5 mg doses of dextroamphetamine and a placebo on the amount of verbal conditioning established by employing 'good' as the positive reinforcer and 'mild electric shock for half a second' as the negative reinforcer in extraverted and introverted groups of subjects. Drug-treatments was the within-subject variable. The extraverts conditioned better with the rewarding reinforcer ('good') under the placebo condition, but with the punishing reinforcer ('electric shock') under the influence of dextroamphetamine, that is, the extraverts' general sensitivity to signals of reward rather than to signals of punishment was reversed by dextroamphetamine. The introverts conditioned better with the punishing reinforcer under the placebo condition; dextroamphetamine did not alter their sensitivity to signals of punishment, but simply decreased their conditioning scores with the punishing reinforcer, while their conditioning scores with the rewarding reinforcer remained uninfluenced. Thus, introverts' conditioning scores, under the influence of dextroamphetamine, decreased only with the reinforcer to which they are generally more sensitive.

Gupta (1984) replicated the experiment using two doses (30 and 100 mg) of phenobarbital instead of dextroamphetamine. Under the influence of the smaller dose of the drug, as compared with the placebo, the conditioning scores of the extraverts increased with the punishing reinforcer but decreased with the rewarding reinforcer. It appeared as if their level of arousal had been enhanced by the smaller dose of the drug, and, consequently, their general susceptibility to reinforcement had been altered. The larger dose produced no effect on extraverts' conditioning scores. Contrarily, the smaller dose was ineffective with introverts while the larger dose decreased their conditioning scores with the punishing reinforcer but not with the rewarding reinforcer.

Cognitive Performance

Gupta (1972) investigated the effects of 100 mg of phenobarbital and 10 mg of dextroamphetamine on the intelligence test scores of 10th and

11th grade school children (aged 15.0–16.5 years) having high, intermediate or low scores on the extraversion or neuroticism dimension of personality (Expt. 2). The criterion measured were Culture Fair Intelligence Test, Scale 2 (CFIT; Cattell, 1965) and the Hindi version (Singh, 1966) of Hundal's (1962) General Mental Ability Test (GMAT). The former contains four subtests, namely series, classification, matrices and topology, while the latter contains seven subtests (number series, analogies, classification, inferences, following directions, opposites and synonyms) is a traditional type of verbal intelligence test. It had been proposed that the reversible short-term fluctuations would have a more pronounced effect on the CFIT scores, which presumably are the measures for a pure behavioural and neuralphysiological function related closely to biological influences on intellectual development than on the GMAT scores, which perhaps represent the results of skills and concepts established through experiential-educative-acculturative influences associated with formally learned experience and habits related primarily to early learning and retained at the physiological level in the form of established neural patterns (Cattell, 1963; Horn, 1966). The study showed that as compared with placebo, phenobarbital decreased and dextro-amphetamine increased the CFIT composite scores of all the extraversion or neuroticism (high, intermediate, low) groups, except for the N+ group where the increase under the influence of dextroamphetamine did not reach the accepted level of significance. All the mean comparisons for the GMAT measure were statistically nonsignificant. The evaluation of the independent drug-effect, with standard deviation as a unit for the CFIT scores, revealed that phenobarbital decreased and dextroamphetamine increased the test scores of the E (intermediate scorers on extraversion dimension), E–, and N (intermediate scorers on neuroticism dimension) groups of subjects only; other mean comparisons yielded statistically non-significant results. Gupta (1972; Expt. 3) also examined the effects of the same doses of phenobarbital and dextroamphetamine on the CFIT and the GMAT scores of subjects having different positions (high, intermediate, low) on Factor G of the 16 PF Questionnaire (Cattell and Eber, 1962). Phenobarbital led to a decrease in the CFIT and the GMAT scores of all the three groups, whereas dextroamphetamine increased the scores of the G+ and G– groups on the CFIT, and that of the G and G– groups on the GMAT. The independent drug-effect (decrease in test scores under the influence of phenobarbital, and increase with dextroamphetamine) was, however, statistically significant for the G– group in the case of phenobarbital and the G+ group in the case of dextroamphetamine.

The effects of dextroamphetamine on the CFIT and the GMAT scores were also examined in a dose-response study on male high school students, aged 15–17 years, differing on both neuroticism and extraversion dimensions of personality (Gupta, 1977). The drug was used in three doses: 5, 10, and 15 mg. As compared to placebo, the 5 and 10 mg doses improved the performance of the N–E+ (less aroused) group while the 15 mg dose led to a sharp decrement in the performance of this group. The drug, in all doses, reliably inhibited the performance of the moderately aroused (N–E– and N+E+) and highly aroused (N+E–) groups, except for the N+E+ group, whose performance decreased under the influence of the 5 mg dose; but, the decrease was not statistically significant. The results, therefore, revealed that dextroamphetamine facilitated the performance in the states of low arousal. The study also showed that the performance of all the personality groups on the GMAT remained unaffected by the drug.

Gupta (1988a) investigated the effects of caffeine on the CFIT performance of male postgraduate students, aged 19–24 years, in a dose-response study, using caffeine in four doses, viz., 1, 2, 3 and 4 mg/kg body weight. The instrument used for measuring cognitive performance was the CFIT, Scale 3, Form A (Cattell, 1965). Caffeine in larger doses (3 and 4 mg/kg body weight) facilitated the performance of N–E+ and N+E+ groups of subjects, but did not produce any effect on the performance of N+E– and N–E– groups.

Gupta (1988b) also examined the effects of caffeine on the CFIT performance of male postgraduate students having high or low scores on the scale of impulsivity. Caffeine was administered in four doses, that is, 1, 2, 3 and 4 mg/kg body weight. Caffeine improved the performance of the high impulsives, but produced no effect on the performance of the low impulsives. The study demonstrated different dose-response trends in the two groups of subjects.

CONCLUSIONS

Dose-response studies appear to be more revealing in drug action and personality theory interactional research than studies where only a single dose of a drug is used. Such studies, by providing optimum conditions, offer greater opportunities for the drug-effects to be expressed into behaviour, and for the drug-by-personality interaction to emerge in its effects on the dependent variable. Moreover, drug-effects on behaviour are not usually linear—this aspect of drug-effects can be revealed only by dose-response studies. Besides, drug-effects are also situation- and task-specific, appearing in certain situations on certain tasks but none on others. Habituation to drugs, and the time of the day when the drugs are administered and the testing of behaviour is done, are other confounding variables which affect an individual's response to drugs. In fact, human responsivity to drugs is affected by a diverse and complex array of variables, and it is just not feasible to control them fully in experimentation (Eysenck, 1983; Trouton and Eysenck, 1981). The occurrence of a state-by-trait interaction (i.e., interaction between drug-effect and personality characteristics) for any behavioural parameter poses a challenge, and, perhaps opens new vistas for the personality theorists who regards personality characteristics as the consistent patterns of behaviour.

References

Boulenger, J.P. and T.W. Unde (1982). 'Caffeine Consumption and Anxiety: Preliminary Results of a Survey Comparing Patients with Anxiety Disorders and Normal Controls', *Psychopharmacology Bulletin,* 18: 53–57.

Cattell, R.B. (1963). 'Theory of Fluid and Crystallized Intelligence: A Critical Experiment', *Journal of Educational Psychology,* 54: 1–22.

Cattell, R.B. (1965). *The IPAT Culture Fair Intelligence Scales 1, 2 and 3,* 3rd edn., Champaign, Illinois: Institute of Personality and Ability Testing.

Cattell, R.B. and H.W. Eber (1962). *Sixteen Personality Factor Questionnaire: Manual for Forms A and B,* Champaign, Illinois: Institute of Personality and Ability Testing.

Cohen, P.J. (1975). 'Signs and Stages of Anesthesia', in L.S. Godman and A. Gilman (eds.), *The Pharmacological Basis of Therapeutics,* 5th edn., New York: Macmillan, pp. 60–65.

Dews, P.B. (1982). 'Caffeine', *Annual Review of Nutrition,* 2: 323–41.

Eysenck, H.J. (1957). *The Dynamics of Anxiety and Hysteria,* London: Routledge and Kegan Paul.

Eysenck, H.J. (1960). 'Drug Postulates, Theoretical Deductions, and Methodological Considerations', in L. Uhr and J.G. Miller (eds), *Drugs and Behaviour,* New York: John Wiley and Sons.

Eysenck, H.J. (ed.) (1963). *Experiments with Drugs,* Oxford: Pergamon Press.

Eysenck, H.J. (1967a) *The Biological Basis of Personality,* Springfield, Illinois: Charles C. Thomas.

Eysenck, H.J. (1967b). 'Intelligence assessment: A Theoretical and Experimental Approach', *British Journal of Educational Psychology,* 37: 81–98.

Eysenck, H.J. (1983). 'Drugs as Research Tools in Psychology: Experiments with Drugs in Personality Research', *Neuropsychobiology,* 10: 29–43.

Franz, D.N. (1975). 'Drugs Acting on the Central Nervous System: Introduction', in L.S. Goodman and A. Gilman (eds), *The Pharmacological Basis of Therapeutics,* 5th edn, New York: Macmillan, pp. 47–53.

Gray, J.A. (1970). 'The Psychophysiological Basis of Introversion-Extraversion', *Behaviour Research and Therapy,* 8: 249–66.

Gray, J.A. (1973). 'Causal Theories of Personality and How to Test Them', in J.R. Royce (ed.), *Multivariate Analysis and Psychological Theory,* London: Academic Press, pp. 409–63.

Gupta, B.S. (1968). 'A Study of Extraversion and Phenobarbitone as Experimental Variables in Verbal Conditioning', *Indian Journal of Experimental Psychology,* 2: 18–20.

Gupta, B.S. (1970). 'The Effect of Extraversion and Stimulant and Depressant Drugs on Verbal Conditioning', *Acta Psychologica,* 34: 505–10.

Gupta, B.S. (1972). 'The Effect of Stimulant and Depressant Drugs on the Test Scores of Fluid and Crystallized Intelligence of High School Children', Unpublished Ph.D. thesis, Panjab University, Chandigarh.

Gupta, B.S (1973). 'The Effect of Stimulant and Depressant Drugs on Verbal Conditioning', *British Journal of Psychology,* 64: 553–57.

Gupta, B.S. (1974). 'Stimulant and Depressant Drugs on Kinaesthetic Figural Aftereffect', *Psychopharmacologia,* 36: 275–80.

Gupta, B.S (1976). 'Extraversion and Reinforcement in Verbal Operant Conditioning', *British Journal of Psychology,* 67: 47–52.

Gupta, B.S (1977). 'Dextroamphetamine and Measures of Intelligence', *Intelligence,* 1: 274–80.

Gupta, B.S. and U. Gupta (1984). 'Dextroamphetamine and Individual Susceptibility to Reinforcement in Verbal Operant Conditioning', *British Journal of Psychology,* 75: 201–6.

Gupta, B.S and S. Kaur (1978). 'The effects of Dextroamphetamine on Kinesthetic Figural Aftereffects', *Psychopharmacology,* 56: 199–204.

Gupta, B.S. and M. Nagpal (1978). 'Impulsivity/Sociability and Reinforcement in Verbal Operant Conditioning', *British Journal of Psychology,* 69: 203–6.

Gupta, B.S. and S.D. Singh (1971). 'The Effect of Extraversion, Neuroticism and a Depressant Drug on Verbal Conditioning', *Indian Journal of Experimental Psychology,* 5: 15–17.

Gupta, S. (1990). 'Impulsivity/Sociability and Reinforcement in Verbal Operant Conditioning—a Replication', *Personality and Individual Differences,* 11: 585–90.

Gupta, S. and A.P. Shukla (1989). 'Verbal Operant Conditioning as a Function of Extraversion and Reinforcement', *British Journal of Psychology,* 80: 39–44.

Gupta, U. (1982). 'Phenobarbitone and Kinaesthetic Aftereffect', *Current Psychological Research,* 2: 171–80.

Gupta, U. (1984). 'Phenobarbitone and the Relationship Between Extraversion and Reinforcement in Verbal Operant Conditioning', *British Journal of Psychology,* 75: 499–506.

Gupta, U. (1988a). 'Personality, Caffeine and Human Cognitive Performance', *Pharmacopsychoecologia,* 1: 79–84.

Gupta, U. (1988b). 'Effects of Impulsivity and Caffeine on Human Cognitive Performance', *Pharmacopsychoecologia,* 1: 33–41.

Gupta, U. (1991). 'Differential Effects of Caffeine on Free Recall After Semantic and Rhyming Tasks in High and Low Impulsives', *Psychopharmacology,* 105: 137–40.

Gupta, U. (1993). 'Effects of Caffeine on Recognition', *Pharmacology Biochemistry and Behavior,* 44: 393–96.

Gupta, U., G.P. Dubey and B.S. Gupta (1994). 'Effects of Caffeine on Perceptual Judgement', *Neuropsychobiology,* 30: 185–88.

Gupta, U. and B.S. Gupta (1990). 'Caffeine Differentially Affects Kinesthetic Aftereffect in High and Low Impulsives', *Psychopharmacology,* 102: 102–5.

Gupta, U. and B.S. Gupta (1994). 'Effects of Caffeine on Perceptual Judgement: A Dose-Response study', *Pharmacopsychoecologia,* 7: 215–19.

Hamilton, P., B. Hamilton and M. Rejman (1977). 'The Place of the Concept of Activation in Human Information Processing Theory: An Integrative Approach', in S. Dornic (ed.), *Attention and Performance,* Vol. 6, New York: Halstead, pp. 463–86.

Horn, J.L. (1966). 'Short Period Changes in Human Abilities', Report 618, National Aeronautics and Space Administration, Denver, Colorado: Denver Research Institute.

Hundal, P.S. (1962). 'A Study of Ability of University Students', Unpublished, Ph.D. thesis, Panjab University, Chandigarh.

Jawanda, J.S. (1965). 'Age, Sex and Personality Variables in Verbal Conditioning and its Modification by Drugs', Unpublished Ph.D. thesis, Panjab University, Chandigarh.

McDougall, W. (1929). 'The Chemical Theory of Temperament Applied to Introversion and Extraversion', *Journal of Abnormal and Social Psychology,* 24: 293–309.

Shagass, C. (1960). 'Drug Threshold as Indicators of Personality and Effect', in L. Uhr and J.G. Miller (eds), *Drugs and Behaviour,* New York: John Wiley and Sons.

Singh, A. (1966). *Hindi Version of Hundal's General Mental Ability Test,* Chandigarh: Panjab University.

Singh, V.K. and B.S. Gupta (1981). 'Personality and Drugs in Visual Figural Aftereffects', *International Journal of Psychology,* 16: 35–44.

Taffel, C. (1955). 'Anxiety and the Conditioning of Verbal Behaviour', *Journal of Abnormal and Social Psychology,* 51: 496–501.

Thayer, R.E. (1978). 'Toward a Psychological Theory of Multi-Dimensional Activation (Arousal)', *Motivation and Emotion,* 2: 1–34.

Trouton, D.S. and H.J. Eysenck (1961). 'Psychological Effects of Drugs', in H.J. Eysenck (ed.), *Handbook of Abnormal Psychology,* London: Pitman.

10 Dimensions of Rural Development Personnel

B.C. Muthayya

In the present context of emphasis on rural development, with an important strategy oriented to serve the needs of the rural poor, not only in identifying their existing conditions but also in evolving programmes which are relevant for them with an inbuilt motivation, the task of the officials who engage themselves in this endeavour becomes important. In this context, the general assumption that any person can serve as a change agent, given the powers and privileges, has not always been found to be true based on the information available. Though as psychologists, we believed that every person has a job, but then it should be found; and we also do not seem to believe that every person can do any job, any time, in any manner, as we have grounded our belief in the theory of individual differences. Therefore, psychologists have always concerned themselves with finding jobs which fit a person. In case they are able to find a job which is suitable to the potentiality of the person, then there is a possibility of maximizing his/her output.

If we assume that rural development, by and large, is aimed at not only bringing about improvement in the level of living of the people by providing them various inputs, but also at making them capable of and responsible for sustaining and improving the programmes undertaken for their betterment, then it calls for an approach which is oriented towards an understanding of the existing situations and taking action to remove the lacunae observed.

For this purpose, we need officers with a missionary zeal, knowledge, skills, and, above all, experience of working effectively with people. In view of this, the key officials who are considered as agents of change are supposed to be in a position to understand the needs of the people and implement the programmes effectively in keeping with the objectives envisaged. By and large, it amounts to saying that these key officials should have qualities of leadership and, more particularly, have a level of motivation which not only provides them the orientation to work in the desired direction but also enthuse others working with them to participate in the venture. However, it may also be added that in case these officials have a rural background and orientation, it may further facilitate their endeavours.

In India, during the initial period of rural development, not much thought seems to have been given to the requirements of the personnel. Most of the officials who had to head the institutions of rural development were expected to bring about certain changes in their thinking, feeling and acting as otherwise, it was felt that, whatever change that is propagated for rural development would not be possible as 'progress is impossible without change, and those who cannot change their minds cannot change anything.' If this should be the guiding principle, then to man development administration, we have to find people who are not only change-prone but also highly adaptable to the changing demands of the job from time to time. For example, when officers were largely drawn from the Revenue Departments of the Government to man the development organizations, it was found that whatever had been learnt in bureaucratic administration was transmitted to the development administration without any regard to its applicability. In view of this, it was observed the inhabitants of the present administrative set-up were hesitant to change.

Every organization that is big enough will develop a bureaucracy. A bureacracy is a form of social organization for administering the affairs of a formal organization. In a sense, bureaucracy can be conceived as a social invention for administering heterogeneous groups of people engaged in a corporate activity. Bureaucratic administration was invented when large formal organizations were developed, bringing together mixed groups of people with dissimilar backgrounds to perform a complex, co-ordinated task. The tremendously swollen bureaucratic apparatus, which seems to be safe from public criticism, develops unpleasant features, and the machinery has an inbound tendency to entrench itself and to perpetuate itself for its own sake.

Some of the qualities of the bureaucracy are impartiality, objectivity, efficiency and impersonality, whatever may be the qualities that are associated with bureaucracy, the tendency of the bureaucrats to be influenced by social values, family and kinship ties, loyality to the class, caste, linguistic groups, etc., is not only imperative, but at times, comes into conflict with their administrative roles. However, in development administration, it was expected of the inhabitants of this system to change their orientation from the original rule and procedure-centred (ritualistic) to people and goal-centred (innovative) behaviour.

We may conceive of administration, structurally, as a hierarchy of subordinate-superordinate relationships within an 'administration' system. Functionally, this hierarchy of relationship is the locus for allocating and integrating roles, and facilities in order to achieve the goals of the administrative system. It is here, in these relationships, that the arrangements of status, provision of facilities, organization of procedure, regulation of activity, and evaluation of performance take place (Bennis, Benne and Robert, 1964).

Administration is always operative in an interpersonal social relationship that makes the nature of this relationship a crucial factor in the administrative process. An administrative system is conceived here as involving two classes of phenomena: (1) the institution with certain roles and expectations that will fulfil the goals of the system; and (2) the individuals inhabiting the system with certain personalities and need dispositions. The observed interactions between the two comprise what we generally call social behaviours (Bennis, Benne and Robert, 1964) .

This social behaviour may be understood as a function of these major elements, viz., institution, roles and expectations, which together constitute the nomothetic or normative dimension of activity in a social system, and the individual, personality and need dispositions, that constitute the idiographic or personal dimension of activity in a social system. The interactional relationship between these two demands, organizational on the one hand and individual on the other, can be expressed as follows (Bennis, Benne and Robert, 1964):

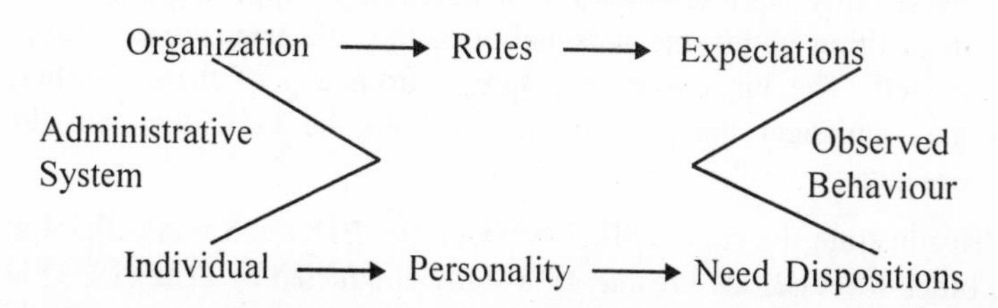

The proportion of role and personality factors determining behaviour will, of course, vary with the specific act, the specific role and the specific personality involved. In any case, however, whether the proportion tends towards one end or the other, behaviour, in so far as it is social, remains a function of both role and personality, although in different degrees. When role is maximized, behaviour still retains some personal aspect. When personality is maximized, social behaviour still cannot be free from role prescription (Bennis, Benne and Robert, 1964).

In any job, more so among the Block Development Officers (BDOs), specification of their role expectations are very important. These role (job) expectations serve as a guiding factor for their job performance. For example, the role of the BDO and the non-official (elected representative of the people) functioning at the block level are supposed to be complementary roles in the Indian set-up of development administration. In a sense, a role is a prescription not only for the given role incumbent, but also for the incumbents in other roles within the organization, so that, in a hierarchical setting, the expectations of one role may to some extent, also or the expectations for a second interlocking role. Inadequate understanding of the role or personality may lead to conflict, affecting one's performance on the job. There can be three types of conflicts resulting from this aspect (Bennis, Benne and Robert, 1964):

1. Role-personality conflict occurs as a function of discrepancies between the pattern of expectations of a given role and the pattern of need-disposition (motivations) characteristic of the role incumbent.
2. Role conflict occurs whenever a role incumbent is required to conform simultaneously to a number of expectations which are mutually exclusive, contradictory or inconsistent, so that adjustment to one set of requirements makes adjustment to the other impossible or, at least, difficult. Role conflicts are the result of the given situation, independent of the personality of the incumbent.
3. Personality conflict occurs as a function of opposing needs and disposition within the personality of the role incumbent himself/herself. The incongruence resulting from any of these conflicts may endanger the productivity or both the individual and the organization.

To illustrate the role conflict between the BDO and non-official at the block level (Block President), a study conducted by Fritz (1973) in Karnataka (a southern state of India) may be cited. The study aimed to investigate the evolution of roles of the BDO and the non-official (President) in the block organization of the local self-government in order to find out whether or not incumbents of these roles in the block organization have evolved common informal role expectations for their roles and relations. The items on which their opinions were sought in terms of who is mainly responsible for taking decisions are: locations of a project or scheme in a block, supervision of extension staff, use of the block jeep, preparation of budget of the block, preparation of agenda for meetings of the block panchayat, organization of special programmes, and selection of a contractor for undertaking works in the block.

The results revealed that the maximum institutionalization (i.e., a greater differentiation of roles of official and non-official in development administration have become formalized) of roles had occurred in selection of location of projects or schemes, followed by supervision of extension staff. The least institutionalized function was choosing a contractor. A moderate degree of institutionalization was found in the remaining functions as in each, both sets of respondents (BDOs and Presidents of the panchayat at block level) tended to see these functions as either joint responsibilities or as administrative responsibilities. This result, by and large, suggests the need for institutionalization of roles for the block-level functionaries like the President of the block level local self-government body and the BDO, so that the confusion and conflict resulting from perceived overlap of roles can be averted. Wherever joint responsibility had been mentioned for any of the functions, it is at best a safeguard than an attitude in order to foster a better work atmosphere. Therefore, proper identification and differentiation of one's job roles is a prerequisite for developing a better orientation to work.

PERSONALITY

A study was undertaken to assess the personality factors of 225 BDOs (Supervisors-Coordinators at the block level) spread over three states of the Indian Union (Muthayya and Kanna,1973). The personality factors studies were dominance, emotional stability, empathy, need achievement, ego ideal, introversion, self-confidence, dogmatism, pessimism and social intelligence. In comparison with the other subordinate functionaries in the block, the BDOs were found to be less dominant, more emotionally stable, more emphathetic, high in need achievement, average in ego ideal, extraverted, less pessimistic, more self-confident, more dogmatic, and more socially intelligent. By and large, the personality of the BDOs studies was positively-oriented. This study suggests that being endowed with a positvely-oriented personality is a basic requirement for one engaged in development administration. However, it is not possible to offer an explanation for the BDOs positively-oriented personality compared with other functionaries, as personality is a measure of the consistent manner in which an individual reacts to the expectations of his environment.

Personality Characteristics and Job Satisfaction

The job satisfaction of these 225 BDOs was studied through a questionnaire which is arbitrarily classified into three aspects—job, personal and interpersonal. The job aspect covered information on pay, work opportunity, lack of technical know-how, promotional opportunities, facilities for work, over or low workload, conflicting work roles, monotony of work, work-expectation of superiors, and authority vested on the job. All these aspects were measured through seventeen items. The personal aspect included ten items and covered information on feelings of inadequacy, security, non-acceptance in the department, under-employment, desire to change the job, and lack of authority and belief in the programme. The interpersonal aspect consisted of seven items covering information on perceived apathy of people towards the programmes, political interference and pressures of one's work and attitude of superior officers.

Dissatisfaction was found to be more on the job aspect, followed by the interpersonal and personal aspects. This result revealed that job demands and avenues for its fulfillment are limited, giving rise to feelings of dissatisfaction and, perhaps, affecting one's motivation to work. There were 36.9 per cent of the BDOs who were highly satisfied on the job, 37.8 per cent were moderately satisfied, and 23.3 per cent were less satisfied. As for their satisfaction with facilities in the work situation, cost of living in the work place, cost of housing, absence of recreational facilities for children and adults, and housing facility were mentioned. This suggests that the absence of certain facilities for the self and the family could also contribute to job dissatisfaction *vis-a-vis* motivation.

It was found that those BDOs who were in the higher age group (43 years and above) were less educated, belonged to a nuclear family, had less than three children, had an annual income between Rs. 5,000 and Rs. 9,000, had held three to four jobs before and had belonged to agricultural families were satisfied on the job. The latter factor reveals that need for a rural background for development personnel is important not only to remain satisfied but also to maintain a certain degree of motivation in work. Similarly, the BDOs who were highly satisfied on the job were self-confident, emotionally stable, optimistic, sociable and socially intelligent.

In a study of Administrative Officers of different development departments, it was found that these officers were relatively introverted (less sociable) and emotionally stable. The upper middle level officers were more extraverted (sociable) but emotionally unstable, whereas the lower middle level officers were less extraverted but more emotionally stable (Muthayya, 1969).

A study on the perceived need satisfaction on the job among administrative officers of development departments revealed that those with needs for self-actualization and autonomy were perceived to be less satisfied on their job. The needs in which greater dissatisfaction was expressed among introverts (less sociable) were self-actualization and autonomy, whereas among extraverts (sociable) these were self-actualization and social needs. Those who were emotionally stable, had expressed dissatisfaction in social and autonomy needs, whereas those who were emotionally less stable had expressed dissatisfaction in needs for security, esteem and self-actualization (Muthayya, 1970).

A study of personality orientation of officers (Muthayya, 1975) associated with command area development projects, revealed that task orientation was the most predominant personality orientation followed by self-orientation. The self-oriented personality style is characterized by an emphasis on self-esteem, status, or other personal gains of this sort. Such an individual is socially bold, egoistic, desirous of self-expression, etc. The task-oriented person depends on the particular goals of the group, and tries his best to help obtain group goals, solves its problems, overcomes barriers preventing the successful completion of the group tasks and persists at his/her assignment until success is achieved. A people-oriented person is concerned with the group as a means for forming friendships, sharing things with others, providing the security of belonging, and, also, fostering strong interpersonal relationships. In development administration, the administrator's need to have a higher proportion of task, and people-centred orientations, and less of self-orientation.

A study was undertaken to assess the hopes and fears of administrative officers (Muthayya, 1969). The majority of administrative officers associated with development departments had expressed their hopes for reduction in the cost of living, self-sufficiency and contentment in life, and also for providing sufficient education for children. Fears expressed were related to family worries, and lack of opportunity for advancement. As for hopes for the nation, the majority of the officers had expressed hopes for honest and self-reliant government, and economic and social advancement. With regard to fears for the country, deterioration in the state of affairs, and corruption and dishonesty were mentioned. As for the influence of personal factors on one's hopes and fears for the self and the country, it was found that occupational level, level of monthly income, and years of experience on the job, to some extent, determine the nature of one's fears and hopes.

In another study among 12 BDOs, Muthayya (1970) assessed the job-related tension index, and the results suggested that job tension was prevalent to a considerably lesser extent among these BDOs. The job aspects in which tension was expressed to a great extent were lack of required authority or a sense of autonomy, too much workload, incompatiable demands by different reference groups (higher officials/non-officials), dearth of required information (communication), taking action against one's convictions, and, finally, lack of a sense of achievement in one's job.

Muthayya and Vijayakumar (1984) in another study found that the most dissatisfied needs among the administrative officers were self-actualization and autonomy. There was no influence of personal data on the perceived need satisfaction. The most frequently perceived subjective job characteristics were difficulty in assessing individual contribution, followed by unpredictability. This was also found to be the trend across the compared groups based on different personal characteristics. Significant interrelationships were found between most of the perceived needs. Many of the interrelationships between the different job characteristics were not found to be significant. As for the interrelationships between perceived need satisfaction and job characteristics; significant and positive correlations were found between self-actualization and discretion, social need and work interdependence, esteem and discretion, and negative but significant correlations were found between social need and discretion; esteem and work inter-dependence; security and difficulty in assessing individual contri-butions; and, autonomy and discretion.

In another study, Muthayya and Vijayakumar (1985) found that autonomy and self-actualization needs were the most dissatisfied ones among the administrative officers while their predominant leadership orientation was task-orientation. Further, they found that the higher the task-orientation of these officers, the lesser the dissatisfaction in the needs of esteem and self-actualization, whereas the higher the interaction orientation, the higher the dissatisfaction in autonomy, esteem, and self-actualization needs, the higher the self-orientation, the lesser the level or dissatisfaction in autonomy needs.

In another study of Integrated Rural Development Programme (IRDP) Personnel and Lead Bank Managers (LBMS) in relation to the personal and social backgrounds, job satisfaction, personality attributes, and leadership styles, the following findings were reported (Muthayya and Vijayakumar, 1985a):

1. Personal and Social Characteristics: The mean age of the officials was 42 years; the Project Officers (POs) as well as the LBMs had a lower mean age of 38 and 40 years, respectively, and the Assistant Project Officers (APOs) and BDOs had a mean age of 43 years. Most of the officials and LBMs were graduates, though 60 per cent of the POs were postgraduates, and 12 per cent had some professional degree. The majority of the officials and LBMs had more than 16 years of service, except in the case of a few POs, who had an experience of 5 years or less. Most of these officials and LBMs had attended one course or the other oriented to subject-matter specialization, or refresher courses concerned with development of certain skills. These officials, as well as the LBMs generally mentioned a large number of problems in their occupations, which were administrative in nature. The administrative problems generally mentioned were the bureaucratic attitude of superior officials, inadequate staff/personnel, irregularity in the release of funds, too much workload, lack of co-ordination with other departments, ineffective feedback of schemes implemented, frequent transfers, lack of administrative powers, and more responsibility with less infrastructural facilities. These problems, by and large, seemed to have affected their job performance, more particularly, in the implementation of the IRDP.

2. Job Satisfaction: The POs as well as the LBMs, were less dissatisfied on the job than the APOs and BDOs who had an equal level of dissatisfaction. Job dissatisfaction was found to be more in the job aspect (covering mostly the different administrative functions) than on the personal and interpersonal aspects. In all these different aspects of job dissatisfaction, the POs were less dissatisfied than the APOs and BDOs. In other words, the POs were generally satisfied with their job compared to their subordinate officers involved in IRDP. Some of the problems mentioned earlier generally cover the job aspect and, hence, the dissatisfaction with the job aspect can usually influence their job performance.

   As for satisfaction with the physical and social facilities at the place of work, the LBMs, followed by the POs, were more satisfied than the APOs and BDOs. The type of facilities, and their accessibility and availability, particularly in relation to the hygiene factor contributed to their satisfaction with the job situation though it may not have motivated them. However, dissatisfaction with these facilities might have contributed to maladjustment to the job, and affected their job performance.

3. Personality Variables: The personality of the officials was studied using a questionnaires assessing nine variables, viz., empathy, ego-ideal, pessimism, introversion, neuroticism, need-achievement, self-confidence, dogmatism and dominance. The LBMs, compared with the officials, more particularly with the POs, were found to be higher on empathy, ego-ideal, need-achievement and self-confidence, and lower on introversion, pessimism, neutroticism, dogmatism and dominance. The POs compared with the APOs and BDOs were more empathetic, less pessimistic, less dogmatic, more in ego-ideal than BDOs, less introverted on par with the BDOs, more emotionally stable than the APOs, higher on need-achievement than the BDOs, and less in self-confidence, less dogmatic and less dominant than the BDOs. Between APOs and BDOs, the APOs were less empathetic, more in ego-ideal, more pessimistic, more introverted, emotionally more unstable, higher on need-achievement, low on self-confidence, more dogmatic and less dominant.

   Generally, it was found that the LBMs and POs had a fairly positive personality disposition (the former exceeding the latter) compared with the APOs and BDOs; the BDOs, in turn, had a fairly positive personality disposition than the APOs. However, both the APOs and BDOs, who belonged to a higher age group and also had more than 16 years of service, seemed to have a personality disposition which does not contribute to the dynamism, by being more pessimistic, more dominant, more dogmatic, and less empathetic, etc. Between APOs and BDOs, the latter were endowed with a more positive personality than the former. One may, therefore, conclude that the personality disposition of the POs is generally in keeping with the expectations of IRDP and, hopefully, they might be in a position to manage the implementation of the programme as effectively as envisaged. However, the supporting functionaries in the IRDP, being not endowed with a similar personality disposition, contribute more to the difficulties in its implementation.

4. Leadership Styles: The leadership styles were assessed using a questionnaire consisting of the five styles, namely direction, delegation, consultation, negotiation and participation. It was found that the predominant leadership style among all the officials as well as the LBMs was 'direction', followed by 'delegation' and 'participation' among the LBMs, POs and APOs, and 'consultation' and 'participation' among the BDOs. In case the IRDP is concevied as a participative effort involving a large number of officials, the predominant style of direction may not bring about the required level of interaction among the concerned officials and bankers, thus affecting the co-ordination required in managing the different functions relating to the programmes. However, this predominant style, being followed by delegation and participation, might make room for a flexible leadership style contingent to the situation and, thereby, one may say that these officials and bankers have the required leadership style to manage the implementation of the programme. It would have been, perhaps, desireable if these officials and bankers had consultation and participation as the predominant leadership styles, so that the involvement of the people as well as the officials for co-ordinative efforts in the implementation of the programmes would have been facilitated to a large extent.

In a study of personality assessment of extension personnel (Block Extension officers and village level workers) covering 100 extension officers and 345 village level workers in five states of the Indian Union, Muthayya and Singh (1992) found that extension officers, as compared with the village level workers could be characterized as dominant, emotionally stable, empathetic, low on need-achievement, less in ego-ideal, less introverted, more pessimistic, low in self-confidence, less dogmatic, and less in social intelligence. The personality qualities that were most needed for extension personnel are self confidence, need-achievement, social intelligence, emotional stability, optimism and sociability.

It is, therefore, suggested that whenever important programmes are to be implemented, selection of personnel, from those available needs to be made, should be on the basis of their personality assessment. Secondly, whenever training programmes are organized for these personnel, their personality should be made in order to evolve methods for personality change.

CONCLUSIONS

A question, therefore, arises about the possibilities to bring about changes in the present administrative set-up to make it development oriented, and also to find incumbents who would further the goals of this administrative system. The following changes are suggested:

1. Structural Changes of the Administration: A system should be evolved which encourages group discussion and participation without being influenced by hierarchy and other administrative constraints as is prevalent in the present system. It may not be out of place here to quote the results of a study that was conducted among the participants of the orientation courses conducted at NIRD over a period of twelve months. Sixty-six government officers of various occupational levels were asked an open-ended question to list out their occupational problems. The problems mentioned by them were analysed for content, and were classified broadly into the following categories.
   (a) Personal: Personal problems were related to self-inadequacies, worries (financial, promotion), inadequate freedom, and inability to adjust to the changing demands of one's work.
   (b) Interpersonal: Interpersonal problems were related to dealing with people's apathy, enlisting people's participation, changing

motivation, non-officials–officials relationships and conflicts and political party pressures and interferences.

(c) Administrative: This category included problems related to authority, decision-making, indifference of higher officials, lack of official support, procedural inadequacy, problems of co-ordination, confusion in the administration, inadequte and inefficient staff, lack of training opportunities, inadequate role differentiation of co-ordinating departments/persons, heavy workload, and problems connected with supervision and related functions.

(d) Financial/material (official): These problems were concerned with inadequate funds for the programmes, lack of provision for providing basic requirements, lack of timely supplies of inputs and other requirements, lack of market facilities for the products, management of inadequate supply, etc.

This analysis revealed that the officer sample mentioned 151 problems. Among these, administrative problems topped the list (52.3 per cent), followed by interpersonal problems (32.5 per cent) (Table 1).

Table 1

Types of Problems	Frequency	Percent
Personal	15	9.9
Interspersonal	49	32.5
Administrative	79	52.3
Financial/Material (Official)	8	5.3

This suggests that problems connected with administrative process are prevalent to a greater extent, indicating structural constraints needing certain changes.

2. Changes in the rules and procedures: The rules and procedures should be made more flexile and goal-directed. These may include changes in the way people work with each other, the structure of working, manner of communication, methods of problem-solving and decision-making, and the exercise of authority and responsibility.
3. Good selection procedures for the recruitment of the right type of personnel: Personnel to man these organizations should have

such qualities which are on par with the desired leadership functions. It goes without saying that one of the reasons for lack of motivation may be that a person on the job may not be suited to it. To work as a development functionary, one needs to have certain personality attributes, such as (a) abstract intelligence, through which it would be possible for the incumbent on the job to visualize the consequences of his/her actions and help in the decision-making process; (b) Social perception, which would enhance awareness of the feelings, opinions and attitudes of others in the group, and enable the incumbent to know what others think; and (c) Emotional Stability, which is the capacity to view the situations/experiences objectively without giving rise to irrational behaviour. Apart from this, several qualities which have been found to be present to a greater extent among leaders in a variety of situations are: intelligence, adjustment, self-confidence, sociability and empathy. Therefore, it is necessary to take clues from studies on personality among leaders, and use those qualities which are associated with positive endeavour to select officers to man development administration.

4. Training of personnel: Training should orient the personnel to the requirements of the developmental administration. It should not be conceptual but practical in changing their outlook and attitudes. When the demands on the jobs keep changing with the changing emphasis and direction of programmes for rural development, training occupies an important place not only in keeping the individual prepared for the changes brought about, but also in generating the type of attitudes as the job demands. This would indirectly facilitate the growth of motivation in the desired direction. The emphasis of the training programmes should be more on changing the outlook and attitudes of the personnel, rather than simply being an exercise of information-giving. The objective of the training should be to change the ways of doing things, and make the procedures and practices more effective.
5. Creating organization climate: One of the ways in which changes can be brought about in the functioning of the incumbents in the organizations *vis-à-vis* motivation is by organizational development. It is a process that attempts developing organization climate based on behavioural science principles for diagnosing and coping with inadequacies in the organization process. It is a complex education strategy intended to change the beliefs,

attitudes, values and structure of the organization, so that they can better adapt to new technologies and challenges. The commonly sought objectives of organizational development are: (a) improvement in interpersonal competence, (b) a shift in values so that human factors and feelings come to be considered as legitimate, (c) development of increased understanding between and within working groups in order to reduce tensions, (d) development of more effective team management and development of the capacity of functioning groups to work more effectively, and (e) development of better methods of conflict resolution. Rather than the usual methods, which rely mainly on suppression, compromise and unprincipled power, more rational and open methods of conflict resolution are sought. More specifically, the goal is to improve communication, to secure more effective participation from subordinates in problem solving, and to move in the direction of increased openness, feedback and support.

In short, a decision has to be made to change the culture to help the organization to meet its goals, and to provide better avenues for initiative, creativity and self-actualization on the part of the members of the organization. Thus, organizational development process would improve faith among human beings, thereby enriching opportunity for self-actualization and self-motivation.

REFERENCES

Benis, W.G., K.D. Benne, and Robert Chin (1964). *The Planning of Change,* New York: Holt Rinehart & Winston, 297–303, 376–84, 422–31.

Fritz, Dan (1973). 'Evaluation of Official and Non-Official Roles in Mysore State's Panchayati Raj', *Indian Journal of Public Administration,* 19 (2): 163–76.

Muthayya, B.C. and I. Gnana Kanna (1973). *Development Personnel-A Psycho-Social Study Across Three States in India,* Hyderabad: (NICD).

Muthayya, B.C., (1969). 'Some Personal and Personality Factors of Administrative Officers', *Behavioural Sciences and Community Development,* 3(2).

Muthayya, B.C. (1970). 'Personality and Personal Orientations to Certain Aspects of the Life Situation of Administrative Officers', *Behavioural Sciences and Community Development,* 4(1).

Muthayya, B.C. (1969). 'Hopes and Fears of Administrative Officers for Self and the Country', *Behavioural Sciences and Community Development,* 3(2).

Muthayya, B.C. (1970). 'A Study of Job Tensions among Block Development Officers', *Psychology Annual,* 4: 13–17.

Muthayya, B.C. (1972). 'Perceived Need Satisfaction on the Job and its Relation to Personal and Personality Variable', *PACT,* 1(2).

Muthayya, B.C. (1975). 'Perceived Need Satisfaction on the Job and Personality Orientation of the Officers of the Command Area Development Projects', *Behavioural Science and Community Development,* 9(2).

Muthayya, B.C. and S. Vijayakumar (1985a). 'IRDP and Lead Bank Personal: A Psycho-Social Study', *Journal of Rural Development,* 4(1).

Muthayya, B.C. and S. Vijayakumar (1984). 'Perceived Need Satisfaction and Subjective Job Characteristics of Administrative Officers', *Journal of Rural Development,* 3(4).

Muthayya, B.C. and S. Vijayakumar (1985). 'Relationship between Perceived Need Satisfaction and Personality Orientations of Administrative Officers', *Psychological Studies,* 30(1).

Muthayya, B.C. and Vikram Singh (1992). 'Extension Personnel-Personality Assessment', *Mimeograph,* National Institute of Rural Development, Hyderabad.

11 What is it to be High-Neuroticism? Drive, Vigilance, or Personal Memory?

Chris Brand

ABSTRACT

Neuroticism/Emotionality (*n*) is a major dimension of personality variation that has yet to be understood in psychological terms. Here, the correlates, distribution and psychogenetic origins of *n* differences are first reviewed; then three psychological theories of *n* are indicated—involving 'drive', 'vigilance' and 'personal memory' (PM). Evidence from studies in Edinburgh show that more details of personal life-events are available to higher-*n* people: estimates of the extent of young adult memories of their adolescent experiences, such as 'receiving first public examination results' and 'first kiss', correlate at around +0.50 with *n*; and the *n*-PM effect is not attributable to high-*n* people having had less enjoyable experiences. A store of full, unretranscribed personal memories may confer advantages in pursuits where sensitivity to individual experience of key events is expected; and in romantic attachments, where loyalty needs to be demonstrated to a partner. Higher levels of *n* may be advantageous in combination with higher intelligence—leading to artistic creativity; and low *n* (in combination with reasonable intelligence) may yield the more distinctly scientific and politico-military attainments of other individuals and nations.

INTRODUCTION

In 1765, R. Whytt made what was perhaps the first record of the particular covariation of human characteristics that was to underpin the concept of 'nervous sensibility'. In his *Observations on the Nature, Causes and Cure of those Disorders which are called Nervous,* Whytt linked the reporting of diverse somatic dysfunctions and symptoms with complaints of mood fluctuations and irritability (Fahrenberg, 1992). Eventually, neuroticism (*n*)—as emotionality was to be somewhat insensitively titled by later psychometrician-psychologists—was quantified by researchers in Holland and London some eighty years ago. In ratings (Heymans and Wiersma, 1909; Burt, 1915; Webb, 1915[1]), *n* distinguished tense and troubled children and adults in a way that was largely independent of other personality variations like extraversion–introversion. Following Woodworth's (1919) development of a 'maladjustment' questionnaire, individual differences in self-reported intensity, and frequency of emotions and moods (especially of the less agreeable varieties) have remained central to differential psychology (e.g., Schonell, 1948: 21; Brand, 1984; Eysenck and Eysenck, 1985). For many years the best-known psychometric variants of *n* were those of Eysenck (1947), Taylor (1953), and Cattell and Scheier (1963)[2].

The Psychometry of *n*

The *n* dimension readily appears in surveys of psychopathology in the general population: Friedman and Booth-Kewley's (1987) review of 101 studies of personality and disease noted the connections between 'depression, anger/hostility, anxiety and possibly other aspects of personality' that would license talk of *generic* proneness to psychosomatic complaints. At both, the empirical and theoretical levels, Luteijn and Bouman (1988) remark that 'the concepts of depression, anxiety and neuroticism are closely linked and hard to demarcate from each other'; and Fujita (1993) found that 'neuroticism and negative affect were indistinguishable at the latent trait level.' Because of pervasive inter-correlation, individual differences in experiences of strong emotion are invariably found in survey work (Gotlib, 1984; Bagozzi, 1993), and currently constitute the best agreed factorial dimension among the 'Big Five-or-Six' dimensions of personality.[3] Higher *n* scores go to people who report themselves, across a range of positively-correlated items, as moody, nervous, easily-stressed, sensitive, passionate, and as having lighter and longer sleep and more dreams[4]; while low-*n* scorers profess stability, confidence, self-esteem, balance, emotional self-control, and relative infrequency of strong emotional experience. Eysenck and Gudjonsson (1989) expect high-*n* people to be depressed, tense, irrational, shy, moody and emotional, and to suffer from low self-esteem and guilt feelings. Measures of general psychological distress correlate substantially with *n* (Waston and Pennebaker, 1989; Wilson, Deary and Malan, 1988, 1991)[5].

Levels of *n* seem higher in art students, children of higher 'musicality'[6], creative painters and sculptors, ballet dancers, actors, musicians, designers, operatic sopranos and tenors, novelists[7], and first-rank philosophers[8] (e.g., Götz and Götz, 1973; Eysenck and Eysenck, 1975: 24–5; Scharfstein, 1981; Prentky, 1980; Wilson, 1984; Bakker, 1988; Wilson and Marchant-Haycox, 1993; Eysenck, 1994); and *n* correlates with extravagant intensity of romantic experience.[9] However, such news seems to bring little cheer to high-*n* scorers themselves. Higher-*n* people normally dislike, and think they would rather do without the 'negative', or, at least, the rather overpowering aspects of *n*—notably, the tendency to swing easily into the four dysphoric mood-states of depression, anxiety, fatigue/boredom and hostility/mistrust. Variability of mood is undoubtedly central to *n*: it correlates very strongly with *n* (e.g., Cameron, 1975; Williams, 1981, 1993) and yields as highest-loaded for *n* the item, 'My moods often go up or down, with or without apparent reason.' It comes as no surprise to high-*n* scorers that high-*n* characterizes psychiatric patients and other groups of unhappy and discontented people. Many high-*n* people themselves think they would prefer the lower *n*-levels found in scientists, welfare officers, police, military aircrew and bomb disposal officers (Eysenck and Eysenck, 1975; Goorney, 1970; Burbeck and Furnham, 1984; Hallam and Rachman, 1980).

While *n* levels are plainly evident to the testees themselves (thus yielding scales having good internal reliabilities), *n* is a rather 'private' variable on which raters often disagree (e.g., Watson, 1989). It is even hard to tell whether people seen daily over seven weeks are high- or low-*n*, except by having them complete standardized questionnaires (Paulhus and Bruce, 1992). Even husbands and wives can be quite surprised to discover 'what it feels like' to be their spouse. Citing several studies attesting the privacy of *n* levels, Borkenau and Ostendorf (1992) remark that 'Neuroticism is the trait....that may be easiest to conceal, even from acquaintances.' Although *n* has only slight negative correlations with measured intelligence (Ley *et al.*,

1966; Crookes *et al.,* 1981), it has often been thought to be associated with some kind of cognitive overload (Hamilton, 1979; Warburton, 1979). Higher-*n* patients often complain of difficulties in concentration, attention learning and memory; and, by objective criteria, they sometimes 'fail to learn information that requires sustained effort or the use of elaborate rather than superficial cognitive operations' (Tariot and Weingartner, 1986)[10], and are somewhat impeded in dual tasks requiring the carrying of heavy short-term memory loads (Macleod and Donnellan, 1993). Females score almost two-thirds of a standard deviation higher than males on many *n* inventories; and, far from this being some peculiarity resulting from a few sex-biased items, it is the items that are traditionally best (factorially) for measuring *n* which show the greatest sex difference (see Francis, 1993). Score distributions on measures of *n* are continuous and bell-shaped, but somewhat positively skewed, thus suggesting the influence of multiple factors plus positive interactions between them. However, it is possible to produce flatter distributions by using ipsative items (e.g., 'Are you best described as calm or passionate?') (Brand and Egan, 1989; Brand, 1994a); and, even though it avoids psychopathological content, this ipsative scale (of sensibility vs. sense) yields in research in Edinburgh, scores that are 1½ standard deviations lower for police officers (mainly male) than for psychology students (mainly female). There are also marked national and/or racial differences in *n*. (Quite the most wide-ranging report is that of Lynn (1971), who used both questionnaire data and criteria such as suicide rates and consumption of caffeine and carbohydrates[11]; Kline (1979) summarizes data from Cattel's questionnaires; and Vernon (1982) especially considers Asians in North America.) Apparently, *n* levels are relatively high in Austria, India, Italy, Germany, Hungary and Japan, and also in North American Asians; while they are generally low throughout the one-time 'White Commonwealth', including Ireland and the USA. Such are the more outstanding, objectively established generalizations about psychometric *n*.

THE PSYCHOGENETICS OF *n*

Can high-*n* be traced to conventionally intelligible origins, for example, to physical handicaps, unhappy childhoods, failed relationships, or major life stresses? Many psychological aspirants would think it likely that sexual unattractiveness, exam failures, jiltings, unemployment, being taken hostage, or living through a nuclear power disaster would increase unhappiness, moodiness, and *n* levels. However, despite a half-century of social-environmentalists' enthusiasm in psychology, there is no systematic evidence of such causation, as is also evident from the following observations:

1. Sometimes correlations between personality and life-stresses are simply so low as to rule out environmental causation: for example, *n* estimates show no demonstrable association with major stressors like bankruptcy (Chown, 1984), learning that one is infertile (Edelman and Connolly, 1986), living in a high-bomb-damage area in the 1939–45 War, or living through the Northern Irish 'Troubles' (Richman, 1993).
2. Sometimes correlations between situation and symptomatology need reintepretation in view of the additional influence of personality. Thus, people who seem to be suffering unhappiness because of a broken marriage or 'mid-life crisis' have usually been high-*n* and unhappy for many years *preceding* their current problems (Costa and McCrae, 1980). From their classic study in working-class South London, Brown and Harris (1978) reported that mild depressive tendencies could be traced statistically to interaction effects between personality and life stresses. However, many of their supposed 'stresses' (and interactions between them) would themselves have resulted from and reflected personological influences (e.g., unemployment, being single, having several children).[12] Bolger and Schilling (1991) observe that 'Neuroticism may lead to distress through exposing people to a greater number of stressful events, through increasing their reactivity to those events, or through a mechanism unrelated to environmental events....' in 339 persons studied over six weeks, they found: 'exposure and reactivity to....minor stressors explained over 40 per cent of the distress differences between high- and low-neuroticism subjects. Reactivity to stressors accounted for twice as much of the distress difference as exposure to stressers.' Even post-traumatic stress disorder is 30 per cent heritable (True *et al.,* 1993) and symptoms can owe as much to sufferers' heavy drinking as to the original stress itself (Cohen, 1994).
3. Unhappy and unloving homes in childhood are quite often reported to have been experienced by less happy and higher-*n* people; but even this remote association does not itself establish

the direction of causation. Today, fulfilling the promise of Bell's (1968) suggestion that parental behaviour is much influenced by children themselves, Plomin *et al.* (1994) report that, even when identical twins are reared *apart,* there are detectable similarities in parental handling and parental relationships that are not attributable to socio-economic similarities between homes.[13] A child's home nurture will reflect the child's own nature.

4. To date, psychogenetic research into *n* (by twin[14] and adoption study[15]) shows (as for most other personality traits) the following developmental contributions:
   (a) a clear heritable component, accounting for some 35 per cent of phenotypic variance;
   (b) a mere 5 per cent contribution from imposed environmental similarities (which should make siblings more similar when they grow up together);
   (c) evidence of genetic-genetic interaction (i.e., of *epistatic* gene packaging) which makes monozygotic twins (r = 0.45) markedly more similar than dizygotic twins (r = 0.15), even though the moderate monozygotic correlation means that the overall broad heritability could not possibly exceed a correlation of 0.40; and
   (d) much remaining variance to be explained, perhaps by within-family factors that push children apart, such as sibling rivalry (see Brand, 1989, 1995) or idiosyncratic parental favouritism, and abuse (beyond those preferences and practices that are triggered by children's own *n* levels).

THE PSYCHOLOGY OF *n*

What, then, is to be made of the psychology of *n*? Whatever the remote developmental origins of *n* differences, are there any real, enduring, underlying differences in *abilities* or *propensities* between high- and low-*n* people? Some three main theories of *n* seem to have attracted modern scientific investigators, as follows:

1. One idea is that *n* is a *drive*-like variable which affects performance and learning, while being sometimes opposed by efforts at suppression or repression. This idea may be traced both to psychoanalytic orgins[16] and to the Yerkes-Dodson Law specifying the general advantage of

moderate levels of emotional arousal. The drive theory of anxiety (alias *n* with a suffusion of introversion) enjoyed special attention in mainstream differential psychology of the 1960s. Just as the era of strict behaviourism was drawing to a close, the idea that *n*, as a drive, multiplied with habit strengths, was even advanced to explain schizophrenia (Storms and Broen, 1969). At low drive (multiplier effect zero), and with no clear, ordered response hierarchy, performance would be unpredictable. At moderate drive, responses having even slightly distinguishable likelihoods would become more spread out, with the best-learned response in a repertoire now being reliably given, thanks to the multiplicative influence of drive. But at high drive (assuming a ceiling for the multiplicatory power of drive), the responses in the hierarchy would reach asymptote (making them all once more of equivalent probability); and behaviour would thus be unpredictable and confused, except in so far as other (e.g., 'cognitive') principles might be brought into play to resolve 'priority disputes' between response options..

The merit of the drive concept is that it serves to predict superior performance when emotion and motivation are operative and when one simple, 'correct' response is required and readily available (whether by instinct or previous learning). By the same token, this formulation predicts poorer learning under emotion when the situation is complex and when many previously established response options might be relevant. Modest support for the facilitating effect of anxiety on learning, when competing responses are eliminated, was recorded by Hamilton (1979). In recent times, *n* is more commonly linked to the much looser notion of 'arousal' (e.g., Humphrey and Revelle, 1984); and the idea that *n* is specially associated with superior conditioning under both reward and punishment has been the special concern of Gray's work on the rat (e.g., 1987, 1991).[17] In the human psychology laboratory, the idea of memory's partial dependence on emotional state ('state-dependent learning') found particular recognition around 1980 (e.g., Teasdale and Taylor, 1981). Today, laboratory studies of suppression show that heightened arousal and presumptive expenditure of cognitive and emotional resources occur when subjects under experimental instructions try to 'suppress' drive-sponsored thoughts, for example, about sex (Wegner *et al.*, 1991, 1993).

Undoubtedly, a weak feature of the drive approach is the failure of modern psychology to agree as yet on the nature and number of the main states of mood, emotion, drive or motivation. Four main mood contrasts may be ventured (e.g., Brand, 1995[18]) and linked to the other four of the Big Five personality dimensions as follows:

Elation–Depression	probably relates to	Extraversion–Introversion
Confidence–Fear	probably relates to	Will–Subdudeness
Alertness–Fatigue	probably relates to	Control–Casualness
Trust–Hostility	probably relates to	Affection–Cynicism

Figure 1 displays the four dimensions in a two-dimensional space so as to indicate how they sometimes collapse into the broader contrasts of Osgood's Potency and Activity dimensions (see Brand, 1995a).

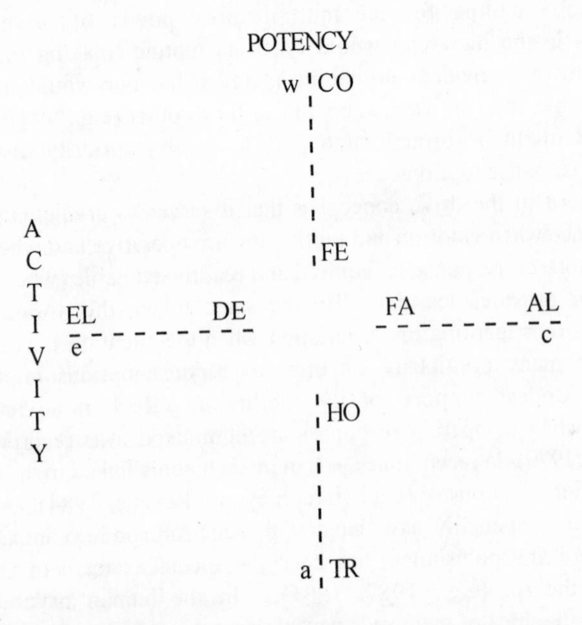

Figure 1 *Shows a specific personality link for each of the four main, specific mood dimensions (see text) while also allowing broader contrasts to be recognized along the lines of Osgood's Potency and Activity factors (see Brand, 1994b). EL = Elation; DE = Depression; FA = Fatigue; AL = Alertness; CO = Confidence; FE = Fear; HO = Hostility; TR = Trust; e = extraversion; c = control; w = will; a = affection.*

However (a) Such a descriptive scheme offers no compelling account of why high-*n* scorers, though more variable in all of these four ways, especially report experiencing the mood states that are less pleasant—towards the centre of Figure 1. (b) It also does not explain why, even at rather high levels of *n*, the unpleasant mood states of anxiety, depression, fatigue and hostility still covary so as to maintain the notable internal consistency of *n* scales. (c) There is obvious role for either suppression or repression, except in so far as some of the mood states are intrinsically less agreeable, and thus more likely to be associated with painful memories.[19] (d) Even if agreement could be envisaged on the 'drives' and drive-related variations underlying and yielding *n* differences between people, it would remain a surprise that many years of work in the drive tradition have not thrown up an agreed finding of any form of human learning, under motivational conditions, at all, at which high-*n* scorers are (to their own surprise as it would be) markedly superior. (e) More generally, the drive theory makes little use of the self-reported variability of high-*n* people.

2. A second theoretical tradition, that of *vigilance,* is to the effect that *n* is a condition of hypersensitivity in which cues to danger are particularly clearly received. Deriving from the ideas of Donald Byrne in the 1960's (e.g., Dana and Cocking, 1969), this tradition gives higher-*n* individuals a better impression as they are 'more in touch with their emotions',even if at the expense of attributing stark insensitivity or repression to low-*n* people. Its strength is the provision of modest confirmatory evidence that high-*n* people are indeed more alert to danger-cues and more likely to concentrate upon them when they appear; and Michael Eysenck (1988) has shown that when the kind of 'repression' associated with sheer hypocrisy (and measurable *via* Lie scales) is controlled, *n* at last shows more than trivial correlations with measures of psycho-physiological arousal. In contrast to undeceitful low-*n* people, high-*n* people are more likely to hear threat-laden homophones, and to devote more processing resources to the ear at which the threat was registered. M.W. Eysenck (1992) thus maintains that higher-*n* people differ not only in higher responsiveness of Gray's 'behavioural inhibition system' but also in 'the amount of processing accorded to threatening stimuli and in the interpretation of ambiguous stimuli and situations.' Thus, high-*n* people are expected to perform poorly on 'working memory' tasks, but to be unimpaired on tasks where only 'automatic' processing is required. However, this account of *n* does not explain why, despite their vigilance, high-*n* individuals should experience internal conflict and uncertainty[20]; it sees *n* as opposed to, or at least reduced by 'repression' (or hypocrisy), whereas

preconscious perceptual defensiveness can be positively associated with *n* (Watt, 1993[21]) (as would be expected of from classical psychoanalytic repression and denial); it does not predict any useful feats of learning or recall, or seem capable of explaining the sometimes glamorous occupational involvements of high-*n* scorers[22]; it neglects that 'working memory', when measured reliably, is largely a matter of general intelligence,[23] in which high-*n* people are only very slightly impaired; and, like the drive theory, Eysenck's model allows no special place for the well-established variability of high-*n* people in mood, behaviour, and laboratory task performance.

3. A third suggestion (Brand, 1984) is that memory, when distinguished from intelligence, is actually central to *n*; and sometimes overloads consciousness when the cognitive resources of a high-*n* person are not ample. Some long-term memories are presumably overlearned and crucial to crystallized intelligence, for example, mathematical formulae, or how to reach Orly airport from Saint Sulpice. But others, for the details of on-off experiences, and the events of one's life, are chiefly of personal significance. The function of retaining the details of such experiences would presumably be that they provide unique, personally relevant, temporally ordered data for which no simpler, conclusive summary ('She beat me', 'I loved him') is yet possible or adequate.

Research into the Memory Hypothesis

Although Freud and Breuer (1896) were the first to nominate a group of clinically neurotic patients (*viz.*, hysterics) as suffering 'mainly from reminiscences'. Mueller (1976) furnished the first relevant evidence from objective testing. Mueller found high-*n* people to show relatively good recall of less organized, acoustic material that they had not clustered into general semantic categories (the normal way of winning memory advantages in the psychological laboratory). Following Crick and Mitchison's (1993) suggestion that unlearning (e.g., *via* random brain stimulation during the night) might be a source of individual differences related to sleep and dreaming, high-*n* people (who are often light and restless sleepers) might be envisaged to retain more fully the details of daily experience. Over time, they might thus be compared to computer programme writers who add 'loops' rather than re-write their programmes. Such retention of old association and routines may sometimes be valuable; but it will add unpredictablity to the functioning of the system, which will become progressively harder to understand or modify (Brand, 1984).

Following up Mueller's result, Deary (1984) began investigations in Edinburgh into the hypothesis that high-*n* subjects especially store task-irrelevant material that may either enrich or disrupt propositional recall. Deary compared high- and low-*n* subjects for their recall of a dense, detailed 400-word 'story', in which relations between characters were summarily presented. (Thirty student subjects, of both sexes, were selected from the top and bottom thirds of the distribution on Cattel and Scheir's (1963) IPAT Anxiety Scale.) Although high-*n* subjects remembered less systematically and less effectively in terms of the pre-established experimental categories regarding what had truly 'happened' in the story, they took markedly more time in free recall ($r = 0.58$, $p < 0.01$) and provided more 'irrelevant' detail, especially about the relationships between the characters ($r = 0.53$, $p < 0.01$). Rather as Mueller had found, but in a quite different experimental paradigm, the high-*n* subjects formed and retained more associations even at the expense of overrearching cognitive schematizations that usually make for strict correctness of recall. Deary also observed a strong association between *n* and common Cognitive Failures ('forgetting what one is looking for', 'putting salt into one's coffee': see Broadbent *et al.*, 1982), suggesting what the everyday effects of routinely carrying a memory overload might be for high-*n* people.[24]

Following the hunch that non-specific, idiosyncratic memory and associations might be enhanced in high-*n* people, Flona Mair (1987) tape-recorded 48 friends and relatives (26 males, 22 females; aged 18–64 years) as they responded to six requests for recall and description. It was hoped that at least some information of each required type would be available to all subjects, so the six requests were as follows:

Describe your childhood room.
Name your primary school teachers.
Describe what was your usual route to secondary school.
Describe your first day at your first-ever job.
Recite the longest poem, quotation or prayer that you know.
Describe what you are wearing at the moment.

In line with the association hypothesis, the length of time for which the testees spoke[25] correlated at +0.45 ($p < 0.001$) with *n*. That the high-*n* 'advantage' was with more personal material was suggested by their having marginally less to say than the low-*n* testees when asked to recite anything they knew by heart ($r = -0.05$, n.s.) However, it could still have been that *n* was somehow linked to talkativeness more than to memory, for *n* correlated at +0.47 with response length to the 'clothes' item—almost as highly as with the best of the questions about past history ('first day in first job', $r = +0.48$). Also, the personal presence of the experimenter could conceivably have influenced results; if, for example, she had somehow gratified any tendency of the higher-*n* testees to say more in response to reassurance or reward.[26] Nevertheless, there is no established empirical generalization in psychology that links *n* to sheer talkativeness, so the 'clothes' item may equally have been tapping richness of personal associations and how much the high-*n* subjects' clothes 'meant to them'. Further research under altered conditions was clearly necessary, if only to ensure that the +0.45 correlation did not reflect some quirk of this unusual testing arrangement. However, it seemed well worth continuing with an 'association' hypothesis, and especially with a version linking *n* to relatively personal memory (PM). If high-*n* people have enhanced PM, this would at once address: (a) the difficulty that high-*n* subjects have in changing their thoughts (and habits); and (b) the variability and unpredictability of mood (and behaviour) that are such central features of *n* (not least to the patients whose own 'fear of fear' and uncertainty are acknowledged parts of their syndromes; see Rachman, 1994; Marks and deSilva, 1994). While allowing the possibilities envisaged by 'drive' and 'vigilance' theorists, to invoke PM as central to *n,* may especially capture (c) the oft-hypothesized cognitive overload. Again, PM differences look promising as explanations of (d) the special association of high-*n* with skill and creativity in the arts. Whereas it is important that members of the uniformed services carry out their duties exactly as instructed, without idiosyncrasy, it is precisely the unique contribution of the human individual, drawing on rich and seldom repeated experiences of complex emotion, that is often expected in the arts. (e) More prosaically, demand for a good memory for particular, 'one-off' details could explain why female receptionists and shop assistants have the highest *n* scores recorded for any occupational group (Eysenck and Eysenck, 1975); for such jobs seem to require especially good recall of many fast-changing local details (of customers and physical objects) that will seldom have wider significance.[27] Such are the advantages of a 'memory' hypothesis that goes beyond the more familiar notion that high-*n* people might have better recall of events that are particularly *aversive*.[28]

Aiming to repeat and extend Mair's research, Wagstaff (1994) and the present author asked young adults to provide written answers concentrating on *what actually happened* on particular 'first' occasions that they were all likely to have experienced. The three selected events were:

The day you received your first important examination results.
The first day at your most recent job.
The day of your first kiss.

For eighteen police officers (15 males, 3 females; aged 21–33 years; all university graduates), allowed a half hour in conditions of group testing, the correlation of total words written (to all three questions) with *n* was +0.47, with the highest single correlation (+0.61) being for the 'exam' question. For eighteen psychology students (8 males), 10 females, aged 19–30 years), given the questions to complete individualy, usually at home, the correlation for total words with *n* was +0.82, and again, the highest single correlation (+0.74) involved the 'exam' question.[29] The *n*-PM correlation did not depend on whether the testees' experiences had been predominantly positive or negative: the higher recall of high-*n* testees was not due to their reporting conspicuously more unpleasant 'first' experiences (about which their reports might have been complaining at greater length).[30]

With the psychology students, Wagstaff also administered the Wechsler Memory Test Battery, and did find a tendency ($r = +0.45$, n.s., $p < 0.1$) for higher-*n* subjects to have better Wechsler memories; however, Wechsler memory was unrelated to PM. Wagstaff further observed that the student records showed strong evidence of more emotion words and phrases (both positive and negative) being used overall by higher-n student testees. (median $r = +0.56$); however, this effect was only found at a significant level for the 'exam' question in the police sample (median $r = 0.00$). To illustrate the overall *n*-PM correlation, here are the records of two extreme subjects who contributed to the positivity of the correlation in their recall of all three experiences.[31] One, a low-*n*-scorer had furnished the following account of his first exam results:

> I remember awaiting the envelope to be delivered, with my own handwriting of the address which had been completed some time before. Trepidation not knowing what they would be, there was some pleasure in having passed so many but disappointment on the grades. Maybe some feeling of anticlimax after it was over.

The other, a high-*n* female, supplied a much fuller account:

> Our family had just returned from a holiday in France, we had driven up from Dover, and due to a puncture it was about two in the morning before we reached Dundee. We were all very tired. There were piles of mail on the kitchen table for each of us. My bundle was quite big because I had a birthday whilst in France and there were loads of cards waiting for me. At the bottom of the pile was a big brown envelope which would contain the results of my Highers. These were my first important exam results, because they would determine my University choices. I can remember Mum and Dad being amazed that I didn't open any of my mail, but went straight to bed. Next morning, bright eyed and bushy tailed, I opened all my mail and got 2 A's and 3 B's much to my delight. My thinking was that I had already had my birthday and that I couldn't do anything about my grades, so it would be better to open them all when I was awake enough to enjoy the moment.

Further examination of *n* and PM undertaken by McNamara (1995). Here, subjects (mainly medical students) were asked to provide information about the following two items:

Your childhood room.
Your first day in your first-ever job.

Instructions especially included a required for 'memorable events' and 'particular incidents'.[32] Seventeen subjects (9 males, 8 females) wrote their responses at home; their combined total words averaged 383 (s.d. 77). Sixteen subjects (8 males, 8 females) were interviewed (including 'gentle prompting') by McNamara, having their responses recorded on a portable cassette recorder; and the total time for which they spoke averaged 219 seconds (s.d. 36). Subsequently, all 33 subjects completed a Short Form of the Eysenck Personality Questionnaire Revised (Eysenck *et al.*, 1985) and had a mean Neuroticism (*N*) score of 5.9 (s.d. 3.0). Analysis by the present author gives correlations between *N* and PM of 0.65 ($p < .01$) and 0.56 (p Ω 0.2) for written and tape-recorded reports respectively; and *N* correlated with the number of specific incidents recalled at 0.40 and 0.50 in the two groups. Lie scores and sex had only slight and quite non-significant correlations with both *N* and memory in these groups. Higher-*N* testees tended to have been more pessimistic in anticipation of their first day at work; but their reports of the day itself were just as happy, on average, as those of the low-*N* scorers. As McNamara observed:

> The fact that the relationship between *n* and the amount of material recalled has been proven again would seem to lend further weight to the

> case for personal memory being inextricably linked with neuroticism as a personality dimension....The qualitative differences of memories appear once again to be the deciding factor in pushing up the total amount recalled. Information concerning names of colleagues, for example, was comparable for individuals at both ends of the *n*.... spectrum. It was the details concerning the precise ordering of childhood rooms and relationships with other individuals which separated the subjects.

Certainly, the *n*-PM effect has turned out to be robust across considerable variations in experimenters, procedures and subjects. With or without any involvement of drive or vigilance, *n* involves enhanced PM.

Whether emotionality (EM) is a *cause* or an *effect* of PM might now be a question to which research could usefully be addressed. To many psychologists, it will seem easier to hypothesize that EM is the primary phenomenon to which, in conjunction with more extreme mood states, enhanced PM is secondary. However, to see PM itself as primary would be compatible with Freud's (e.g., 1896) view that neurosis results from a failure to 'retranscribe' memories during the course of development, resulting in the retention of more primitive and disorganized 'psychic material' from earlier periods.[33] Higher PM would seem likely to yield greater variety and extremes in response options, greater cognitive load, and thus some advantages from suppression and even from classical Freudian repression. At least, it deserves consideration that, over time, EM and PM have reciprocal links such that each potentates the other, thus helping explain the good reliability of *n* scores even though *n* is a variable on which many people wish to change their characteristic levels (usually to lower them). The failure to 'retranscribe' material and release what is no longer strictly needed could presumably result in cognitive overload and increasing unpredictability of behaviour, as envisaged by Freud and by Crick and Mitchison. Above all, making PM central to the psychology of *n* would recognize the distinctive experiential resource that high-*n* people can bring to the world of the arts, so long as they can call on good general intelligence to mitigate cognitive overload.[34] By contrast, the combination of low *n* with high *g* seems more conducive to scientific discovery (see Eysenck, 1994). Notoriously, science does not concern itself with one-off events that cannot be replicated. Involving PM in *n* would also respond to Epstein's (1994) call for recognition by modern psychology not only of rational, *propositional thinking* but also of rapidly made but slow-to-change *narrative associations.* (Whereas differential psychologists cannot escape the need to deal with aspects of personality other than intelligence, modern 'cognitive psychologists' have capriciously ignored emotion and motivation in their focus on 'working memory', when not entirely hypnotized by the bloodless electronic computer.) It was Aristotle who first recognized that thinking is 'particular' as well as 'universal', and that psychology should be concerned with *both* aspects of mentality. Today, psychology's successful exploration of propositional thinking ability in terms of psychometric *g* can perhaps be complemented by researches that link personal narrative richness to emotionality, and to what are, thanks to the empirical endeavours of differential psychologists, the well-established phenomena of psychometric *n*.

Conclusions and Psychotelic Speculations

Three modern psychological accounts of *n* that it especially involves:

1. drive (and reinforcement-responsiveness) (e.g., Gray, 1987, 1991);
2. vigilance (and reallocation of cognitive resources) (e.g., M.W. Eysenck, 1992); or
3. PM and the resulting cognitive overload (e.g., Brand, 1984). Each theory has its own area of purchase on data, though none currently provides any very definite place for the operation of classical repression as an explanatory process. The PM theory now has firm support from several groups of subjects and testing paradigms; it links best to the variability of emotional people by presuming that current mood will trigger state-dependent recall; it offers an explanation of the stronger artistic sensibilities of emotional people; and, by posting a risk of cognitive overload in extreme mood states of *any* kind, it suggests high-*n* people might find quite wide uses for suppression and repression.

An important task for the future will be to explore differential advantages that accrue to high- and low-*n* people—especially in the area of sociosexual endeavour (cf. Buss, 1989, 1994; Barkow, 1991). Several advantages of higher *n* level are as follows:

1. If higher PM reflects unresolved conflict, higher-*n* people might seek conflict resolution and pattern maintenance through the dramatic voyages of emotional recreation that many art forms

provide; high-*n* people may find it reassuring to experience their own emotions being carried forward and resolved satisfactorily thanks to the understanding and expertise of a composer or a novelist. (The powerful attraction that adolescent females, at the peak age for *n*, feel for unattainable and largely unsophisticated male singers may be one striking, low-level expression of this phenomenon.[35])

2. Because of their emotional range, high-*n* people may be more able to bond uniquely in romantic relationships, offering that assurance of unique and remarkable attachment that a man is usually held by sociobiologists to expect of a woman as an assurance of his paternity of her children[36].
3. The higher level of *n* that is found in countries like Austria, France, Germany, Hungary, India and Italy may be associated with the somewhat stronger interests of the people of these countries in romance and music, in contrast with the lower emotionality and high incidence of tone-deafness, tastelessness, and artistic indifference (with their happier correlates of tolerance, humour and fortitude) that are sometimes remarked among the English-speaking peoples of the British Isles, the White Commonwealth, and the USA. [It is perhaps of some interest that English-speaking authors reach the highest levels of achievement and international recognition as playwrights (Shakespeare, Wilde, Shaw, Becket, Osborne) rather than as novelists. While plays require fast-moving and surprising dialogue, novels require a well-stocked memory for places, faces, mannerisms, and even furniture. Notoriously, novelists' characters are based on people who are literally well known to them.]

In view of the strong and robust correlations that *n* now has outside the questionnaire realm, it is time to give it the *psychotelic* treatment of its biological and social importance that has so far been provided only for psychometric *g* (e.g., Jensen 1980; Brand, 1987; Harrnstein and Murray, 1994). In particular, psychologists must protest at the countless 'social surveys' of people's dissatisfaction (with their spouses, jobs, lack of jobs, national parliaments, etc.) that do not include measures of what is probably after *g*, differential psychology's most important variable. To those who will say 'But you don't know what *n* really is', enhanced PM in high-*n* people can now be offered as a postulate that has the requisite scientific potential. As well as explaining the special effects indicated in the present chapter, it is compatible with others' empirical findings of enhanced simple conditioning and cognitive overload in high-*n* people. At the same time, it squares with Freud's original idea of neurosis as involving a return of material that has been retained and repressed in the course of development (rather than being simply forgotten or sensibly retranscribed). Still more importantly, *n* promises to be, next to *g*, the second variable in differential psychology of which a fairly full and secure account can be offered: rather than being just a source of population variance on which evolution has not bothered to select, *n* differences are probably rich in meaning and adaptive value when considered in conjuction with other features. Whereas high *n* may help in the retention and development of a sophisticated culture, low *n* may assist the exploration and colonization of uncharted territories—be the territories geographical or intellectual—and in the defence of countries and systems that find themselves coming under novel forms of attack. Such differences may be of great practical significance: low-*n* Britain and the USA have no great reputation themselves as countries of art and romance; yet they proved able to help preserve the high and romance-rich cultures of Hindu India, France and Italy.

ACKNOWLEDGEMENTS

I gratefully acknowledge the assistance of Zuleika von Meck, Andrew Sadler and Professor Alan Thompson.

NOTES

[1] The studies involved ratings by teachers, supervisors of college halls of residence, and school teachers. Webb's 'will' (w) factor was usually taken by the London School as the simple reverse of the factor that Burt called 'emotionality' (e).

[2] More than other workers, Eysenck has maintained over the years the independence of neuroticism from extraversion—in line with Jungian more than with Freudian conceptions, as he and his wife once put it (Eysenck and Eysenck, 1969). However, to this day, measures titled 'neuroticism' (and 'anxiety') usually have a modest negative correlation with extraversion. Eysenck's explanation is that, at high levels of *n*, midbrain activation begins

to force up cortical arousal, and thus to yield the behavioural inhibition of the introvert.

[3] By the 1980s, the 'Big Five-or-Six' personality dimensions were fairly widely agreed by psychometrician-psychologists as the largest and most reliable factorial dimensions in empirical studies using questionnaires and rating scales (e.g., Brand, 1984; Deary and Matthews, 1993). There was particularly strong consensus on Neuroticism and Extraversion—Eysenck's two 'classic' and best known dimensions. However, argument continued as to whether Conscientiousness and Agreeableness were best considered to be variants of Eysenckian *non-Psychoticism*; and as to whether Openness should be split into two separate components of affection/tender-mindedness and intellect/intelligence. (Brand and Egan, 1989; Eysenck, 1992; Matthews and Oddy, 1993; Brand, 1994a, b.)

[4] Long sleepers sleep more lightly, have more REM sleep, are less confident, and are more shy, depressed and inhibited (Hartmann *et al.,* 1971). Dream frequency, intensity, and duration—especially of fearful dreams, are all correlated with *n* (Cohen, 1977; Lang and O'Connor, 1984).

[5] More widely, *n* probably has a negative relation to general physical health; and higher *n* is especially found in people who suffer from angina pectoris and premenstrual tension (Wood, 1985; Kissen and Eysenck, 1992; Eysenck, 1993; Grossarth–Maticek *et al.,* 1993). However, Adler and Watts' (1984) review of the literature, while noting claims for 'emotional distancing' in cancer patients, records no significant tendency to lower anxiety or depression in cancer sufferers.

[6] Salter (1973) defined 'musicality' as 'the imaginative, intelligent or sensuous response to music which necessitated no specific musical abilities such as the discrimination of pitch or rhythm'. He had assessed it in children and found it related to Neuroticism scores on the Junior Eysenck Personality Inventory.

[7] The novelist Edna O'Brien once remarked 'I'm a very anxious person. I don't know a writer who isn't.' (BBC IV UK, interviewed by Dr A. Clare, 28 viii 1987.) Distinguished modern American novelists have been remarked to have a near-100 per cent of alcoholism. Mohan and Tiwana (1985) report *n* levels in well-known Indian writers that are almost one standard deviation above population norms.

[8] An account of the 'artistic, moody and intuitive' Wittgenstein, and of his almost daily despair and rage was left by Bertrand Russell (Clark, 1975). Carl Jung wrote to Arnold Kunzli in 1943 that 'neurosis saddles the brain of every philosopher'; and Russell records that he himself had often contemplated suicide as a youth. Like other highly successful groups, first-rank philosophers have experienced high rates of parental loss in childhood. Russell, for example, lost both parents by age two.

[9] Manic love correlates strongly with *n* (Lester and Phibrick, 1988).

[10] Tariot and Weingartner especially noticed that depressive patients who perform badly at laboratory tasks requiring attention nevertheless show good

'incidental' learning (of the furniture in the room, etc.). Their capacity for the more 'automatic' types of learning is thus well preserved during their illness.

[11] Levels of *n* and self-reported anxiety are correlated negatively (if modestly, at around –0.25) with self-reported intake of caffeine and carbohydrates.

[12] Oatley (1992) summarizes the Brown and Harris study as follows: 'Although nine out of ten women who had breakdowns had suffered at least one severe event or difficulty, only a fifth of those who experienced such an event or difficulty broke down. [There were four vulnerability factors—single, maternal loss before 11, several young children, unemployed—which operated by increasing the risk of breakdown only if an event occurred.] Severe events and difficulties, in conjuction with vulnerability factors...explained much of the incidence of depression among the urban women...by far the largest proportion of psychiatric distress is occasioned not by anything intrinsically wrong with them, but by serious adversities in people's lives.' However, all the supposed 'vulnerability' factors would themselves have been likely to reflect influences of *personality*.

[13] Modern research indicates that genetic influence operates during people's childhoods on what they experience by way of 'parenting, childhood accidents, television viewing, classroom environments, peer groups, social support, work environments, life events, divorce, exposure to drugs, education and socio-economic status.' (Plomin *et al.*, 1994), For whatever reason—presumably genetic—even monozygotic twins who have been reared separately show significant similarities in 'life events'.

[14] For a review see Bouchard, 1994. Allowing for the unreliability of personality measurement and including *all* genetic influences (not just those that are passed 'additively' from parents to children), Bouchard estimates that 'about two-thirds of the reliable variance in measured personality traits is due to genetic influence.' The remaining 25 per cent (or so) of reliable variation that does not arise from a family's effects on *all* its children arises presumably from forces that drive children *apart* (such as sibling rivalry and unique occupation by siblings of their own psychological *niches* within the family).

[15] The best modern adoption studies show little similarity for emotionality between children and their biological parents (the correlations are actually around 0.00 over the first seven years of life), or between adoptees who grow up together. Apparently, there is little effect of either additive (transmissible) genetic effects or (between) family environmental differences (Plomin *et al.*, 1991). Research thus gives reason for thinking that either epistasis or sibling competition may be important: even if additive-genetic and between-family environmental effects were at work, epistasis and sibling competition could reduce siblings' phenotic similarities to the remarkably low rates that are commonly observed (Brand, 1984, 1989). (However, intelligence has lately shown higher heritability in older people, who are more in charge of their own environments than are children; so it must be borne in mind that similar effects might yet be observed in the study of emotionality.)

[16] In 1910, Freud wrote '...a certain degree of neurosis is of inestimable value as a drive, especially to a psychologist' (Brandon, 1990).
[17] Gray (1987) explains: '...neuroticism is above all characterized by strong emotions which are easily aroused....It is a simple step to translate 'strong emotions' into a general sensitivity to all reinforcing events, whether rewarding or punishing.'
[18] A very similar linkage of four specific dimensions of mood to the four dimensions of personality (other than *g* and *n*), Exvia (*e*), Control (*c*), Pathemia (*a*) and Independence (*w*) was made by Cattel and Scheier, 1961 (see also Cattell and Kline, 1977, Chapter 11).
[19] It may even be envisaged that attempts at suppression will be counterproductive: Wegner *et al.,* (1991) observe that...trying not to think about sex, like thinking about sex, elevates skin conductance level in comparison to thinking about or not thinking about less exciting topics ['dancing', 'Mom', 'our student Dean']....the suppression of exciting thoughts might be involved in the production of chronic emotional responses such as phobias and obsessive pre-occupations.'
[20] For the wide agreement today that humans (and animals) prefer predictable to unpredictable aversive events, see Rachman, 1994: 688. For the particular fear of loss of control experienced by high-*n* people, see Marks and de Silva, 1994: 765.
[21] Watt (1993) used a modified two-field tachistoscope to present drawings judged emotionally 'unpleasant' or 'neutral' for duration at which subjects were unable to detect the contents of the drawing. Indeed, in Watt's 'Pandora's Box' procedure, testees are not even aware that a picture is being displayed; testees merely indicate when progressive illumination allows them to detect the *frame* of a picture. In two experiments, the more 'defensive' participants (who needed brighter illumination to identify the outline of the 'unpleasant' drawing and did worse with these stimuli than with 'neutral' drawings or with scrambled versions of either type of drawing) had *higher* EPI N scores ($p<0.01$, $p<0.05$).
[22] As to the less artistic occupations, low vigilance does not seem an obvious requirement for a member of the uniformed services in modern conditions. Such low-*n* occupations probably require a judicious combination of reasonable sensitivity to input with courage and self-control.
[23] Kyllonen and Chrystal (1990) first noticed the high correlation between intelligence and working memory, once tests of the latter are corrected for their usually considerable unreliability.
[24] A strong correlation between *n* and Cognitive Failures was also reported by Hogg (1983), reaching +0.66 for 26 adults selected as being of lower intelligence (Cattel Culture Fair Test).
[25] Subjects spoke to a tape-recorder that was left running so that there were no distractions; but the final research record discounted speech pauses.

[26] As far as possible, subjects were given *no* encouragement during the testing session: for each question, the tape-recorder was simply turned off when the subject first came to a halt.

[27] Eysenck and Eysenck (1975) report data for females in 35 occupations, 26 receptionists, 224 factory workers, 140 shop assistants, 41 art students, 15 transport workers and 54 actors, designers and musicians made up the groups having the highest *n* scores. (For contrast: the lowest-*n* female groups were 16 occupational therapists, 27 medical students, 9 scientists, 15 physiotherapists, 23 welfare officers, and 37 civil servants.)

[28] For example, Penelope Davis (1987) found high-*n* people (vs 'repressors') to display a greater 'accessibility [of] personal, real-life affective memories that was particularly pronounced for fear and self-consciousness experiences.' (However, Rapee *et al.* (1994) did *not* find higher memory bias in phobic patients towards unpleasant information.)

[29] If the police and student groups are considered together, the correlation between total account length and *n* is +0.42 (p≤.01) [and not +0.28 as stated at one point in the text of Wagstaff's thesis]. This is still a clear effect, but it is weaker than the effects found *within* each of the two groups. The police were markedly lower than the students in *n;* but their stories were not correspondingly shorter. However, the police sample differed in their age, in their higher extraversion, and in their higher conscientiousness (and thus perhaps in attention to detail). More relevant, probably, the police were tested under *group* conditions in which testees who finished earlier might have felt a little uncomfortable; perhaps especially not wanting their colleagues seated nearby to infer they had little to say about their 'first kiss'!

[30] For example, the five *most anxious* testees (all students, IPAT scores >49, see Wagstaff's Appendix V) wrote that they were, variously, 'pleased', 'quite pleased', 'relieved', 'delighted' and 'pretty ecstatic' about their results. The five *least anxious* students (IPAT <39) recorded: 'I did quite well on the whole, though I remember being disappointed to get a B for German', 'It was fab'; 'all the marks I wanted', 'a family friend....stopped me because I looked happy'; and (as the total answer) 'No chance, all I remember was being given [the results] by our register teacher, and drawing on the brown envelope."

[31] These two examples are derived using Wagstaff's graph on p. 34 and her Appendix V. The low-*n* scorer, Subject 2 [Code: ASIC] (IPAT Anxiety = 8, Words = 172), is a policeman; the high-*n* scorer, Subject 32 [Code:DALA] (IPAT Anxiety = 53, Words = 573) is a student.

[32] The detailed instructions were as follows. (1) *Room.* 'Give an account of your childhood room, that is, the one you had when you were between approximately 5 and 10 years old. Include, if you can, details about the physical characteristics of the room, any associations that these or the room might have for you, and any events that occurred there that are particularly memorable to you'. (2) *Job.* 'Give an account of your first day at your first-ever job. Include, if you can, details of what the job entailed, the names of

any relationships (friendly or otherwise) that you formed with your colleagues; and any particular incidents that may have occurred that day.'
[33] Freud (1896) explains his view to his friend Wilhelm Fliess as follows: '....I am working on the assumption that our psychic mechanism has come into being by a process of stratification: the material present in the form of memory traces being subjected from time to time to a *rearrangement* in accordance with fresh circumstances—to a *retranscription*. Thus what is essentially new about my theory is the thesis that memory is present not once but several times over, that it is laid down in various kinds of indications.... I should like to emphasize the fact that the successive registrations represent the psychic achievement of successive epochs of life. At the boundary between two such epochs a translation of the psychic material must take place. I explain the peculiarities of the psychoneuroses by supposing that this translation has not taken place in the case of some of the material....' Freud maintains that early failures to transcribe material occur as a 'normal' defence against 'the unpleasure that would be generated by a translation'; whereas later, 'pathological' repression (at least in hysteria, obsessional disorder and paranoia) is the continuing struggle to repress the untranscribed material from an earlier stage. Freud gives an example of a female patient whose older brother admitted during the course of her analysis with Freud that he had liked to suck he toes when she was in bed as a child. This confession released an earlier memory on the patient's part (dating from age four) of seeing her father sucking the toes of the family wet nurse while *in flagrante delicto* with her. This recall in turn triggered violent headaches on the patient's part. Her brother had told her he himself had experienced headaches after being accidentally kicked on the head by his father's boot while hiding under a bed where his father was making love.
[34] The vigilance ('sensitization') concept of Byrne was originally held to predict that 'sensitizers' would be both neurotic and creative (see Cohen, 1977); but the linking of vigilance to creativity no longer seems to form part of M.W. Eysenck's theorizing.
[35] The use of song in human sexual competition is explored by Ridley, 1993. Another example of music showing the way out of emotional turmoil might be what is sometimes said to be the attraction that higher-*n* people feel for the music of Tchaikovsky until they become more musically sophisticated. Tchaikovsky—himself emotionally remarkable, with his struggles against his homosexuality, his suicide bid after three months of marriage to a young admirer, and his ten-year long-distance affair with Madame von Meck (whom he never met)—notoriously provides in his music, melodrama and its natural complement of clear and firm resolution (Swafford, 1992). Certainly the importance of music for some people cannot be overestimated: Nietzsche said, 'Without music, life would be a mistake'; and the American composer, Charles lves insisted, 'Music does not represent life. It is life!' Swafford notes it being said of nineteenth-century Russia that 'after piano recitals, young ladies were

known to shoot themselves because they felt the rest of their lives would be an anticlimax.'

[36] That neuroticism/emotionality has especial associations with romantic bonding is suggested by recent research conducted by third-year students and myself in Edingurgh. Sixty-six friends and fellow students responded anonymously (*via* internal University mail) to questions about their romantic and sexual relationships. They were asked to describe in turn their 'best love affair', 'best steady relationship' and 'the best sex you have ever had'; then they were asked whether the same partner had been involved *in all three selections.* Such 'sexual/romantic consistency' correlated at 0.39 ($p < 0.001$) with self-rated emotionality (using the reversed *ego* factor from Brand and Deary, 1989); and this correlation held up for both the 24 males and the 42 females separately (0.57, 0.41). Although more emotional testees reported slightly less love at home ($r = 0.31$) and slightly more sexual partners since age 16 ($r = 0.32$), they had apparently been more able to achieve, at least at some point, the ideal romantic relationship in which love, steady companionship, and sexual satisfaction are conjoined. In line with their experience, the higher-*n* people were a little more likely to believe in 'one true love' ($r = 0.26$).

References

Adler, Nancy and Karen Watts (1994). 'Health Psychology: Why do Some People get Sick and Some Stay Well?' *Annual Review of Psychology,* 45: 229–59.

Bagozzi, R.P. (1993). 'An Examination of the Psychometric Properties of Negative Affect in the PANAS-X Scales', *Journal of Personality and Social Psychology,* 65: 836–60.

Barkow, J.H. (1991). 'Precis of Darwin, Sex and Status: Biological Approaches to Mind and Culture', *Behavioral & Brain Sciences,* 14 (2): 295–334.

Bakker, F.C. (1988). 'Personality Differences Between Young Dancers and Non-Dancers', *Personality & Individual Differences,* 9(1): 121–32.

Bell, R.Q. (1968). 'A Re-Interpretation of the Direction of Effects in Studies of Socialization', *Psychological Review,* 75(2): 81–95.

Bolger, N. and Elizabeth A. Schilling (1991). 'Personality and the Problems of Everyday Life: the Role of Neuroticism in Exposure and Reactivity to Daily Stressors', *Journal of Personality,* 59(3) 355–86.

Borkenau, P. and F. Ostendorf (1992). 'Social Desirability Scales as Moderator and Suppressor Variables', *European Journal of Personality,* 6: 199–214.

Bouchard, T.J., Jr. (1994). 'Genes, Environment and Personality', *Science,* 264, 17vi, 1700–01.

Brand, C.R. (1984). 'Dimensions of Personality: an Overview', in J.Nicholson Halla Beloff, *Psychology Survey,* 5, pp. 175–209, Leicester: British Psychology Society.

Brand, C.R. (1987). 'The Importance of Intelligence', in S. Modgil and Celia Modgil, *Arthur Jensen: Consensus and Controversy,* pp. 251–65, Brighton, UK: Falmer.

Brand, C.R. (1989). 'A Fitting Endeavour', *Nature,* 341: 7 ix, p. 29.

Brand, C.R. (1994a). 'Open to Experience–Closed to Intelligence: Why the 'Big Five' are Really the 'Comprehensive Six', *European Journal of Psychology,* 8(4): 299–310.

Brand, C.R. (1994b). 'How Many Dimensions of Personality? The 'Big Five', the 'Gigantic Three' and the 'Comprehensive Six', *Psychological Belgica,* 4(4) 257–75.

Brand, C.R. and V. Egan (1989). 'The 'Big Five' Dimensions of Personality? Evidence from Ipsative, Adjectival Self-Attributions', *Personality & Individual Differences,* 10: 1165–71.

Brandon, Ruth (1990). *The New Women and the Old Men,* London: Secker.

Broadbent, D.E., P.F. Cooper, P. Fitzgerald and Katharine R. Parkes (1982). 'The Cognitive Failures Questionnaire (CFQ) and its Correlates', *British Journal of Social and Clinical Psychology,* 21(1): 1–16.

Brown, G.W. and T.O. Harris (1978). *The Social Origins of Depression,* London: Tavistock.

Burbeck, Elizabeth and A. Furnham (1984). 'Personality and Police Selection: Trait Differences in Successful and Non-Successful Applicants to the Metropolitan Police', *Personality & Individual Differences,* 5(3): 257–64.

Burt C. (1915). 'The General and Specific Factors Underlying the Primary Emotions', *British Association Annual Report,* 84: 694–96.

Buss, D.M. (1989). 'Sex Differences in Human Mate Preferences; Evolutionary Hypotheses Tested in 37 Cultures', *Behavioral & Brain Sciences,* 12: 1–49.

Buss, D.M. (1994). 'The Strategies of Human Mating', *American Scientist,* v/vi, 238–50.

Cameron, P. (1975). 'Mood as an Indicant of Happiness: Age, Sex, Social Class and Situational Difference', *Journal of Gerontology,* 30: 216–24.

Cattel, R.B. and P. Kline (1977). *The Scientific Analysis of Personality,* New York: Academic.

Cattel, R.B. and I.H. Scheier (1961). *The Meaning and Measurement of Neuroticism and Anxiety,* New York: Ronald.

Cattel, R.B. and I.H. Scheier (1963). *Handbook of the IPAT Anxiety Scale,* Champaign, IL: Institute for the Study of Personality and Ability Testing.

Chown, S.M. (1984). Review of T.K. Hareven and K.J. Adams, *Life Course Transitions: An Interdisciplinary Perspective,* London, Tavistock. *British Journal of Psychology,* 75(1): 121–22.

Clark, R.W. (1975). *The Life of Bertrand Russell,* London: Cape/ Weidenfeld & Nicolson.

Costa, P.T. and R.R. MaCrae (1980). 'Still Stable After all These Years: Personality as a Key to Some Issues in Childhood and Old Age', in P.B.Baltes and O.G.Brim Jr., *Lifespan Development and Behavior,* Vol. 3, pp. 65–102, New York: Academic.

Cohen, D.B. (1977). 'Neuroticism and Dreaming Sleep: a Case for Interactionism in Personality Research', *British Journal of Social and Clinical Psychology,* 16: 153–63.

Cohen, S.J. (1994). *Letter, British Medical Journal,* 309. Issue 8. vol. 73.

Crick, F. and G. Mitchison (1983). 'The Function of Dream Sleeps', *Nature,* 304: (14vii) 111–14.

Crookes, T.G., P.R. Pearson, L.J. Francis and Marian Carter (1981). 'Extraversion and Performance on Raven's Matrices in 15–16 Year Old Children: An Examination of Anthony's Theory of the Development of Extraversion', *British Journal of Educational Psychology,* 51: 109–11.

Dana, R.H. and R.R. Cocking (1969). 'Repression-Sensitization and Maudsley Personality Inventory Scores: Responsee Sets and Stress Effects', *British Journal of Social and Clinical Psychology,* 8(3): 263–69.

Davis, Penelope J. and G.E. Schwarts (1987). 'Repression and the Inaccessibility of Affective Memories', *Journal of Personality and Social Psychology,* 52(1): 155–62.

Deary, I.J. and G. Matthews (1993). 'Personality Traits are Alive and Well', *The Psychologist,* 6(vii): 299–311.

Deary, V.A.H. (1984). 'The Neurotic Memory: a Study of its Task-Oriented Relevance and Efficiency', Edinburgh University Final Honours Thesis (B.Sc. Med. Sci. with Honours in Psychology).

Edelman, R.J. and K.J. Connolly (1986). 'Psychological Aspects of Infertility', *British Journal of Medical Psychology,* 59: 209–19.

Epstein, S. (1994). 'Integration of the Cognitive and the Psychodynamic Unconscious', *American Psychologist,* 49(8): 709–24.

Eysenck, H.J. (1947). *Dimensions of Personality,* London: Routledge & Kegan Paul.

Eysenck, H.J. (1992). 'Four Ways Five Factors are not Basic', *Personality & Individual Differences,* 13: 667–73.

Eysenck, H.J. (1993). 'Prediction of Cancer and Coronary Heart Disease Mortality by Means of a Personality Inventory: Results of a 15-Year Follow-Up Study', *Psychological Report,* 72: 499–516.

Eysenck, H.J. (1994). 'A Biological Theory of Intelligence' in D.K. Detterman, *Current Topics in Human Intelligence,* Vol. IV, pp. 117–50, Norwood, NJ: Ablex.

Eysenck, H.J. and S.B.G. Eysenck (1969). *Personality Structure and Measurement,* London: Routledge & Kegan Paul.

Eysenck, H.J. and S.B.G. Eysenck (1975). *Manual for the Eysenck Personality Questionnaire,* London: Hodder & Stoughton.

Eysenck, H.J. and M.W. Eysenck (1985). *Personality and Individual Differences: A Natural Science Approach,* New York: Plenum.

Eysenck, H.J. and G. Gudjonsson (1989). *The Causes and Cures of Criminality,* New York: Plenum.

Eysenck, M.W. (1988). 'Anxiety and Attention', Anxiety Research, 1: 9–15.

Eysenck, M.W. (1992). 'The Nature of Anxiety', in A. Gale and M.W. Eysenck, *Handbook of Individual Differences: Biological Perspectives,* pp. 157–78, Chichester: Wiley.

Eysenck, S.B.G., H.J. Eysenck and P. Barrett (1985). 'A Revised Version of the Psychoticism Scale', *Personality & Individual Differences,* 6(1): 21–29.

Fahrenberg, J. (1992). 'The Psychophysiology of Neuroticism and Anxiety', in A. Gale and M.W. Eysenck, *A Handbook of Individual Differences: Biological Perspectives,* pp. 179–226, Chichester: Wiley.

Francis, L.J. (1993). 'The Dual Nature of the Eysenckian Neuroticism Scales: a Question of Sex Differences', *Personality & Individual Differences,* 15(1): 43–59.

Freud, S. (1896). 'Letter to Wilhelm Fliess', 6 xii, in J.M. Masson (ed.), *The Complete Letters of Sigmund Freud to Wilhelm Fliess, 1887-1904,* pp. 207–15, Cambridge, MA: Harvard University Press.

Freud, S. and J. Breuer (1896). Studies on Hysteria in the Complete Psychological Works of Sigmund Freud' (*ed. James Strachy & Anna Freud*) 1957, London: Hogarth Press.

Friedman, H.H. and Stephanie Booth-Kewley (1987). 'The "Disease-Prone Personality": a Meta-Analytic View of the Construct', *American Psychologist,* 42: 539–55.

Fujita, F. (1993). 'Anxiety and Neuroticism in Students', Paper Read at the 6th Meeting of International Society for the Study of Individual Differences, Baltimore.

Goorney, A.B. (1970). 'MPI and MMPI Scores, Eorrelations and Analysis for a Military Aircrew Population', *British Journal of Social and Clinical Psychology,* 91(2): 164–70.

Gotlib, I.H. (1984). 'Depression and General Psychopathology in University Students', *Journal of Abnormal and Social Psychology,* 93.

Götz K.O. and K. Götz (1973). 'Introversion and Extaversion and Neuroticism in Gifted and Ungifted Arts Students', *Perceptual & Motor Skills,* 36: 675–78.

Gray, J.A. (1987). *The Psychology of Fear and Stress,* 2nd edn., London: Weidenfeld & Nicolson.

Gray, J.A. (1991). 'Brain Systems that Mediate Both Emotion and Cognition', in J.A. Gray, *Psychobiological Aspects of Relations between Emotion and Cognition,* pp. 269–88, Hove, UK: Lawrence Erlbaum Associates.

Grossarth-Maticek, R., H.J. Eysenck and P. Barrett (1993). 'Prediction of Cancer and Coronary Heart Disease as a Function of Method of Questionnaire Administraion', *Psychological Reports,* 73: 943–59.

Hallam, R.S. and S.J. Rachman (1980). 'Courageous Acts or Courageous Actors?' *Personality & Individual Differences,* 1(4): 341–46.

Hamilton, V. (1979). 'Anxiety: Trait, State and Cognition', in V. Hamilton and D.M. Warburton, *Human Stress and Cognition,* Chichester: Wiley.

Hartmann, E., F. Baekland, G. Zwilling and P. Hoy (1971). 'Sleep Need: How Much and What Kind?' *American Journal of Psychiatry,* 127: 1001–8.

Herrnstein, R. and C. Murray (1994). *The Bell Curve,* New York: The Free Press.

Heymans, G. and E. Wiersma (1909). 'Beiträge zur speziellen Psychologie of Grund einer Massenuntersuchung', *Zeitschrift für Psychologie,* 51: 1–72.

Hogg, Lorna (1983). 'The Psychological Correlates of Ageing: Inspection Time, Intelligence, Cognitive Factors and Personality', Final Honour Thesis, Department of Psychology, Edinburgh University.

Humphreys, M.S. and W. Revelle (1984). 'Personality, Motivation and Performance: a Theory of the Relation Between Individual Differences and Information Processing', *Psychlogical Review,* 91(2): 153–84.

Jensen, A.R. (1980). *Bias in Mental Testing,* London: Methuen

Kissen, D.M. and H.J. Eysenck (1992). 'Personality in Male Lung Cancer Patients', *Journal of Psychosomatic Research,* 6: 123–37.

Kline, P. (1979). *Psychometrics and Psychology,* London: Academic.

Kyllonen, P.C. and K.P. Christal (1990). 'Reasoning Ability is (little more than) Working Memory Capacity?' *Intelligence,* 14(4): 389–433.

Lang, R.J. and K.P. O'Connor (1984). 'Personality, Dream Content and Coping Style', *Personality & Individual Differences,* 5(2): 211–20.

Ley, P., M.S. Spelman, Ann D.M. Davies and S. Riley (1966). 'The Relationships Between Intelligence, Anxiety, Neuroticism and Extraversion', *British Journal of Educational Psychology,* 36: 185–91.

Lester, D. and J. Philbrick (1988). 'Correlates of Styles of Love', *Personality & Individual Differences 9,* 3, 689–90.

Luteijn, F.J. and T.K. Bouman (1988). 'The Concepts of Depression, Anxiety and Neuroticism in Questionnaires', *European Journal of Personality,* 2.

Lynn, R. (1971). *Personality and National Character,* Oxford: Pergamon.

Macleod, C. and Avonia M. Donnellan (1993). 'Individual Differences in Anxiety and the Restriction of Working Memory Capacity', *Personality and Individual Differences,* 15(2): 163–73.

Marks, Melanie and P. de Silva (1994). 'The Match/Mismatch Model of Fear: Empirical Status and Clinical Implications', *Behaviour Research & Therapy,* 32(7): 759–70.

Matthews, G. and K. Oddy (1993). 'Recovery of Major Personality Dimensions from Trait Adjective Data', *Personality & Individual Differences,* 15(4): 419–31.

McNamara, N. (1995). 'Neuroticism, Introversion and the Quality of Experience: an Investigation of Personal Memory', Final Honours Thesis, Department of Psychology, Edinburgh University.

Mohan, Vidhu and R. Chopra (1987). 'Personality Variation as an Effect of Premenstrual Tension,' *Personality & Individual Differences,* 8(4): 763–5.

Mohan, J. and M. Tiwana (1985). 'Personality and Alienation of Creative Writers: a Brief Report', *Personality & Individual Differences,* 8(3): 449.

Mueller, J.H. (1976). 'Anxiety and Cue Utilization in Human Learning and Memory', in M. Zuckerman and C.D. Spielberger, *Emotions and Anxiety: New Concepts, Methods and Applications,* Potomac, MD: Erlbaum.

Oatley, K. (1992). *Best Laid Schemes: the Psychology of the Emotions,* New York: Cambridge University Press.

Paulhus, D.L. and M.N. Bruce (1992). 'The Effect of Acquaintanceship on the Validity of Personality Impressions: A Longitudinal Study', *Journal of Personality and Social Psychology,* 63(5): 816–24.

Plomin, R., Hilary Coon, G. Carey, J.C. DeFries and D.W. Fulker (1991). 'Parent-Offspring and Sibling Adoption Analyses of Parent Ratings of Temperament in Infancy and Childhood', *Journal of Personality,* 59(4): 706–32.

Plomin, R., M.J. Owen and P. McGuffin (1994). 'The Genetic Basis of Complex Behaviour', *Science,* 264(17vi): 1733–39.

Prentky, R.A. (1980). *Creativity and Psychopathology,* New York: Praeger.

Rapee R.M., S.L. McCallum, L.F. Melville, H. Ravenscroft and J.M. Rodney (1994). 'Memory Bias in Social Phobia', *Behaviour Research & Therapy,* 32(1): 89–100.

Richman, Naomi (1993). 'Annotation: Children in Situations of Political Violence', *Journal of Child Psychology and Psychiatry,* 341(8): 1286–302.

Rachman, S. (1994). 'The Overprediction of Fears: A Review', *Behaviour Research & Therapy,* 32(7): 683–90.

Ridley, M. (1993). *The Red Queen,* New York: Viking.

Scharfstein, B-A. (1981). *The Philosophers,* Oxford: Blackwell.

Schonell, F. (1948). *Backwardness in the Basic Subjects,* Edinburgh; Oliver & Boyd.

Salter, F.W. (1973). 'Neuroticism as a Correlate of Musicality', *Bulletin of the British Psychological Society,* 26(92): 269–70.

Storms, L.H. and W.E. Broen (1969). 'A Theory of Schizophrenic Behavioural Disorganisation, *Archives of General Psychiatry,* 20(2): 129–44.

Swafford, Jan (1992). *The New Guide to Classical Music,* New York: Random House.

Tariot, P.N. and H. Weingartner (1986). 'Psychobiologic Analysis of Cognitive Failure: Structure and Mechanisms', *Archives of General Psychiatry,* 43: 1183–88.

Talyor, Janet A. (1953). 'A Personality Scale of Manifest Anxiety', *Journal of Abnormal Psychology,* 48, 285–90.

Teasdale, J.D. and R. Taylor (1981). 'Induced Mood and Accessibility of Memories: An Effect of Mood State or of Induction Procedure?', *British Journal of Clinical Psychology,* 20(1): 39–48.

True, W.R., J. Rice, S.A. Eisen, A.C. Heath, J. Goldberg, M.J. Lyons and J. Nowak (1993). 'A Twin Study of Genetic and Environmental Contributions to Liability for Posttraumatic Stress Symptoms', *Archives of General Psychiatry,* 50, 257–64.

Vernon, P.E. (1982). *The Abilities and Achievements of Orientals in North America,* New York: Academic.

Wagstaff, Heather (1994). 'Do We All Experience the Same?: A Comparative Study of High- and Low-*n* Scorers Memory', Final Honours Thesis, Department of Psychology, Edinburgh University.

Warburton, D.M. (1979). 'The Neurotransmitters and Anxiety', in V. Hamilton and D.M. Warburton, *Human Stress and Cognition,* Chichester: Wiley.

Watson, D. (1989). 'Strangers' Ratings of the Five Robust Personality Factors: Evidence of a Surprising Convergence with Self-Report', *Journal of Personality and Social Psychology,* 57(1): 120–8.

Watson, D. and J.W. Pennebaker (1989). 'Health Complaints, Stress and Distress: Exploring the Central Role of Negative Affectivity', *Psychological Review,* 96: 234–54.

Watt, Caroline (1993). 'The Relationship Between Performance on a Prototype Measure of Perceptual Defence/Vigilance and *psi* Performance', Ph.D. Thesis, Department of Psychology, Edinburgh University.

Webb, E. (1915). 'Character and intelligence', *British Journal of Psychology Monographs,* 1(3): 1–99.

Wegner, D.M. and R. Erber (1993). 'The Hyperaccessibility of Suppressed Thoughts', *Journal of Personality and Social Psychology,* 63(6): 903–12.

Wegner, D.M., J.W. Shortt, A.W. Blake and M.S. Page (1991). *Journal of Personality and Social Psychology,* 58(3): 409–18.

Williams, D.G. (1981). 'Personality and Mood: State-Trait Relationships', *Personality and Individual Differences,* 2(4): 303–10.

Williams, D.G. (1993). 'Are Personality Effects upon Average Mood Due to Personality Effects upon Mood Variation?', *Personality & Individual Differences,* 14(1): 199–208.

Wilson, G. (1984). 'The Personality of Opera Singers', *Personality & Individual Differences,* 5: 195–201.

Wilson, J.A., I.J. Deary and A.G.D. Maran (1988). 'Is Globus Hystericus?', *British Journal of Psychiatry,* 153: 335–39.

Wilson, J.A., I.J. Deary, and A.G.D. Maran (1991). 'The Persistence of Symptomsin Patients with *Globus Pharyngis*', *Clinical Otoloryngology,* 16: 202–5.

Wood, C. (1985). 'The Healthy Neurotic', *New Scientist,* 105, No. 1442, 7th February, 12–15.

Woodworth, R.S. (1919). *Personal Data Sheet,* Chicago: C.H.Stoertling.

12 Word Association Test: Its Diagnostic Potential

V.V. Upmanyu and Sushma Upmanyu

Word Association Test (WAT) is one of the oldest procedures used in personality study. It is a versatile and powerful diagnostic device. It has been widely used for: clinical diagnosis, identification of areas of emotional disturbance, detection of guilt, investigating repression and recall, description of interest patterns and attitudes, description of thought processes, and tracing language development in children. Several studies of word association (Pons and Ecolasse, 1982; Pack and Pons, 1985) recently gave evidence that a cognitive parameter, related both to commonness anu repetition of word responses, identifies an associative trait characteristic of the personality of the subject. Most studies of schizophrenic thinking based on associative disturbance have utilized the word association technique to investigate disturbed thought processes. In recent years, investigators have increasingly turned their attention to the study of diagnostic potential of the word association test in psychiatrically normal populations.

Historical Perspective and Recent Studies

Word association technique has a long history. Although Galton (1879), Cattell and Bryant (1889), Kraepelin (1892), Munsterberg (1907), and Wundt (1911) showed keen interest in the association process, the most influential formulation of the relation between response faults on the word association test and emotional disturbance was made by Jung (1910), who launched the word association test as a clinical diagnostic tool with a psychoanalytic rationale. In a series of extremely significant studies by Jung, Riklin, Wehrlin and other members of the Bluuler–Freudin School of psychiatry, two things stand out: (1) classification and analysis of the kinds of responses given by various types of normal and pathological individuals (content analysis); and (2) enunciation of various signs (e.g., long reaction time, idiosyncratic responses, commonality of responses, reproduction failure, response repetition, perseveration) indicative of emotional disturbance (formal analysis). The utility of a given type of complex sign, however, depends chiefly upon two facts: (a) the relative frequency of the appearance of a particular sign; and (b) the diagnostic power of the sign when it does appear.

Jung's work stimulated a ceaseless search (e.g., Hull and Lugoff, 1921; Rapaport, Gill, and Schafer, 1946; Symonds, 1931; Tendler, 1945) to verify the validity of earlier findings, and for locating new indicators that might help in identifying complexes and clinical diagnosis. Although the research interest in word associations declined considerably after 1910 and mostly remained dormant till 1945 when Tendler (1945) initiated a new series of experiments, the last few decades have seen a wealth of empirical studies of word meanings and word associations. A prodigious literature (Bradley and Baddeley, 1990; Chapman and Chapman, 1973; Eysenck and Wilson, 1973; Green and Galbraith, 1986; Hundal and Upmanyu, 1974, 1981; Kline, 1981; Levinger and Clark, 1961; Miller and Chapman, 1983; Pack and Pons, 1985; Parkin, Lewinsohn and Folkad, 1982; Pons and Ecolasse, 1982; Pons, Nurnberger and Murphy, 1985; Pons *et al.,* 1986; Rierden, 1980; Silverstein and Harrow, 1980; Silverstein and Harrow, 1983a, b; Upmanyu, 1981, d; Upmanyu and Kaur, 1986, 1988; Upmanyu and Singh, 1984; Upmanyu and Upmanyu, 1988; Upmanyu, Gill and Singh, 1982), which appears to contain many stimulating hypotheses concerning variegated facets of association process, has developed during the last two decades.

A perusal of the extensive research literature using the word association test indicates that although the word list devised by Kent and Rosanoff, dating back to 1910, is still frequently employed, there have been a number of investigations (e.g., Galbraith and Sturke, 1974; Levinger and Clark, 1961) which have used other stimulus items. The variation in the nature of word lists, indices for assessing associative disturbance and single response versus continuous association paradigm, leads to an unfortunate problem in the word association literature, in which it becomes difficult to compare results across different studies. Despite these methodological problems, the available literature provides evidence that word association test offers promise as an instrument for studying cognitive and personality disturbances in schizophrenia and other psychiatric conditions, as well as psychiatrically normal population. Long reaction time, repetition of stimulus word before responding, response repetition (response with same reaction word at two or more different stimulus words), defective reproduction of original reaction at the second presentation of the stimulus word, perseveration, and rare responses have been found useful indicators of psychiatric disturbance.

From a series of studies on the personality variable of sex guilt (Galbraith, 1968; Galbraith and Mosher, 1970; Galbraith and Struke, 1974; Galbraith, Hahn and Leiberman, 1968; Mosher, 1965; Schill, 1972), the evidence seems clear that individual differences in sex guilt affect the content of associations to double-entendre sexual words. In addition, high-sex-guilt subjects showed better recall for associations elicited under the control condition than low-sex-guilt subjects. Conversely, low-sex-guilt subjects showed better recall under the sexual condition than high-sex-guilt subjects. The results also suggested that the 'sexuality–asexuality' of the stimulus words might be a significant factor in the recall errors of high- and low-sex-guilt subjects.

In addition, uncommon word associations have long been valued as indicators of schizophrenic thought disorder (Miller and Chapman, 1983). This finding of rare associates in schizophrenia was first reported by Kent and Rosanoff (1910), who reported that their 108 dementia praecox patients gave 34.3 per cent individual responses, that is, responses not given by any subject in a normative group, whereas 1,000 normal control subjects gave only 6.8 per cent individual responses. The authors noted that an increased number of 'unclassified responses, mostly of the incoherent type' was one of the characteristics of schizophrenics. Bleuler (1911, 1950) regarded incoherence as one of the basic symptoms of schizophrenics who seem to have lost some of the cues that normally organize and guide thinking. He suggested that the mechanism underlies all schizophrenic symptomatology. Since the writings of Bleuler, loosening of associative threads has occupied an important position, and for some, has been considered the primary disturbance in schizophrenia. In clinical practice, incoherence of associations is still one of the main diagnostic criteria of schizophrenia when clearness of consciousness is preserved. Astrup and Flekkoy

(1968, 1969, cited in Flekkoy, 1973) found that incoherent association differentiated best between normals and schizophrenics, and between schizophrenics and the other main diagnostic groups. Flekkoy (1973) in a single-word, free association situation (Kent–Rosanoff, 1910) found that the production of incoherent associations was related to: (1) intrusion of unrelated thought processes, (2) restriction, and (3) instability of the representational meaning of the stimulus words.

More recent studies (e.g., Sackheim and Shapiro, 1981; Shakow, 1980; Penk, 1978) using the traditional single-response word association test also found more rare associates by schizophrenics than by control subjects. According to Silverstein and Harrow (1982), these studies, with the exception of an investigation by Griffith *et al.* (1980) and Rierdan (1980), have tended to emphasize single word associations to the relative neglect of multiple associative responses, which may assess breakdowns in purposive thinking as one formulation addressed by Bleuler. The authors argued that the continuous association technique may have promise in identifying individuals who are vulnerable to developing schizophrenia, as well as individuals who succumb to the disorder.

Rierdan (1980) examined the word associations of socially-isolated adolescents. It was hypothesized that social isolates would emit a greater number of idiosyncratic associations than non-isolates (taken to indicate greater acquisition of deviant behaviours), and would emit idiosyncratic associations earler in a series of associations than non-isolates (taken to indicate greater probability of manifesting deviant behaviours). Socially isolated and non-isolated adolescents, 32 in each group, performed two word association tasks, each of which required giving a series of associations to stimulus words. The isolates emitted a significantly greater proportion of idiosyncratic associates than did the non-isolates, and the isolates emitted an idiosyncratic associate significantly earlier in a series of associations than the non-isolates. These differences, which were particularly clear for girls, suggested that social isolation was correlated with the acquisition of deviant behaviour. The author argued that noncontextual responding by social isolates might reflect a schizophrenic-like inability to attend to the contextual demands of the word association task.

Silverstein and Harrow (1982), using a continuous association technique with 42 schizophrenic and 30 non-schizophrenic psychiatric patients concluded that 'the continuous word-association method offers promise as an instrument for studying thought disorder involving associative processes in schizophrenia and other psychiatric conditions. Differential performance on continuous-association tasks relative to single word-association tasks as well as the differential nature of associative thinking in the two procedures, awaits further research' (p. 808). Further, Miller and Chapman (1983), using a continued word-association procedure in hypothetically psychosis-prone college students, also found results similar to the aberrant/idiosyncratic/unusual associations found in schizophrenic populations for the single-response word-association task. These results, however, were found on tasks (unstructured tasks) with relatively few contextual restrictions.

More recent studies in India (Hundal and Upmanyu, 1981, Upmanyu and Kaur, 1986; Upmanyu and Singh, 1984; Upmanyu and Upmanyu, 1988; Upmanyu, Gill and Singh, 1982), using the traditional single-response Kent–Rosanoff word association test also yielded positive and significant associations between unusual word associations and psychosis proneness as measured by Eysenck Personality Questionnaire (Eysenck and Eysenck, 1975). In addition, Upmanyu and Singh (in press) in an investigation with non-clinical sample of college students found that rare word associations are a strong marker of a predisposition to psychoticism. The authors concluded: 'Until we have more definitive evidence from follow-up studies of these subjects, the present study gives tentative evidence that at least some of the subjects giving more of rare associates are psychosis-prone.'

It should be noted, however, that this firmly established finding of more rare (either fewer common or more individual) associates by schizophrenics or psychosis-prone subjects as revealed by the Eysenck Personality Questionnaire has been questioned by some researchers. As representative of published negative findings, failure to distinguish between schizophrenics and normal subjects on commonality and a number of idiosyncratic (individual) responses (Dokecki, Polidoro and Cromwell, 1965; Fuller and Kates, 1969; Wynne, 1963), and between schizophrenic and tubercular subjects (O' Brain and Weingartner, 1970), and process and reactive schizophrenics in high-stress conditions (DeWolfe and Youkilis, 1974). Schwartz (1978) also questioned the entire published evidence that schizophrenics give more rare associates than normal subjects. In his review of word associations studies, Schwartz (1978a: 240) commented; 'Taken as a whole, the results of these studies have been interpreted to demonstrate that schizophrenics give fewer common word associations than nonschizophrenics. When each study is examined individually, however, the support for this contention is unimpressive.'

Despite these atypical reports, there is substantial evidence (Miller and Chapman, 1983; Upmanyu and Singh, 1996) possessing merit to indicate more unusual (rare) word associates by schizophrenics or psychosis-prone subjects than by normal subjects. However, a difficulty in equating unusual word associations only with psychiatric malfunctioning and aberrations of perception is occasioned by the fact that word associations that go more or less completely out of context (rare associates) are also known from past work (Barron, 1965, 1969; Guilford *et al.,* 1951; Maltzman, 1960; Mednick, 1962) to be indicative of creative attainment. Gough's (1976) investigation showed that moderately infrequent word associations were more strongly related to creativity than were associations of extreme remoteness or common occurrence. The author concluded, 'Associations of a moderate but not extreme atypicality may furnish a better index of creative potential than very rare or distant responses.' This study did not reveal information about the nature of emotional disturbance associated with the word association test performance, because there was no response-specific criterion of psychiatric disturbance in the design of the study. As such, it is clearly perilous to infer only creativity rather than psychiatric disturbance even from moderately infrequent word associations (1–10 per cent). The inclusion of creativity measures, with a complete exclusion of emotional disturbance measures in the data, may make it much harder to discern simple creativity correlates of word associations.

Further, the reported difficulty in the literature in relating unusual word associations to personality and cognitive variables could be due to a heavy reliance on unusualness of word association responses. It appears that the inclusion of different types of word associations (extremely remote word associations, moderately remote word associations, less common word associations, common word associations, very common word associations) and measures of psychiatric disturbance, as well as creativity within the purview of a single study are essential for examining the demonstrable value of the word association test for studying creativity and psychopathology. Studies focusing either on psychiatric disturbance measures or on cognitive measures in isolation suffer from important omissions, because a comprehensive investigation which attempts to relate word associations to various measures of ability and psychopathology could only reveal the essential features of word association test performance. This methodological problem was overcome in a series of studies by Upmanyu and associates.

In addition, another major limitation of the studies exploring creativity–word associations relationship has been a heavy reliance upon psychometric measures of creativity. Emerging evidence, however, suggests that creativity might be much wider in its meaning. It has been contended that while the psychometric measures are adequately appropriate for novelty type of creativity, meaning type may be tapped most fruitfully by projective measures, specially the Rorschach human movement response (Minhas, 1981; Minhas and Kaur, 1983; Stark, 1965a, b). As such, it is imperative that both indices of creativity are essential for tapping the total spectrum of creative potential, and should be included in any study concerned with the examination of creativity correlates of word association test performance.

Nature of the Stimulus Words and Emotional Indicators

The nature of the words bearing the heaviest burden of complex signs next engages our attention. This is particularly interesting in view of the ample literature that assigns a significant role to the characteristics of the stimulus words in a word association test. The findings of several studies suggest that the stimulus characteristic may be an important variable in accounting for personality differences in word association test performance, and point to a factor which may account for contradictions in the literature, as well as paucity of personality correlates of words association test performance among normal subjects.

Cofer and Shevitz (1952) found that the words which occur with high frequency in the language elicit more responses than do low frequency words, and that nouns elicit more responses than adjectives. Lambert (1955) also found that nouns, particularly concrete nouns, elicit more responses than do adjectives. Lisman and Cohen (1972) demonstrated that schizophrenic–non-schizophrenic group differences varied appreciably with stimulus word type: schizophrenics gave fewer popular responses when stimulus words were 'ambiguous' and more popular responses when stimulus words were 'unambiguous'.

Past research has also highlighted the role of the following in word association test performance:

1. response entropy of the stimulus words,
2. affective connotation of the stimulus words, and
3. idiodynamic set in word association test performance.

Response Entropy and Word Association Test Performance

Response entropy, a measure of randomness of associations, take into account not only the number of different responses to a stimulus word, but also the percentage of subjects giving each response. Laffal (1955: 268) concluded: 'response faults in word association, it is seen, are largely a function of the nature of the associational response hierarchy of the stimulus word. Response faults are most likely to occur where there are many competing responses in the response hierarchy, and less likely to occur where there are strongly dominant responses in the hierarchy. Such an analysis does not completely rule out the role of emotional factors in the production of response disturbances. It would seem, however, that emotional factors might be most reasonably adduced to explain response faults only in words with strongly dominant responses. In such case, the fault might reflect the subject's need to avoid the dominant 'response'. Cramer (1968: 277) attributes word association to a process of activation of associative domains, or associative response hierarchies. In addition, Upmanyu (1981) examined the role of response entropy in emotional indicators elicited by the stimulus words in Kent–Rosanoff word association test. The author concluded that it is imperative to control response entropy while examining the diagnostic potential of the Kent–Rosanoff word association test. Several other recent studies (Hundal and Upmanyu, 1981; Kaur, 1992) using the Kent–Rosanoff word association test yielded the same finding.

Stimulus Affectivity and Word Association Test Performance

Further, in word association research, stimulus effectivity (i.e., emotional impact) is also known to be a potent variable influencing word associations (Cramer, 1968). Bodin and Geer (1965), using word graded along a dimension of hostility found that highly hostile words were responded to more slowly than moderately hostile words, which were responded to more slowly than non-hostile words. Pollio and

Lore (1965) demonstrated that affectively unpleasant words have longer associative latencies than affectively pleasant words, and that the latencies to unpleasant stimulus words increased as a function of the number of unpleasant context words that immediately preceded the unpleasant stimulus words of focal attention. Levinger and Clark (1961) asked subjects to give associations to 30 'emotionally' toned words (e.g., pity, love, bad) and 30 'neutral words' (e.g., lamp, sing, month). As predicted, longer latencies were associated with the emotionally toned words, and stimulus words rated highly emotional by (a) the experimenters, and (b) the subjects, were far more likely to elicit associations which were later forgotten than were those stimuli which were rated low on emotionality. It was proposed that the forgetting of word associations is a function of both emotional and non-emotional determinants. In discussing the observed influence of emotional factors in the forgetting of word associates, the authors concluded, 'it seems unlikely that an 'emotionless' theory of association can explain these findings' (p. 104). Although Levinger and Clark suggested that their results were compatible with the concept of repression, they were, however, careful to avoid any direct Freudian interpretation. Instead, they merely suggested that emotional responses (whether good or bad) are subject to some form of 'emotional inhibition', the nature of which was not clearly specified (see Parkin, Lewinsohn and Folkard, 1982: 389–90).

The Levinger and Clark (1961) study has been criticized, however, by Eysenck and Wilson (1973) and Parkin *et al.* (1982). Eysenck and Wilson (1973) regarded the results as an instance of an effect noted by Kleinsmith and Kaplan (1963, 1964), whereby highly arousing material is more likely than less arousing material to be forgotten after a short delay, but more likely to be remembered after a one-week interval. Bradley and Baddeley (1990) also found that the associations to emotional material were less well recalled immediately than the associations to material which was low in emotional valence, but tended to be better recalled a month later. The findings were compatible with those of Parkin *et al.* (1982), who found a significant interaction between recall interval and emotional content. The authors observed that the associates of emotional words were less well recalled immediately than the associates of neutral words, but after an interval of one week, the reverse was the case. These finding indicate that arousal interferes with short-time recall but facilitates long-term recall (for a review see M.W. Eysenck, 1976). A few studies (Jones,

O'Gorman and Byrne, 1987; Rossmann, 1984) cast doubt on the intepretation of forgetting of the associates of emotional and neutral words advanced by Eysenck and Wilson (1973) and Parkin *et al.* (1982) as the results of these studies indicated that forgetting was greater for the associates of emotional than neutral words irrespective of the recall interval. There was no significant interaction between emotionality and retention interval. Upmanyu, Singh and Panda (in press) also found similar results using the Kent–Rosanoff word association test.

In addition, Brown (1970), Innes (1971), Galbraith and Sturke (1974), Kuntz (1974), Penk (1978), Shiomi (1979) and Panda (1993) also found that stimulus effectivity is an important variable in accounting for personality differences in word-association behaviour. Personality findings with neutral stimulus words may fail to be confirmed with emotional stimulus words on account of the differential role of stimulus affectivity.

These studies clearly posit that stimulus affectivity is an important variable and needs careful attention in any study interested in the analysis of personality and cognitive correlates of the word association test performance. Panda (1993) found that dependent variables (emotional indicators) in the traditional single-response word association test are significantly influenced by stimulus affectivity.

Idiodynamic Set and Word Associations

Numerous investigators have commented on what might be called idiodynamic sets in word associations. In the traditional single-response word association test, some individuals tend to give predominately one charactristic 'category' of associate to different word lists in the context of their enduring idiodynamic associative sets. Several studies have demonstrated a tendency for certain subjects to respond with opposites on the standard word association tests (Carroll, Kjeldegaard and Carton, 1962; Kjeldegaard, 1962; Moran, Meffered and Kimble, 1964; Wynne, Gerjuoy and Schiffman, 1965). Three such sets have been described by Moron *et al.* (1964): (1) Object-referent set, characterized by a preponderance to give functional associates, (e.g., foot–shoe, boat–dock); (2) Concept-referent set, characterized by a preponderance to respond with synonym (e.g., small–little) and superordinate (e.g., cabbage–vegetable) associates, and (3) speed set, characterized by a fast contrast (e.g., apple–orange) associates, involving a set for speed in responding. Moran (1966) added a fourth such tendency being referred to as idiodynamic set, perceptual-referent.

Word association test performance is significantly influenced by an interaction between the subject's idiodynamic set and the set compatibility of the stimulus words. Response faults (e.g., delayed reaction time, blank, multiword, etc.) occur less frequently to stimulus words that are most compatible with the subject's set. Commonality score (degree to which a subjects' associates correspond to those of a normative group) is a partial function of the number of stimulus words in the list that happen to be compatible with the subject's set.

CONCLUSIONS

Since the publication of Jung's pioneering studies on word association, there has been a steadily increasing number of studies directed towards verifying the diagnostic potential of the word association test. The last few decades have seen a wealth of important investigations of word meaning and word association. One might believe that the multitude of investigations would have led to some reasonably secure conclusions about the relationship between emotional disturbance and word association emotional indicators as derived from word association test performance. Yet, this is not the case.

A variety of emotional indications have long been valued as signs of psychopathology. For example, we regard the more rare associates by disturbed psychotics than by non-psychotics as a firmly established finding. Likewise, long reaction time and other features of word association test performance (e.g., response repetition, reproduction failure, to mention just a few) have been widely accepted as indicators of emotional disturbance. Most studies of schizophrenic thinking based on associative disturbance have utilized the word association technique to investigate disturbed thought processes.

Furthermore, since there is ample evidence that the characteristics of stimulus words demonstrably affect association test performance, it is clearly perilous to infer 'psychiatric disturbance' or 'creativity', or 'both' rather than the role of 'stimulus characteristics' from a particular instance of idiosyncratic, rare or common word associations and other features of word association performance. In the context of these studies emphasizing the role of stimulus characteristics, the problem of understanding associative disturbances in schizophrenic and non-schizophrenic populations has become still more problematic. This conclusion is bound to be disquieting to experimenters wishing to use verbal materials to investigate perceptual defence, repression, etc. It is not, however, necessarily the final conclusion. Studies of personality and cognitive correlates of word associations, which failed to take into account the response entropy and affective connotation of the stimulus items, may bear re-evaluation in terms of these variables. It implies that any researcher looking for demonstrable value of word association tests for clinical diagnosis must concentrate either on the control or the manipulation of stimulus characteristics.

The results of several studies provide evidence that by paying close attention to the selection of the stimulus words, word association tests would meet our current standards as an acceptable instrument for clinical diagnosis. Rather, it is to emphasize that the frequently employed Kent and Rosanoff word association test, dating back to 1910, in the current form maybe unacceptable as a routine device for individual or differential diagnosis.

References

Astrup, C. and K. Flekkoy (1969). 'Verbal and Electrical Stimulation in Psychiatric Patients and Normal Controls', Cf. K.M. Flekkoy (1973) 'Some Hypothetical Mechanisms Underlying Associative Incoherence in Schizophrenics', *British Journal of Medical Psychology,* 46: 281–98.

Astrup, C. and K. Flekkoy (1968). 'Association Experiments in Psychiatric Patients and Normal Controls', Cf. K.M.Flekkoy (1973) 'Some Hypothetical Mechanisms Underlying Associative Incoherence in Schizophrenics', *British Journal of Medical Psychology,* 46: 271–78.

Barron, F. (1965). 'The Psychology of Creativity', in T.M. Newcomb (ed.), *New Directions in Psychology, II,* New York: Holt, Rinehart and Winston.

Barron, F. (1969). *Creative Person and Creative Process,* New York: Holt, Rinehart and Winston.

Bleuler, E. (1950). *Dementia Praecox or the Group of Schizophrenics,* Translated by J.Zenkin, New York: Inernational Universities Press.

Bodin, A.M. and J.H. Geer (1965). 'Association Responses of Depressed and Non-Depressed Patients Towards Their Hostility', *Journal of Personality,* 33: 392–408.

Bradley, B.R. and A.D. Baddeley (1990). 'Emotional Factors in Forgetting', *Psychological Medicine,* 20: 351–55.

Bown, W.P. (1970). 'Individual Differences in Associating to Neutral and Emotional Words', *Journal of Consulting and Clinical Psychology,* 34: 33–36.

Carrol, J.B., P.M. Kjeldegaard, and A.S. Carton (1962). 'Opposites vs. Primaries in Free Association', *Journal of Verbal Learning and Verbal Behaviour,* 1: 22–30.

Cattell, J.M. and S. Bryant (1889). 'Mental Association Investigated by Experiment', *Mind,* 14: 230–50.

Chapman, L.J. and J.P. Chapman (1973). *Disordered Thought in Schizophrenia,* Englewood Cliffs, N.J.: Prentice Hall.

Cofer, C.N. and R. Shevitz (1952). 'Word Association as a Function of Word Frequency', *American Journal of Psychology,* 65: 75–79.

Cramer, P. (1968). *Word Association,* New York: Academic Press.

Dewolfe, A.S. and H.D. Youkilis (1974). 'Stress and the Word Association of Process and Reactive Schizophrenics', *Journal of Clinical Psychology,* 30: 151–53.

Dodecki, P.R., L.G. Polidoro and R.L. Cromwell (1965). 'Commonality and Stability of Word Association Responses in Good and Poor Pre-Morbid Schizophrenics', *Journal of Abnormal Psychology,* 70: 312–16.

Eysenck, H.J. and S.B.G. Eysenck (1975). *Manual of Eysenck Personality Questionnaire (Junior and Adult),* London: Hodder and Stoughton.

Eysenck, H.J. and S.B.G. Eysenck (1976). *Psychoticism as a Dimension of Personality,* London: Hodder and Stoughton.

Eysenck, H.J. and G.D. Wilson (1973). *The Experimental Studies of Freudian theories,* London: Methen.

Flekky, K.M.(1973). 'Some Hypothetical Mechanisms Underlying Associative Incoherence in Schizophrenics', *British Journal of Medical Psychology,* 46: 271–73.

Fuller, G.D. and S.L. Kates (1969). 'Word Association Repertoires of Schizophrenics and Normals', *Journal of Consulting and Clinical Psychology,* 33: 497–500.

Galbraith, G.G. (1968). 'Effects of Sexual Arousal and Guilt Upon Free Associative Sexual Responses', *Journal of Consulting and Clinical Psychology,* 32: 707–11.

Galbraith, G.G., K. Hahn and H. Leiberman (1968). 'Personality Correlates of Free-Associative Sex Responses to Double-Entendre Words', *Journal of Consulting and Clinical Psychology,* 32: 193–97.

Galbraith, G.G. and D.L. Mosher (1970). 'Effects of Sex Guilt and Sexual Stimulation on the Recall of Word Associations', *Journal of Consulting and Clinical Psychology,* 34: 67–71.

Galbraith, G.G. and R.W. Sturke (1974). 'Effects of Stimulus Sexuality, Order of Presentation and Sex Guilt on Free Associative Latencies', *Journal of Consulting and Clinical Psychology,* 6: 828–32.

Galton, F. (1879). 'Psychometric Facts; Nineteenth Century', in H.H. Andersen and G.L. Andersen (1951) An Introduction to Projective Techniques. Eaglewood Clipps, NJ: Prentice Hall Inc. 274–94.

Gough, H.G. (1976). 'Studying Creativity by Means of Words Association Tests', *Journal of Applied Psychology,* 61: 348–53.

Green, P.D. and G.G. Galbraith (1986). 'Associative Responses to Double Entendre Drug Words: A Study of Drug Addicts and College Students', *Personality and Social Psychology Bulletin,* 12: 31–39.

Griffith, J.J., S.A. Mednick, F. Schulsinger and B. Diderrichsen (1980). 'Verbal Associative Disturbances in Children at High Risk for Schizophrenia', *Journal of Abnormal Psychology,* 89: 125–31.

Guilford, J.P., R.C. Wilson, P.R. Christensen and D.J. Lewis (1951). 'A Factor-Analytic Study of Creative Thinking. Hypotheses and Description of Tests', Reports from the Psychological Laboratory (No. 4), Los Angeles: University of Southern California.

Hull, C.L. and L.S. Lugoff (1921). 'Complex Signs in Diagnostic Free Association', *Journal of Experimental Psychology,* 4: 111–36.

Hundal, P.S. and V.V. Upmanyu (1974). 'Emotional Indicators in Word Association and Their Relation with Psychometiric Measures of Anxiety and Neuroticism', *International Review of Applied Psychology,* 23: 111–20.

Hundal, P.S. and V.V. Upmanyu (1981). 'Nature of Emotional Indicators in Kent–Rosanoff Word Association Test: An Empirical Elaboration', *Personality Study and Group Behaviour,* 1: 50–61.

Innes, J.M. (1971). 'Word Association, Associative Structure and Manifest Anxiety', *British Journal of Psychology,* 62: 519–25.

Jones, E.B., J.G. O'Gorman and B. Byrne (1987). 'Forgetting of Word Associates as a Function of Recall Interval', *British Journal of Psychology,* 78: 79–89.

Jung, C.G. (1910). 'The Association Method', *American Journal of Psychology,* 21: 219–69.

Kaur, K. (1992). 'An Investigation into the Nature of Word Associations in Relation to Pathology, Intelligence and Creativity', Unpublished Ph.D. Thesis, Panjab University, Chandigarh.

Kent, G.H. and A.I. Rosanoff (1910). 'A Study of Association in Insanity', *American Journal of Insanity,* 67: 37–96, 317–90.

Kjeldegaard, P.M. (1962). 'Commonality Scores Under Instructions to Give Opposites', *Psychological Reports,* 11: 219–20.

Kline, P. (1981). *Fact and Fantasy in Freudian Theory,* London: Methuen.

Kleinsmith, L.J. and S. Kaplan (1963). 'Paired Associates Learning as a Function of Arousal and Interpolated Interval', *Journal of Experimental Psychology,* 66: 190–96.

Kleinsmith, L.J. and S. Kaplan (1964). 'Interaction of Arousal and Recall Interval in Nonsense Syllable Paired Associate Learning', *Journal of Experimental Psychology,* 67: 124–26.

Kraepelin, E. (1892). *An Introduction to Projective Techniques,* Cf. H.H. Anderson and G.L. Anderson (1951), Englewood Cliffs, New Jersey: Prentice-Hall Inc., pp. 279–94.

Kuntz, D. (1974). 'Response Faults on Word Association as a Function of Associative Difficulty and of Affective Connotation of the Words', *Journal of Consulting and Clinical Psychology,* 42: 231–35.

Laffal, J. (1955). 'Response Faults in Word Association as a Function of Response Entropy', *Journal of Abnormal and Social Psychology,* 50: 265–70.

Lambert, W.E. (1955). 'Associational Fluency as a Function of Stimulus Abstractness', *Canadian Journal of Psychology,* 9: 103–6.

Levinger, G. and J. Clark (1961). 'Emotional Factors in the Forgetting of Word Associations', *Journal of Abnormal and Social Psychology,* 62: 99–105.

Lisman, S.A. and B.D. Cohen (1972). 'Self-Editing Deficits in Schizophrenia: A Word-Association Analogue', *Journal of Abnormal Psychology,* 79: 181–88.

Maltzman, I. (1960). 'On the Training of Originality', *Psychological Review,* 67: 229–42.

Mednick, S.A. (1962). 'The Associative Basis of the Creative Process', *Phychological Review,* 69: 220–32.

Münsterberg, H. (1907). *An Introduction to Projective Techniques,* New Jersey: Prentice Hall Inc., pp. 279–94.

Miller, E.N. and L.J. Chapman (1983). 'Continued Word Association in Hypothetically Psychosis-Prone college students', *Journal of Abnormal Psychology,* 92: 468–78.

Minhas, L.S. (1981). 'A Factor Analytic Study of Psychometric and Projective Indices of Creativity and Those of Intelligence and Personality', *Personality Study and Group Behaviour,* 2: 29–38.

Minhas, L.S. and F. Kaur (1983). 'A Study of Field-Independent Cognitive Styles in Relation to Novelty and Meaning Context of Creativity', *Personality Study and Group Behaviour,* 3: 20–34.

Moran, L.J. (1966). 'Generality of Word-Association Response Sets', *Psychological Monographs: General and Applied,* 80: 1–25.

Moran, L.J., R.B. Meffered, Jr. and J.P. Kimble, Jr. (1964). 'Idiodynamic Sets in Word Association', *Psychological Monographs: General and Applied,* 78: 1–22.

Mosher, D.L. (1965). 'Interaction of Fear and Guilt in Inhibiting Unacceptable Behaviour', *Journal of Consulting Psychology,* 29: 161–67.

O'Brian, J.P. and H. Weingartner (1970). 'Associative Structure in Chronic Schizophrenia', *Archives of General Psychiatry,* 22: 136–42.

Pack, D. and L. Pons (1985). 'Correlation Between Two Indices of Commonality and of Repetition in Free Word-Association Responses', *Psychological Reports,* 56: 931–38.

Paivio, A., J.G. Yuille and S.A. Madigan (1968). 'Concreteness, Imagery and Meaningfulness Values for 925 Nouns', *Journal of Experimental Psychology, Monograph Supplement,* (Part 2) 71: 1.

Panda, S.N. (1993). A Study of Word Associations to Neutral and Emotional Words', Unpublished M.Phil Dissertation, Panjab University, Chandigarh.

Parkin, A.J. (1984). 'Comment on 'Parkin *et al.* Reconsidered' by Rossmann', *Psychological Research,* 45: 389–94.

Parkin, A.J., J. Lewinsohn and S. Folkard (1982). 'The Influence of Emotion on Immediate and Delayed Retention: Levinger and Clark reconsidered', *British Journal of Psychology,* 73: 389–93.

Penk, W.E. (1978). 'Effects of Ambiguous and Unambiguous Stimulus Word Differences on Popular Responses of Schizophrenics', *Journal of Clinical Psychology,* 34: 838–43.

Pollio, H.R. and R.K. Lore (1965). 'The Effect of Semantically Congruent Context on Word Association Behaviour', *Journal of Psychology,* 61: 17–26.

Pons, L., M. Bielecki, B.L., Chevalier, C. Schupp and F. Morin (1986). 'Responses of Parkinsonian Patients to a Successive Free Word-Association Test', *Psychological Reports,* 58: 67–72.

Pons, L. and M. Ecolasses (1982). 'Commonality and Reproduction of a Word Associated Response in Three Samples of French, American and Japanese Students', *Psychologia,* 25: 205–12.

Pons, L., J. Nurnberger and D. Murphy (1985). 'Mood-Independent Aberrancies of Word Responses and Action of Lithium on Their Repetition in Manic-Depressed Illness', *Psychiatric Research,* 14: 315–22.

Rapaport, D., M. Gill and R. Schafer (1946). *Diagnostic Psychological testing,* Vol.II, Chicago: Year Book Publication.

Rierdan, J. (1980). 'Word Association of Socially Isolated Adolescents', *Journal of Abnormal Psychology,* 89: 98–100.

Rossmann, P. (1984). 'On the Forgetting of Word Associations: Parkin *et al.* reconsidered', *Psychological Research,* 45: 377–88.

Sackheim, H.A. and H.E. Shapiron (1981). 'Schizophrenic Cognition: Regression or Yielding to Normal Biases', *The Journal of Nervous and Mental Disease,* 169: 591–98.

Schill, T.R. (1972). 'Need for Approval, Guilt, and Sexual Stimulation and Their Relationship to Sexual Responsibility', *Journal of Consulting and Clinical Psychology,* 38: 31–35.

Schwartz, S. (1978a). 'Do Schizophrenics Give Rare Word Association?', *Schizophrenia Bulletin,* 4: 248–51.

Shakow, D. (1980). 'Kent-Rosanoff Association and its Implications for Segmental Set Theory', *Schizophrenia Bulletin,* 6: 676–85.

Shiomi, K. (1979). 'Differences in Reaction Times of Extraverts and Introverts to Rapaport's Word Association Test', *Psychological Reports,* 45: 75–80.

Silverstein, M.L. and M. Harrow (1980). 'Auditory Misperceptions of Word-Association Stimuli in Schizophrenia', *Perceptual and Motor Skills,* 50: 1192–94.

Silverstein, M.L. and M. Harrow (1983a). 'Word Association: Multiple Measures and Multiple Meanings', *Journal of Clinial Psychology,* 39: 467–70.

Silverstein, M.L. and M. Harrow (1983b). 'Goal-Directed Thinking in Schizophrenic Associations', *Journal of Personality Assessment,* 47: 161–66.

Sinton, C.M. (1981). 'Sex Differences in the Interaction of Emotional Factors with Memory', *International Journal of Neuroscience,* 14: 211–18.

Stark, S. (1965a). 'An Essay in Romantic Genius, Rorschach Movement and the Definition of Creativity', *Perceptual and Motor Skills,* 20: 409–18.

Stark, S. (1965b). 'Toward a Psychological Knowledge Hypothesis Recording Rorschach Movement and Creativity', *Perceptual and Motor Skills,* 21: 839–59.

Symonds, P.M. (1931). *Diagnosing Personality and Conduct,* New York: Appleton-Century-Crofts Inc.

Tendler, A.D. (1945). 'Significant Features of Disturbance in Free Association', *Journal of Psychology,* 20: 65–89.

Upmanyu, V.V. (1981). 'Study of Kent-Rosanoff Word Association Test in Relation to Response Entropy', *Personality Study and Group Behavior,* 1: 1–52.

Upmanyu, V.V., P.S. Gill and S. Singh (1982). 'Nature of Unusual Responses in Kent–Rosanoff Word Association Test in Relation to Response Entropy', *Personality Study and Group Behavior,* 2: 44–53.

Upmanyu, V.V. and K. Kaur (1986). 'Diagnostic Utility of Word Association Emotional Indicators', *Psychlogical Studies,* 32: 71–78.

Upmanyu, V.V. and K. Kaur (1988). 'Word Association Test Performance in Relation to Anxiety and Stimulus Characteristics', *Journal of Personality and Clinical Studies,* 4: 121–26.

Upmanyu, V.V. and S. Singh (1984). 'Word Association Test Response: An Index of Pathological Characteristics or Creativity', *Personality Study and Group Behavior,* 4: 39–49.

Upmanyu, V.V. and S. Singh (1996). 'Word Association Emotional Indicators: Associations with Anxiety, Neuroticism, Psychoticism and Creativity', *Journal of Social Psychology* (Accepted).

Upmanyu, V.V. and S. Upmanyu (1988). 'Utility of Word Association Emotional Indicators for Predicting Pathological Characteristics', *Personality Study and Group Behavior,* 8: 13–22.

Wundt, W. (1911). Cf. H.H. Anderson and G.L. Anderson (1951). *An Introduction to Projective Techniques,* Englewood Cliffs, New Jersey: Prentice Hall Inc., pp. 279–94.

Wynne, R.D. (1963). 'The Influence of Hospitalization on the Verbal Behaviour of Chronic Schizophrenics', *British Journal of Psychiatry,* 109: 380–89.

Wynne, R.D., H. Gerjuoy and H. Schiffman (1965). 'Association Test Antonym-Response Set', *Journal of Verbal Learning and Verbal Behavior,* 4: 354–59.

13 Coronary Artery Disease and Essential Hypertension in Relation to Personality Stress Questionnaire: Validation in India

H.J. Eysenck, Jitendra Mohan and Meena Sehgal

ABSTRACT

Research in the last few years by H.J. Eysenck and Grossarth-Maticek has clearly demonstrated that there is a strong evidence concerning the relationship between personality and diseases like cancer and Coronary Heart disease. They developed a questionnaire to measure six different reaction types, the contention being that persons prone to certain kinds of illnesses show different types of reaction to interpersonal stress. This system of typology can predict the occurrence of cancer and Coronary Heart Disease in people, based on their reaction types. An attempt was made to establish cross-cultural validity of this questionnaire by administering it to 100 coronary Heart disease patients, 100 Essential Hypertension patients, and 200 healthy controls in the age range of 40–50 years. The implication of results in using PSQ as a screening device are discussed.

INTRODUCTION

There is a long history of belief, more than 2,000 years long, originating in the works of Hippocrates, Galen and Sushrut, that psychosocial factors play an important role in causation and development of psychosomatic diseases, especially cancer, hypertension, and Coronary Heart Disease (CHD). These beliefs resurfaced in the 20th century, and were vigorously tested by Le Shan (1959, 1977), Friedman and Rosenman (1959), and Kissen and Eysenck (1962). These early studies were positive, yet some reviews also led to the conclusions that prevalence of negative results precluded any overall positive evaluation (Fox, 1978, 1981). Eysenck (1990, 1993), however, stated that these negative evaluations are unjustified because they are based on erroneous assumption, and may have reviewed studies not based on good theoretical foundations or appropriate methods of investigation. Eysenck (1991, 1993) argued that there is now sufficient evidence that personality and stress are as important risk factors for cancer and CHD as other risk factor like smoking, heredity, cholesterol level, hypertension and physiological variables. The cancer-prone personality is characterized by a tendency to suppress the expression of emotions, and an inability to deal with stress, leading to feelings of hopelessness/helplessness and, finally, depression (Eysenck, 1990). The CHD-prone personality is characterized by strong, easily aroused feelings of anger, hostility and aggression (Eysenck, 1990). Bortner and Rosenman (1967) and Rosenman and Chesney (1980) gave evidence that Type A behaviour Pattern (TABP) is related to and predictive of CHD.

In India, a recent study by Dhamija and Bhattacharya (1996) found that CHD patients in comparison to healthy persons (in the age range of 40 to 55 years), scored significantly higher on anxiety, neuroticism, and extraversion. Earlier, Mohan and Sehgal (1998, 1999) also found personality factors, viz., neuroticism, hostility and stress to be related to CHD.

In this connection, a series of prospective studies carried out by Grossarth-Maticek and H.J. Eysenck (Eysenck, 1983, 1984, 1988, 1991; Eysenck *et al.,* 1991; Grossarth-Maticek, 1986, 1982; Grossarth-Maticek and Eysenck, 1990, 1991; Grossarth-Maticek *et al.,* 1982, 1985, 1988) clearly demonstrated that personality is a major risk factor in cancer and CHD. They found that persons prone to certain kinds of illnesses showed different types of reactions to interpersonal stress. For this purpose, they developed a questionnaire to measure six different reaction types. These different behaviour types are related to cancer, CHD, and endogenous depression (Schmitz, 1992). A brief description of the six behaviour types, based on descriptions by Grossarth-Maticek and Eysenck (1990) and Schmitz (1992), is presented in the following sections.

Type I Behaviour: Under-Stimulation

Persons of this type show a permanent tendency to regard an emotionally highly valued object as the most important condition for their own well-being and happiness. Type I is defined by a conformist dependency on a valued, withdrawing object. A Type I person tries permanently and intensively to approach highly valued targets (persons, objects, situations), which are, unfortunately, inaccessible for him/her. The stress produced by the continued withdrawal or absence of this object is experienced as an emotionally traumatic event. Type I individuals fail to distance themselves from the object, and remain dependent upon it. Thus, individuals of this type do not achieve success in reaching the object, and remain distant and isolated from this highly valued and emotionally important object. As a result, they experience great stress. Persons belonging to this type lack autonomy, and are highly dependent on others. They show depressive tendencies, are rigid, and are inhibited in showing and communicating their feelings.

Type II Behaviour: Overarousal

Persons of this type show a continued tendency to regard an emotionally highly important object as the most important cause for their particular distress and unhappiness. Rejection by the object (if a person), or failure to reach it (as in the case of occupational success) is experienced as an emotional trauma, but persons of this type fail to achieve disengagement from the object, rather, they feel more and more helplessly dependent on the object. Thus persons of this type remain in constant contact with these negatively valued and emotionally disturbing people and situations, and fail to distance themselves and free themselves from dependence on the disturbing object. Where persons of Type I behaviour keep on seeking nearness to the object of their desires, and experience their failure in terms of hopelessness and helplessness, persons of Type II behaviour fail to disengage themselves from the object, and experience anger, aggression and arousal.

Type II, in contrast to Type I, behaviour, is defined by a conformist dependency on a disturbing object. Type II persons try fruitlessly to escape or emancipate themselves from a person or an object which is emotionally very important for them. Their behaviour is also very rigid and, often, depressive. Like Type I persons, Type II persons have difficulties in showing their feelings, particularly feelings of anger and annoyance. CHDs are considered to be related to Type II behaviour pattern.

Type III Behaviour

Type III behaviour pattern is described by a non-conformist dependency on an object which is both withdrawing and disturbing. Persons of this type show a tendency to shift from the typical reaction of Type I to the typical reaction of Type II, and back again. As Grossarth-Maticek (1986) put it, 'This type shows a permanent tendency to regard an emotionally highly valued object alternatively as the most important condition for his own well-being, and as the main cause for his own unhappiness.' Thus, in individuals of this type, there is an alternation of feelings of hoplessness/helplessness and of anger/arousal. It seems that depressive tendencies and anxiety are partially related to this type of behaviour. Eysenck states that this behaviour type may be related to hysterical behaviour by virtue of the alternations of the moods involved.

Type IV: Personal Autonomy

Type IV behaviour is characterized by autonomy. This type is the 'healthy type'. The typical reactions of Types I, II and III indicate a dependence on the highly valued object, and their reactions are characterized by constant contradiction between expected consequences and the actual consequences of their actions. For persons of Type IV behaviour pattern, there is a strong tendency to regard their own autonomy, and the autonomy of the persons with whom they wish to be in contact, as the most important condition for their own well-being and happiness. This enables persons of Type IV to experience realistically the approach or avoidance behaviour of the object of their desires, and, thus, enables them to accept the autonomy of the object. In other words, persons of Types I and II show dependence on the important object which engage their emotions but cannot remain autonomous when these emotional objects withdraw or remain unattainable; it is this that constitutes the stress, which, according to the theory, leads to cancer or CHD. Persons of Type IV are able to deal with this situation by virtue of their autonomy-preserving ability, and, thus, avoid the stress reaction. Type IV is healthy autonomous type of behaviour pattern that survives best.

Type V Behaviour

Persons of Type V show 'rational and anti-emotional' tendencies. It is predicted that this type would be prone to endogenous depression. Typical reactions of a person belonging to this behaviour type are: 'I can only express feelings when they have a rational basis' or 'I can only express happy emotions when they have a rational basis'. Type V shows rational and anti-emotional tendencies and would be prone to depression and cancer.

Type VI behaviour

Type VI behaviour pattern is characterized by 'anti-social and possibly psychopathic behaviour'. Persons belonging to this behaviour type are prone to drug addiction. Typical reactions of persons of this typology are: 'When a person is emotionally important to me, I usually experience strong contradictory feelings, like love and hate, attraction and dislike, etc.' or 'I often feel the need to attack other people aggressively and to upset them.'

Table 1
Summary Description of Six Behaviour Types
(Grossarth-Maticek et al., 1986)

Type I	Conformist dependency on a withdrawing object. Disposition: prone to Cancer.
Type II	Conformist dependency on a disturbing object. Disposition: prone to Cardiovascular Diseases.
Type III	Non-conformist dependency on an object which is both withdrawing and disturbing. Disposition: prone to Chronic Anxiety.
Type IV	Appropriate autonomy; a permanent self-regulation, which brings independence in the satisfaction of needs. Disposition: prone to Healthy Behaviour.
Type V	Rational anti-emotional tendencies. Disposition: prone to Endogenous Depression.
Type VI	Anti-social tendencies. Disposition: prone to Criminal Behaviour, Drug Addiction.

Type VI is clearly antisocial and, possibly, criminal and prone to drug addiction. Grossarth-Maticek and Eysenck (1990) stated that Types III, IV and VI are relatively healthy types, as opposed to Type I, II and V, which are unhealthy.

Grossarth-Maticek (1986) further stated that failure in relation to emotionally highly valued people and/or life goals is experienced by persons of Type I and II as 'unavoidable', whereas persons of Type IV possess the ability to cope with the situation, and hence the stress is 'avoidable' given that unavoidable stress is closely related with disease, whereas avoidable stress is not (Sklar and Anisman, 1979, 1981), it is clear that Type IV should be less likely to suffer from cancer and heart disease than Types I or II. Type III may also be protected to some extent by changing its reaction to the stressful situation from behaviour typical of Type I to behaviour typical of Type II, and back; in this way, persons of Type III may avoid, to some extent, the build-up of behaviour patterns related to cancer or CHD, respectively.

The emotional reactions of persons of these types follow from what has been said. Persons of Type I react with depressions and hopelessness to the loss of the idealized object, whereas persons of Type II react with anger and arousal to the feeling of being helplessly delivered to a hostile object. Emotional reactions of persons of Type III vary from anxiety and fear to aggressive tendencies stimulated by the recalcitrance of the object (Eysenck and Grossarth-Maticek, 1990).

According to Grossarth-Maticek (1986), typical reactions of persons of these various types are largely moulded by specific dynamics of their family life and early development. Thus, persons of Type I experience early rejection by parents combined with parental demands to idealize and love them. Persons of Type II typically experience positive emotional attachment and attraction to one parent. It should not be assumed, of course, that even though there may be statistical relationships of these kinds, these must have a causal role. It is more plausible to think of the relationship being mediated by genetic factors (Grossarth-Maticek, 1986).

These types of behaviours are reactions to stressful situations, and as research shows (Grossarth-Maticek, Eysenck and Vetter, 1988) they are partially influenced by the individuals' life experiences and, consequently, can be modified by therapeutic interventions.

THE PRESENT STUDY

Aims

Cardiovascular diseases are the leading cause of death in India. Today, the biopsychosocial model of health and illness highlights the role of psychological factors like personality, stress, and lifestyle in chronic ailments. In the same vein, Grossarth-Maticek and Eysenck (1990) developed and inventory measuring six personality types which can prospectively predict CHD and cancer.

Specifically, Type II dimension was said to be linked with Cardiovascular disease and Type IV with healthy behaviour. As the disease groups included in the present study were CHD Essential Hypertension patients, exploring the role of these two typologies and their link with health and disease status was of special significance in the present study.

Method

For this purpose, 400 subjects comprised the sample. There were 100 CHD patients, 100 Essential Hypertension patients, and 200 healthy controls. Inclusion criteria for the patients was chronicity of disease, that is, subjects who were suffering from the disease for not less than 6 months and not more than 5 years. The controls did not suffer from any disease. All the subjects were males in the age range of 40 to 50 years, and were drawn from different professions. They were administered the Personality Stress Questionnaire-short form (Grossarth-Maticek and Eysenck, 1990).

Results and Discussion

Over hundreds of years, medical orthodoxy believed firmly in the existence of a strong relation between personality and specific diseases like cancer and CHD. The cancer-prone personality was described as repressing emotions and finding it difficult to cope with stress, giving up easily, and developing the feeling of hopelessness and helplessness (Eysenck, 1991; Temoshok and Dreher, 1992). Sir William Osler, often called the father of English medicine, said in 1910, 'It is often more important what person has the disease than disease the person has'. Earlier clinical observation of CHD patients revealed that for a long time CHD was found to be linked with personality traits of impatience, hyperalertness, aggressiveness and proneness to anger (Osler, 1910; Kemple, 1945; Menninger and Menninger, 1936). These observations were put together into the concept of Type A behaviour by the cardiologists (Friedman and Rosenman, 1959), who reported that majority of the CHD patients showed a set of behaviour patterns and emotions similar to that shown in previous clinical observations (Price, 1982). One may state, therefore, that in the 1950s serious scientific study began to show that the anecdotal evidence of past centuries had a backing of truth (Eysenck, 1993). The work of pioneers like Leshan (1977) verified many of the old theories in relation to cancer. Type A concept has done the same for CHD, although according to Eysenck (1993), subsequently only parts of this TABP (aggressiveness, hostility and anger) appear to have survived replication.

An alternative method of assessing a personality type along more holistic lines and prospective in nature was developed by Grossarth-Maticek, Eysenck and Vetter (1988). The Personality Stress Questionnaire (PSQ) yields six personality types, which were said to be related to differential susceptibility to certain diseases. Detailed description of these has already been given earlier in the text. This system of typology is geared to the prediction of cancer and cardiovascular diseases in people.

> *Type I personalities are more susceptible to cancer, Type II personalities to Coronary Heart Diseases, Type III to Chronic Anxiety, Type IV to Health and Autonomy, Type V to Depression and Cancer and Type VI to Antisocial tendencies, Criminal behaviour and greater inclination to become addicted to drugs.*

Such a claim by Eysenck and Grossarth-Maticek was linked with the possibility of using behaviour therapy for prevention of illness in cancer-prone and cardiovascular disease-prone individuals (Grossarth-Maticek and Eysenck, 1991).

However, there has been considerable controversy over these claims (Amelang, Rathjens and Mathews, 1996). The present study made an attempt to test these claims in the Indian population. Earlier also, Mohan, Eysenck and Eysenck (1987), Mohan and Kaur (1986), Mohan and Rattan (1987), Mohan and Tiwana (1987), Mohan (1994, 1995, 1997, 1998a) and Mohan and Sehgal (1999a, b) attempted to establish cross-cultural norms for Eysenck Personality Questionnaire-Revised. More specifically, keeping in view the two disease groups chosen—

CHD and Essential Hypertension—it was expected that in line with the predictions made by Grossarth-Maticek and Eysenck, these two groups should score the highest on Type II, and healthy controls should score the highest on Type IV.

Table 2 shows the means, SDs and t-ratios for the six behaviour types obtained by Group I (healthy controls), Group 2 (Essential Hypertensions patients), and Group 3 (CHD patients), respectively, For Type I, significant differences emerged between Group 1 and Group 2 (Group 2 > Group 1) and Group 2 and Group 3 (Group 2 > Group 3). Insignificant differences emerged between Group 1 and Group 3, with Group 1 obtaining higher mean scores than Group 3.

On Type II, which is of primary significance in the present study as this typology tests susceptibility to cardiovascular disease, it was found that as expected, the CHD group scored significantly higher than the control and Essential Hypertension groups (Table 2). The t-ratio was almost significant between Groups 1 and 2, with Group 2 (Essential Hypertension) scoring higher than Group 1 (healthy controls). The results validate Grossarth-Maticek and Eysenck's claim that Type II measures proneness to cardiovascular diseases.

On Type III, which measures proneness to chronic anxiety, again, the CHD group scored significantly higher than the Essential Hypertensive patients and controls. A comparison between Group 1 (healthy controls) and Group 2 (Essential Hypertension) revealed that though the t-ratio was insignificant the Essential Hypertension group obtained higher mean scores than the control subjects. These findings also make sense as anxiety and stress have been found to play a crucial role in disease groups.

On Type IV, which measures disposition to health and autonomy, the healthy controls scored significantly higher than the Essential Hypertension and CHD groups. No significant differences between Essential Hypertension and CHD groups emerged on this dimension. Again, these results validate Grossarth-Maticek & Eysenck's (1990) findings that Type IV measures health proneness.

On Type V, which measures depression proneness, the controls obtained significantly higher mean scores than the Essential Hypertension and CHD groups. The Essential Hypertension group scored significantly higher than the CHD group. The finding that the healthy controls scored the highest on this dimension, is a little perplexing.

On Type VI, which is a disposition to criminal behaviour, the Essential Hypertension group scored significantly higher than the CHD

Table 2

Means, SDs, and t-ratios for all the Three Groups.

	Group 1 n=200		Group 2 n=100		t-ratios b/w groups	Group 3 n=100		t-ratios b/w groups	t-ratio b/w groups
	M	SD	M	SD	1&2	M	SD	1&3	2&3
Type I: Cancer-Prone	4.06	1.98	4.96	3.2	2.58	3.77	2.11	1.15	3.11
Type II: Cardiovascular Disease Prone	4.20	2.43	4.63	2.11	1.58	6.16	1.83	7.8	5.48
Type III: Chronic Anxiety Prone	3.50	1.98	3.76	1.58	1.23	5.01	1.66	6.96	5.46
Type IV: Healthy Type	13.25	3.01	11.32	3.00	5.24	11.26	2.04	6.75	.17
Type V: Depression-Prone	6.17	1.53	5.78	2.25	5.04	4.96	1.75	5.22	2.88
Type VI: Anti-Social Behaviour	2.60	2.01	3.77	1.72	5.25	3.24	1.90	2.7	2.07

Group 1. Healthy Controls (HC)
Group 2. Essential Hypertension (EHT)
Group 3. Coronary Heart Disease (CHD)

* Significant at 0.05 levels
** Significant at 0.01 levels

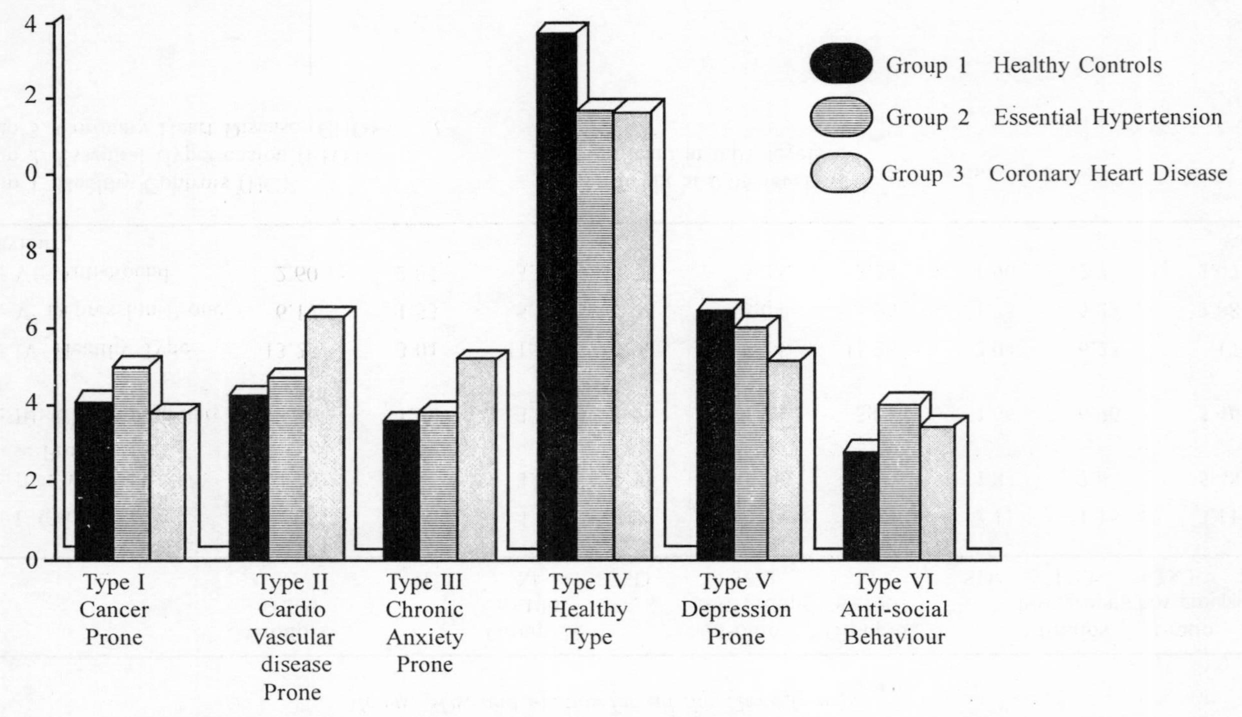

Figure1. *Mean Scores of the Three Groups on Six Personality Types.*

group and the controls. The CHD group scored significantly higher than the controls. Again, this finding as to why the cardio-vascular group shows more psychopathic tendencies needs further investigation.

The role of Type II, Type III and Type IV in health and disease, when tested through t-tests, was clearly established, but certain confounding results also emerged. Whereas Type II, Type III, and Type IV differentiated between healthy participants and disease groups in the predicted direction, the same cannot be said for Type I, Type V and Type VI. Contrary to the expectations, healthy participants scored the highest on Type V, and both the disease groups scored higher on Type VI. Similar confounding results, as regards the role of Type I, Type V and Type VI in distinguishing the disease groups like cancer and CHD, were reported by Amelang *et al.* (1996) in Heidelberg, Germany.

In conclusion, it could be safely stated that, Type II and Type IV dimensions of the PSQ have shown clear discriminant validity, and may serve as a valid and promising screening device to successfully identify in advance, individuals prone to developing cardiovascular diseases. More studies are needed with different disease groups to check the claims of Eysenck and Grossarth-Maticek (1990) regarding the role of Type I, Type V and Type VI behavioural typologies in the causation and development of disease.

The cross-cultural validation of the roles of the six behavioural typologies and their link with disease is a complex phenomenon and cannot be accepted and generalized in its entirety. These claims need more replications, and may be accepted ultimately with certain culture-based modifications. More than anything else, the present study adds to the growing body of evidence that psychosocial factors play an important and definite role in health and disease.

References

Amelang M., C.S. Rathjens and G. Matthews (1996). 'Personality Cancer and Coronary Heart Disease: Further Evidence on a Controversial Issue', *British Journal of Health Psychology.*, 1: 191–205.

Bortner, R.W. and R.H. Rosenman (1967). 'The Measurement of Type-A Pattern: A Behaviour', *Journal of Chronic Disease,* 20: 525–33.

Dhamija, S.C. and T. Bhattacharya (1996). 'Psycho-Social Correlates of Cardiac Patients', *Social Science International,* 12: 142.

Eysenck, H.J. (1983). 'Stress Disease, and Generality: the "Inoculation Effect"', in C.I. Cooper (ed.), *Stress Research,* London: Wiley, pp. 121–46.

Eysenck, H.J. (1984). 'Lung Cancer and the Stress Personality Inventory', in C.L. Cooper (ed.), *Psychosocial Stress and Cancer,* London: Wiley, pp. 49–71.

Eysenck, H.J. (1988). 'The Respective Importance of Personality, Cigarette and Interaction Effects for the Genesis of Cancer and CHD', *Personality and Individual Differences,* 9: 453–64.

Eysenck, H.J. (1990). 'The Prediction of Death from Cancer by Means of Personality/Stress Questionnaire: "Too Good to be True"?', *Perceptual and Motor Skills,* 71: 216–18.

Eysenck, H.J. (1991). *Smoking Personality and Stress: Psycho-Social Factors in the Prevention of Cancer and Coronary Heart Disease,* New York: Springer Verlag.

Eysenck, H.J. (1993). 'Prediction of Cancer and Coronary Heart Disease Mortality by Means of Personality Inventory: Results of a 15-Year Follow-Up Study', *Psychological Reports,* 72: 499–516.

Eysenck, H.J., Grossarth-Maticek and B. Everitt (1991). 'Stress, Smoking and Genetic Predisposition as Synergistic Risk Factors for Cancer and Coronary Heart Disease', *Integrative Physiological and Behavioural Science,* 26(4): 309–22.

Fox, B.H. (1978). 'Premorbid Psychological Factors as Related to Incidence of Cancer', *Journal of Behavioural Medicine,* 1: 45–133.

Fox, B.H. (1981). 'Behavioral Issues in Cancer', in S.M. Weiss, J.A. Herd, and B.H. Fox (eds), *Perspectives on Behavioral Medicine,* London: Academic Press, pp. 101–34.

Friedman, M. and R.H. Rosenman (1959). 'Association of Specific Overt Behavior Patterns with Blood and Cardiovascular Findings', *Journal of the American Medical Association,* 169: 1286–96.

Grossarth-Maticek, R. (1986). 'Psychosociale Verhalte stypen unchronische Erkrankungen', Der Kassenarzi, 39: 26–35.

Grossarth-Maticek, R., J. Bastiaans and D.T. Kanazir (1985). 'Psychosocial Factors as Strong Predictors of Mortality from Cancer, Ischaemic Heart Disease and Stroke: Yugoslav

Prospective Study', *Journal of Psychosomatic Research,* 29: 167–76.

Grossarth-Maticek, R. and H.J. Eysenck (1990). 'Personality, Stress and Disease Description and Validation of a New Inventory', *Psychological Reports,* 66: 355–73.

Grossarth-Maticek, R. and H.J. Eysenck (1991). 'Creative Novation Behaviour Therapy as a Prophylactic Treatment', *Behaviour Research and Therapy,* 29: 1–16.

Grossarth-Maticek, R., D.T. Kanazir, P. Schmidt and H. Vetter (1982). 'Psychosomatic Factors in the Process of Cancero-Genesis', *Psychotherapy and Psychosomatics,* 28: 284–302.

Grossarth-Maticek, R., H.J. Eysenck, H. Vatter and R. Frentzel-Beyme (1986). 'The Heidelberg Prospective Intervention Study', Paper presented at the 1st International Symposium of Primary Prevention and Cancer in Antwerp, Belgium, March 19–22.

Grossarth-Maticek, R., H.J. Eysenck and H. Vatter (1988). 'Personality Type, Smoking Habit and their Interaction as Predictors of Cancer and Coronary Heart Disease', *Personality and Individual Differences,* 9: 479–95.

Kemple, L. (1945). 'Rorschach Method and Psychosomatic Diagnosis: Personality Traits of Patients with Rheumatic Disease, Hypertension, Cardiovascular Disease, Occlusions and Fracture', *Psychosomatic Medicine,* 7: 85–89.

Kissen, D.M. and H.J. Eysenck (1962). 'Personality in Male Lung Cancer Patients', *Journal of Psychosomatic Research*, 6: 123–27.

Le Shan, L. (1959). 'Psychological States as Factors in the Development of Malignant Disease: a Critical Review', *Journal of the National Cancer Institute,* 22: 1–18.

Le Shan, L. (1977). *You can Fight for Your Life; Emotional Factors in the Causation of Cancer,* New York: M. Evans.

Menninger, R.A. and W.C. Menninger (1936). 'Psychosomatic Observations in Cardiac Disorder', *American Heart Journal,* 11: 10–21.

Mohan, J., (1994). 'Recent Advances in Yoga & its Application in Sports', Keynote Address, 23rd International Congress of Applied Psychology, 20–24 July, Madrid, Spain.

Mohan, J. (1995). 'Cross-Cultural Psychology: The Indian Perspective', *Indian Journal of Social Psychiatry,* 11(1): 40–45.

Mohan, J. (1997). 'Sports Stress and Personality', Symposium, 9th World Congress of Sports Psychology, 5–9 July, Israel.

Mohan, J. (1998a). 'Personality & Sports', Keynote Address, 11th National Conference of Sports Psychologhy, Hyderabad, India.

Mohan, J. (1998b). 'Cross-Cultural Experience of Collaboration in Personality Research', Invited Lecture at 24th International Congress of Applied Psychology, 9–14 August, 1998, San Fransisco, USA.

Mohan, J., H.J. Eysenck and S.B.G. Eysenck (1987). 'The Eysenck Personality Questionnaire: An Indian Experience', *Personality Study and Group Behaviour,* Vol. 7(2): 61–64.

Mohan, J and Parmajit Kaur (1986). 'Standardization of PQ on Indian students', *Journal of Personality and Clinical Studies,* 2(2): 127–33.

Mohan, J. and N. Rattan (1987). 'A Study of Effectiveness, Personality and Achievement Motivation of Executives', Paper included in the National Seminar on Management Science, April 1987, Chandigarh, India.

Mohan, J. and M. Sehgal (1998). 'A Survey of Determinants of Stressors in CHD and Essential Hypertension Patients' (Communicated).

Mohan, J. and M. Sehgal (1999). 'Role of Personality Factors in Chronic Disease' (Communicated).

Mohan, J. and M. Tiwana (1987). 'Personality and Alienation of Creative Writer: A Brief Report', Personality and Individual Differences, 8(3): 449.

Osler, W. (1910). 'Lecture on Angina Pectoris', Lancet, 1: 839–44.

Price V.A. (1982). Type A Behaviour, New York: Academic Press.

Rosenman R.H. and M.A. Chesney (1980). 'The Relationship of Type A Behaviour Pattern to Coronary Heart Disease', *Activitas Nervosa Superior,* 22: 1–45.

Schmitz, P.G. (1992). 'Personality, Stress-Reactions and Disease', *Personality and Individual Differences,* 13(6): 683–91.

Sklar. L.L. and H. Anisman (1979). 'Stress and Coping Factors Influence Tumor Growth', *Science,* 205: 513–17.

Sklar, L.S. and H. Anisman (1981). 'Stress and Cancer', *Psychological Bulletin,* 89: 396–406.

Temoshok, L. and H. Dreher (1992). *The Type C Connection,* New York: Penguin Books.

14 Empathy and Its Development

Anuradha Bhandari and Komila Parthi

Analysis and understanding of human behaviour in the recent years has moved from concrete to very subtle forms. This might be primarily due to appreciation on finer and delicate strands of response patterns, or due to interpersonal nature of determinants of these forms of responses. Prosocial behaviour has assumed academic as well as training importance for behavioural scientists. One of the highly valued but least researched form of prosocial behaviour—empathy—deserves systematic investigation from the developmental angle in terms of personality development, interpersonal perception, and training and socialization. From infant to child, to adolescent, to adult, and to the aged, empathy has a great meaning as well as implication in terms of feeling and behaviour.

Historically, the notion of empathy, or Einfuhlung, grew out of earlier works in aesthetics by Visher (Wind, 1963) and in psychology by Lipps (1903), who explained it as the tendency of an observer to fuse with the object that absorbs his/her attention. When Titchner (1909) translated Lipps's notion of Einfuhlung as empathy, he meant to preserve the idea of the self projected into the perceived object. He harbingered two different concepts of empathy as a way of knowing another's affect and as a kind of social-cognitive bonding. Sullivan (1953) suggested that empathy is important in the personality development and socialization of the young child. Through empathy the infant can feel and be affected by the attitudes and emotions of significant people even before it is able to understand the signs of emotional expression. Whatever the mother's emotional feelings are, the child is sensitive to them, Fabes *et al.* (1990) opined that the concept of empathy and sympathy, and an understanding of their development are of considerable importance to the study of social development.

Sympathy refers to a process whereby the pain of the sufferer is brought home to the observer, leading to an unselfish concern for the other person. Empathy refers to the process whereby one person tries to understand accurately the subjectivity of another person, without prejudice. Although both have as their object the emotions of another person—the sufferer or the client—they have different psychological processes. Empathy is a way of 'knowing', while sympathy is a way of 'relating' (Wispe, 1986).

The term empathy appears to have been used to refer to at least four different qualities: (a) knowing what another person is feeling (Dymond, 1949: a component of 'content accuracy' according to Lekes *et al.,* 1990); (b) feeling what another person is feeling (Eisenberg *et al.,* 1989); (c) responding compassionately to another person's distress (Coke, Batson and McDavis, 1978); and (d) learning that one values the welfare of a person in need (Batson *et al.,* 1995). Vymetal (1997) believes that empathy is the understanding of another person through identification.

Components of Empathy

Empathy is a complex process regulated by both cognitive and affective components interacting in a systematic manner to produce an emotional understanding. The affective elements of empathy have been considered to include: sensitiveness to another person's feelings (Rogers, 1980), ability to share another person's emotions (Truax and Carkhuff, 1967), and momentary identification with another person's status (Tahka, 1970).

The psychoanalytic school and especially the more recent ego psychology emphasize the affective components of empathy (Kalliopuska. 1983). Empathy is looked upon as an affective understanding of the state of emotion of another person reached through momentary identification. The ability to reach genuine empathy reflects psychic maturity, enabling one to regard another individual with affection without threat or fear of losing one's identity, or of the breaking of boundaries of the self (Kohut, 1971: Kernberg, 1972).

Some researchers conclude that a pure emotional type of empathy is unpleasant for the empathizing person. Wise and Cramer (1988) opined that because of the personal distress, anxiety and discomfort when confronted with another's negative experience, it indicates a sort of vulnerability and excessive sensitivity. Furthermore, it does not probably function very well in everyday life, because, in a critical situation, if somebody only suffers together with a person in trouble, he will not be efficient enough concerning the solution of the problem (Kozeki and Berghammer, 1992).

From the angle of cognitive psychology, empathy is often likened to an ability to adopt a role. The adoption of another person's point of view and an identification with his role are presuppositions to an understanding of another's emotions and state of life, and to accurate prediction of the thoughts, feelings and actions of another person. The most prominent representatives of this approach have been Dymond (1949) and Hoffman (1975). Kalliopuska (1983) opined that with development, the cognitive factors acquire a central role at the expense of the previously dominant uncontrolled affectivity which results in harmonious interaction of both the components. Kozeki and Berghammer (1992) examined the pure cognitive type of empathy, and found that it can be a characteristic trait of a good leader, but also that of a despot, always calculating and trying to foresee others' feelings and reactions. Prosocial and antisocial behaviour, that is, the ethically positive or negative use of this knowledge depends on how developed the person's morality is.

Hoffman (1975) and Feshbach (1978) have opted for a conception of empathy that integrates cognitive and affective components. One such integrative conception has been succinctly stated by Iannotti (1978) as 'an emotional response to the perspective of another'. Davis (1983) maintains that a multidimensional approach to studying empathy is needed, a sentiment echoed by Chlopan *et al.* (1985), Riggio *et al.* (1989) have suggested that empathy is a constellation of many constructs, some of which relate to cognitive perspective-taking, while others seem to be connected with the ability to respond affectively to emotional communication. Kozeki and Berghammer (1992) have proposed that there are three aspects of empathy—affective, cognitive and moral or adaptive empathy.

Models of Empathy

A variety of theoretical perspectives of empathy have been proposed to account for its role in prosocial behaviour. One of the early models to explain empathic understanding was proposed by Katz (1963), which suggested that there are four phases in the empathic process identification, incorporation, reverberation and detachment.

Coke, Batson and McDavis (1978) proposed a two-stage model of empathic mediation of helping behaviour. They contended that adopting the perspective of others is associated with greater feelings of sympathy and concern (empathic emotion). The two stages of the model are: (1) Taking the perspective of a person in need tends to increase one's empathic emotional response, and (2) Empathic emotion, in turn, increases motivation to see that the person's need is reduced. Although this model postulates that cognitive perspective-taking and empathic feelings both contribute to the motivation to help, it predicts that perspective-taking affects helping only as a result of its effects on one's empathic emotional response.

Hoffman (1976, 1982) has proposed an influential developmental model of age-related changes in empathy and the relation of empathy to prosocial behaviour. The theory emphasizes both the cognitive and affective aspects of empathy. According to this model, in the first year of life, before the child has developed the understanding of person permanence, distress cues emanating from others elicit global distress reactions, and the child does not try to help distressed others but himself becomes upset. As children develop some understanding of person permanence they increasingly differentiate between their own and others' distress. However, young children cannot clearly differentiate between their own internal state and those of others. Therefore, as they start to try to assist distressed others at about one year of age, their helping behaviour, are often 'egocentric'. Hoffman (1976) suggested that these very early prosocial behaviours are 'quasi hedonistic' in motive in that a child may assist others to alleviate his or her own distress. At a slightly advanced stage, children are likely to try to comfort others with means that comfort themselves.

In the second and third years of life, children develop the ability to take others' perspectives. As a consequence, children's prosocial actions are more appropriate and responsive to others' particular needs. Moreover, with the development of language, children can derive information about others' state from symbolic cues, rather than from facial and other physical expressions, and can begin to empathize with a wider range of emotions. Finally, in late childhood, children's vicarious responding is affected by their developing an understanding that the self and others are individuals with different and separate histories and identities, and that people have feelings beyond the immediate situation. Consequently, children can experience empathy (or related reactions) for the poor, the ill, or others with chronic problems, even without immediate information about their distress.

The arousal, cost-reward model by Piliavin, Rodin and Piliavin (1969) and Piliavin *et al.* (1981, 1982) identifies two conceptually separate but functionally interdependent components that influence helping. The first factor-arousal, is an emotional response to the need or distress of others. People are aroused by the distress of others, and exhibit emotionally empathic reactions to the problems and crisis of others. Emergencies of greater clarity and severity generate higher levels of arousal. Furthermore, the distress of others with whom one is closer generates a stronger empathic reaction. These affective reactions appear quite early developmentally. The second factor, a cost-reward component, involves the cognitive processes by which bystanders assess and weigh anticipated costs and rewards associated with action and inaction.

Elizur (1985) put forward an integrated developmental model of empathy. According to him, empathy has four principal components, perceptual, affective, cognitive and object relations. Since empathy helps to promote prosocial behaviours, any intervention programmes should be based on empathic object evaluation. Markowitz (1987) has proposed a model of empathy, which attempts to synthesize Kohut's (1971) self psychology and Loevinger's (1976) ego development theories. Kohut believes that optimal empathy is essential to the development of a cohesive self. For him, empathy is the ability to grasp another's thoughts and feelings which requires self-others differentiation. Loevinger's post conformist individuals evidence self-other differentiation. They also appear to have the capacity to take the role and to value individual differences. These capacities are inherent in empathic interaction. Markowitz (1987) argues that the development of conscience appears integral to both ego development and empathy.

Kozeki and Berghammer (1992) have proposed a developmental theory of empathic function, and its connections with intimacy, time factors and social values. They opine that empathy is a complex personality trait which needs affection, mental reflection and behavioural control. It is not merely a state of emotion, but also a certain action towards the other person, that is, the object of empathy. On the basis of their research finding showing a strong correlation of empathy with moral motivation, they have added to the existing and differentiated emotional and cognitive type of empathy a third one, a sort of 'adaptive' or 'moral' empathy, which is full of ethical content, develops in a tight relationship with moral motivation, and guarantees high levels of social values and character building. Affective empathy manifests itself in a person, who, seeing a suffering child, begins crying. Cognitive empathy characterizes the competing pupil, empathizing with his partner in order to calculate probable reactions. Moral or adaptive empathy is characteristic of a responsible leader, who, considering the interest of his group, is capable of self-denial.

Socialization and Developmental Issues

Some studies have focussed on the processes through which empathy-related responses develop and are socialized. The family has been considered the primary agent for socializing empathic behaviour (Hoffman, 1977; Barnett, 1987), but there is relatively little research directly examining parental correlates of empathy.

Children who have secure attachments with their care-givers tend to exhibit more empathy than do children with insecure attachments (Iannotti *et al.* 1978; Kestenbaum, Faber and Sroufe, 1989). Maternal empathy and supportive parenting (especially by mothers) have been positively associated with offsprings' emotional responsivity to others (Fabes, Eisenberg and Miller, 1990).

The patterns of findings regarding the development of children's vicarious emotional responsiveness appear to vary in strength across studies for boys and girls. For example, Feshbach (1978) found that empathy in girls was positively related to positive mother–daughter interactions, whereas for boys empathy was inversely related to father's encouragement of competition. In contrast, Eisenberg-Berg and Mussen (1978) found significant positive relations between sons' (but not daughters') empathy and the maternal qualities of being affectionate, egalitarian, non-restrictive and non-punitive. Barnett *et al.* (1980) found a positive relation between empathy and gender stereotypic patterns of parental empathy. They suggested that when the mother is considerably more empathic than the father, empathy may be identified as distinctly gender-appropriate for women, thereby enhancing its development in girls. No relations were found between boys' empathy scores and the empathy scores for either parent.

Empathy has been linked to maternal warmth, sensitivity and involvement with the child (Feshbach, 1987). Theoretically, maternal empathy and sympathy should foster close relationships and secure attachments between mother and child. Eisenberg *et al.* (1989) have pointed out that the moderating effects of maternal affective arousal in the socialization of children's empathic responding are complex.

Hoffman (1976, 1982) contended that parents should allow their children to be exposed to a broad range of experiences and emotions so as to foster their sensitivity to the feelings of others. A child who is shielded from particular distressful experiences may have difficulty empathizing with a needy other, whose problem or emotional reaction may be perceived as foreign and unfamiliar. Feshbach (1982) suggested that the empathic responsiveness of some individuals may be enhanced by having weathered a dysphoric experience, such as a serious familial illness or loss.

Barnett (1987) indicated that a child's tendency to empathize with others appears to thrive in an environment that satisfies his or her own emotional needs and discourages excessive self concern, thereby enabling the emotions and needs of others to become more salient. It is quite likely that people who are more other-oriented in a given situation are more likely to attend to details regarding another's distress or need and, consequently, are more likely to perspective-take, empathize, and sympathize.

Gender Differences in Empathy

Empathy is more frequently attributed to females than to males. This stereotypic perception has most likely been derived from the broader belief that females are more nurturant and interpersonally oriented than males—a stereotype that itself is a natural consequence of traditional feminine and masculine roles (Parsons and Bales, 1955). Freud (1925, 1961) asserted that since females do not fear castration, they do not resolve the oedipal complex as completely as do males. Consequently, they develop weaker egos and super egos. This inferior developmental status purportedly results in females relying more on emotions and less on rational principles than do males. Some other psychoanalytic theorists also think along the same lines. They describe females as being more concerned than males with inner space (a concept relating to maternal functioning) and less concerned with external world (Erikson, 1965), as well as being more intuitive (Deutsch, 1975).

Brehm *et al.* (1984) on the basis of their research have proposed an interesting relationship between empathy, gender and age. They hypothesized that during the early school years empathy operates more 'cognitively' for males and more 'affectively' for females. Larrieu and Mussen (1986) have reported that in the course of socialization, girls are more likely than boys to acquire general prosocial tendencies and broad concepts of prosocial behaviour. They found that boys were no less likely than girls to share possessions or to help others, but they showed significantly less caring (expressive behaviour), less empathy, and less regard for prosocial goals. Riggio *et al.* (1989) studied gender differences in empathy and social skill inventories, and found that women are more sensitive and expressive than men, but that men may be more adept at regulating and controlling emotional displays. Eisenberg *et al.* (1991) opined that girls were higher than boys on self-reported sympathy and dispositional sympathy and empathy, while boys were higher on self-monitoring. Litvack-Miller, McDongall and Romney (1997) studied the structure and development of dispositional empathy during middle childhood. They found that girls were more empathic than boys, and older children showed more empathic concern than younger children.

Eisenberg and Lennon (1983) found that gender differences in empathy varied greatly as a function of the type of empathy index used. There was a huge gender difference favouring females for self-report measures in experimental contexts, and no gender differences in facial and physiological indices. Gender differences on the picture-story indices vary as a function of sex of the experimenter, with children scoring higher if interviewed by same sex adults.

Correlates of Empathy

The literature on cognitive and emotional empathy has increased substantially in the recent years (Clark, 1980). Several researchers have attempted to investigate the relationship between empathy and other psychological variables. Low empathic abilities have been implicated in many forms of psychopathology, including child abuse (Letourneau, 1981), deviant behaviour (Kurtz and Eisenberg, 1983), psychoticism (Eysenck, 1992), neuroticism, (Eysenck and Eysenck,

1978; Rushton *et al.,* 1989), and aggression (Feshbach and Feshbach, 1986). High empathy and related concepts have been proposed as playing a counter-force to power in social interaction (Clark, 1980), as key elements of moral conduct and character (Shelton and McAdams, 1990), as necessary and sufficient conditions for effective psychotherapy (Rogers, 1980), and as an instrumental factor in attitude change towards stigmatized groups (Batson *et al.,* 1997). Empathy has also been related to a number of other variables, such as helping and sharing (Fabes *et al.* 1991), relationship satisfaction (Davis and Oathout, 1987), affiliative tendency (Mehrabian, 1976), and sociopolitical intelligence (Daurio, 1978).

Altruism and Empathy

Altruism refers to acts of concern for others, such as, sharing, helping, showing concern and consideration, reassuring, and defending, that are performed independent of hope of reward or fear of punishment from external sources (Grusec, 1991). The most frequently proposed source of altruism has been empathy, Batson *et al.* (1986) reported that if there are sources of altruistic caring other than empathy, they have yet to be found. Batson and Oleson (1991) have agreed that the human capacity for altruism is limited to those for whom we feel empathy. When empathy for the person in need is low, the pattern of helping suggests underlying egoistic motivation. According to them, it is not that we never help people for whom we feel little empathy; we often do, but only when it is in our best interest.

Several researchers (e.g., Hoffman, 1975, 1976; Batson, Darley, and Coke, 1978; Batson and Coke, 1981) have reported that empathic emotion leads to motivation directed toward the altruistic goal of increasing others' welfare. This suggestion has been called the empathy-altruism hypothesis (Batson and Coke, 1981). The empathy-altruism hypothesis contradicts the common assumption in psychology that all motivation, including all prosocial motivation, is ultimately directed towards the egoistic goal of increasing one's own welfare (Wallach and Wallach, 1983).

Batson (1987) proposed possible new egoistic explanations for all or part of the evidence presented in support of the empathy-altruism hypothesis. Briefly, he suggested that apart from any general rewards and punishments associated with helping, there are empathy-specific rewards or punishments. Feeling empathy changes the anticipated reward or punishment structure of the situation, making helping more beneficial to the self, and so increasing the egoistic motivation to help. Batson *et al.* (1988) designed and conducted five studies to test these proposed egoistic alternatives to this hypothesis. Results of these five studies did not support either the empathy-specific reward or the empathy-specific punishment hypothesis. Instead, the results of each study supported the empathy-altruism hypothesis, that is, empathic emotion evokes altruistic motivation.

Batson and Olesan (1991) studied the status of empathy-altruism hypothesis and concluded that it was valid. They opine that empathy-induced altruistic motivation is a potentially important psychological resource, which, if harnessed and put to work, may yield important practical as well as theoretical benefits.

In spite of continued challeges to the empathy-altruism hypothesis, Batson (1997) opines that strong and extensive research evidence exists that justifies acceptance of the empathy-altruism hypothesis.

Our Studies in India

Bhandari and Grewal (1988) administered scales of empathy, personality, self-concept and moral judgement to 200 school children (100 boys and 100 girls) in the age range of 9 to 11 years. They also took their subjects' scores on aggression, which were based on parents' ratings and teachers' ratings. The girls were found to score significantly higher on empathy in comparison to boys. Empathy was positively associated with neuroticism in girls and negatively associated with parent-rated aggressiveness in boys. Factor analysis indicated that the structure of empathy was different in boys and girls.

Bhandari (1991) explored the relationship between empathy and aggression in children. It was found that Fifth and Sixth grade girls, in contrast to boys, scored higher on Bryant's test of empathy and lower on parents' ratings of aggression at home and teachers' ratings of aggression in school. It was felt that the greater senstivity and affective understanding of girl child, combined with her lower scores on aggression, makes her uniquely suited for playing a significant role in the helping and caring professions.

Bhandari and Parthi (1994) studied gender differences in the relationship between empathy and altruism. A total of 400 university students (200 males and 200 females) were administered emotional, cognitive and multidimensional measures of empathy. Results revealed that females scored higher on emotional empathy perspective-taking, fantasy scale, empathic concern and personal distress, No gender differences emerged on cognitive empathy. Cognitive empathy was positively associated with altruism in males but not in females. An insignificant correlation emerged between emotional empathy and altruism. Empathic concern and fantasy scale correlated positively with altruism, while personal distress correlated negatively with altruism in both the gender groups. They concluded that empathy is a complex process regulated by both cognitive and affective components. The empathy-altruism relationship is influenced both by gender differences and the nature of self-report measure of empathy used.

Parthi and Bhandari (1994) examined the correlates of empathy among 200 male and 200 female college and university students. In men, cognitive empathy was positively related to altruism, irritability, needs for Achievement, Power and Approval. In women, cognitive empathy was correlated positively with need for Achievement. Emotional empathy in both men and women was found to show significant correlations with some subscales of Buss-Durkee Hostility Inventory only. Specifically, in both the gender groups emotional empathy was found to be positively related to resentment. Additionally, in men it was negatively related to assault, negativism and guilt, while in women it was positively related to irritability. Perspective-taking was found to be positively related to resentment, while in women it was found to be negatively related to the need for Achievement. Fantasy scale showed to have a positive association with psychoticism, altruism, verbal hostility and the need for Power and Approval in women only. Empathic concern was found to have a positive relationship with Altruism in both men and women, but in men it was also positively related with resentment and negatively related with indirect hostility. Personal distress showed a positive association with psychoticism, neuroticism and assault in both men and women. Further, in men it was positively related to resentment, while in women it was found to be negatively related to assault. The factorial structure of empathy was found to be different among men and women. The results indicated that the nature of empathy is determined by the kind of sample as well as the measure of empathy employed.

Bhandari and Parthi (1995) examined the relationship between emotional empathy, cognitive empathy and the need for Achievement,

Affiliation, Power and Approval. Two studies were separately carried out on 400 university students. In the first study, students high (25 per cent top scorers) and low (25 per cent bottom scorers) on emotional empathy were compared on the tests of the four motives. Results showed that high emotional empathy scorers obtained significantly higher scores on need for Achievement and need for Affiliation. In the second study, students high and low on cognitive empathy were compared on the measures of the four motives. Results revealed that high cognitive empathy scorers obtained significantly higher scores on need for Achievement, Affiliation and Approval. Taken together, the results of the two studies clearly indicated that the students high on both affective and cognitive components of empathy seem to be achievement-oriented, sensitive and interested in seeking warm personal relationships with others. However, the high and low empathy groups do not differ in the need for Power.

Bhandari and Parthi (1998), using the same design as in the 1995 study, compared high and low cognitive and emotional empathy scorers on the Buss-Durkee Hostility Inventory. Differences on hostility between high and low empathy subjects emerged only on emotional empathy. High emotional empathy females scored significantly lower on resentment and suspicion, but significantly higher on indirect hostility. These findings suggest that high emotional empathy females score lower on the 'attitudinal' component of hostility, but higher on the 'motor' component of hostility. High and low emotional empathy males do not differ on hostility.

Conclusion, Implications and Future Research

The following broad conclusions can be made on the basis of the review of researches conducted on the concept of empathy in the last couple of decades:

1. Empathy is a multidimensional concept regulated by both affective and cognitive components.
2. Empathic emotions have a physiological base. Genetic factors may produce differences in the individuals capacities to experience empathy.
3. Supportive parenting, that is, parents who are responsive, inductive, warm and accepting of their children's emotional reactions have offsprings who are socially competent and emotionally responsive to others.

4. Empathy enhances the development of prosocial behaviour.
5. Empathy is a source of moral action. However, empathy-induced altruism and moral motives may sometimes compete and sometimes co-operate.
6. Empathy inhibits the development of aggressive antisocial behaviour. Empathy training brings about more positive social behaviours and positive self-evaluation in aggressive persons.
7. Methodological refinements in the measures of empathy continue even as researchers continue to emphasize using multiple measures of empathy.
8. Empathy has been identified as a necessary condition for effective counselling and a sufficient condition for therapeutic personality change. Individuals exposed to empathy enhancement training programmes significantly improve their levels of empathic understanding and counselling skills.

The authors of this chapter believes that the complex personality trait of empathy require adopting a dynamic and multifaceted view of the empathic process, and highlight the need for more research on empathy, both as an independent and an intervening variable.

References

Barnett, M.A., L.M. King, J.A. Howard and G.A. Dino (1980). 'Empathy in Young Children: Relation to Parents Empathy, Affection and Emphasis on the Feelings of Others', *Developmental Psychology,* 16(3): 243–44.

Barnett, M.A. (1987). 'Empathy and Related Responses in Children', in N. Eisenberg and Strayer (eds), *Empathy and its Development,* pp.146–62, Cambridge: Cambridge University Press.

Batson, C.D., J.M. Darley and J.S. Coke (1978). 'Altruism and Human Kindness: Internal and External Determinants of Helping Behaviour', in L. Pervin and M. Lewis (eds), *Perspectives in Interactional Psychology,* pp. 111–40, New York: Plenum Press.

Batson, C.D. and J.S. Coke (1981). 'Empathy: A Source of Altruistic Motivation of Helping?', in J.P. Rushton and R.M. Sorrentino (eds), *Altruism and Helping Behaviour: Social Personality and Developmental Perspectives,* pp. 167–87, Hillsdale, N.J.: Erlbaum.

Batson, C., Daniel, Michelle M. Bolen, Julie A. Cross and Helen E. Neuringer-Benefiel (1986). 'Where is the Altruism in the Altruistic Personality?', *Journal of Personality and Social Psychology,* 50(1): 212–20.

Batson, C.D. (1987). 'Prosocial Motivation: Is it Even Truly Altruistic?', in L. Berkowitz (ed.), *Advances in Experimental Social Psychology,* Vol. 20, pp. 65–122, New York: Academic Press.

Batson, C.D. (1987). 'Self-Other Merging and the Empathy-Altruism Hypothesis: Reply to Neuberg *et al.* (1997)', *Journal of Personality and Social Psychology,* 73(3): 517–22.

Batson, C.D., J.R. Dyck, J.T. Brandt, J.G. Batson, A.L. Power, M.R. McMaster and C. Griffitt (1988). 'Five Studies Testing Two Egoistic Alternatives to the Empathy-Altruism Hypothesis', *Journal of Personality and Social Psychology,* 55(1): 52–77.

Batson, C.D., T.R. Klien, L. Highberger and L.L. Shaw (1995). 'Immorality from Empathy-Induced Altruism: When Compassion and Justice Conflict', *Journal of Personality and Social Psychology,* 68(6): 1042–54.

Batson, C.D. and K.C. Olesan (1991). 'Current Status of Empathy Altruism Hypothesis', in M.S. Clark (ed.), *Prosocial Behaviour,* London: Sage Publications.

Batson, C.D., C.L. Turk, L.L. Shaw and T.R. Klein (1995). 'Information Function of Empathic Emotion: Learning that we Value the Others' Welfare', *Journal of Personality and Social Psychology,* 68(2): 303–13.

Batson, C.D., M.P. Polycarpou, E. Harmon-Jones, H.J. Imhoff, E.C. Mitchener, L.L. Bednar, T.R. Klein and L. Highberger (1997). 'Empathy and Attitudes: Can Feeling for a Member of a Stigmatized Group Improve Feelings Toward the Group?', *Journal of Personality and Social Psychology,* 72(1): 105–18.

Bhandari, A. and J. Grewal (1988). 'A Study of Empathy in Children', Unpublished Manuscript, Panjab University, Chandigarh.

Bhandari, A. (1991). 'Empathy in the Girl Child', Paper presented at National Seminar on Psychological Aspects in the Social Acceptability of Girl Child, Kurukshetra University, Kurukshetra.

Bhandari, A. and K. Parthi (1994). 'Gender Differences in the Relationship Between Empathy and Altruism', Paper presented at fifth conference of National Academy of Psychology, University of Allahabad, Allahabad.

Bhandari, A. and K. Parthi (1995). 'Empathy and Motives', Unpublished manuscript..

Bhandari, A. and K. Parthi (1998). 'Empathy and Hostility in College Students', Paper presented in the ninth conference of National Academy of Psychology, Jodhpur University, Jodhpur.

Brehm, S.S., L.K. Powell and J.S. Coke (1984). 'The Effects of Empathic Interactions Upon Donating Behaviour: Sex Differences in Young Children', *Sex Roles,* 10: 405–16.

Chlopan, B.E., M.L. McCain, J.L. Carbonell and R.L. Hagen (1985). 'Empathy: Review of Available Measures', *Journal of Personality and Social Psychology,* 48(3): 635–53.

Clark, K.B. (1980). 'Empathy; a Neglected Topic in Psychological Research', *American Psychologist,* 35: 188

Coke, J.S., C.D. Batson and K. McDavis (1978). 'Empathic Mediation of Helping: A Two-Stage Model', *Journal of Personality and Social Psychology,* 36: 752–66.

Daurio, S.P. (1978). 'The Development of Sociopolitical Intelligence', Unpublished doctoral dissertation, John Hopkins University.

Davis, M.H. (1983). 'Measuring Individual Differences in Empathy: Evidence for a Multidimensional Approach', *Journal of Personality and Social Psychology,* 44: 113–26.

Davis, M.H. and H.A. Oathout (1987). 'Maintenance of Satisfaction in Romantic Relationships: Empathy and Relational Competence', *Journal of Personality and Social Psychology,* 53(2): 397–410.

Deutsch, F. (1975). 'Effects of Sex of Subject and Story Character on Preschooler's Perceptions of Affective Responses and Inter-Personal Behaviour in Story Sequences', *Developmental Psychology,* 11: 112–13.

Dymond, R.F. (1949). 'A Scale for the Measurement of Empathic Ability', *Journal of Consulting Psychology,* 13: 127–33.

Eisenberg-Berg, N. and P. Mussen (1978). 'Empathy and Moral Development in Adolescents', *Developmental Psychology,* 14: 185–86.

Eisenberg, N., R.A. Fabes, M. Schaller and P.A. Miller (1989). 'Sympathy and Personal Distress: Development, Gender Differences and Interrrelations of Indexes', in N. Eisenberg (ed.), *Empathy and Related Emotional Responses,* San Francisco: Jossey-Bass.

Elizur, A. (1985). 'An Integrated Development Model of Empathy', *Israel Journal of Psychiatry and Related Sciences,* 22(1&2): 29–39.

Erikson, E.H. (1965). 'Inner and Outer Space: Reflections of Womanhood', in R.J. Lifton (ed.), *The Woman in America,* Boston: Houghton Mifflin.

Eysenck, S.B.G. and H.J. Eysenck (1978). 'Impulsiveness and Venturesomeness: Their Position in a Dimensional System of Personality Description', *Psychological Reports,* 43: 1247–55.

Eysenck, H.J. (1992). 'The Definition and Measurement of Psychoticism', *Personality and Individual Differences,* 13(7): 757–85.

Fabes, R.A., N. Eisenberg and P.A. Miller (1990). 'Maternal Correlates of Children's Vicarious Emotional Response', *Developmental Psychology,* 26(4): 639–48.

Feshback, N.D. (1978). 'Studies of Empathic Behaviour in Children', in B.A. Maher (ed.), *Progress in Experimental Personality Research,* Vol. 8, New York: Academic Press.

Feshbach, S. and N.D. Feshbach (1986). 'Aggession and Altruism: A Personality Perspective', in C. Zahn-Waxler, E.N. Cummings, and R. Iannotti (eds), *Altruism and Aggression: Biological and Sociological Origins,* pp. 189–217, Cambridge: Cambridge University Press.

Feshbach, N.D. (1987). 'Parental Empathy and Child Adjustments/Maladjustment', in N. Eisenberg and J. Strayer (eds), *Empathy and Its Development,* pp. 271–91, Cambridge: Cambridge University Press.

Freud, S. (1925, 1961). 'Some Psychical Consequences of the Anatomical Distinction Between the Sexes', in J. Strachey (Ed. and Trans.), *Standard Edition of the Complete Psychological Works of Sigmund Freud,* Vol. 19, London: Hograth Press, 1961 (Originally Published in 1925).

Grusec, J.E. (1991). 'The Socialization of Altruism', in M.S. Clark (ed.), *Prosocial Behaviour,* London: Sage Publications.

Hoffman, M.L. (1975). 'Developmental Synthesis of Affect and Cognition and its Implications for Altruistic Motivation', *Developmental Psychology,* 11: 607–22.

Hoffman, M.L. (1976). 'Empathy, Role-Taking, Guilt and Development of Altruistic Motives', in T. Lickona (ed.), *Moral Development and Behaviour: Theory, Research and Social Issues,* New York: Holt, Rinehart and Winston.

Hoffman, M.L. (1977). 'Sex Differences in Empathy and Related Behaviour', Psychological Bulletin, 84: 712–22.

Hoffman, M.L. (1982). 'Development of Prosocial Motivation: Empathy and Guilt', in N. Eiservberg (ed.), *Development of Prosocial Behaviour,* pp. 281–313, New York: Academic Press.

Iannotti, R.J. (1978). 'Effect of Role-Taking Experiences on Role-Taking, Empathy, Altruism and Aggression', *Developmental Psychology,* 14(2): 119–24.

Ickes, W., L. Stinson, V. Bissonnette and S. Garcia (1990). 'Naturalistic Social Cognition: Empathic Accuracy in Mixed-Sex Dyads', *Journal of Personality and Social Psychology,* 59: 730–42.

Katz, R.L. (1963). *Empathy: Its Nature and Uses,* London: Free Press.

Kalliopuska, M. (1983). 'Verbal Components of Emotional Empathy', *Perceptual and Motor Skills,* 56: 487–96.

Kernberg, O. (1972). 'Early Ego Integration and Object Relations', *Annals of the New York Academy of Sciences,* 193: 233–47.

Kestenbaum, R., E.A. Faber and L.A. Sroufe (1989). 'Individual Differences in Empathy Among Preschoolers: Relation to Attachment History', in N. Eisenberg (ed.), *New Directions in Child Development,* Vol. 44, pp. 51–64, San Francisco: Jossey-Bass.

Kohut, H. (1971). *The Analysis of Self,* New York: International Universities Press.

Kozeki, B. and R. Berghammer (1992). 'The Role of Empathy in the Motivational Structure of School Children', *Personality and Individual Differences,* 13(2): 191–203.

Kurtz, C.A. and N. Eisenberg (1983). 'Role-Taking Empathy and Resistance of Deviation in Children', *The Journal of Genetic Psychology,* 142: 85–95.

Larrieu, J. and P. Mussen (1986). 'Some Personality and Motivational Correlates of Children's Prosocial Behaviour', *Journal of Genetic Psychology,* 147: 529–42.

Letouneau, C. (1981). 'Empathy and Stress: How They Affect Parental Aggression', *Social Work,* 26: 383–89.

Lipps, T. (1903). 'Einfushlung, inner Nachahmung, and Organ-Umpfindungern', (Empathy, Inner Imitations and Sensations), *Archive Fur Die Gesamte Psychologie,* 2: 185–204.

Litvack-Miller, W., D. McDongall and D.M. Romney (1997). 'The Structure of Empathy During Middle Childhood and its Relationship to Prosocial Behaviour', *Genetic Social General Psychology Monograph,* 123(3): 303–24.

Loevinger, J. (1976). *Ego Development,* San Francisco: Jossey-Bass.

Markowitz, P.F. (1987). 'A Synthesis of Self Psychology and Ego Developmental Perspectives: Toward a Model of Emphathy', Education Department, Boston University, *Psychological Development,* 48(8): 2477.

Mehrabian, A. (1976). 'Questionnaire Measure of Affiliative Tendency and Sensitivity to Rejection', *Psychology Report,* 38: 199–209.

Parsons, T. and R.F. Bales (eds) (1955). *Family Socialization and Interaction Processes,* New York: Free Press.

Parthi, K. and A. Bhandari (1994). 'A Study of Correlates of Empathy Among College and University Students', Unpublished manuscript, Panjab University, Chandigarh.

Piliavin, I.M., J. Rodin and J.A. Piliavin (1969). 'Good Samaritanism: An Underground Phenomenon', *Journal of Personality and Social Psychology,* 13: 289–99.

Piliavin, J.A., J.F. Dovidio, S.L. Gaertner and R.D. Clark III (1982). 'Responsive Bystanders: The Process of Intervension', in V.J. Derlega and J. Derlega and J. Grzelak (eds), *Co-operation and Helping Behaviour: Theories and Research,* pp. 279–304, New York: Academic Press.

Riggio, R.E. J. Tucker and D. Coffaro (1989). 'Social Skills and Empathy', *Personality and Individual Differences,* 10(1): 93–99.

Rogers, C.R. (1980). *A Way of Being,* Boston: Houghton Mifflin.

Rushton, J.P., D.W. Fulker, M.C. Neale, D.K. Nias and H.J. Eysenck (1989). 'Ageing and the Relation of Aggression, Altruism and Assertiveness Scales to the Eysenck Personality Questionnaire', *Personality and Individual Differences,* 10(2): 261–63.

Shelton, C.M. and D.P. McAdams (1990). 'In Search of an Everyday Morality: the Development of a Measure', *Adolescence,* 25(100): 923–43.

Sullivan, H.S. (1953). *The Interpersonal Theory of Psychiatry,* New York: W.W. Norton.

Tahka, V. (1970). *Psykotoraplan Perustoot,* Porvoo, Finland: Wsoy.

Titchner, E. (1909). *Elementary Psychology of the Thought Processes,* New York: Macmillan.

Truax, C.B. and R.R. Carkhuff (1967). *Toward Effective Counselling and Psychotherapy,* Chicago, IL: Aldine.

Vymetal, J. (1997). 'Empathy—Understanding Through Identification', *Sb Lek,* 98(4): 317–25.

Wallach, M.A. and L. Wallach (1983). *Psychology's Sanction for Selfishness: The Error of Egoism in Theory and Therapy,* San Francisco: Freeman.

Wind, E. (1963). *Art and Anarchy,* London: Faber and Faber.

Wispe, L. (1986). 'The Distinction Between Sympathy and Empathy: To Call Forth a Concept, a Word is Needed', *Journal of Personality and Social Psychology,* 50: 314–21.

Wise, P.S. and S.H. Cramer (1988). 'Correlates of Empathy and Cognitive Style in Early Adolescence', *Psychological Bulletin,* 63: 179–92.

15 Cultural Influences on the Development of Identity: India and England

Pittu Laungani

INTRODUCTION

That cultures vary along several identifiable parameters is a truism, For, even a casual observation reveals that there are political, social, economics, physical, and other environment differences between cultures. For instance, the life experiences and the social arrangements of people living in Alaskan regions, where temperatures are often known to drop to 40^0 C below zero, are likely to be very different from those living in Cheerapunji, where it rains over 400" a year! Several studies, including the one by Berry (1967), have demonstrated that there are significant differences in the levels of independence and conformity between the food gathering communities and the food-hunting communities. But, more importantly, cultures vary not only with respect to their physical and geographical environments, but also in relation to their value systems.

The existing value systems have a significant bearing on the religious and social beliefs, the rites and rituals, the kinship patterns, and the social arrangements of the people of that culture, and on the development of individual (personal) and social identities (Camilleri and Malewska-Peyre, 1997; Greenfield, 1997; Kakar, 1979, 1992; Laungani, 1999 (in press); Roland, 1988). Values are best defined as the currently held normative expectations underlying individual and social conducts (Laungani, 1995). Smith and Bond (1993) see values as universalistic statements about what we think is desirable or attractive. This, however, is a narrow definition because it overlooks the fact that values are both positive and negative. They guide us in terms of actions (behaviours) which are considered to be desirable and therefore need to be pursued and emulated, and actions which are considered to be undesirable, and, consequently, need to be avoided and discarded. The ethical components of values define for us appropriate and inappropriate behaviours. The author's views related to values and the functions served by values have been re-echoed elsewhere by Smith and Schwartz, 1997).

Our major beliefs concerning right and wrong, good and bad, normal and abnormal, appropriate and inappropriate, proper and improper, and the like, are, to a large measure, influenced by the values which prevail in our culture, particularly the sub-culture to which we belong and into which we are socialized (Brown, 1965; Danziger, 1970; Smith and Schwartz, 1997). We may be unable to explain *why* we hold such and such a belief and why this is important and that less so. Yet, values, like air, pervade our cultural atmosphere, and we imbibe them often without a conscious awareness of their origins. Values form the basis of social, political and religious order. They are often the result of past religious, political and philosophical legacies. Since these beliefs are passed on over centuries, their roots get deeper and deeper and are not easily severed. Thus values become an integral part of our psychological and existential make-up. We carry our values as securely as a fish its gills.

However, values are subject to change. Several factors, for example, migration from one culture to another; political, religious, scientific and technological upheavals; war; insurrection; and devastating epidemics, may bring about dramatic changes in our value systems, forcing us to re-examine our evaluations of ourselves, our beliefs, our behaviour, often in unpredictable ways. The process of change, however, may vary from culture to culture, being slow in some and rapid in others.

Given the cultural-specificity of certain values, it follows that many of our beliefs, attitudes and behaviours, both private and public, are likely to be culture-specific. Thus, one would expect to find both within and between cultures, similarities and differences in the manner in which a variety of problems, such as health, illness, mental illness, grief, bereavement, stress, patterns of child rearing and socialization, acquisition of identity, child abuse, attitudes to work, relationships, etc., are defined, conceptualized, and acted upon by peoples of those cultures.

THEORETICAL MODEL OF CULTURAL DIFFERENCES

Since private and social behaviours, to a large extent, are influenced by a set of core values prevalent in a given culture, it would help to posit a theoretical model which would articulate clearly the similarities and differences between different cultural groups, in particular, between Eastern and Western cultures. A theoretical model proposed by Laungani (1990, 1991, 1991a and b, 1992, 1993, 1994, 1995, 1996, 1996a, 1997) argues that there are four interrelated core values or factors which distinguish Western cultures from Eastern cultures, and more specifically, British culture from Indian culture in terms of their salient value-systems. The proposed four theoretical constructs are:

Individualism–Communalism (Collectivism)
Cognitivism–Emotionalism
Free-Will–Determinism
Materialism–Spiritualism

It needs to be made clear that the two concepts underlying each factor are not dichotomous. They are to be understood as extending along a continuum, starting at, say, individualism, at one end, and 'extending into communalism (or collectivism) at the other. A dichotomous approach, however, tends to classify people in 'either–or' terms. Such an approach is limited in its usefulness. An acceptance of the dichotomous approach, as Schwartz (1990) in his critique of individualism–collectivism, postulates 'that individualist and collectivist values form two coherent syndromes that are in polar opposition' (p. 140). People seldom fit into neat theoretically formulated and/or empirically derived categories. The sheer complexity and variability of human behaviours and responses precludes serious attempts at such dichotomous classifications.

A dimensional approach, on the other hand, takes account of human variability. It has the advantage of allowing us to measure salient attitudes and behaviours at any given point in time and over time. It also enables us to hypothesize expected theoretical and empirical shifts in positions along the continuum, both within and between cultural groups. Each of the hypothesized dimensions subsumes within it a variety of attitudes and behaviours which, to a large extent, are influenced by the norms and values operative within that culture. The theoretical bases of these factors have been described at length elsewhere (see Laungani, 1990, 1991, 1991a, and b, 1992, 1995, 1996,

1997). Sachdev (1992) has provided an empirical validation of the four factors. In her research study, she by means of specifically designed questionnaires, compared the beliefs and values of the British-born Indian school children with those of the Caucasian school children in West London. The two groups of children—though both born and socialized in a predominantly Western culture—showed marked preferences in items of their favoured value-systems. Her research also enabled her to predict the sets of conditions under which an individual's position is likely to shift—*in either direction*—along each continuum. Several sets of related hypotheses have also been subjected to rigorous empirical tests in India (Sachdev, 1992). The analysis of the data lends further support to the above model.

Further empirical validation of the theoretical model has also been provided by Laungani and Sookhoo (1995), Sookhoo (1995), and Laungani, (1997a; 1998, in press). In their studies on coronary heart patients suffering from myocardial infarction, a set of questionnaires was administered to the two sample groups, one of which consisted of Asian (males and females of Indian origin) patients and the other of white Caucasian patients. The patients for the study were randomly drawn from the cardiology department of a medical ward in a hospital in East London. The analysis of the questionnaires revealed that the two groups showed significant preferences for their favoured value-systems. In-depth, one-to-one interviews with each of the subjects revealed that the Asian subjects, to a large extent, conceptualized their myocardial infarction, its onset, etiology, its course of treatment, and its eventual prognosis in terms of determinism and spiritualism, whereas the Caucasian subjects saw their infarction in terms of free will. The close-knit family structures of the Asian subjects also enabled them to seek the comfort and security, which they believed would assist them in the process of recovery. The Caucasian groups, on the other hand, either did not have the close-knit family structures, or preferred not to show any dependence on their family members.

The factors, being discussed in the following pages, clearly show the British vs. Indian positions on each of the dimentional factors.

INDIVIDUALISM–COMMUNALISM (COLLECTIVISM)

Over the years, much has been written on the concepts of individualism and collectivism (Hofstede, 1980, 1991; Hui and

Triandis, 1986; Kagitcibasi, 1997; Kim, Triandis and Yoon, 1992; Kim *et al.,* 1994; Matsumoto, 1996, Schwartz, 1990; Triandis, 1994), and they have come to mean different things to different people. Many authors have construed the concepts in dichotomous terms, arguing that the sets of values related to each concept are in polar opposition (Schwartz, 1990).

In so far as the concept collectivism is concerned, the author prefers the word communalism. The concept collectivism is of dubious value. It is an undesirable legacy which cross-cultural psychologists in the Third World countries have inherited from Western psychologists. Although the notion of collectivism appears to be seemingly neutral, upon closer examination it turns out to contain a set of implicit values, some of which, when examined critically turn out to contain a set of implicit values, some of which, when, examined critically, turn out to be pejorative (Laungani, 1998). The author prefers the use of the concept communalism, notwithstanding its diverse subjective connotations. The arguments for the retention of the word communalism instead of collectivism, have been discussed elsewhere (Laungani, 1999, in preparation). Suffice to say that in employing the term collectivism there is the unvoiced danger of reintroducing the old notions of 'group mind' which were abandoned several decades ago. Although the term collectivism appears neutral in its connotation, it does convey a vague impression of large, amorphous crowds of people gathered together, responding to collectivism values.

Individualism

One of the distinguishing features of the Western society is its increasing emphasis on individualism. At an abstract level, the concept itself has come to acquire several different meanings: an ability to exercise a degree of control over one's life; the ability to cope with one's problems; an ability to change for the better; reliance upon oneself; being independent, autonomous, and responsible for one's actions; self-fulfilment; and self-realization of one's internal resources. As Triandis (1994) points out, individualism, in essence, is concerned with giving priority to one's personal goals over the goals of one's in-group. Individualism has also been the subject of considerable debate among Western thinkers (Ballah, 1985; Kagitcibasi, 1997; Lukes, 1973; Matsumoto, 1996; Riesman, 1954; Schwartz, 1990; Spence, 1985; Triandis, 1994; Waterman, 1981). Some writers, however, have been unhappy with the concept of individualism, and have argued that the notions of individualism are incompatible, even antithetical, with communal and collective interests. The 'dog-eat-dog' philosophy is seen as being divisive, inimical in terms of the promotion of communal goals, and in the long run, it alienates fellow-beings from one another. However, there are others—among them, Sampson (1977) being the more outspoken of the defenders of individualism—who extol its virtues. Individualism, it is argued, is in keeping with the philosophy of humanism, which emphasizes, among other things, the notion of 'diginity of man', its disentanglement from theology and religion, and its espousal of scientific enterprise as the fundamental bases for understanding the universe (Cooper, 1996). In recent years, the increasing popularity of individualism can also be attributed to the Weberian spirit of capitalism and free enterprise. Sampson (1977) sees no reason why the philosophy of individualism should not also nurture a spirit of co-operation and coexistence.

How does the notion of individualism help us to understand the development of identity?

1. Identity, in Western society, is construed by psychologists and psychiatrists of virtually all theoretical persuasions, in developmental terms, which start from infancy. And in the process of development, one's identity, according to received wisdom, passes through several critical stages in adolescence, into adulthood. To acquire an appropriate identity, which asserts one's strengths, which is located in reality, which separates the individual from others and is thereby kept distinct from those of others, which reflects one's true inner being, and which leads to the fulfilment or the realization of one's potential, is by no means easy. It often results in conflict, which if unresolved, leads to severe stress and in extreme cases to an identity crisis (Camilieri, 1990; Erikson, 1963; Maslow, 1970, 1980; Rogers, 1961, 1970).
2. Individualism tends to create conditions which do not permit an easy sharing of one's problems and worries with others. As Camus (1956) pointed out several years ago, individualism creates in people an *existential loneliness*, compounded by a sense of the absurd. The emphasis upon self-reliance, the inability to merge one's identity into those of others—familial or social, the inability to reconcile conflicting identities within oneself thereby forming an integrative whole, all imposes severe stress upon the individual, and may make the search for one's 'true' identity a life-long quest.

3. Another dominant feature of individualism lies in its recognition of and respect for an individual's physical and psychological space. People in the West do not normally touch one another. Touching is seen as an encroachment of one's physically defined boundaries. Secondly, physical contact, particularly between two males, for example, an innocent holding of hands in public, may also be misconstrued; it arouses connotations of homosexuality. The taboos related to physical touch are so strong that even in times of grief, they are not easily violated (Laungani, 1997). Even eye-to-eye contact between two people is normally avoided. Several studies have shown that the effects of violating another person's physical space leads to severe stress and in extreme cases, to neurosis (Greenberg and Firestone, 1977; Rohner, 1974).
4. Closely related to the concept of physical space is that of 'psychological space'. Psychological space is concerned with defining boundaries which separate the psychological self from others. It is an idea of immense value in the West, respected in all social situations. It comes into play in all social encounters, from the most casual to the most intimate. One hears of people feeling threatened, upset, angry, confused, etc., when they feel that their subjectively defined space is violated by others. For instance, bereavement in the family is perceived largely as an individual problem, of sole concern to the affected family. Outsiders respect the desire of the bereaved to be 'left alone' and, consequently, do not intrude, for fear of invading the other person's psychological space. As has been pointed out elsewhere (Laungani, 1992), the notion of physical and psychological space is intertwined with the concept of *privacy*. Privacy implies a recognition of and respect for another person's individuality. Even the most casual encounters between people, both in social and familial situations, are dictated by a tacit recognition and acceptance of the other person's privacy. Several studies have demonstrated that the invasion of privacy leads to severe stress (Spielberger, 1979).

The need for privacy and independence is inculcated in children right from an early age. Most parents ensure that their new born infant sleeps with them in their room, so that they may be able to look after the baby in the night and attend to all its needs. A few months later the baby is moved into a separate room, this brings about an abrupt separation between themselves and their child. Such a separation is considered to be of extreme importance in the development of the child's independence. It might be construed as form of 'psychological weaning'.

Communalism (or Collectivism)

Indian society, has been and continues to be community-oriented (Kakar, 1981; Koller, 1982; Lannoy, 1976; Laungani, 1988; Mandelbaum, 1972; Sinari, 1984). Most Indians grow up and live in *extended-family* networks. It is and has been for centuries a family-oriented and community-based society. A community, in the sense in which it is understood in India, has several common features. People within a group are united by a common caste-rank or *jati,* religious grouping and linguistic and geographical boundaries. The members within a community generally operate on a ranking or a hierarchical system. On important issues, the members of a community may meet and confer with one another, and any decisions taken are often binding on the rest of the members within the community.

A microcosm of such a ranking or hierachical system is also to be found within each extended-family network. A typical extended family usually consists of the mother and the father. The father, in most parts of India, is seen as the head of family. The extended family would normally include all their children: their married sons and their wives, and their children (if any), their unmarried sons, their unmarried daughters, and other relatives, such as the father's younger brothers, their wives and children, the father's widowed sister, all of whom would live under the same roof. In such a family structure, incomes are pooled and are redistributed according to the needs of the respective members within the family. Elders are accorded special status within the family, and their important role is very clearly recognized. Elders, whether they come from rural areas or from large metropolitan cities, are generally deferred to.

In an Indian family life, one's individuality is subordinated to collective solidarity, and one's ego is submerged into the collective ego of the family and one's community. It may be of passing interest to note here that Indians often use the collective pronoun 'we' in their everyday speech. The use of the pronoun we or *hum* (in Hindi) signifies the suppression of one's individual ego into the collective ego of one's family and community. Thus, one speaks with the collective voice of others, and, in so doing, gains they approbation. When a problem—financial, medical, psychiatric or whatever—affects an individual, it affects the entire family. The problem becomes one of concern for the whole family. The problems are discussed within the interlocking network of family (hierachical) relationships, and attempts are made to find a feasible solution. Only occasionally will the family members turn to members of their sub-community for a solution of their problems.

However, it should be emphasized that for an individual to stay as an integral part of the family and of the community, it is expected that the individual will submit to family and communal norms, and will not deviate to an extent where it becomes necessary for severe sanctions to be imposed upon the deviant or, as an extreme measure, for the deviant to be ostracized. The pressure to conform to family norms and expectations can and does cause acute stress in individual members in the family, leading, in some instances, to psychotic disorders and hysteria (Channabasavanna and Bhatti, 1982; Sethi and Manchanda, 1978).

Identity in India, to a large extent, is *ascribed,* and, to a lesser extent, *achieved.* By virtue of being born into one of the four hereditary castes (this applies mainly to the Hindus who comprise over 82 per cent of the total population of India), one's identity is ascribed at birth. There are both advantages and disadvantages in such a traditional arrangement. On the one hand, the individual in an Indian family set-up does not have to pass through the critical stages in the process of developing an identity, as is normally the case with children in Western individualistic cultures. On the other hand, an ascribed identity tends to restrict the choices open to the individual. While personal choice is central to an individualistic society, it is seen as an exception in a communalistic society. Occupations are largely caste-dependent, and caste, of course, is hierachical and determined by birth. While movement from the lower caste to a higher caste is virtually impossible, it is, of course, possible (as a result of certain 'caste-polluting' actions) to lose one's caste and drop from a higher to a lower caste. Although the pattern of caste-related occupations is beginning to undergo a transformation in the urban areas of India, there is little evidence of such changes in the rural areas of the country, which are inhabited by nearly 80 per cent of the Indian population. One has little choice even in terms of one's marriage partner. Marriages are arranged by the parents of the prospective spouses. Although the 'style' of arranged marriages has undergone a modest change within the Indian society, particularly among the affluent members of society in the urban sectors of the country, they are still the norm.

One is born into a given caste, and is destined to remain in it until death. One's friends too are an integral part of one's extended-family network; pressures from the elders and threats of ostracism ensure that one strays within the confines of one's caste and community, and seldom or never strays away from it. Major features of individualism and communalism with respect to the acquisition of identity are summarized in Table 1.

Table 1

Individualism	Communalism
Emphasis on high degree of self-control.	Such emphasis unnecessary.
Emphasis on personal responsibility.	Emphasis on collective responsibility.
Emphasis on self-achievement.	Emphasis on collective achievement.
Identity achieved.	Identity ascribed.
Anxiety is related to the *acquisition* of identity.	Anxiety may be related to the *imposition* of a familial and caste-related identity.
Emphasis on nuclear families.	Emphasis on extended families.

With the exception of the caste-system, which is a singularly unique feature of the Indian society, other collectivist cultures, including China, Taiwan, Korea, Hong Kong, Philippines, Thailand, Nepal, Pakistan, Iran, Turkey, Portugal, Mexico, Peru, Venezuela and Colombia, also share most of the features described above (Cheng, 1996; Gulerce, 1996; Hofstede, 1980; Jing and Wan, 1997; Kim, 1997; Matsumoto, 1996; Sinha, Mishra and Berry, 1996; Ward and Kennedy, 1996; Yang, 1997). For instance, Yang (1997) in his excellent analyses of the traditional Chinese personality, refers to the tight, close-knit bond between the individual and his/her family. He points out that:

> Chinese familism disposes the Chinese to subordinate their personal interests, goals, glory, and welfare to their family's interest, goals, glory, and welfare to the extent that the family is primary and its members secondary.... (1997: 245).

Again, Yang (1997: 245) points out that in order to attain harmony within the family it is essential for the individual to 'surrender or merge into his or her family, and, as a result, lose his or her individuality and idiosyncrasies as an independent actor.

COGNITIVISM–EMOTIONALISM

This is concerned with the way in which the British (the English, in particular) construe their private and social worlds, and the ways in which they form and sustain social relationships. In broad terms, it has been suggested by Pande (1968) that British society is a *work-and-activity-centred* society and in contradistinction, the Indian society is *relationship-centred.* It should be emphasized that these different constructs are result of their different philosophical legacies.

Cognitivism

1. In a *work-and-activity-centred* society, people are more likely to operate on a cognitive mode, where the emphasis is on rationality, logic and control. Public expression of feelings and emotions, particularly among the middle classes in England, is often frowned upon. The expression of negative feelings causes mutual embarrassment, and is often construed as being vulgar. Negative feelings and emotions, when they are expressed, are done in an oblique and understated manner. The process of exercising restraint over their negative feelings and emotions starts during infant socialization, and by the time the infants reach adulthood, the process gets internalized and becomes an integral part of their behavioural repertoire.

   Within a cognitivist framework, there is a cultural expectation that persons in most social situations will exercise a high degree of self-control. This, combined with the cultural embargo on the expression of feelings and emotions in public, can often lead to severe stress. Even in situations where it would seem legitimate to express feelings openly, without inhibition, at funerals, for instance, the English are guided by control, which suggests that one must not cry in public, one must at all times put on a 'brave' face, one must above all, never lose one's diginity. Diginity is preserved or even perpetuated through restraint. If one *has* to cry, one must do so in the silence of one's heart and the privacy of one's home. The unwillingness or the inability to express emotions openly is a theme that has caused some worry to other writers in the field (Gorer, 1965; Hockey, 1993).

Obviously, in a work-and-activity-centred society, a need often arises for the creation of professional and semi-professional settings which permit the legitimate expression of specific feelings and emotions, and their handling by experts trained in the specific areas. Thus, one sees in Western society the growth of specialist counsellors, including bereavement counsellors, cancer and AIDS counsellors, marriage guidance counsellors, family therapists, rational-emotive therapists, and, last, but not the least, psychotherapists and psychoanalysts of different theoretical persuasions.

2. Given the emphasis on work and activity, relationships in such a society are formed on the basis of *shared commonalties*. One's relationships too, to a large extent, grow out of one's work. Thus relationships become a byproduct of work. One is expected to 'work at a relationship' in a marriage, in a family situation, with friends, with colleagues at work, and even with one's children. In a work-and-activity oriented society, one's identity, self-image, and self-esteem work defines one's sense of worth.
3. Work and its relations to self-esteem acquire meaning only when seen against the background of time. Our conception of time is both objective and subjective. At an objective level, time is seen in terms of an Einsteiniun dimension, where each hour is divided into fixed moments of minutes, seconds and milli-seconds. Each moment (at least on earth) expires at the same speed. An hour passes not a moment sooner, not a moment later. At a subjective level, however, there are variations in our perceptions of time. In a work-and-activity centred society, one's working life, including one's private life, to a large measure, is organized around time. To ensure the judicious use of time, one resorts to keeping appointment books, calenders, computer-assisted diaries; works to fixed time-schedules, sets deadlines; and tries to keep within one's time-limits. One is constantly aware of the swift passage of time, and to fritter it away is often construed as an act of criminality. Time, therefore, comes to acquire a significant meaning in a work-and-activity centred society. McClelland (1961) has shown that people in general, and high achievers in particular, use metaphors such as 'a dashing waterfall', 'a speeding train', etc., to describe time. The fear of running out of time is seen as one of the

greatest stressors in Western society. Even casual encounters between friends, between colleagues at work, are time-related, and operate on convert agendas. One seldom meets people as an end in itself, meeting people is construed as a means to an end, with time playing a significant role.

Emotionalism

1. Non-western societies, to a large extent, are *relationship-centred* and operate on an *emotional* mode. The fact that people live in close physical proximity and share their lives with one another, forces them to relate with one another on an emotional mode. In such a society, feelings and emotions are not easily repressed, and their expression, in general, is not frowned upon. Crying, dependence on others, excessive emotionality, volatility and verbal hostility, both in males and females, are not in any way considered as sign of weakness or ill-breeding. Since feelings and emotions—both positive and negative—are expressed easily, there is little danger of treading incautiously on others' sensibilities and vulnerabilities, such as might be the case in work-and-activity centred societies; given the extended-family structure of relationships, emotional outbursts, as it were 'taken on board' by the family members. Quite often, the emotional outburst are of a symbolic nature and even highly stylized and ritualistic. To appreciate fully the ritualistic component of emotional outbursts among Indians, be they Hindus or Muslims, one must visualize it against the backdrop of the living conditions in India. In the urban areas, for those who are fortunate enough to live in brick houses, it is not at all uncommon for a family of eight to ten persons to be living together in one small room. Given the extreme closeness of life, the paucity of amenities, the absence of privacy, the inertia evoked by the overpowering heat and dust and the awesome feeling of claustrophobia, it is not at all surprising that families do often quarrel, fight and swear at one another (and from time to time assault one another too). But their quarrels and outbursts are often of a symbolic nature, for otherwise, such quarrels would lead to a permanent rift, the consequences of which would be far more traumatic than those of living together. There is, in such outbursts, a surrealistic quality, for, at one level, they are frighteningly real (the words and

abuses hurled at one another), callous and hurtful, yet at another, bewilderingly unreal. They serve no function other than the relief which such 'cathartic' outbursts bring.

However, in a hierachical family structure, each member within the family soon becomes aware of his or her own position within the hierarchy, and, in the process of familial adjustment, learns the normative expressions of emotionality permissible to the person concerned.

2. One of the major disadvantages of being in a relationship-centred society is that one is forced into relationships from which one cannot or is unable to opt out without severe sanctions being imposed upon the individual. Several studies have shown that one's inability to severe enforced relationships based on birth and caste often leads to severe stress and neurosis (Channabasavanna and Bhatti, 1982).
3. The factor of time which, as we saw, is so important in the Western societies, does not have the same meaning in a relationship-centred society. At an objective level, time is construed in virtually the same way as it is in the West. But at a subjective level, time in India is seen in more flexible and even relaxed terms. Time in the Indian metaphysics, is not conceptualized in linear terms. A linear model of time signifies a beginning, a middle, and an end, or, in other words, a past, a present, and a future. Time, in Indian Philosophy, is conceptualized in circular terms, which means that time has no beginning, no middle, and no end, or, if there is a beginning, it remains unknown. These differential conceptualizations have serious implications in our understanding a variety of social behaviours in both the cultures.

For instance, on a day-to-day observational level, one does not notice among Indians the same sense of urgency which appears to have become the hallmark of the Western society. Time in India is often viewed as a quiet, 'motionless ocean', 'a vast expanse of sky'. It is interesting to note that in Hindi there is only one word—*kal*—which stands for both, yesterday and tomorrow. One gauges the meaning of the word from its context. The Indians' flexible attitude to time is often reflected in their social engagements: they tend to be quite casual about keeping appointments; being late for an appointment, keeping another person waiting; all this does not appear to cause them any undue stress.

There are, however, exceptions to this flexible construction of time. They occur in those situations which are considered auspicious: undertaking an important journey; fixing the time of christening, betrothals, weddings, and funerals, in particular. In such auspicious situations one is expected to consult the family Brahmin priest, who then consults an almanac from which he (most Brahmin priests are male) calculates the most auspicious time for the commencement of that particular activity. Such events, because of their religious significance, are seldom left to chance; one seeks divine guidance in their planning and execution.

The major features of cognitivism and emotionalism, and their relative differences are summarized in Table 2.

Table 2

Cognitivism	Emotonalism
Emphasis on rationality and logic.	Emphasis on feelings and intuition.
Feelings and emotions kept in check.	Feelings and emotions expressed freely.
Relations based on shared interests.	Relations caste and family-based.
Relationships often seen as a means to an end.	Relationships seen as ends in themselves.
Emphasis on work-and-activity.	Emphasis on relationships.

Free–Will Determinism

Prior to Newton's spectacular achievements, determinism was entangled in its theistic and metaphysical connotation. But after the publication of Newton's *Principia* in 1687, the concept of determinism was partially freed from its theistic connotations and a non-theistic and mechanistic view of determinism in science, and indeed in the universe, gained prominence. A scientific notion of determinism with its emphasis on casualty, or conversely, its denial of non-causal events, found favour among the rationalists philosophers who embraced it with great fervour (Popper, 1972). However, it was not until the emergence of quantum mechanics in the early twentieth century that determinism in science, if not in human affairs, once again came to be seriously questioned. In keeping with his own views on the subject, Popper (1988) avoids the terms determinism and free will altogether, and proposes the term indeterminism, which, he argues, is not the opposite of determinism nor is it the same as free will.

Notwithstanding the unresolved debates in philosophy on the subject, there is a peculiar dualism in Western thinking concerning free will and determinism. Scientific research in medicine, psychiatry, biology, and other related disciplines, including psychology, is based on the acceptance of a deterministic framework; hence the concern with seeking causal explanations, and with predictability in accordance with rational, scientific procedures of prediction. Yet, at social, psychological and commonsense levels there is a strong belief in the notion of free will, which manifests itself in the constant proverbs, homilies, poems and popular advice offered freely to children and adults, often by the very people who adopt a deterministic model in the course of their professional and scientific work (Laungani, 1992).

Free Will

What do we mean by free will? Free will might be defined as a non-causal, voluntary action. However, at a commonsense level, it is defined as exercising voluntary control over one's action. Thus, free will allows an individual to do what he/she wills, and, in so doing, take 'credit' for his/her successes, and accept blame for his/her failures as mishaps. As a result, one is locked into the consequence of one's own actions. One is entrapped into one's own existential predicament, from which there does not appear to be an easy way out.

Determinism

Indians, by virtue of subscribing to a deterministic view of life, in a teleological sense at least, are prevented from taking final responsibility for their own actions. The notion of determinism plays an extremely crucial role in Indian thinking. The *law of karma,* which involves determinism and fatalism, has shaped the Indian view of life over centuries (O'Flaherty, 1976; Sinari, 1984; Weber, 1963). In its simplest form, the *law of karma* states that happiness or sorrow is the predetermined effect of actions committed by the persons either in his present life or in one of his numerous past lives. Things do not happen because *we* make them happen. Things happen because they were *destined* to happen. If one's present life is determined by one's actions in one's previous life, it follows that any problem that affects an individual was destined to happen because of past actions.

A belief in the *law of karma* does not necessarily negate the notion of free will. As von Furer-Haimendorf (1974) has pointed out, in an important sense *karma* is based on the assumption of free will. The theory of *karma* rests on the idea that an individual has the final moral responsibility for each of his/her actions, and hence the freedom of moral choice.

Pandey, Srinivas and Muralidhar (1980), in a study of informants of psychiatric patients in India, found that the most commonly stated causes of psychotic disorders was attributed to sins and wrong deeds in their previous and present lifes. These findings have been corroborated by Srinivasa and Trivedi (1982), who, in their study of 266 respondents selected from three villages in South India, attributed, among other factors, 'God's curse' as one of the most common causes of stress leading to mental disorders. Such a belief has its advantages: it takes away the blame which might otherwise be apportioned to the individual concerned.

A belief in determinism is likely to engender in the Indian psyche, a spirit of passive, if not resigned, acceptance of the vicissitudes of life. This prevents a person from experiencing feelings of guilt, a state from which the Westerners, because of their fundamental belief in the doctrine of free will, cannot be protected. The main disadvantage of determinism—and there are many—lies in the fact that it often leads to a state of existential, and in certain instances, moral resignation, compounded by a profound sense of *inertia*. One does not take immediate *proactive* measures; one merely accepts the vicissitudes of life without qualms. While this may prevent a person from experiencing stress, it does not allow the same person to make individual attempts to alleviate his unbearable conditions.

The major features of free will and determinism are summarized in Table 3.

Table 3

Free Will	Determinism
Emphasis on freedom of choice.	Freedom of choice limited.
Proactive.	Reactive.
Free Will is relevant only to one's present life.	Determinism affects one's past, present, and future lives.
Success or failure due largely to individual effort.	Although effort is important, success or failure is related to one's *karma*.
Self-blame or guilt is a residual consequence of failure.	No guilt is attached to failure.
Failure may lead to victim-blaming.	No blame is attached to victim.

MATERIALISM–SPIRITUALISM

Materialism

Materialism refers to a belief in the existence of a material world or a world composed of matter. What constitutes matter is itself debatable; the questions have never been satisfactorily answered (Trefil, 1980). If matter consists of atoms, it appears that atoms are made of nuclei and electrons. Nuceli, in turn, are made up of protons and neutrons. What are protons and neutrons made of? Gell-Mann (see Davies, 1990) coined the word quarks. But quarks, it appears, have their own quirks. In other words, the assumed solidity of matter may indeed turn out to be a myth (Davies, 1990).

The notion of the solidity of matter was robustly debated by Heisenberg in his now famous research paper on indeterminacy in quantum theory in 1927 (Heisenberg, 1930). Such debates, however, are confined to journals of philosophy and science. At a practical, day-to-day level, however, aided by empiricism, one accepts the assumed solidity of the world which one inhabits—but not without paying a heavy price. For, such an acceptance gives rise to the popular myth that all explanations of the phenomena, ranging from lunar cycles to lunacy, need to be sought within the (assumed) materialist frame-work. This is evidenced by the profound reluctance among psychiatrists, medical practitioners and psychologists in general to entertain any explanations which are of a non-material or supernatural nature. Non-material explanations are treated at best with skepticism, and at worst with scorn.

A materialist philosophy also tends to engender in its subscribers the belief that our knowledge of the world is external to ourselves; reality is as it were, 'out there', and it is only through objective scientific enterprise that one will acquire an understanding of the external world and, with it, and understanding of 'reality'.

The few psychiatrists and psychologists who have steered away from materialistic explanations, or have shown the willingness to consider alternative non-material explanations, comprise a very small minority. Most of them are only too aware that anyone offering such explanations of phenomena is in danger of incurring the wrath of the scientific community. Non-material explanations fall within the purview of the pre-scientific communities, or in other words, superstitious and backward societies, to be found mainly in under-developed countries and by implications, in the collectivist societies.

Let us consider an example to illustrate such forms of thinking in the Western society. For over two thousand years, *yogis* in India have made claims about their abilities to alter their states of consciousness at will, thereby bringing their autonomic nervous states under voluntary control (Radhakrishnan, 1923, 1989). In the *hathayoga,* yogic exercises—or *asanas* as they are called—were claimed to have therapeutic effects for a variety of physical and psychological disorders. Such claims were seldom taken seriously by the Western scientists. They were dismissed as unsubstantiated exaggerations. It was not untill 1969, when Neal Miller successfully trained his laboratory rats to lower and raise their blood-pressure by selective reinforcement (Miller, 1969) that it began to dawn on the Western mind that there might, after all, be some substance in the claims made by yoga. Using a similar selective reinforcement strategy, Miller found that he could train his students to exercise voluntary control over their autonomic responses. Suddenly, the claims made by the yogis began to acquire credibility. Miller's performing rats did the trick! Miller's findings opened the doors to yoga in the American Universities, and research into altered states of consciousness, followed by its applications into techniques of bio-feedback, became respectable. It is therefore hardly an accident when one realizes the importance given to yogic *asanas* in a variety of stress management exercises designed by Western experts.

In Indian thinking, the notion of materialism is a relatively unimportant concept. The external world to Indians is *not* composed of matter. It is seen as being *illusory.* It is *maya.* The concept of *maya,* as Zimmer (1989) points out, 'holds a key position in Vedantic thought and teaching' (p. 19). Since the external world is illusory, reality, or its perception, lies *within* the individual, and not, as Westerners believe, *outside* the individual. This, according to Zimmer (1989), tends to make Indians more *inward looking* and Westerners more *outward looking.* Also, given the illusory nature of the external world, the Indian mind remains unfettered by materialistic boundaries. It resorts to explanations where material and spiritual, physical and metaphysical, natural and supernatural explanations of phenomena coexist with one another. What to a Western mind—weaned on Aristotelian logic; nourished on a scientific diet; socialized on materialism, empiricism and positivism might seem an irreconcilable contradiction, leaves an Indian mind relatively unperturbed. To a Westerner if A is A, A cannot then be not –A. If dysentery is caused by certain forms of bacteria, it cannot then be due to the influence of the 'evil-eye'. The two are logically and empirically incompatible. But contradictions to Indians are a way of life. A is not only A, but under certain conditions, A may be not –A. This differential construction of one's physical world has an important bearing on the development of identity and patterns of their social relationships.

Spiritualism

Indian beliefs and values revolve round the notion of spiritualism. The ultimate purpose of human existence is to transcend one's illusory physical existence, renounce the world of material aspirations, and attain a heightened state of spiritual awareness (Radhakrishnan, 1923, 1989; Zimmer, 1951, 1989). Any activity—particularly yoga—which is likely to promote such a state is to be encouraged.

The major features of Materialism and spiritualism are shown in Table 4.

Table 4

Materialism	Spiritualism
The world is solid, 'real', physical.	The world is illusory—it is *maya.*
Rejection of contradictory explanations of phenomena.	Co-existence of contradictory explanations of phenomena.
Reality is external to the individual.	Reality internal to the individual.
People in general tend to be outward-looking.	People in general tend to be inward looking.
Reality perceived through scientific enterprise.	Reality is perceived through contemplation and inner reflection.

Conclusions

All cultures, as we have seen, exercise a powerful influence on the development of one's identities, and in initiating, sustaining, and controlling behaviours. Behaviours which fall outside the established conventional norms may be seen as deviations, and depending on the importance and the functional value of the behaviour concerned, pressures, from mild to severe, may be brought to bear upon the individual to conform to the norms. And when that fails, sanctions may be imposed upon the deviant individual, ranging from confinement, incarceration to ostracism, etc. Certain forms of deviations in certain instances may be construed as forms of mental aberrations, and once identified, are dealt with in culturally-appropriate ways; for example, confinement, medication, exorcism, etc., may be dealt with by a culturally accepted 'expert' who is trained in such practices.

Thus, each culture devises its own internally consistent sets of rules. To understand a given pattern of behaviour in another culture, it is necessary to understand the system of rules and the assumptions which guide the private and social behaviours of people in that culture.

This suggests an adoption of a relativistic position. It is often assumed that the adoption of a relativistic position would put an end to any form of pejorative (or racist) judgements of other cultures, because one then attempts to understand from within the culture's own consistent system of rules (emic perspectives) and not from the investigator's cultural standpoint (etic perspectives). Thus, there would be no need to 'order' cultures on a measurable scale of superiority or inferiority, civilized or primitive, etc. Such an approach would also help to dilute, if not dissolve altogether, the oft-voiced accusations of scientific, educational and economic imperialism which have been levelled against the Western countries by the developing countries.

But the acceptance of relativistic doctrines creates its own peculiar problems. How does one make sense of the internal rules of another culture? One might learn the language in order to learn the rule of the cultural system, but that alone is not enough to guarantee a clear understanding of the principles underlying the rules of the culture. One of the main weaknesses of the relativistic principle, as Doyal and Harris (1986) point out, lies in the fact that in an attempt to understand the rules of the culture through translations, one would have to suspend judgement concerning whether a given rule was true or false, rational or irrational. If the rules of the language of another culture do not have built into them the canons of formal logic and conceptions of rationality, it becomes difficult, if not impossible, to interpret behaviours in any meaningful manner. No judgements of behaviours would ever be possible.

Although one can see the value of adopting a relativistic position, it does not lend itself to a ready acceptance. Relativism as a valid explanatory concept has come to be seriously questioned by several authors, including Gelner (1985). It has also been argued that relativism in recent years has come to acquire a variety of ideological connotations, and is often used as a gag to stifle any recognition of genuine differences in opinions, beliefs, values and behaviours across cultures. In that sense, therefore, it is potentially dangerous to adhere to a relativistic position, for its blanket acceptance has no room in it for any genuine understanding of cross-cultural differences in a variety of fields. The uncritical acceptance of relatives, as Popper (1963) has demonstrated, leads to an epistemological *cul-de-sac*. It does not permit one to transcend one's cultural boundaries. One is forever doomed to languish within the narrowly-defined boundaries of one's culture.

However, to question relativism does not necessary mean that there are not behaviours which are not culture-specific. Some obviously are, and have been specifically recognized as such. Clear catalogues of culture-specific behaviours, particularly in the field of mental disturbances, have been examined by various authors working in this area (Draguns, 1981, 1990; Verma, 1988). It therefore seems reasonable to assume that some behaviours are culture-specific and some universalistic.

This chapter highlighted the salient value systems of people in India and in England. Although India and England were singled out for a closer examination, it is clear that, to a large measure, the value systems described in this chapter are also applicable to other individualist and collectivist cultures. The chapter also examined the influence of cultural values on a variety of private and public behaviours of the peoples of the two cultures.

The postulated conceptual model allowed us to describe each of the dominant value systems as extending along a continuum, thus suggesting that the perceived differences in the behaviours of people may, more often than not, be a matter of degree and not of kind. Such a formulation has one or two distinct advantages over a dichotomous formulation. First, it enables one to measure any changes in value systems which may occur in an individual due to migration from one culture to another (e.g., a person moving from a collectivist to a individualistic culture, and vice versa). Second, it enables one to measure the influence of acculturation of second generation children of parents who have emigrated to another culture; that is, to what extent do children imbibe the values of the new culture into which they are born, and to what extent do they internalize the values of the parents' culture. Third, it enables one to hypothesize the source and types of variations in attitudes, values and behaviours which are more likely to be influenced by those living in another culture.

Most psychologists, until recently, have been concerned with finding invariant universal patterns of behaviours, and have often ignored the fact that we are all products of our culture. We are influenced by our culture and, in turn, we influence our own culture. It is only in recent years, with the growth to cross-cultural psychology and the development of indigenous approaches to psychology, that the situation is beginning to undergo a change and, in the years to come, may provide a radical and much-needed paradigm shift.

References

Bellah, R.N. (1985). *Habits of the Heart: Individuation and Commitment in American life,* Berkeley: University of California Press.

Berry, J.W. (1967). 'Independence and Conformity in Subsistence-Level Societies', *Journal of Personality and Social Psychology,* 7: 415–18.

Brown, R. (1965). *Social Psychology,* London: Collier Macmillan.

Camilleri, C. and H. Melewska-Peyre (1997). 'Socialization and Identity Strategies', in J.W. Berry, P.R. Dasen, T.S. Saraswathi (eds), *Handbook of Cross-Cultural Psychology,* 2nd edn, Vol. 2, pp. 41–67, Boston: Allyn & Bacon.

Camilleri, C. (1990). 'Identite et gestion de la disparite culturell: Essai d'une typologie', in C. Camilleri *et al., Strategies identiaires,* pp. 85–110, Paris: Presses Universitaires de France.

Camus, A. (1955). *The Myth of Sisyphus,* London: Hamish Hamilton.

Channabasavanna, S.M. and R.S. Bhatti (1982). 'A Study on Interactional Patterns and Family Typologies in Families of Mental Patients', in A. Kiev and A. V. Rao (eds), *Readings in Transcultural Psychiatry,* pp. 149–61, Madras: Higginbothams.

Cheng, C.H.K. (1996). 'Towards a Culturally Relevant Model of Self-Concept for the Hong Kong Chinese', in *Asian Contributions to Cross-Cultural Psychology,* J. Pandey, D. Sinha, and D.P.S. Bhawuk (eds), pp. 235–54, New Delhi: Sage Publications.

Cooper, D.E. (1996). *World Philosophies: A Historical Introduction,* Oxford: Blackwell.

Danziger, K. (ed.) (1970). *Readings in Child Socilaization,* Oxford: Pergamon Press.

Davies, P. (1990). *God and The New Physics,* London, England: Penguin Books.

Doyal, L., and R. Harris (1986). *Empiricism, Explanation and Rationality: An Introduction to the Philosophy of the Social Sciences,* London: Routledge.

Draguns, J.G. (1981). 'Psychlogical Disorders of Clinical Severity', in H.C. Traindis and W.R. Brislin (eds), *Handbook of Cross-Cultural Psychology,* Vol. 5, Boston, Mass: Allyn & Bacon, Inc.

Draguns, J.G. (1990). 'Normal and Abnormal Behaviour in Cross-Cultural Perspective: Specifying the Nature of Their Relationship', in J.J. Berman (ed.), *Nebraska Symposium on Motivation, 1989,* Lincoln, NB: Nebraska University Press.

Erikson, E. (1963). *Childhood and Society,* London, England: Penguin.

Gelner, E. (1985). *Relativism and the Social Sciences,* Cambridge: Cambrıdge University Press.

Gorer, G. (1965). *Death, Grief, and Mourning in Contemporary Britain,* London: Cresset Press.

Greenbeg, C.I. and I.J. Firestone (1977). 'Compensatory Response to Crowding: Effects of Personal Space and Privacy Reduction', *Journal of Personality and Socail Psychology,* September, 35(9): 637–44.

Greenfield, P.M. (1997). 'Culture as Process: Empirical Methods for Cultural Psychology', in J.W. Berry, Y.H. Poortinga, and J. Pandet (eds), *Handbook of Cross-Cultural Psychology,* Vol. 1, pp. 301–46, Boston: Allyn & Bacon.

Gulerce, A. (1996). 'A Family Structure Assessment Device for Turkey', in J. Pandey, D. Sinha, and D.P.S. Bhawuk (eds), *Asian Contributions to Cross-Cultural Psychology,* pp. 108–18, New Delhi: Sage Publications.

Heisenberg, W. (1930). *The Physics of the Quantum Theory,* Berkeley: California University Press.

Hockey J. (1993). 'The Acceptable Face of Human Grieving?: The Clergy's Role in Managing Emotional Expression During Funerals', in D. Clark (ed.), *The Sociology of Death,* 129–48, Oxford: Blackwell Publishers.

Hofstede, G. (1980). *Culture's consequences: International Differences in Work-Related Values,* Beverly Hills, CA: Sage.

Hofstede, G. (1980). *Cultures and Organizations: Sotware of the Mind,* London: McGraw-Hill.

Hui, C.H. and H.C. Triandis (1986). 'Individualism-Collectivism: A Study of Cross-Cultural Researchers', *Journal of Cross-Cultural Psychology,* 17: 222–48.

Jing, Q. and C. Wan (1997). 'Socialization of Chinese Children', in H.S.R. Kao and D. Sinha (eds), *Asian Perspectives on Psychology,* pp. 25–39, New Delhi: Sage Publications.

Kagitcibasi, C. (1997). 'Individualism and Collecitivism', in J.W. Berry, M.H. Seagall, and C. Kagitcibasi (eds), *Handbook of Cross-Cultural Psychology,* Vol. 3, Boston: Allyn & Bacon.

Kakar, S. (1979, 1992). (ed.), *Identity and Adulthood,* Delhi: Oxford India Paperbacks.

Kakar, S. (1981). *The Inner World—A Psychoanalytic Study of Children and Society in India,* Delhi: Oxford University Press.

Kim, U., H.C. Triandis, and G. Yoon (1992). (eds), *Individualism and Collectivism: Theoretical and Methodological Issues,* Newbury Park, CA: Sage.

Kim, U. (1997). 'Asian Collectivism: An Indigenous Perspective', in H.S.R. Kao and D. Sinha (eds), *Asian Perspectives on Psychology,* pp. 147–63, New Delhi: Sage Publications.

Koller, J.M. (1982). *The Indian Way: Asian Perspecties,* London: Collier Macmillan.

Lannory, R. (1976). *The Speaking Tree,* Oxford: Oxford University Press.

Laungani, P. (1989). 'Cultural Influences on Mental Illness', *Political & Economic Weekly, Bombay,* 28, October, pp. 2427–30.

Laungani, P. (1990). 'Turning Eastward—An Asian View on Child Abuse', *Health & Hygiene,* 11(1): 26–29.

Laungani, P. (1990a). *'Family Life and Child Abuse: Learning from Asian Culture',* Paper presented at the 3rd International Child Health Congress, Kensington Town Hall, London, 19–22 March.

Laungani, P. (1991). 'Preventing Child Abuse and Promoting Child Health across cultures', Paper presented at the United Nations Conference on Action for Public Health, Sundsvall, Sweden, 9–15 June.

Laungani, P. (1991a). 'The Nature and Experience of Learning. Cross-cultural perspectives', Paper presented at a Conference on Experiential Learning, University of Surrey, Guildford, 16–18 July.

Laungani, P. (1991b). 'Stress Across Cultues: A theoretical Analysis', Paper presented at the Conference of The Society of Public

Health on Stress and the Health Services, Royal Society of Medicine, Wimpole Street, London, 25 July.

Laungani, P. (1992). 'Assessing Child Abuse Through Interviews of Children and Parents of Children at Risk', *Children and Society,* 6(1): 3–11.

Laungani, P. (1994). 'Cultural Differences in Stress: India and England', *Counselling Psychology Review,* 9(4): 25–37.

Laungani, P. (1995), 'Stress in Eastern and Western Cultures', in J. Brebner, E. Greenglass, P. Laungani, and A. O'Roark (eds), *Stress and Emotion,* Vol. 15, pp. 265–80, Washington DC: Taylor & Francis.

Laungani, P. (1995a). 'Patterns of Bereavement in Indian and English Societies', *Bereavement Care,* 14(1): 5–7.

Laungani, P. (1996). 'Research in Cross-Cultural Settings; Ethical Considerations', in E. Miao (ed.), *Cross-Cultural Encounters, Proceedings of the 53rd Annual Convention of International Council of Psychologists,* pp. 107–36, Taipei, Taiwan: General Innovation Service (GIS).

Laungani, P. (1996a). 'Death in a Hindu Family', in C.M. Parkes, P. Laungani and W. Young (eds), *Death and Bereavement Across Cultures,* London: Routledge (in press).

Laungani, P. (1997a). 'Patterns of Bereavement in Indian and English Societies', in J.D. Morgan (ed.), *Readings in Thanatology,* pp. 67–76, Amityville, New York: Baywood Publishing Co. Inc.

Laungani, P. (1997a). 'Cross-Cultural Investigations of Stress, Anger, and Coronary Heart Disease', in *Rage and Stress: Proceedings of the National 1996 Conference of the International Stress Management Association,* pp. 16–50, London: ISMA Publications.

Laungani, P. (1988). 'Coronary Heart Disease in India and England: Conceptual Considerations', *International Journal of Health Management* (in press).

Laungani, P. (1998a). *India and England: A Psycho-Cultural Analysis,* Amsterdam, The Netherlands: Hardwood Academic Publishers (in press).

Laungani, P. (1999). *India and England: A Psycho-Cultural Analysis,* Reading, England: Harwood Academic Publishers (in preparation).

Laungani, P., and D. Sookhoo (1995). *'Myocardial Infarction in British White and Asian Adults: Their Health Beliefs and*

Health Practices', Paper presented at the 4th European Congress of Psychology, Athens, Greece.

Lukes, S. (1973). *Individualism,* Oxford: Basil Blackwell.

Mandelbaum, D.G. (1972). *Society in India,* Vol.2., Berkeley: University of California Press.

Maslow, A. (1970). *Motivation and Personality,* 2nd edn., New York: Harper & Row.

Maslow, A. (1980). *The Farther Reaches of Human Nature,* New York: McGraw-Hill.

Matsumoto, D. (1996). *Culture and Psychology,* CA, USA: Brooks/ Cole Publishing Co.

McClelland, D.C. (1961). *The Achieving Society,* Princeton: Van Nostrand.

Miller, N.E. (1969). 'Learning of Visceral and Glandular Responses', *Science,* 163, No. 3866, January, 31, pp. 434–35.

O'Flaherty, W.D. (1976). *The Origins of Evil in Hindu Mythology,* Berkeley, California: University of California Press.

O'Flatherty, W.D. (1980). *'Karma and Rebirth in Classical Indian Traditions,* Berkeley: University of California Press.

Pande, S. (1968). 'The Mystique of 'Western' Psychotherapy: An Eastern Interpretation', *The Journal of Nervous and Mental Disease,* June, 146: 425–32.

Pandey, R.S., K.N. Srinivas and D. Muralidhar (1980). 'Socio-Cultural Beliefs and Treatment Acceptance', *Indian Journal of Psychiatry,* 22: 161–66.

Popper, K. (1963). *Conjectures and Refutations,* London: Routledge & Kegan Paul.

Popper, K. (1972). *Objective Knowledge: An Evolutionary Approach,* Oxford: The Clarendon Press.

Popper, K. (1988). *The Open Universe: An Argument for Indeterminism,* London, England: Hutchinson.

Radhakrishnan, S. (1923, 1989). *Indian Philosophy,* Vol. 2, Centenary Edition, Delhi: Oxford University Press.

Riesman, D. (1954). *Individualism Reconsidered,* New York, USA: Doubleday Anchor Books.

Rogers, C. (1961). *On Becoming a Person,* Boston: Houghton Mifflin.

Rogers, C. (1970). *On Encounter Groups,* New York: Harper-Collins.

Rhoner, R.P. (1974). 'Proxemics and Stress: An Empirical Study of the Relationship Between Space and Roommate Turnover', *Human Relations,* September 27(7): 697–702.

Roland, A. (1988). *In Search of Self in India and Japan,* New Jersey: Princeton University Press.

Sachdev, D. (1992). 'Effects of Psychocultural Factors on the Socialisation of British Born Indian Children and Indigenous British Children Living in England', Unpublished Ph.D. thesis, South Bank University, London.

Sampson, E.E. (1977). 'Psychology and the American Ideal', *Journal of Personality and Social Psychology,* 15: 189–94.

Schwartz, S.H. (1990). 'Individualism-Collectivism: Critique and Proposed Refinements', *Journal of Cross-Cultural Psychology,* 21: 139–57.

Sethi, B.B. and R. Manchanda (1978). 'Family Structure and Psychiatric Disorders', *Indian Journal of Psychiatry,* 20: 283–88.

Sinari, R.A. (1984). *The Structure of Indian Thought,* Delhi: Oxford University Press.

Sinha, D., R.C. Mishra and J.W. Berry (1996). 'Some Eco-Cultural and Acculturation Factors in Intermodal Perception', in J. Pandey, D. Sinha and D.P.S. Bhawuk (eds), *Asian Contributions to Cross-Cultural Psychology,* pp. 151–64, New Delhi: Sage Publications.

Smith, P.B. and M.H. Bond. (1993). *Social Psychology Across Culture: Analysis and Perspectives,* Hemel Hempstead, England: Harvester Wheatsheaf.

Smith, P.B. and S. Schwartz (1997). 'Values', in J.W. Berry, M.H. Segall, and C. Kagitcibasi (eds), *Handbook of Cross-Cultural Psychology,* Vol. 3, Boston: Allyn & Bacon.

Sookhoo, D. (1995). 'A Comparative Study of the Health Beliefs and Health Practices of British Whites and Asian Adults with and without Myocardial Infarction', Paper presented at the 53rd Annual Convention of the International Council of Psychologists, August, Taipei, Taiwan.

Spence, J.T. (1985). 'Achievement American Style: The Rewards and Costs of Individualism', *American Psychology,* 40: 1285–95.

Spielberger, C.D. (1979). *Understanding Stress and Anxiety,* London: Harper & Row.

Srinivasa, D.K., and S. Trivedi (1982). 'Knowledge and Attitude of Mental Diseases in a Rural Community of South India', *Social Science Medicine,* 16: 1635–39.

Trefil, J. (1980). *From Atoms to Quarks: An introduction to the Strange World of Particle Physics,* London: Charles Scribner.

Triandis, H.C. (1994). *Culture and Social Behaviour,* New York, USA: McGraw-Hill Inc.

Verma, S.K. (1988). 'Mental Illness and Treatment', in J. Pandey (ed.), *Psychology in India: The State-of-the-Art,* Vol. 3, New Delhi: Sage Publications.

Von-Furer-Haimendorf, C. (1974). 'The Sense of Sin in Cross-Cultural Perspective', *Man,* 9: 539–56.

Ward, C.A. and A. Kennedy (1996). 'Cross Cultures: The Relationship between Psychological and Socio-Cultural Dimension of Cross-Cultural Adjustment', in J. Pandey, D. Sinha and D.P.S. Bhawuk (eds), *Asian Contributions to Cross-Cultural Psychology*, pp. 289–306, New Delh: Sage Publications.

Waterman, A.A. (1981). 'Individualism and Interdependence', *American Psychologist,* 36: 762–73.

Weber, M. (1963). *The Sociology of Religion,* 4th edn, London: Beacon Press.

Yang, K.S. (1997). 'Theories and Research in Chinese Personality: An Indigenous Approach', in H.S.R. Kao and D. Sinha (eds), *Asian Perspectives on Psychology,* pp. 236–64, New Delhi: Sage Publications.

Zimmer, H. (1951, 1989). *Philosophies of India,* Bollingen Series XXVI, New Jersey: Princeton University Press.

16 Cross-Cultural Experience of Collaboration in Personality Research*

Jitendra Mohan

Introduction

Advancement as well as proliferation of research is indicative of three basic elements in terms of acceptance of theoretical models—dependability of the instrument across cultures, a sense of co-operation among investigators belonging to different cultural backgrounds, and professional training. This is much more evident in the field of personality than any other area because of its appeal, range, and unending possibilities. The concord certainly does not mean concurrence. Sometimes, it yields results which express differences rather than similarities.

In a span of almost thirty years of research collaboration and co-operation with distinguished personality experts like, Professor H.J. Eysenck, Professor P.F. Merenda, Professor R. Lynn, Professor P. Kline, and more recently Professor Charles D. Spielberger, using different theoretical models, instruments and populations, the present researcher had to come to terms with many issues. Some of the research references have culminated in an edited volume of its own nature and character. Eysenck and Mohan (1998), Mohan, Eysenck, and Esyenck (1987), Merenda, Mohan and Migliorino (1985) and other works were reviewed in 1995, and are being discussed in the light of about 200 papers of Mohan and associates and about fifty

---

* Based on an invited lecture of the author delivered at the 25th International Congress of Applied Psychology, at San Fransisco, USA on 14th August 1998.

Doctoral theses supervised by the author on the background of the latest works of Lynn and Martin (1997) and Eysenck and Mohan (1998).

The entire experience is characterized by a basic appreciation of the usefulness of collaboration in terms of scientific co-operation. It also raises methodological problems in terms of selection of culturally-coloured items and their historical as well as semantic meaning; it tends to bring on a comparative platform some of the models of personality, and helps in the evolution of concepts. The five-factor theory also gets another look in the context of our research experience.

Psychometrically as well as behaviourally, the experience raises some of the questions related to administration and norms. This chapter has the possibility of opening up another debate, which might be slightly disturbing, but undoubtedly useful and valuable in personality research at the turn of the century.

Though western thinking always starts with the Greeks and certainly the Chinese, the Indians and the Egyptians have their own precursors of interactions and concern for others' cultures. But some of the most pervasive influences in cross-cultural comparisons drew from the belief in social evolution by Darwin, in development of religion by Tylor, in the family by Lubbock, in arts by Haddon, in industry by Mortgan, in modes of thought by Conte, in mentality by Levy-Bruchi, and in economics and social structure by Marx. Psychologists were doing their bit in understanding others, and their ways of beliefs and actions. Folk psychology, social mind, primitive mind, and primitive behaviour were the various labels used for cross-cultural investigations. But the pioneering works of Boas and his students, Sullivan, Ruth Benedict, Kluckhon, Hall, and Margaret Mead stand as examples of serious analysis of cultures. A truly inter-disciplinary penetration came with Hargreaves of the World Health Organization. Some of the issues taken up included language and thought; perception and memory; projective techniques and their interpretation; psychoanalysis; Genetic psychology; problems of national character; national stereotypes; and more recently the study of cross-cultural perception of psychopathology (most relevant to this International Symposium on Cultural Psychiatry); authoritarianism; leadership and social climate; field independence; acceleration and cultural changes; and the achievement motive. In any case, cross-cultural concerns have become increasingly acceptable in spite of being dubbed as American fads to begin with. Today, after about 30 years or so, cross-cultural psychology has become a field of collaboration, co-operation, and communication among psychologists from different lands. One of the most significant events in the growth of this field was the publication of a six-volume *Handbook of Cross-Cultural Psychology,* edited by Triandis and Lambert (1980), covering Perspectives, Methodology, Basic Process, Developmental Psychology, Social Psychology and Psychopathology; it was truly a teamwork of an international standard, and influenced the entire field in the years to come, in which cross-cultural psychology became a discipline in its own right. The *Journal of Cross-Cultural Psychology* started in 1970, and the International Association of Cross-Cultural Psychology had its first meeting in Hong Kong in 1972. And with these, cross-cultural psychology evolved an identity.

Cross-cultural psychology is concerned with the systematic study of behaviour and experience as it occurs in different cultures (Triandis, 1994). Culture is a complex, multidimensional and multi-meaning concept, but broadly refers to 'man-made' part of the human environment. The term cross-cultural refers to comparisons of culture, either in terms of cult units or larger units like nations.

A major purpose of cross-cultural psychology is to test the generality of psychological laws. It also attempts to explain behaviour in terms of cultural unity, dissimilarity, similarity and oddities. Cult units provide nature-quasi experiments, which need to be studied in terms of different ecological settings. Since cultures shape aspects of psychological functioning, cross-cultural studies help in revealing how ecological and psychological variables are interrelated. It also helps in understanding what is universally and fundamentally common in all cultures, and what tends to be transformed or moulded due to cultural differences. It further helps in understanding the variations in a concept or behavioural form in different cultures in terms of semantics and operations. Furthermore, cultures differentiate between concepts within cognitive domains, which need to be studied in terms of differentiation, integration, discrimination, and formation. Cross-cultural studies help in improving communication of experiences in different cultures in terms of categories, definitions, implications, applications and organization. In a way, cultural complexity in itself is a remarkable area of research, as well as an issue deserving analysis in terms of its measures, dimensions and expressions. The domain of cross-cultural psychology is more in terms of methodology rather than theory. It has become clearer that one cannot take a psychological method and use it in another culture without drastic modification. A major aspect of methodology is in terms of universal dimension called 'etic' and culture-specific dimension called 'emic' descriptions. This applies to the constructs as well as measurement techniques. It could be assumed that cross-cultural psychology attempts to establish a framework within which differences or similarities could be interpreted, and at the same time keeps on improving the methodology so that the estimates of cultural differences could be attempted at more acceptable and rational levels.

The system of variables could be in terms of the ecology, the subsistence system, the socio-cultural system, the individual system, and the inter-individual and projective systems, but, certainly, it needs to distinguish between the interactions system and cultural system (artifacts vs. facts of culture). In any case, cross-cultural psychology refers to some issues, concerns, and problems of human experience and behaviour which cannot be simply labelled as merely anthropological, sociological, economic, technological or psychological. It is concerned much more with collaboration, inter-relation, and interpretation.

Cross-Cultural Psychology Research in India

The Beginning

In the first survey of research in psychology, Rath (1972) reviewed cross-cultural studies undertaken by Indian psychologists, relating to values, attitudes, stereotypes, and some personality characteristics. These emphasized cross-cultural differences found in habitual response preferences indicating anxiety (Singh and Retting, 1962); belongingness, anxiety, and self-sufficiency (Anant, 1971), social-desirability judgements (Mukherjee, 1967), occupational ratings (Sharma and Sinha, 1968); ascendance-submission reactions (Ray Choudhary, 1959), Rosenzwieg P.F. study (Pareek, 1958), Rorschach (Prabhu, 1967), and Allport–Vernon–Lindzey study of values (Ray Choudhary, 1959). A factorial study of cross-cultural values and related biographical data was reported by Sinha and Ralph (1983b), Roy (1963) reported a study of persons within the industrial belt of Calcutta; Beg (1966), Bhatnagar (1967), and Singh, Huang and Thompson (1962) reported cross-cultural studies of values and attitudes of British, Chinese, American and Indian students. Rath (1972) viewed these studies as cross-national, and suggested studies with different cultural groups living in various parts of India to be named as real cross-cultural studies.

Later Developments

In the survey of research in psychology (1971–76) some cross-cultural studies have been reported. Kakkar (1972) made a cross-cultural study of response sets, and found that for each sex, Japanese subjects marked undecided responses four to five times more than Indian subjects. Sundburg and Tyler (1970) reported a study conducted on American, Dutch and Indian adolescent boys and girls to find out the number of occupations, free-time activities, and acquaintances each of them could list; the study revealed significant cross-cultural differences. Muralidharan and Sharma (1971) found insignificant differences in the anxiety levels of American, French, Japanese and Indian boys from high-fee schools. Indian girls were higher on anxiety than the Japanese girls; girls were higher on anxiety than boys in high-fee schools, but in low-fee schools, boys were higher an anxiety. Anant (1971) reported that Indians were lower on anxiety than the Canadians on the whole, and Indian girls were lower than Canadian girls on extraversion and neuroticism. Mehta *et al.* (1972) found insignificant differences in the median time attributed to seven expected life events, between Indian and American adolescents. However, Indian boys showed greater diversity. The lower class was concerned with more short-term events; however, no sex differences were reported.

Husain (1974) studied achievement motivation and self-esteem of 115 American students and 67 Indian students, and reported a positive correlation between the achievement motivation and self-esteem among the American students, but only a marginal correlation among the Indian students.

Extending the model of Rogers and collaborators (1970) on diffusion on innovation in Brazil and Nigeria on a large sample of 10,000 peasants reporting change-agent-contact to be important in introducing innovations than mass media, Jaiswal, Singh and Singh (1971) found highly significant correlation between innovative behaviour and contact with extension agency. Pareek and Rao (1977) have discussed in detail, with examples from Indian experience, the various dimensions of sampling and inter-viewing in cross-cultural research, especially researches in the field of social change.

Research Trends

In a very critical and revealing manner, with reference to the best construction and development of tests, Kulkarni and Puhan (1988) refer to a seminar conducted by National Test Library, NCERT, in which Verma (1984) reviewed 21 tests, including the oft-used ones like Pareek's Battery of Preadolescent Personality, Kundu's Introversion–Extraversion Scale, A.K.P. Sinha's Adjustment Inventory, and P. Sinha's Indian Frustration Scale. It was pointed out that many manuals of tests provide inadequate descriptions of the construct, sample, and generalizability (reliabilities, validities) of the test; and in many cases the items appear ambiguous and misleading. Verma also reviewed seven widely used personality tests supposedly adapted for use in India, namely Eysenck's Maudsley Personality Inventory (Jalota and Kapoor), Children Personality Questionnaire (Kapoor), Ego Strength Scale (Hasan), T.A.T. (Chowdhary); Newman Kohilstdt Diagnostic Test (Prakash); IPTA Anxiety Scale (Kapoor). In many of these, adaptation meant mere translation and elimination of items, which the authors thought were culturally not relevant. Sinha (1986) confessed that he was himself a victim of the tendency (in case of test of anxiety, based on Taylor's test) to use the foreign tests and constructions indiscriminately and uncritically, as in case with some others who developed tests measuring achievement motivation, anxiety, level of aspiration, self-concept, social change, frustration, authoritarianism, etc. These were some examples of psychometrically indefensible and overrated instruments.

Assessment in cross-cultural context can be divided into two categories of studies. The first category includes studies in which tools developed in foreign cultures are used on Indian samples. (e.g., Kumar, 1978; Saha and Biswas, 1980; Sengupta, 1982). The second category includes studies in which two or more culturally different groups are studied specifically on certain common cognitive and personality dimensions, usually with same or equivalent tools (Kline and Mohan, 1978; Singhal, 1978). In the first category, again, there are studies where foreign tests have been blindly used assuming their original reliability and validity in the Indian settings. Mukherjee (1980) and Sinha (1983a, b) ruthlessly exposed this slavish mentality among Indian researchers. Puhan (1975a) discussed the issues inherent in psychological assessment in India. Mohanty and Puhan (1980) pointed out the problems arising out of the 'imposed etic' approach following in personnel selection/recruitment in the developing countries.

As one of the rare cross-cultural studies in creativity, Raina, Kumar, and Raina (1980) compared the opinions of 165 Indian fathers regarding characteristics to be encouraged or discouraged in children with the opinions of American parents and experts on creativity. Interesting cross-cultural data on the perception of life-satisfaction by 80 Asian-Indian and 780 American retired citizens was provided by Fry and Ghosh (1980). The attributions of the Asian group showed religious faith, service to others, family ties, and luck as being important factors contributing to life satisfaction. In contrast, more Americans reported that hard work, personal abilities, travel, recreation and social status had significantly influenced their life satisfaction. Sahota (1977) conducted a cross-cultural study of ecology and educability of children in Brazil, India and USA. The focus was on three ecological variables, that is, parents, (particularly mother's) education, family income (or income inequalities), and home environment (especially the quality of the house); it was concluded that parents' education is the most effective way of raising the educational level of children.

Chadha and Sahni (1991) studied job evolvement at a cross-cultural plane. Chadha and Stevenson (1988) studied 326 cases of reincarnation to suggest some common correlates. Sehgal and Rana (1994) in a recent study of Nepalese and Indian managers observed the commonalties as well as differences between the two groups. Mishra (1994) discusses at length the cultural perspectives on human nature, which have important consequences for the shaping of human nature. Non-western cultures have their own distinct notions which cannot be ignored by the 'main-stream' psychology if it has to take care of the diversity. However, the thrust of other Indian psychologists working in the field of cross-cultural psychology indicate that the Indian segment of cross-cultural research is active as well as impressive.

Exclusive Experience

Many cross-cultural collaborative studies were undertaken by the author on diverse issues. Using Activity Vector Analysis (AVA;

Merenda and Clarke, 1959), an instrument of international repute in the field of research and application, a wide range of studies were completed. These focused on cross-cultural perceptions of Nehru and Ideal Self; Nehru and Shastri; Mahatma Gandhi and Abraham Lincoln; Johnson and Kosygin; Nixon and Humphrey; DeGaulle; Wilson; Mao; Wallace; Indira Gandhi; King Husein; Shah of Iran; perceptions of Yahya Khan, Mujibur Rahman, and Zulfigar Ali Bhutto before and after the emergence of Bangladesh in 1971; and perceptions of Ideal Self, Ideal leader, Ideal Teacher and Business Executive. The AVA includes factors of Sociability, Emotional control, Aggressiveness, and Social Adaptability, covered by 81 non-derogatory adjective checklist. These studies were in confirmation with the hypothesis that the perceptions of the personalities and ideals differ in different cultures and change due to the national positions and international events in history (Merenda and Mohan, 1966, 1967, 1968, 1970; Merenda *et al.,* 1968, 1971, 1973, 1975 and Mohan, 1975). Using a little less known personality test, Ai3Q used to measure Anal characters or obsessional personalities, Kline and Mohan (1974) studied the personality of Indian, Ghanian and British students. The study showed clear cultural differences, which may be due to attitudinal factors, discrete and transmatric events, and the cultural bias in the items of the test.

Table 1
Activity Vector Analysis Profile.

	AVA Dimensions			
	Aggressi-veness	Sociability	Emotional Control	Social Adapta-bility
Z. Ali Bhutto (Pre-War)	9	6	2	3
Z. Ali Bhutto (Post-War)	9	6	2	3
Yahya Khan (Pre-War)	9	5	3	3
Yahya Khan (Post-War)	9	6	3	2
Mujibur Rehman (Pre-War)	6	9	2	3
Mujibur Rehman (Post-War)	5	9	3	3
Ideal Self	4	9	4	3
Ideal Leader	4	9	4	3
Ideal Teacher	4	9	4	3
Indira Gandhi	5	9	3	3

Contd.

Table 1 Contd.

	AVA Dimensions			
	Aggressiveness	Sociability	Emotional Control	Social Adaptability
Business Executive	6	9	1	4
Stereotype Khrushchev	9	5	3	3
Ideal US President	5	9	1	5
Administrative Pattern	9	7	1	3
Nixon	9	7	1	3
Humphery	9	7	1	3
Shastri (Cluster 1)	1	7	7	5
Shastri (Cluster 2)	5	9	4	2
Nehru	AVA Dimensions closest to Ideal US President.			
Gandhi Lincoln	Gandhi and Lincoln are closest on AVA Dimensions.			

Merenda and Mohan (1967, 1968, 1970); Merenda, Mohan, Clark, Schulz, Strehse and Winneke (1968) and Merenda, O'Brien and Mohan (1973); Merenda, Shaw and Mohan (1975).

In a comprehensive study of foreign and Indian students on Eysenck Personality Questionnaire (Eysenck and Eysenck, 1975) and Lynn's Achievement Questionnaire (Lynn 1969), Mohan (1980) reported the difference between the two groups on the different dimensions studied, with differences on Extraversion, Psychoticism and Neuroticism favouring Indians and those on Social desirability and Achievement Motivation favouring foreigners. In a cross-cultural study of university students, Merenda, Mohan and Migliorino (1985) reported differences of identification of problems and their solutions by students in Rhode Island, Chandigarh and Palermo, Mohan, Eysenck and Eysenck (1987) related the Indian experience of using EPQ on Indian students (both sexes) of different faculties, foreign students from Nepal, Nigeria, Iraq and Thailand; and professionals from different fields, viz., Doctors, IAS, ISP, IRS officers, Army officers, creative writers, and university teachers. The study supported the contention that EPQ is a reliable tool in different cultural groups and professions, provided the medium of instruction is English. Lynn (1992) conducted a massive study on economic behaviour in 41 countries with 43 collaborators (including the author) and tried to relate national economic development with the

Table 2

S.N.	Group	N	Extra-version	Neuro-ticism	Psycho-ticism	Social Desira-bility
1.	Boys	450	16.43	10.62	7.18	20.90
2.	Girls	450	15.14	12.96	5.92	20.58
Faculties						
3.	Architecture	50	16.24	11.86	9.28	18.52
4.	Arts	50	16.42	11.21	7.26	20.52
5.	Bio-science	50	16.12	11.64	7.14	20.28
6.	Commerce	50	19.36	10.22	6.64	17.56
7.	Education	50	15.34	11.72	6.98	24.36
8.	Engineering	50	16.04	11.80	8.32	18.64
9.	Fine Arts	50	16.08	11.58	8.64	21.24
10.	Home Science	50	17.24	13.94	6.02	17.76
11.	Languages	50	16.02	13.06	6.96	22.88
12.	Nursing	50	14.88	12.48	7.22	23.76
13.	Science	50	15.94	10.42	6.74	23.48
14.	Social Science	50	16.86	9.74	6.16	17.24
		1500	16.29	11.66	7.17	20.55
Foreigners						
15.	Thailand	50	16.22	9.88	6.82	18.82
16.	Iraq	50	18.28	11.96	7.96	20.26
17.	Nepal	50	17.58	10.28	7.28	20.14
18.	Nigeria	50	22.76	8.24	5.48	19.26
		200				
Professions						
19.	Doctors	100				
20.	I.A.S.	25	14.30	10.12	7.28	22.32
21.	I.P.S.	25	13.58	7.34	5.52	25.36
22.	I.R.S.	25	13.86	8.64	5.46	22.46
23.	Army	25	15.36	9.82	6.32	24.24
24.	Creative Writers	100	14.66	19.46	8.46	21.44
25.	Teachers	50	13.26	12.28	5.66	23.68
		350				

concepts of money, work ethics, achievement motivation, and competitiveness. Mohan and Gyani (1978) studied differences in personality and recognition of advertisement among Indian and foreign students studying in India. In a more recent study, Mohan and Agochia (1994) studied personality, values and altruistic behaviour of youth workers of Bangladesh, Hongkong, India, Malaysia, Singapore, Sri Lanka, Australia and New Zealand. It was reported that on Extraversion, Psychoticism, Neuroticism, Social desirability, values and altruism, youth workers from different countries showed differences, though they were doing similar work. Some of the ongoing research projects are in the field of inteligence, biorhythms, anxiety model, aesthetic appreciation and personality.

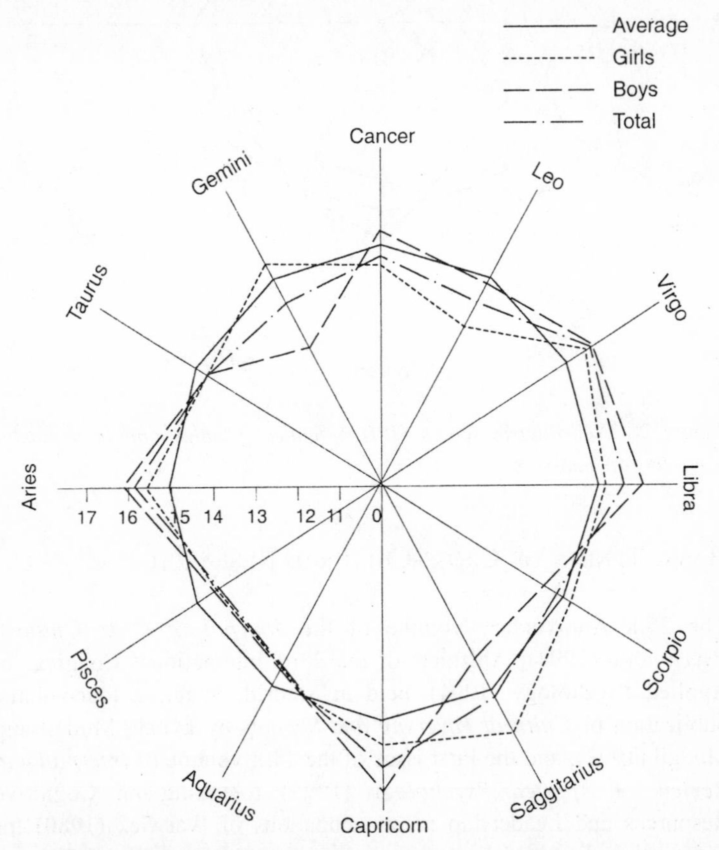

Figure 1. *Extraversion Scores (JPI) of males, females and total sample according to Sun-sign.*

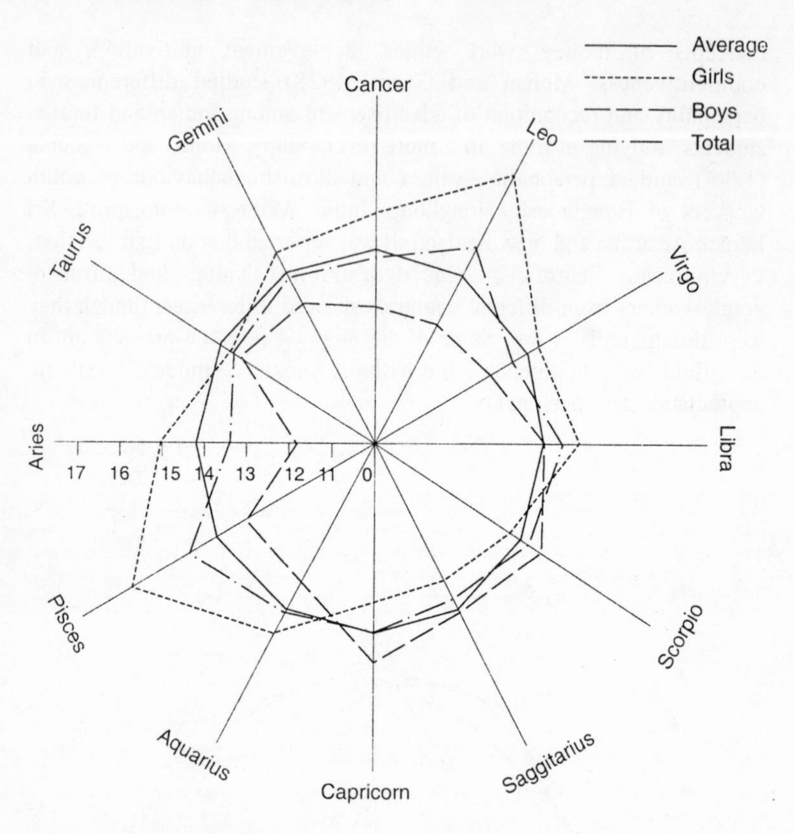

Figure 2. *Neuroticism scores (JPI) of males, females and total sample according to Sun-sign.*

BASIC TENETS OF CROSS-CULTURAL RESEARCH

The 25th Anniversary volume of the *Journal of Cross-Cultural Psychology* (1994); Abstracts of the 23rd International Congress of Applied Psychology (1994), held in Madrid, Spain; a four-volume publication of *Cultural Diversity and Schools* by Lynch, Modgil and Modgil (1992); and the First issue of the 44th volume of *International Review of Applied Psychology* (1995) focussing on Cognitive Resources and Leadership recommendations of Warwick (1980) for cross-cultural research in psychology, recommend the following professional and ethical issues:

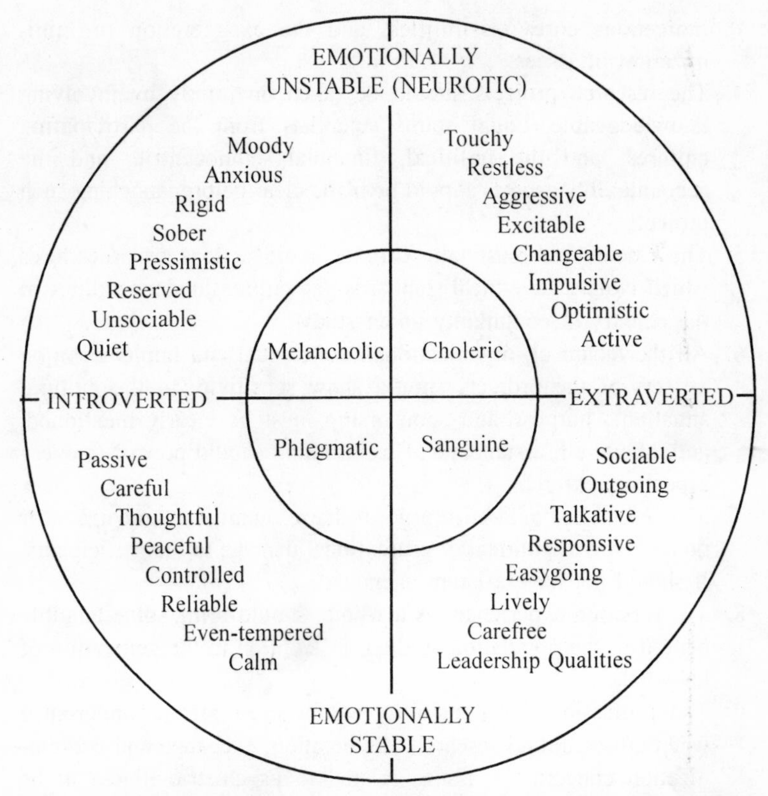

(From *Personality and Individual Differences* by H.J. Eysenck and M.W. Eysenck, Plenum Publishing, 1958. Reprinted by permission.)

Figure 3. *A two-dimensional classification of personality.*

1. The search for universals in the face of cultural differences implies serious consideration of the diversity of determinants of human behaviour.
2. While adapting/developing/standardizing tests originating from one culture to other, *'ad hoc'* subjective criteria should be replaced by the systematic consideration of the local milieu, culture, language, forms and patterns of behaviour. It requires a second look at the over-publicised psychometric achievements, which could at best be culture-fair rather than culture-free or universal.
3. The diagnosis, classification and treatment of mental problems and sicknesses cannot ignore the culture-based standards and norms,

indigenous cure possibilities, and the exaggeration or minimization of issues.

4. The research projects should be taken up jointly by involving knowledgeable, equal status scientists from the participating cultures, and the political, financial, ethnocentric, and the accountability aspects should be made clear before launching such projects.
5. The researchers must take care to avoid actions or procedures which violate the ethical standards and cultural understandings of the country or community under study.
6. All the technical, organizational, conceptual and implementation aspects of the projects should show sensitivity to the cultural situations; purpose and sponsorship must be clearly mentioned, and, above all, a standard of truth-telling should prevail in every aspect of research.
7. The research should ensure not to harm, humiliate, embarrass, or do any type of political or professional damage to the participants. It should not have a latent agenda.
8. The research experience, as a whole, should bring some tangible benefit to the population studied, in addition to the generation of knowledge.
9. The professional responsibility attains even greater importance when cross-cultural research, deliberation, exchange and communication concern the issues related to psychiatric illness in its entirety, that is, diagnosis, assessment, classification, treatment and rehabilitation.

The ongoing work of the author on the Big Five (Costa and McCrae 1995), and Abstracts of the 9th European Conference on Personality (7–11 July, 1998), and the 25th International Congress of Applied Psychology (9–14 August, 1998) have clearly hinted that the dimensions of Extraversion, Agreeableness, Conscientiousness, Emotional Stability and Culture are the consensual points of research in the field of personality. In a strange coincidence, the ancient Indian concept of Five Sheaths (*Koshas*) of the Physical Body, Energy Sheath, Mental Sheath, Intuitive Sheath, and the Blissful Sheath deserve deeper probing in the early years of the next century. The overlapping of about three of Eysenckian personality dimensions among the Big Five suggests some acceptable common ground among the psychologists.

Table 3
Five-Factor Model of Personality.

Investigators	Factor I	Factor II	Factor III	Factor IV	Factor V
Tupes & Christal (1961)	Surgency	Agreeableness	Dependability	Emotional Stability	Culture
Norman (1963)	Surgency	Agreeableness	Conscientiousness	Emotional Stability	Culture
Goldberg (1981, 1989)	Surgency	Agreeableness	Conscientiousness	Emotional Stability	Intellect
McCrae & Costa (1985a)	Extraversion	Agreeableness	Conscientiousness	Neuroticism	Openness to Experience
Conley (1985a)	Social Extraversion	Agreeableness	Impulse Control	Neuroticism	Intellectual Interests
Others	Confident	Social	Conformity	Emotional	Inquiring
	Self-Expression	Adaptability	Task Interest	Control	Intellect
		Likability	Will to Achieve	Emotionality	Intelligence
	Assertiveness	Friendly		Ego Strength	Intellect
	Power	Compliance	Impulse	(Anxiety)	Culture
		Agreeableness	Control	Emotional	
		vs	Work	Instability	
		Coldheartedness		Dominant-	
		Agreeable		Assured	
		Stable		Satisfaction	
		Love		Affect	

Adapted from John, 1990, p. 72.

Table 4
Five Dimensions of Personality.

Factor	Scales
Extraversion	Talkative versus silent
	Frank, open versus secretive
	Adventurous versus cautious
	Sociable versus reclusive
Agreeableness	Good-natured versus irritable
	Not jealous versus jealous
	Mild, gentle versus headstrong
	Co-operative versus negativistic
Conscientiousness	Fussy, tidy versus careless
	Responsible versus undependable
	Scrupulous versus unscrupulous
	Persevering versus quitting, fickle
Emotional Stability	Poised versus nervous, tense
	Calm versus anxious
	Composed versus excitable
	Not hypochondriacal versus hypochondriacal
Culture	Artistically sensitive versus artistically insensitive
	Intellectual versus unreflective, narrow
	Polished, refined versus crude, boorish
	Imaginative versus simple, direct

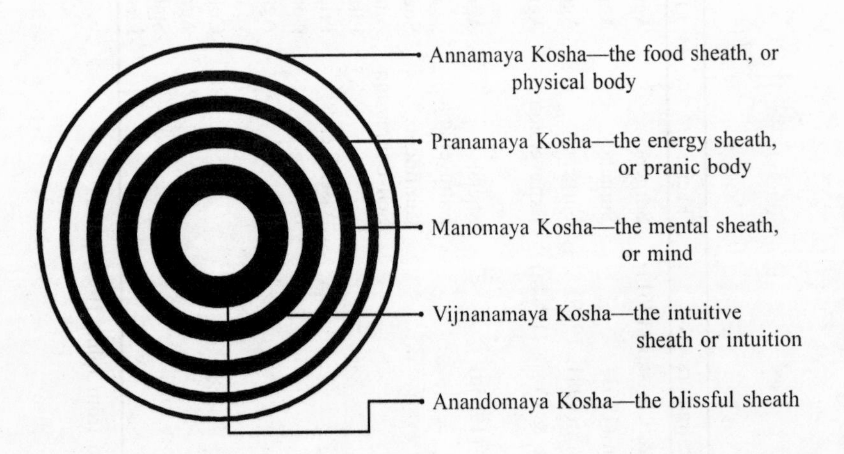

Figure 4

Table 5
Examples of Behaviours Used to Infer the Big Five Personality Dimensions.

Behaviours that indicate Extraversion	Behaviours that indicate Agreeableness
• Has high enthusiasm and energy level	• Expresses sympathy to partner
• Speaks in a loud voice	• Seems to enjoy interaction
• Is talkative	• Behaves in a cheerful manner
Behaviours that indicate Neuroticism	**Behaviours that indicate Conscientiousness**
• Shows signs of tension or anxiety	• Speaks fluently
• Expresses guilt	• Displays ambition
• Seeks reassurance	• Exhibits high degree of intelligence
Behaviours that indicate Openness	
• Seems interested in what partner says	
• "Interviews" partner	
• Discusses philosophical iss' es	

Adapted from Funder & Sneed, 1993

At the confluence of the 20th and 21st centuries, the personality research appears to be at a starting point of consensus of Western theories, and awakening to the Eastern models of personality.

CONCLUSIONS

Considering the experience of research collaboration with stalwarts like H.J. Eysenck, Peter F. Merenda, Richard Lynn, Paul Kline and Charles D. Spielberger, using different theories, concepts models, tests and populations, the following conclusions are warranted:

The activity vector analysis, Eysenck personality questionnaire. psychoanalytical inventory, and state-trait anxiety/stress models get duly confirmed, by the five factors, extracted on the basis of review of personality research.

Personality still remains as a multi-layered entity with more masks to hide than to express the inner reality. The cognitive and the semantic problems of the cross-cultural research can not be ignored.

However there is a need to develop a survey model by the personality researchers, similar to the one's used by the WHO and economic or demographic surveys, large enough to cover major nationalities, religions languages and gender and age groups to arrive at a more lasting and acceptable personality model.
Of course, this would not mean that the science of personality will arrive at a final agreement at the turn of the century.

Finally, it could be submitted that some of the eastern models could also be taken into consideration before the five factor model that could be taken as the point of consensus at the turn of the century. Certainly, the twenty-first century deserves a clearer, broader and more acceptable model.

REFERENCES

Abstracts: 23rd International Congress of Applied Psychology, July 17–22, 1994, Madrid, Spain.

Anant, S.S. (1971). 'A Cross-Cultural Study of Belongingness, Anxiety, Neuroticism and Extraversion', *ICSSR Research Abstracts,* 1(2): 42–8 (IPA, 1: 255).

Beg, Moazziz, A. (1966). 'Value Orientations of Indian & American Students: A Cross-Cultural Study', *Psychologia,* 9(2): 111–19.

Bhatnagar, J.K. (1967). 'The Values & Attitudes of some Indian and British Students', *Race,* 9(1): 27–35.

Chadha, N.K. and Ian Stevenson (1988). 'Two Correlates of Violent Death in Cases of Reincarnation Type', *Journal of the Society for Psychical Research,* 55(81): 71–79.

Chadha, N.K. and Vinod Sahni (1991). 'Job Involvement as a Function of Background Variable; A Cross-Cultural Study', *Prachi Journal of Psycho-Cultural Dimensions,* 7.2, 1–10.

Eysenck, H.J. and S.B.G. Eysenck (1975). *Manual of the Eysenck Personality Questionnaire,* London: Hodder & Stougher.

Eysenck, H.J. (1991). 'Dimensions of Personality; 16, 5 or 3?: Criteria for a Taxonomic Paradigm', *Personality Individual Differences,* 12(8): 727–90.

Eysenck, H.J., J.Mohan and M. Seghal (1998). *A Cross-Cultural Study of Personality, EHT and CHD.* (in press).

Fry, P.S. and R. Ghosh (1980). 'Attributional Differences in the Life Satisfactions of the Elderly: A Cross-Cultural Comparison of

Asian and United States Subjects', *International Journal of Psychology,* 15: 201–12.

Husaini, Bagar A. (1974). 'Achievement Motivation and Self-Esteem; A Cross-Cultural Study', *Indian Journal of Psychology,* 49(2): 100–8 (IPA, 8: 131).

Jaiswal, N.K. N.N. Singh and B.N. Singh (1971). 'A Study of Interactional Association of Selected Factor with Innovativeness in Farming', *Indian Journal of Extension Education,* 7(34): 110–16 (IPA, 1: 445)

Journal of Cross-Cultural Psychology (1994). 25th Anniversary Volume, New Delhi: Sage.

Kakar, S.B. (1972). 'A Cross-Cultural Study of Response Sets', *Indian Journal of Applied Psychology,* 8: 75–82 (IPA, 1: 302).

Kline, P. and J. Mohan (1974). 'Cultural Differences in Item Endorsements in a Personality Test—Ai3o in India, Ghana and Great Britian', *The Journal of Social Psychology,* 94: 137–38.

Kline, P. and J. Mohan (1978). 'Oral Personality Traits Among Female Students in North India: A Cross-Cultural Study', *Psychological Studies,* 23: 1–4.

Kulkarni, S.S. and B.N. Puhan (1988). 'Psychological Assessment: Its Present and Future Trends', in J. Pandey (ed.), *Psychology in India: The State-of-Art,* New Delhi: Sage Publications.

Kumar, U. (1978). 'Self-Actualization and Organizational Climate: A Study of Indian Managers', *Indian Journal of Applied Psychology,* 15: 9–14.

Lynch, James, Celia Modgil and Sohan Modgil (1992). *Cultural Diversity & Schools,* Vol. IV, London: The Falmer Press.

Lynn, R. (1969). 'Achievement Motivation Inventory', *British Journal of Psychology,* 60: 529–34.

Lynn, R. (1991). 'Magic of the Modern Economy', London: Social Science Research Council.

Mehta, P.H., P.K. Rohila, N.D. Sundberg and L.E. Tyler (1972). 'Future Time Perspective of Adolescents in India and the United States', *Journal of Cross-Cultural Psychology,* 3(3): 203–302.

Merenda, P.F. and W.V. Clarke (1959). 'Factor Analysis of a Measure of Social-Self', *Psychological Report,* 5: 597–605.

Merenda, P.F. and J. Mohan (1966). 'Perception of Nehru and the Ideal-Self in the Indian Culture', *Perceptual Motor Skills,* 22: 865–66.

Merenda, P.F. and J. Mohan (1967). 'Comparison of Indian Students' Perceptions of Nehru and Shastri', *Perceptual Motor Skills,* 24: 1309–10.

Merenda, P.F. and J. Mohan (1968). 'Perception of Ideal Self, Nehru and Shastri', *Psychological Studies,* 8–11.

Merenda, P.F. and J. Mohan (1968). 'Indian Students' Perceptions of Mahatma Gandhi and Their Comparable American Ideal, Abraham Lincoin', *Perceptual Motor Skills,* 26: 721–22.

Merenda, P.F. and J. Mohan (1970). 'Indian Students' Pre- and Post-Election Perceptions of Nixon and Humphery', *Perceptual Motor Skills,* 30: 677–78.

Merenda, P.F., J. Mohan, W.V. Clarke, H. Schulz, W. Strehse and G. Winneke (1968). 'Cross-Cultural Perceptions of Johnson and Kosygin', *Perceptual Motor Skills,* 26: 843–47.

Merenda, P.F., J. Mohan and W.V. Clarke (1971). 'Indian Students' Perceptions of Eight International Known Personalities', *Perceptual Motor Skills,* 33: 611–14.

Merenda, P.F., J. Mohan and Migliorinog (1985). 'A Cross-Cultural Study of Problems of Students', A WHO Report.

Merenda, P.F., J. Mohan and G. Migliorino (1985a). 'A Cross-Cultural Study of Products of Students', A WHO Report.

Merenda, P.F., J. Mohan and J. Obrian (1973). 'Indian Students' Perceptions of Yayha Khan, Mujibur Rahman, and Z.A. Bhutto Before and After Emergence of Bangladesh', *Perceptual Motor Skills,* 36: 1111–14.

Merenda, P.F., J. Mohan and B.J. Shaw (1973). 'Indian Students' Perceptions of the Ideal Self, the Ideal Leader, the Ideal-Teacher, Indira Gandhi and the Business Executive', *Perceptual Motor Skills,* 40: 611–15.

Mishra, G. (1994). 'Psychology of Control; Cross-Cultural Considerations', *Journal of Indian Psychology,* 12 (1 and 2): 8–14.

Mitra, S.K. (ed.) (1972). *A Survey of Research in Psychology,* Bombay: Popular Prakashan.

Mohan, J. (1980). ' "Honoured Guests" in our Academic Institutions', *Social Sciences Research Journal,* Vols. 1 and 2, March and July, 55–56.

Mohan J. and D. Agochia (1994). 'Personality, Values and Altruistic Behaviour of Youth Workers of Different Cultures', Abstract Guide, 23rd International Congress of Application Psychology, 23–28 July, Madrid, Spain.

Mohan, J. (1995). 'Cross-Cultural Psychology: The Indian Perspective', *Indian Journal of Social Psychiatry,* 11(1): 40–45.

Mohan, J. (1998). 'Personality and Sports', Keynote Address, Proceedings of 9th National Conference of Sports Psychology, Hyderabad, India.

Mohan, J., H.J. Eysenck and S.B.G. Eysenck (1987). 'The Eysenck Personality Questionnaire: An Indian Experience', *Personality Study and Group Behaviour,* July, 7(2): 67–70.

Mohan, J. and R. Gyani (1978). 'A Study of Determinants of Advertisement Recognition', A Research Report.

Mohanty, A.K. and B.N. Puhan (1980). 'Strategy in Cross-Cultural Testing and Personnel Selection in Developing Countries', *ISPT Journal of Research,* 4(2): 1–17.

Mukherjee, B.N. (1980). 'Psychological Theory and Research Methods', in V. Pareek (ed.), *A Survey of Research in Psychology, 1971–76,* Part I, pp. 3–135, Bombay: Popular Prakashan.

Mukherji, J. (1967). 'Modern Science and Technology and Their Impact on Spiritual Values and Tradition', *Science and Culture,* 31(2): 616–20.

Muralidharan, R. and A. Sharma (1971). 'Manifest Anxiety in Indian Children', *Indian Educational Review,* 6(2): 67–68 (IPA, 1: 426).

Pandey, J. (ed.) (1988). *Psychology in India: The State-of-Art,* Vol. I, New Delhi: Sage Publications.

Pareek, U. (1958). 'Reliability of the Indian Adaptations of Rosenzweig PF Study (Children's Form)', *Journal of Psychological Researches,* 2: 18–23.

Pareek, Udai (ed.) (1980). *A Survey of Research in Psychology, 1971-76,* Part I, Bombay: Popular Prakashan.

Costa, Paul T. Jr. and Robert R. McCrae (1995). 'Primary Traits of Eysenck's P.E.N. System: Three and Five Factors Solution', *Journal of Personality and Social Psychology,* 69(8): 773–90.

Pareek, Udai (1980). *A Survey of Research in Psychology, 1971–76,* Part II, Bombay: Popular Prakashan.

Pareek, Udai and T.V. Rao (1977). 'Cross-Cultural Surveys and Interviewing in H. Triandis (ed.), *Handbook of Cross-Cultural Psychology,* New York: McGraw Hill.

Prabhu, G.G. (1967). 'The Rorschach Technique with Normal Adult Indians', *Indian Psychological Review,* 3(2): 97–106.

Puhan, B.N. (1975a). 'A Call for the Assessment of Psychometric Invariance of Tests Adopted and Developed in India', *Indian Psychological Review,* 12(2): 1–4.

Raina, M.K., G. Kumar and V.K. Raina (1980). 'A Cross-Cultural Study of Parental Perception of the Ideal Child', *Creative Child and Adult Quarterly,* 5: 234–41.

Rath, R.N. (1972). 'Social Psychology: A Trend Report', in *A Survey of Research in Psychology,* Project sponsored by the Indian Council of Social Science Research, New Delhi, 362–82.

Ray Chaudhaury, K. (1959). 'Allport-Vermon-Lindzey Study of Values (old Form) in Indian Situation: II. Reliability & Item Analysis', *Indian Psychological Bulletin,* 4: 7–15.

Richard, Lynn (1922). *Miracle of Modern Economy,* UK: R.C. Publication.

Richard, Lynn and Terrence Martin (1997). Gender Differences in E N and P in 37 Nations, *Journal of Social Psychology,* 137(3): 369–73.

Rogers, Everett M. *et al.* (1970). 'Cross-Cultural Generalizations about the Diffusion of Innovations Research in Brazil, Nigeria and India', Paper presented at the 7th world Congress of International Sociological Association, 18(5).

Saha, G.B., and S.K. Biswas (1980). 'A Cross-Cultural Study of the Eysenck Personality Inventory', *Manas,* 27: 5–8.

Sahota, C.K. (1977). 'The Ecology and Educability of Children: A Three-Country Study', *Dissertation Abstracts International,* 38 (6–A): 3265–66.

Sehgal, M. and A. Rana (1994). 'Job Satisfaction and Correlates Among Indian and Nepalese Managers: A Cross-Cultural Comparison', Paper abstracted in 23rd International Congress of Applied Psychology, July 17–22, Madrid.

Sengupta, M. (1982). 'Purdue Creativity Test: 'Psychometric Properties on an Indian Sample', *Psychological Studies,* 27: 23–25.

Sharma, K.L. and S.N.A. Sinha (1968). 'Note on Cross-Cultural Comparison of Occupation of Occupational Ratings', *Journal of Social Psychology,* 75(1): 233–84.

Singh, P.N., C. Huang Sophia and George A.C. Thompson (1962). 'A Comparative Study of Selected Attitudes, Values and Personality Characteristics of American, Chinese and Indian students', *Journal of Social Psychology,* 57(1): 123–38.

Singh, P.N. and S. Retting (1962). 'Cross-Cultural Difference in Habitual Response Preferences as an Index of Anxiety', *Journal of Social psychology,* 58(1): 9–15.

Singhal, S. (1978). 'Cultural Variations in Students Affects', *Indian Journal of Psychology,* 53: 44–48.

Sinha, D. (1983a). 'Human Assessment in Indian Context', in S.H. Iwine and J.W. Berry (eds), *Human Assessment and Cultural Factors*, pp. 17–34, New York: Plenum Press.

Sinha, D. (1983b). 'Reflections on Measurement of Human Motivation in India', *Psychological Studies,* 29: 197–206.

Sinha, D. (1986). *Psychology in a Third World Country: The Indian Experience,* New Delhi: Sage Publications.

Sundberg, N.D. and L.E. Tyler (1970). 'Awareness of Vocation Possibilities of Indian, Dutch and American adolescents', *Journal of Cross-Cultural Psychology,* 1(3): 153–57.

Spielberger, C.D., Jitendra Mohan and Meena Sehgal (1998). *Anger, Anxiety and Type A Behaviour as Determinants of EHT and CHD* (in press).

Triandis, H.C. (1994). Culture and Social Behaviour, New York: McGraw Hill Inc.

Triandis, H.C. and W.W. Lambert (1980). *Handbook of Cross-Cultural Psychology,* Vol. 6, London: Allyn & Bacon.

Verma, J. (1984). 'Personality Tests in Use in India: Their Deficiencies', Paper presented at the Meeting of the National Test Library, NCERT, New Delhi.

17 The Future of Personality Measurement

Paul Kline

In this chapter it is argued that personality measurement and, consequently, modern personality theory, which must be based in measurement, are at crossroads. Measurement has certainly progressed in the last fifty years, but how it should now proceed is no longer as obvious as it once appeared to be. It is commonplace that there are three kinds of personality tests—questionnaires, projective tests, and objective tests, as they have been defined by Cattell and Warburton (1967). Nevertheless, it makes sense to consider the arguments separately in relation to each of these modes of measurement and this is what is done in the following sections.

Personality Questionnaires

There is no question that for the scientific study of personality, personality questionnaires are the measurement devices preferred by the majority of researchers. This is simply because they can be made reliable over time and are internally consistent, and these characteristics are essential for adequate measurement, as has been extensively documented by Kline (1993a) and Nunnally (1978) amongst others. In addition, of course, with personality questionnaires it is easy to gather good normative data and to investigate validity. However, as shall be seen, many of the claims made for the validity of many personality questionnaires are far from being accepted, and there are problems with these kind of tests which have still to be overcome. For example, they are easily faked and are subject to the systematic bias of response sets such as acquiescence and social desirability, that is, tendency to endorse an item because it is socially desirable so to do. There is one further difficulty which should be mentioned. This concerns the argument that personality questionnaire items are too simplistic (Heim, 1975). Heim made the point that intelligent subjects especially often find it difficult to answer personality test items other than in the usually useless doubtful category. In addition, when the personality test items are given careful consideration it is difficult to believe that they could embrace the richness of personality.

Perhaps the greatest advantage of personality questionnaires compared with the projective and objective tests is that they have a clear statistical rationale, at least when they have been adequately constructed. This rationale is concerned with the theory of measurement error. It assumes that a reliable, univariate test is the best measure of the notional true score for any variable, thus minimizing measurement error. Among personality tests, only personality quest-ionnaires can reach these standards of reliability and validity. To understand this it will be necessary to discuss the different methods of test construction since not all of them necessarily lead to the reduction of measurement error. Before scrutinizing these methods it should not be forgotten that a major practical advantage of personality questionnaires lies in the fact that they can be given to large groups at a time, and can be easily scored and interpreted even by computers. This ability to encompass large samples is important, especially if it is compared to the time and effort required to administer and score the Rorschach (e.g., Exner, 1986), even assuming that this test were valid, an issue which will be dealt with briefly in a later section of this chapter.

Constructing Personality Questionnaires

The different methods of constructing personality questionnaires will be described briefly, with emphasis on their statistical models.

Criterion Keyed Tests

In this method of test construction, items are retained if they can discriminate one criterion group from another or from normals, for example, depressives from other clinical groups. The Minnesota Multiphasic Personality Inventory (MMPI) is the best example of this method of test construction. It is one of the most widely used questionnaires, and has recently been updated (Butcher, 1990).

However, as has been fully discussed in Kline (1993a), there are several severe problems with this method of which the most serious is the lack of psychological meaning to scales constructed in this way. This is because groups are likely to differ on a number of characteristics, and items which discriminate groups may be measuring any of these traits. Thus, a criterion keyed scale will not necessarily be homogeneous. This means that the scores are not comparable. A score of X, for example, could be composed differently for two individuals even if the scale measured only two traits, let alone if it measured a large number. This demand for a univariate measure, an essential of any decent test, will be further discussed in the section below on factor-analytic tests.

The fact that a scale discriminates one group from the other does not allow one to infer any psychological meaning. Indeed, this psychological inanity means that the use of the criterion keyed tests can actually hinder the development of knowledge. Their only value is in screening. Thus, for example, if it can be shown that accident-prone tank drivers can be selected by such a test, it is reasonable to use it since it is of little interest to the military as to why this should be the case.

Item-Analytic Tests

Item analysis is used where there is a demand for homogeneous tests. In principle, in this method items are selected if they correlate with the total score on the test. Thus, an item pool is administered to a trial sample, and the correlation of each item with the total score on the pool is calculated (for full details see Kline, 1993a). This can produce an effective test which is bound to be homogeneous. Its only weakness is that if the item pool contains items in fact measuring two distinct but correlated factors item analysis will be unable to distinguish among these items, and the resulting scale will not be unifactorial. In practice, this is probably a rare occurrence, although certainly possible, and it has led most test constructors to prefer to use factor analysis rather than item analysis.

Actually, where only one factor runs through the item pool, item and factor analysis are highly correlated, as was shown by Barrett and Kline (1982) with the EPQ. Since, especially with personality items rather than those used in the field of ability, one can never be certain that only one factor is present, factor analysis is preferable. Indeed, item analysis was used only because before the days of high speed computers and good statistical packages, factoring items was a huge task. Of the reputable modern test constructors, Jackson is one of the few to favour item analysis (Jackson, 1974).

Factor-Analytic Tests

It might be thought, therefore, that only factor-analytic tests should be used and, ideally, this is the case. However, there are severe technical problems in the use of factor analysis, especially in test construction, and this has led to many poor tests, as has been fully documented in Kline (1993a, 1994). The main technical problems, which have made many factored tests of dubious worth, concern the coefficients used to correlate the items, the number of factors rotated in the solution, and the failure to reach simple structure. The last problem is a vital one. This is because there is an infinity of different, but numerically equivalent solutions to any factor analysis. To select one rather than another, is therefore of critical significance. As Cattell (1978) has argued, where there are many hypotheses, the simplest is to be preferred—an example of Occam's razor. Thus, a simple structure must be obtained, because this is the most simple solution, simple structure must being defined by factors with a few high loadings and the majority zeroes. As Cattell (1978) has shown, simple structure factors are replicable. In his studies of factor analysis Cattell (1978) was able to demonstrate that many published examples were so technically defective that there was no simple structure. This accounted for, in his view, the plethora of different solutions and claims about the number of personality factors.

All this is indeed the case. Recently, however, there are packages available which enable test constructors to reach simple structure, and there is good agreement on how this can be achieved, even though, lamentably, there are many instances of technically defective tests. In brief, direct oblique rotation of factors selected by the Scree test, provided that there is a large sample of subjects and a satisfactory subject to variable ratio (at least 2:1), will come close to simple structure.

No more will be said about the technical problems of factor-analytic test construction because these are dwarfed beside the conceptual or logical problems which are far less understood by test constructors. Furthermore, it is these which are most germane to the subject of this chapter, that is, the further of personality tests, and these must now be examined in greater detail. In all that will be said it is assumed that simple structure has been reached, and that the technical problems of factor analyses have been resolved.

Conceptual Problems in Factor Analysis: Originally, factor analysis was used in psychology in an attempt to account for the determinants of academic success. It was used to answer the question as to why human abilities are positively correlated. The modern answer to this question, that there is a small number of ability factors which account for most of the ability variance (Carroll, 1993), is not radically different from the original solution. In the field of abilities the identification of factors is not difficult since the items in the tests, in the main, are examples of the ability itself. For example, a mathematical ability factor consists of mathematical items.

This is not the case with personality questionnaires. Personality questionnaire items clustering on a factor are not examples of the behaviour. They are simply self-reports of behaviour or feelings. The investigator can have no idea whether they are true or false, whether the subjects are deliberately lying or are deluded, or, indeed, what the determinants of claiming, for example, 'I sleep badly', are. Thus, the identification of personality factors simply from the content of the items loading on them is highly dubious on *a priori* grounds. It is simply face validity which is a poor guide to true validity. A cluster of personality items is a far different thing from a cluster of ability items where correct solution of the items is *ipso facto* evidence of the ability.

This means that, in the case of personality tests, item factors must be externally validated. There validity must depend on more than item content. In the case of the best test constructors this problem has been recognized. Thus, Cattell (1957) and Eysenck (1967) have both supplied impressive external validation for extraversion and anxiety in particular, as well as for a number of other factors. These factors have, in the light of such evidence, a clear psychological meaning independent of their item content. Indeed, the only personality factors which should be taken seriously are those with such external validation.

This point has been clearly made by Cattell throughout his long career. He has consistently pointed out that in the field of personality it is easy to write items which are essentially paraphrases of each other. It is hardly surprising, therefore, that if such items are factored, they load a factor. All such loadings demonstrate that subjects understand the meaning of the words, that those who say, for example, that they like gardening, also like flowers, like seeing things grow, do not hate gardening, and enjoy seeing displays of plants. Such factors are labelled as bloated specifics or tautologous factors.

That such factors can be produced means that, firstly, it is impossible to set out a definitive list of personality factors. Secondly, it means that the routine test construction procedure of writing items, factoring them, and finding a factor and, thus, a test is futile, without external validation of the test. If a test is simply a bloated specific it will not correlate with anything in the real world. As was pointed out in Kline (1993a) many published tests are of this kind. In some cases, indeed, test constructors have factored an item pool and taken items loading on the first principal component as evidence that a scale exists. This is a conceptual and mathematical error, a phenomenon not uncommon in the social sciences.

Recognition of Real Factors: Since the identification of factors cannot be based reliably on the content of items, even if a factor will correlate with some external criterion, it may be difficult to identify. As Cattell (1978) pointed out, one of the reasons for the plethora of factors discovered in the field of personality was that essentially the same factor was given a different name because identification was based on items rather than on external validation. Of course, another source of confusion was that factors were improperly rotated, a point which has been already discussed.

The only sensible approach to this problem of factor recognition and identification is to factor all factors, take all tests which claim to measure a distinct factor, and rotate them to simple structure. With the advent of modern, fast computers, which can handle large correlation matrices, this has been increasingly the approach adopted by modern workers in the field of personality questionnaires, and it is this work which will now be scrutinized.

There is now some consensus, though not complete, on the important personality factors in questionnaires. There are too many studies to go through in detail in a chapter of this length, and this work has been extensively reviewed (e.g., Wiggins, in Press; Kline, 1993b). Here, the main findings will be summarized, and the future of personality measurement will be examined in their light.

Costa and McCrae (1992) have argued in many publications that five factors, the Big Five, best account for the variance in personality. These are extraversion, agreeableness, conscientiousness, anxiety and open-mindedness, although in some studies the names of these factors may vary slightly. Eysenck (1992), on the other hand, has argued, cogently, that three factors best account for the variance, needless to say, the factors measured in his questionnaire—extraversion, neuroticism and tough-mindedness. The thrust of Eysenck's argument is that the big five are intercorrelated with each other and with Eysenck's Psychoticism, Extraversion and Neuroticism. Costa and McCrae (1992) try to counter this argument by claiming that these intercorrelations are spurious, affected by biases in self-ratings—arguments which do not appear convincing.

In this chapter it is not intended to settle this point as to how many factors account for the main personality variance. Kline and Barrett (1994), for example, have shown that four factors might be a meaningful solution as open-mindedness and conscientiousness are better conceptualized as one variable—the obsessional personality. However, this debate exemplifies and highlights the problems for the future of personality measurement using questionnaires.

Thus, as has been argued, discussion as to how many factors there are is futile, given that tautologous factors may always be constructed. This is the point made by Eysenck (1992) that bedevils accounts of personality which rest primarily on factor analysis. Thus, there should be a strong theoretical rationale for any model, over and above the factors analysis or powerful external support for the factors. This is where the future for personality measurement by questionnaires must lie. What is required is careful, non-factor-analytic study of the factors which have been identified.

Physiological correlates of the factors are obviously of considerable interest, and Eysenck (1967) discusses just such a basis for extraversion and neuroticism, as indeed does Zuckerman for sensation-seeking (Zuckerman, 1984). Similar and even more impressive evidence for the psychological significance of factors can be obtained from biometric studies in which the proportion of variance attributable to genetic determinants for the factors is estimated. If a factor has a considerable genetic determination it is difficult to argue that it a mere specific or an artifact of the factor-analytic method. Furthermore, modern biometric procedures allow the calculation of the between and within family determinants of the variance. These findings are of considerable theoretical interest since the sociological accounts of human development would require that between family variance was important. Significantly, this is almost never the case. It is the within family variance, the unique experiences of each individual, which appear to be important (Eaves, Martin and Eysenck, 1989). Finally, external correlations, as has been suggested, can be an impressive support for the validity of a factor. The best example of this comes from the ability sphere where there are huge numbers of external correlates of g, as is fully documented in Jensen (1980), with academic success, job success and even happiness.

This is where, in the author's view, the future of personality research seems to be the most hopeful—in genetic and physiological research—together with a study of the discriminatory power of the factors. This must be stressed because there is a strand of research, which is still being woven, to continue the metaphor, which seems far less profitable. This is the elaboration, and indeed complication of the factorial methods.

Factors-Analytic and Multivariate Methods: As has been argued, until recent years there were considerable technical deficiencies in published studies of personality where factor analysis had been used (Cattell, 1978). There can be no doubt that many apparently anomalous findings resulted from these deficiencies. More recently, however, there has been agreement as to how a simple structure can be reached, and computer programmes are freely available to achieve this end. Certainly most of the leading workers in the field produce technically sound work.

However, with the advent of improved computers simple structure analyses are no longer regarded as necessarily satisfactory. Indeed, exploratory factor analysis, which describes most of the work on which personality tests are based, has been relegated to some extent. It is now but one of a number of multivariate techniques. Now the favoured approach is that of structural modelling, especially one aspect of it—confirmatory analysis, and this section of this chapter will conclude with a brief discussion of the use of this method.

Confirmatory Factor Analysis: Structural equation modelling has been developed by Joreskog (Joreskog and Sorbom, 1984) and substantiated into the LISREL programme. There are two aspects to this—the structural model and the measurement model; the latter includes confirmatory analysis, and it is this which will be scrutinized. These techniques are complicated mathematically and computationally; a good related text is that of Loehlin (1987) while Kline's (1994) contains a simplified description.

Confirmatory analysis, which uses maximum likelihood methods, thus giving a statistical test for the number of factors, differs from exploratory analysis in that the user sets a target matrix of factor loadings. Confirmatory analysis gives a set of factors which either fits the target statistically or fails to do so. It thus appears to overcome the main problem of exploratory analysis, namely the necessity to choose one of an infinite set of solutions when the choice (simple structure) is essentially arbitrary. Furthermore, the ability to test hypotheses makes the procedure resemble scientific methods, although refutation rather than confirmation is their essence.

However, it is argued that, at least as regards the study of personality, these advantages are more apparent than real for the following reasons:

1. In the field of personality, there are few well-established theories as the study of any text will indicate (e.g., Pervin, 1990). Thus, it is difficult to set up a realistic target matrix. If, on the other hand, a simplified matrix is supplied, with a few high loading and the rest zeroes, the target is easy to hit.
2. Even where a target is hit, the factors are not necessarily meaningful. For example, one can factor a set of test items, and confirm the previous analysis in a new sample. However, confirmation of the previous analysis does not mean that the factors are not bloated specifics or subject to bias of response sets such as acquiescence.
3. As Loehlin (1987) has pointed out, that the fact a target matrix has been confirmed does not mean that is the only matrix that could be confirmed. Thus, unless the target matrix is embedded in a good theory of personality confirmation may not mean much.
4. There are severe problems with the indicators of fitness. Often they do not agree among themselves. Furthermore, there are sampling difficulties. When samples are large, as they should be for an adequate maximum likelihood factor analysis, small differences between the target matrix and the results are sufficient for rejection. On the other hand, if the samples are small, confirmatory analysis finds it difficult to reject targets.

For all these reasons it is argued that the future of personality questionnaires does not lie in the improvement or refinement of statistical methods. These are more than sufficient for the data obtained from such tests. Confirmatory analysis on its own will not provide the answers. Rather, the future of personality questionnaires lies in the intensive study of the factors which are found in them, especially in research concerned with their genetic determination, their physiological correlates and their external referents. When these are known the factors will be psychologically meaningful and ready to form the basis of a good theory of personality.

Projective Tests

The majority of projective tests consist of ambiguous stimuli which subjects are asked to describe, although there are variants which require subjects to complete sentences, or to draw. These productions are then interpreted by the scorer on the theory that the ambiguity of the task forces the subject to project himself or herself into the descriptions or drawings. The most used—and they are widely used—projective tests all fit this categorization, for example, the Rorschach (Rorschach, 1921) and the Thematic Apperception Test (TAT; Murray, 1938).

Projective tests have been extensively criticized by academic psychologists on the grounds of low reliability and validity (e.g., Eysenck, 1959; Vernon, 1964). This low reliability should be obvious from the description above since there is clearly considerable subjectivity in interpretation and scoring. Given these defects, it might be asked why they are still in use and whether or not they are worthy of even brief discussion in this chapter.

There are several reasons for this. One concerns the simplistic nature of personality inventories. Many clinicians feel that projective tests, despite their problems, are better able to capture the richness of personality. Furthermore, many projective test users follow the distinction drawn, especially by Allport (1937), between nomothetic tests, of which personality questionnaires are a good example, and idiographic measures. Nomothetic tests seek to measure what is common between individuals. This is the basis of factor analysis and psychometrics. Idiographic tests, on the other hand, aim to measure what is particular, private, to each person, material considered by many clinicians to be of far more interest than common traits. Furthermore, it can be argued that in the hands of highly skilled practitioners projective tests have yielded impressive data, the work or Murray (1938) being an excellent example.

The future of projective testing would appear to be clear. One straightforward approach would be to try to make the scoring and interpretation far more reliable and precisely defined, thus, at least, eliminating unreliability. It would then become possible to investigate the validity of these relatively error-free scores. In fact, considerable efforts are being made towards this end with the Rorschach by Exner and his colleagues (Exner, 1986), who have developed a detailed scoring system with extensive norms. Other workers have also attempted similar schemes; the work of Allison *et al.* (1988) at Yale is a good example. These methods attempt to combine the idiographic approach with psychometric rigour. A full description of these methods can be found in Kline (1993a).

Some researchers have attempted to subject the protocols of projective tests to a content analysis, reducing all features to a set of ones and zeroes, representing presence or absence. Thus, if subject A describes a stimulus as resembling a bat—then bat is scored one. All respondents who put 'bat' receive a one, all others zero. These matrices are then subjected to multivariate analysis in an attempt to discriminate meaningful groups of subjects. Holley (1973) developed a special form of analysis, G Analysis, specifically for these matrices although it is doubtful if this is any more effective than other multivariate methods such as discriminant functions. He was able to make powerful discriminations between clinical groups, and Hampson and Kline (1977) found it to be a useful technique with offenders.

Thus, it is argued that projective tests, given clear, reliable scoring schemes, and subjected to appropriate multivariate analyses, might provide valuable data which could not be obtained from questionnaires. This, indeed, is why it is useful to persevere with projective tests, and to attempt to overcome their psychometric deficiencies, because they are unique sources of data.

Before leaving projective techniques it will be valuable to discuss briefly percept-genetics, which is an essentially Swedish approach to the measurement of defence mechanisms. Kragh and Smith (1970) have an excellent description of the theory of percept-genetics and some of the associated tests. Kline (1993a) contains a summary of much of the recent research.

Percept-genetics is concerned with the development of percepts. The theory assumes that perception is a creative process which reflects both the stimulus perceived and all our experiences. Percept-genetics aims to lay open for inspection these normally unconscious perceptual processes.

The Defence Mechanism Test (DMT; Kragh, 1984), which is the most general percept-genetic measure, consists of two stimulus cards adapted from the TAT. Each card consists of a hero figure, an attribute of the hero and a threat figure in the periphery of the picture. This threat figure ensures that the DMT is a measure of defences since the scores obtained from the test reflect the distortions of this peripheral threat.

Each card is presented to the subject in series through a tachistoscope, first below the threshold of perception and then at gradually increasing levels of illumination. At each presentation subjects are required to draw and describe what they saw. Distortions and changes in these descriptions through the series of presentations are held to reflect and represent the inner conflicts and experiences which affects perception in that individual. Thus, it is clear why it can be argued that the DMT is a measure of defence mechanisms.

Examples of scoring will clarify the nature of the test. Repression is scored if the hero or threat figure is not human or both are objects. Denial is scored when the threat is denied. Reaction formation is scored when the threat figure is described as angelic.

Scoring the DMT is a skilled and lengthy process, although there is evidence in its manual that it can be reliably scored. As for validity, this is a more contentious point. In general, the Scandinavian workers simply tend to report results on the assumption that the DMT is valid. Cooper and Kline (1989) did show that an objectively scored version of the DMT yielded a repression factor which was useful in pilot selection, a function for which the DMT has been used in Scandinavia. It would be incorrect to say that there is clear evidence for the validity of the DMT, but there is some support; and there is no doubt that it is an interesting test, different from almost all others, which deserves further rigorous research.

Objective Tests

Before concluding this chapter objective tests must be briefly mentioned. Cattell (1957) defined an objective personality test as one which could be objectively scored and the purpose of which could not be guessed by subjects. This, in principle, would make them particularly valuable in applied psychology, where deliberate distortion or even falsification in not unknown.

Cattell and his colleagues devoted considerable efforts to developing a sound rationale for the construction of objective tests, necessary because, as should be clear from the definition, it is not obvious what an objective test might measure. If it were, the test would not be objective. Works of Cattell and Warburton (1967) and Kline (1993a) contain discussions of the rationale of constructing such tests. In general, any task which discriminates well among individuals is suitable for investigation as an objective test. The emphasis here must be on investigation. Thus, in their compendium of tests Cattell and Warburton list 800 or so devices from which more than 2,000 variables have been constructed. However, most of these were at that date of unknown validity, and nearly thirty years later, this is still the case! It was hoped that clinical and other applied psychologists would use these tests, and thus build up a body of evidence relevant to their validity, but practitioners have not taken them up because they were of unknown validity. This is not as surprising as it might seem when the nature of objective tests is considered. A few examples will illustrate this point. Some of the typical objective tests are:

1. *Slow line drawing:* Subjects are told to draw a line as slowly as possible. The scores derived include the length of the line, and whether the subjects cheated (e.g., stopped drawing).
2. *Signature:* Subjects are required to write their names. The scores are the pressure used in writing and the sizes of the letters.
3. *Fidgetometer:* Here, subjects sit in a special chair, wired to measure movements. The scores are the amount of movement, whether it is feet, and/or arms, and so on.

These three examples illustrate how difficult it would be to fake these tests, or to guess what they may measure. Unfortunately, the few studies of the validity of any of these objective tests have not been convincing. Kline and Cooper (1984) investigated the validity of the O-A Battery (Cattell and Schuerger, 1976), ten tests regarded by Cattell as the most valid and reliable of these objective tests. However, their validity could not be confirmed, and most of the tests measured composites of ability and personality factors.

In respect of objective tests, it may be concluded that these are potentially of great value, especially in applied research, but an intensive research programme needs to be initiated to select measures that are useful.

CONCLUSIONS

It is clear that of the three types of personality tests, only the personality questionnaires reach the criterion of reliability and validity necessary for scientific measurement. With these questionnaires, the future lies not in ever more complex and elaborate factor analyses, although these are valuable in relating variables to each other and discovering what the tests actually measure; rather the future must be taken up with the external validation of the factors which emerge—investigating their genetic determination, their physiological correlates, and their relationship with other known factors. As far as the projective and percept-genetic techniques are concerned, the emphasis must lie in improving their psychometric qualities, so that reliable variables can be extracted from them. When that has been done, these can be investigated in the same way as has been suggested for personality questionnaires. Finally, the whole field of objective tests requires exploratory factor analysis so that sets of reliable objective test factors can be extracted. When this is done, these again can be studied alongside personality questionnaires. Thus, a huge but well defined research programme lies ahead in the field of personality measurement.

REFERENCES

Allison, J., S.J. Blatt and C.N. Zimet (eds) (1988). *The Interpretation of Psychological Tests,* Washington Hemisphere.

Allport, G.W. (1937). *Personality: A Psychological Interpretation,* New York: Holt, Rinehart and Winston.

Barrett, P. and P. Kline (1982). 'The Itemetric Qualities of the Eysenck Personality Questionnaire: A Reply to Helmes', *Personality and Individual Differences*, 3: 73–80.

Butcher, J.N. (1990). *MMPI-2 in Psychological Treatment,* New York: Oxford University Press.

Carroll, J.B. (1993). *Human Cognitive Abilities,* Cambridge: Cambridge University Press.

Cattell, R.B. (1957). *Personality Motivation Structure and Measurement,* Yonkers: World Book Company.

Cattell, R.B. (1978). *The Scientific Use of Factor Analysis,* New York: Plenum.

Cattell, R.B. and J. Schuerger (1976). *The O-A (Objective-Analytic) Test Battery,* Champaign: IPAT.

Cattell, R.B. and F.W. Warburton (1967). *Objective Personality and Motivation Tests,* Champaign: University of Illinois Press.

Cooper, C. and P. Kline (1989). 'A New Objectively Scored Version of the Defence Mechanism Test', *Scandinavian Journal of Psychology,* 30: 228–38.

Costa, P.T. and R.R. McCrae (1992). 'Reply to Eysenck', *Personality and Individual Differences*, 1: 861–65.

Eaves, L.W., N.G. Martin and H.J. Eysenck (1989). *Genes Culture and Personality,* London: Academic Press.

Exner, J.E. (1986). *The Rorschach: A Comprehensive System,* New York: Wiley.

Eysenck, H.J. (1959). 'The Rorschach', in *5th Mental Measurement Yearbooks,* O.K. Buros (ed.), Highland Park: Gryphon Press.

Eysenck, H.J. (1967). *The Biological Basis of Personality,* Springfied: C.C. Thomas.

Eysenck, H.J. (1992). 'Four Ways Five Factors are not Basic', *Personality and Individual Differences*, 13: 667–73.

Hampson, S and P. Kline (1977). 'Personality Dimensions Differentiating Certain Groups of Abnormal Offenders from Non-Offenders', *British Journal of Criminology,* 17: 310–31.

Heim, A.W. (1975). *Psychological Testing,* London: Oxford University Press.

Holley, J.W. (1973). *Rorschach Analysis,* 119–55 in P. Kline (ed.) (1973), New Approach in Psychological Measurement, Chichester: Wiley.

Jackson, D.N. (1974). *The Personality Research Form,* New York: Research Psychologists Press.

Jensen, A. (1980). *Bias in Mental Testing,* New York: Free Press.

Joreskog, K.G. and D. Sorbom (1984). *LISREL: User's Guide,* Mooresville: Scientific Software.

Kline, P. (1973). *New Approaches in Psychological Measurement,* Chichester: Wiley.

Kline, P. (1993a). *The Handbook of Psychological Testing,* London: Routledge.

Kline, P. (1993b). *Personality: The Psychological View,* London: Routledge.

Kline, P. (1994). *An Easy Guide to Factor Analysis,* London: Routledge.

Kline, P. and P. Barrett (1994). 'Studies with the PPQ and the Five Factor Model of Personality', *European Review of Applied Psychology,* 44: 35–42.

Kline, P. and C. Cooper (1994). 'A Construct Validation of the Objective-Analytic Test Battery (OATB)', *Personality and Individual Differences,* 5: 328–37.

Kragh, U. (1984). *The Defence Mechanism Test,* Stockholm: Persona.

Kragh, U. and G.S. Smith (eds) (1970). *Percept-Genetic Analysis,* Lund: Gleerups.

Loehlin, J.C. (1987). *Latent Variable Models,* Hillsdale: Erlbaum.

Murray, H.A. (1938). *Explorations in Personality,* Oxford: Oxford University Press.

Nunnally, J.O. (1978). *Psychometric Theory,* New York: McGraw-Hill.

Pervin, L. (1990). *Handbook of Personality Theory and Research,* New York: Guilford.

Rorschach, H. (1921). *Psychodiagnostics,* Berne: Hans Huber.

Vernon, P.E. (1964). *Personality Assessment,* London: Methuen.

Wiggins, J.S. (ed.) (in press) *Theoretical Perspectives for the Five-Factor Model,* New York: Guilford.

Zukerman, M. (1984). 'Sensation-Seeking: A Comparative Approach to a Human Trait', *The Behavioural and Brain Sciences,* 7: 413–71.

Author Index

Subject Index